HARRIET TUBMAN

HARRIET TUBMAN

MYTH, MEMORY, AND HISTORY

Milton C. Sernett

DUKE UNIVERSITY PRESS

DURHAM AND LONDON

2007

© 2007 Duke University Press
All rights reserved
Printed in the United States
of America on acid-free paper ⊗
Designed by Amy Ruth Buchanan
Typeset in Janson by
Tseng Information Systems, Inc.
Library of Congress Cataloging-in-
Publication Data appear on the
last printed page of this book.

*Generous support for this publication
was provided by* SYRACUSE UNIVERSITY
through THE DEPARTMENT OF AFRICAN
AMERICAN STUDIES *in* THE COLLEGE
OF ARTS AND SCIENCES.

*Production of this work was also made
possible through the assistance of*
THE MARY DUKE BIDDLE
FOUNDATION.

To

AMANDA MAY HEACOCK,

our first grandchild,

born September 29, 2004.

"Hold to that Bright Shining Star!"

CONTENTS

ACKNOWLEDGMENTS

I wish I could say that this book came to me in a dream or that I had a vision of it in completed form from the beginning of the journey. I cannot claim, as have some Harriet Tubman enthusiasts, that the spirit of Black Moses spoke to me while I was standing at her grave in Auburn's Fort Hill cemetery. I am therefore thankful for the many people who enabled me to move this project forward.

Tubman scholarship is finally achieving a level of recognition within the academy worthy of the woman herself. I am particularly grateful to several of Tubman's recent biographers, whose books were published as I was bringing my own research and writing to closure. When I was on the library and archive trail, guest registers at many depositories indicated that Jean Humez had been there before me. I was soon to learn that she was assembling a wealth of primary sources from which a more accurate life of Harriet Tubman could be constructed. She generously shared information and allowed me to read her manuscript prior to publication. Her theoretical insights enriched my reflections on the interplay of myth, memory, and history in the process by which Tubman has become an American icon.

Kate Clifford Larson deserves first honor for having done more than any Tubman biographer, past or present, to unravel the folds in the record and recover a more faithful portrait of Tubman's life and times. An extraordinarily generous scholar, Kate readily shared from her amazingly rich research files and helped me find my way through a thicket of questions that arose as I delved deeper into the conflation of fact and fiction that surround Tubman in the popular imagination. Her Tubman biography is at present the gold standard.

I cannot recall exactly when I first discovered Jim McGowan's pioneering attempt to break through the curtain of silence that has obscured an honest appraisal of Harriet Tubman as an American worth remembering generation after generation. Since coming to know him as both scholar and friend, it seems as if he was there from the beginning, giving encouragement and passing on the torch. Many of us who have joined the ranks of Tubman scholars have been pursuing answers to questions first raised by Jim McGowan and have been inspired by Jim's passion for sorting out fact and fiction.

This book is an extended conversation with the reader about how a black woman, once enslaved but self-liberated, came to occupy an extraordinarily prominent place in the American collective memory. In my explorations of the overlay of memory and history, I benefited from assistance provided by a host of Tubman admirers. I think now of Paul and Christine Carter and others at the Harriet Tubman Home in Auburn, New York; of Pauline Copes-Johnson and Judith Bryant and others who claim ancestral ties to Tubman; of Doug Armstrong and Bonnie Ryan, archaeologists with unique skills; of investigators from the National Park Service; and of the staff at many historical agencies and depositories. I especially thank Angela Williams, director of the Martin Luther King Jr. Memorial Library at Syracuse University. She has been invaluable in the establishment and development of the Harriet Tubman collection in the library and a constant source of encouragement.

Students at Syracuse University, where I taught for nearly three decades, took a risk enrolling in the course "Harriet Tubman: Myth, Memory, and History" that I developed, the first of its kind in the nation. Though they came to our study of Tubman with no more knowledge of her than can be gleaned from books written for children, they readily joined my endeavor to provide the space she deserves in circles where students and professors share a passion for academic excellence. I march now in the emeritus faculty ranks, but I will not soon forget the students and colleagues in the Department of African American Studies at Syracuse University. Linda Carty, as chairperson of my academic unit, and Cathryn Newton, dean of the College of Arts and Sciences, facilitated financial support at a critical time, when I was feeling overwhelmed with the magnitude of the task before me.

Reynolds Smith of Duke University Press, as with several other book-publishing endeavors of mine, deserves a large share of the credit for making this tribute to Tubman possible. He understood early on that my

Tubman book was something unique and that it deserved to see the light of day.

Now that my Tubman book is complete, I have more time for family and friends and the freedom to explore new ventures in retirement. This book is dedicated to Amanda May Heacock, born September 29, 2004. She is too young to know much about Harriet Tubman, but she will soon hear of her, as so many children do. Someday she may even read this book and learn something of her grandfather's hope that all Americans recognize the values of courage and self-sacrifice that Harriet Tubman embodied.

INTRODUCTION

In 1986, Diane Ravitch and Chester Finn published a report of a national survey indicating that more eleventh-grade students recognized Harriet Tubman than knew of Winston Churchill. Students remembered that Tubman had been a conductor on the Underground Railroad, but few of them could name a commanding general of America's Revolutionary War army.[1] When the National Council for History Standards published its recommendations in 1994, Harriet Tubman received six citations, while previous centerpieces of American schoolbooks, such as Paul Revere, Thomas Edison, Alexander Graham Bell, and the Wright brothers, failed to make the grade, much to the consternation of critics of multicultural education.[2] In 1999, as the second millennium drew to a close, the Arts and Entertainment cable TV network broadcast a series called *Biography of the Millennium: 100 People—1,000 Years*, based on interviews with scholars, politicians, and theologians who had been asked to identify which one hundred personalities had most affected the world, "for better or worse," between A.D. 1000 and 2000. Harriet Tubman emerged in the seventy-first slot, ahead of Princess Diana, the Beatles, Joseph Stalin, Elizabeth I, Ronald Reagan, Jonas Salk, Louis Armstrong, and Tubman's contemporary and friend, the women's rights activist Susan B. Anthony of Rochester, New York.[3]

As I write, there are efforts to have the U.S. Congress grant Harriet Tubman veteran status for her services to the Union Army, and some Tubman champions would like to see her receive the Congressional Medal of Honor posthumously. Others, not satisfied with half a loaf of bread in the day of commemoration awarded her in 2003 in New York State, continue to campaign for an actual holiday in her honor. Other Tubman enthusiasts want a national public holiday in her memory. In

1978, the U.S. Postal Service unveiled the first issue of a stamp with a face value of thirteen cents in honor of Harriet Tubman at a ceremony held at Metropolitan African Methodist Episcopal Church, the oldest black church in Washington, D.C. *Jet* magazine hailed the event as "the first major step taken by the government to recognize this indomitable Black leader who for thirty-seven years of her life unsuccessfully sought federal compensation for her years of service as a Union Army spy and nurse during the Civil War" and called Tubman "the 'first lady' of Black American heroines."[4] Tubman, the first African American woman with a stamp to her credit, was again honored with a stamp in 1995, this time with a face value of thirty-two cents. The illiterate black woman whom contemporaries called "the Moses of her people" had by the last decade of the second millennium become a fixture in American iconography.

"Moses" is but one of the many eponyms ascribed to Harriet Ross Tubman (c. 1822–1913). She has been variously referred to as the "Queen of the Underground," the "Black Joan of Arc," "Homespun Heroine," "General Tubman," "Greatest Heroine of Her Age," "Healer," "Liberator," "Missionary," "Modern Amazon," "The Most of a Man," "The Molly Pitcher of Her Day," "The Female John Henry," "Mother Tubman," and "Aunt Harriet." These ascriptions, each reflective of particular contours in the historical process of Tubman's canonization, mask the fact that the flame of Tubman's fame has not always burned as brightly as it now does. Though many constituencies (some with opposing ideologies) and special interest groups such as feminists, advocates for the elderly and disabled, African American sororities, and caucuses for racial reconciliation have adopted Tubman as their symbol, her name has not always been highly negotiable in the marketplace of good causes. Nevertheless, Americans, black and white, have long constructed images of Harriet Tubman mirroring their own experiences and the progress made in the United States (and the world) toward the social goods with which Tubman is identified.

This book is an exploration of the interplay of history and memory in the process by which Harriet Tubman has entered into the American cultural Valhalla, occupying a seat among the worthies of the past, such as Abraham Lincoln and Frederick Douglass. Obstacles have marked the path, for at various times, both before and after her burial on a cold March day in 1913, Tubman's reputation has suffered neglect. In the aftermath of the Civil War and Reconstruction, for example, she held an honored position in the consciousness of very few Americans. The intersubjective process by which certain personalities from the past gain and lose stature in the American memory is convoluted and often clouded by the interjection of myth.

My intent in the chapters that follow is not to present a biographical portrait of Harriet Ross Tubman in the traditional manner of historical biographers. Instead, I focus on why it is that someone whose life story has been characterized by the distinguished African American historian Benjamin Quarles as a "tissue of improbabilities verging on the impossible" has captured the American imagination so strongly, especially in the recent past.[5] Nevertheless, it is hoped that this attempt to sort out the "legend" from the "lady" will enable readers to learn about the woman who has become a cultural icon. This book undertakes two tasks. It seeks to recover the "historical" Tubman in the fashion, for example, of New Testament scholars searching for the historical Jesus behind the literary accretions of the Gospel writers. But it is primarily about the remembered Tubman—that is, about the myth that draws on the factual core but is often in tension with it. To borrow a phrase from Carla Peterson's insightful analysis of Sojourner Truth's place in the American memory, this book is fundamentally about the "overdetermined" Tubman. I am interested in "how a historical figure comes to us mediated by perceptions of contemporaries and later historians."[6]

The canonization of Harriet Tubman, perhaps more so than that of any other figure in African American history, is a mirror in which Americans of varying social and ethnic identities, situated in differing places and times, reveal something of themselves. The historian David Blight asserts that Harriet Tubman has "long been a malleable icon of America's antislavery past."[7] In what is to follow, I affirm this but also argue that Tubman may be America's most malleable icon, with significance for much more than how we are to remember the nation's struggle with the issue of slavery. It is this resilience, and this pliability, that I want to look at, for by learning of Harriet Tubman and her place in the American memory, we learn about ourselves as the American people.

While the ten chapters that follow are constructed thematically, there is a chronological movement to the book as a whole, shaped by the trajectory of Tubman's life story. In chapter 1, I discuss the core myth about Harriet Tubman that has become enshrined in stories told to and written for children. I argue that this venue gives us the clearest picture of the "distilled" and inherited American memory about Tubman. We see something of the potency of this distillation in the national debates during the 1980s over multiculturalism and the rewriting of American history textbooks and curriculums.

Chapter 2 introduces Harriet Tubman in the context of those years before, during, and after the Civil War when she first emerged in the public consciousness of Americans as "Black Moses." This foundational chapter focuses on the use of Tubman as the iconic figure most representative of the Underground Railroad. In a foreword to the 1970 edition of William Still's *The Underground Rail Road*, Quarles affirmed: "Of the blacks who worked in the underground railroad all names pale before that of Harriet Tubman, whose base of operations included the slave states themselves." [8] There are many Americans today who identify Tubman as the preeminent Underground Railroad conductor, black or white, and not a few mistakenly think that she started or invented the Underground Railroad itself. Chapter 2 examines the roots of this powerful mythic memory.

Chapter 3 explores how Tubman's experiences during the Civil War as nurse, scout, and spy have been extrapolated and codified and then merged into the image of her as "General Tubman"—a characterization that in some circles is nearly as important as that of her as "Black Moses." This militant portrayal of Tubman touched a nerve among Americans already alarmed by the extent of violence in their communities, but it rang true to radical critics of social injustice. In chapter 3, I study Tubman's wartime period with the goal of better understanding the possibilities therein for continued iconic representation and utilization.

Some time after Harriet Tubman took up residence in Auburn, New York, she met Sarah Hopkins Bradford, a white woman whose "biography" of Black Moses is a major watershed in the evolution of the Tubman legend. First issued in 1869, then revised and enlarged in an 1886 edition, Bradford's rendition of the Tubman story has infected, for good or ill, almost all subsequent biographical portraits. Chapter 4 analyzes the construction and impact of Bradford's framing of "Moses." Given the unique nature of the Bradford–Tubman relationship, the pecuniary motivation for the publication of the Bradford volumes, and the orally based vignettes Bradford stitched together, I argue that we must deconstruct the heroic and heavily mediated tale that Bradford wove about her subject.

In the post-Reconstruction decades, Tubman's symbolic importance declined, a victim of America's yearning to bury the bitter fruit of the Civil War. The custodianship of her reputation was left to a small but dedicated band of friends and supporters. Many of them had ties to Auburn, New York, where Tubman lived out her days after retiring from her wartime service. Chapter 5 centers on Tubman's long Auburn period, a time during which further aspects of the Tubman myth solidified. Harriet Tubman emerged as a "homespun heroine" with remarkable seer-like powers, honed since her youthful years and used during her raids on a hostile South but now, as she grew older, folded into the notion of her as the model Christian—pious, saint-like, and self-sacrificing. In addition, it is during her Auburn period that Tubman is called on to play yet another role: that of a suffragist or women's rights supporter.

Chapter 6, "The Apotheosis of 'Aunt Harriet,'" begins with a detailed examination of the symbolic import of the Tubman funeral in 1913 and the events about a year later when Booker T. Washington went to Auburn to help dedicate a memorial tablet to the town's most famous black resident. Had it not been for African American women's groups and the African Methodist Episcopal Zion church, to which Harriet Tubman belonged, the mystical chord of memory might have been cut once the crowds at the funeral and memorial services dispersed. It is important, therefore, to look at how America reacted when Black Moses departed this earthly existence. In the dying, the death, and the funeral of Tubman, we have a temporal moment in which the inner structures of the Tubman myth are revealed. These elemental sentiments become enshrined (and preserved for posterity) in the formal process of canonization that took place in 1914 when Booker T. Washington, said to be America's most important black leader, went to Auburn to participate in memorial ceremonies.

"Earl Conrad and the Book That Almost Wasn't" is the title of the seventh chapter. This naming, awkward by intent, reflects the trouble that this Auburn native and crusading journalist had in writing and getting published his book-length biography of Harriet Tubman in 1943.[9] I discuss Conrad's creation of another symbolic Tubman, one in keeping with his own political views and ideology about race, his efforts to garner information on Tubman's life apart from the Bradford legacy, his use of documentary and oral sources, and his struggle with potential publishers. Conrad's biography of Harriet Tubman and, to a lesser extent, his other writings about her have been a major influence on all subsequent authors who have attempted to tell the story of "The Moses of Her People."

Chapter 8, "Spirits Rising," looks at the effusion of the Tubman myth into American culture (at multiple levels) in the post–Conrad years, in spite of the lack of interest in her by professionally trained historians. Writers of fiction fueled the popularization of the iconic Tubman, of course. However, Tubman was seemingly everywhere in the visual and creative arts. Her story was being told in mediums as seemingly disparate as opera and rap. More and more Americans laid claim to the Tubman legacy in the last quarter of the twentieth century. Public debates erupted about how to best honor her. In spite of these controversies, Tubman's iconic value escalated to the point at which it became as much commodity as cultural phenomenon.

Chapter 9 gives primacy to the question of place. Using the overarching themes of preservation and pilgrimage, I examine efforts to "ground" or create space for enshrining the Tubman myth and life history in tangible ways in various parts of the United States and, to a limited extent, in Canada. The Tubman-related properties in Auburn, New York, merit considerable attention, of course, but I also discuss Dorchester County, Maryland, and other places where there has been an effort to capitalize on Tubman's name. This chapter also assesses the significance of the placement by communities of the Tubman name on everything from schools to street signs. Cultural geographers, adept at reading our symbolic landscape, might well marvel at the degree to which Harriet Tubman, once obscure except in the circles of her friends and admirers, is now being firmly anchored to place. To be able to say, "Tubman was here in this spot," is to honor her memory by taking pride in place.

Chapter 10, the last chapter, raises the question, "Why is it that Harriet Tubman has resisted being demythologized?" Here I explore the intersections of history, memory, and myth against the backdrop of the previous chapters. Despite the scarcity of scholarship pertaining to the historical Tubman, or perhaps because of it, the iconic Tubman is more centrally located in the American memory than ever before. In 2003–2004, three new scholarly studies about Tubman appeared.[10] This was a watershed moment. Never before have we had professional historians give such serious attention to Harriet Tubman. No so-called biography had appeared about Tubman since Conrad's book in 1943. Though he sought out primary sources, documentary and human, Conrad was a journalist, not a trained historian. This chapter discusses the significance of the latest Tubman scholarship in light of the Tubman legend or myth and poses the question of whether or not the new biographies escape the limitations of commemorative memory.

Before leaving this introductory note, I should say something about my use of such elusive words as "history" and "memory." Scholarly debates about these concepts have been going on for decades, and an entire subdiscipline called "memory studies" has come into being.[11] Though I purposely have not larded chapter contents and references with technical discussions drawing on this scholarly enterprise, I am indebted to its practitioners for insights that have informed my thinking about the remembered Tubman. I am especially appreciative of the insightful work of the historian David W. Blight, whose ruminations on "the confluence of history and memory" have centered on topics of special interest to me—for example, Frederick Douglass, the Civil War, and the Underground Railroad.[12] I am also indebted to the pioneering and monumental labors of the American historian Michael Kammen, who reminds us that the study of memory centers on "the phenomenon of a society becoming its own historian—for better or worse."[13] Finally, I would be remiss if I did not acknowledge finding instructive parallels to my concentration on tracing the changing image of Harriet Tubman over time in the compelling work that the historian Merrill D. Peterson has done on the place of Abraham Lincoln in American thought and imagination.[14] The sociologist Barry Schwartz's book *Abraham Lincoln and the Forge of National Memory* also provided me with theoretical grounding for a better understanding of the way that the remembered past serves social and cultural functions at any given moment in time.[15]

"History" and "memory" jostle together in confusing fashion in the public mind. While professional historians explore the past with the intent of discovering "the way it really was," none have been totally successful in extracting themselves from "the politics of memory." All of us, this writer included, come to the topic of Harriet Tubman's place in the American memory conditioned by being situated in a particular consciousness. Having acknowledged this, the historian nevertheless analyzes the past with a critical—and, as Blight reminds us—more secular eye than the keepers of "memory." "Memory," Blight, argues, "is often treated as a sacred set of potentially absolute meanings and stories, possessed as the heritage of a community. Memory is often owned; history, interpreted. Memory is passed down through generations; history is revised. Memory often coalesces in objects, sacred sites, and monuments; history seeks to understand contexts and the complexity of cause and effect. History asserts the authority of academic training and recognized canons of evidence; memory carries the often powerful authority of community membership and experience."[16]

"Memory," it is said, is a "social construction" to suit the needs of individuals and groups of one kind or another. "Memory" selectively gleans the past for what is useable in the day-to-day struggles of various segments of society for a place at the national table where goods and services are distributed. Since the past cannot be remembered in its totality, individuals and groups create their histories out of selective memories, conflating and confusing the analytical categories of "memory" and "history" about which the scholars talk. It is necessary, therefore, to heed Kammen's advice as we begin examining the process by which Harriet Tubman has become an American icon: "What history and memory share in common is that both merit our mistrust, yet both must be nevertheless nourished."[17]

"History" often sets itself in judgment over "memory." Nevertheless, historical writing can have a fictive element, just as public and social memory can have a factual core. There are many stories told about Tubman that depart from what can be documented or substantiated in some other manner. Some of these are base fabrications and need to be placed in the category of legend. But others are riffs or elaborations of aspects of the core historical narrative and therefore reveal as much about the mythmakers as they do about Tubman herself. I am interested in both lines of inquiry—the historical Tubman and the symbolic or iconic Tubman—as well as the interplay of myth and history in the crucible of memory. Consequently, the chapters that are to come make use of primary evidence from the best reliable sources (documentary and oral) as well as the "dreamed up" testaments employed by hagiographers (the mythologizers). Folklore, even when embellishing the facts, also speaks to the durability of Harriet Tubman in the American cultural memory.

During the research and writing of this book, I encountered many individuals who shared their personal impressions of Tubman. They have found inspiration, hope, and healing by deep reflection on her ability to overcome. However, this book is not about these essentially privately constructed memories. It is not about what is silent or hidden from the public. I focus on what might be called the Harriet Tubman "public-awareness" campaign, the agency by which Tubman evolved from a little-known or celebrated historical figure into a symbol of national prominence. This book tells the story of the construction of an American icon; it is about collective or national memory. My principal focus is on those individuals who have "gone public," as it were, and thereby contributed to a treasury of memories that is accessible to all who care to consider her significance. "Collective memory," Schwartz argues, "is a representation of the past embodied in *both* historical evidence and commemorative symbolism."[18] Collective memory transcends individual memories and has, says Schwartz, "superpersonal" properties, such as "narratives, pictorial objects, monuments and shrines, place names, and observances, which are accumulated and transmitted across generations."[19]

Harriet Tubman's larger-than-life image has until very recently overpowered the historical evidence available about the real person. Why the collectively remembered Tubman has flourished at the expense of the historian's Tubman has been due in large part to the power of commemorative symbolism. Collective memories weaken, may even die, when they are no longer needed by social groups in their struggles to position themselves in relation to the socially constructed symbols or icons of other groups. Tubman's symbolic currency has varied in value, weak among some segments of American society, strong among others, according to the dictates of the politics of memory. As of this writing, she fares exceedingly well on the national stage, but, as our review of the evolution of her iconic life will reveal, there have been periods when she was relegated to a minor role in the national drama.

In summary, this book chronicles the life history of the commemorated Tubman (the symbol) in relation to the historical Tubman (the life) insofar as we can know her on the basis of biographical and historical facts. By foreshadowing questions of evidence when examining the tension between the remembered Tubman and biographical Tubman, I do not mean to diminish the importance of mythmaking for a better understanding of how Americans conceive of themselves as "we the people." It would be a tragedy if the nation suffered a memory crisis and once again forgot the black woman known to her contemporaries and their children, and their children's children, and so on, as "Moses." Let us not dis-remember Tubman. In so doing, this nation as a democratic society founded on egalitarian ideals would signal retreat from the "promised land" of freedom for which Tubman worked so heroically.

CHAPTER ONE

"MINTY"

Kareem Abdul-Jabbar, the American basketball sensation, tells of a teacher friend who tests students during Black History Month at an elementary school outside Atlanta. "Her kids," Abdul-Jabbar writes in *Black Profiles of Courage*, "know so little about black history that they answer Harriet Tubman for everything."[1] We might read Abdul-Jabbar's disclosure as symptomatic of the failure of American educators to integrate the culture and history of peoples of African descent into school curriculums. We could also interpret the children's ready naming of Tubman as illustrative of a high-water mark in the canonization process of Tubman in the American memory. Earlier generations of children might have called to mind Martin Luther King Jr. or George Washington Carver, if students of the twentieth century, and Booker T. Washington or Frederick Douglass, if queried about nineteenth-century African American heroes. If we must judge by the plethora of books about Tubman in the field of juvenile literature as well as by the many other ways in which young people are taught about her, Harriet Tubman is the all-comprehending black hero of our time.

Listen to the stories adults create for children, and you gain access to the contents of a society's treasure house of memory. In cultures without books as well as in literate ones, the stories passed down to children winnow that which is thought worth preserving from that which fades away as one generation succeeds another. In traditional West African cultures, including the one from which Harriet Tubman's ancestors came, the definition of immortality centered on being remembered. The "living dead" were kept from fading into anonymity by being called to life in communal story, song, and dance.

Remembering, whether by written or oral means, is an act of distillation. Some memories fall away; others survive, are embellished, and become stronger with the passage of time. Stories written for children make up the decanter in which the base elements of the Harriet Tubman myth are revealed. By examining children's literature, sometimes called juvenile literature, we discover not only what Americans have thought worth remembering about Tubman, but also how the Tubman myth has been shaped and reshaped in the crucible of American history. The curricular wars that erupted among educators and politicians in the late twentieth century prove to be an especially revealing window on America's struggle to come to terms with the meaning and importance of Harriet Tubman. By examining this controversy and the emergence of Tubman as a staple in juvenile literature, we can understand the essential elements of the Tubman myth.

Harriet Tubman was herself an inveterate and powerful storyteller. Though she had no children of her own, she enjoyed telling young people of her adventures. This was especially the case during her matriarchal years when she would show up at the homes of her Auburn benefactors. Their children sat before the elderly Tubman and heard of her marvelous exploits on the Underground Railroad and in the South during the Civil War. Samuel Hopkins Adams, a renowned storyteller in his own right whose great-aunt Sarah Hopkins Bradford acted as Tubman's biographer, recalled that it was a "gala day" in the late 1870s when "Old Harriet" arrived at his grandfather's Grant Avenue mansion on the outskirts of Auburn, New York. The children gathered around her, transfixed by her dramatic storytelling ability. They did not fully understand her historical significance, for, as Adams says, "The postwar ebb of patriotic fervor left her stranded." However, they found her to be a fascinating "tribal teller of tales, a never-failing source of adventure and romance."[2]

Some of the stories Tubman told passed from parent to child to grandchildren. In 1939, Alice L. Brickler informed Earl Conrad that, when she closed her eyes, she could "feel again the thrills of adventure & terror as my mother use[d] to tell me the stories of Aunt Harriet." Alice Brickler, the former Alice Lucas, daughter of Margaret Stewart, the young woman whom Tubman allegedly kidnapped in 1862, was approximately fifteen when Tubman died in 1913.[3] Harkless Bowley, another of Conrad's informants, recalled how Tubman, who had aided his parents in escaping to Canada West, as Ontario was known from 1841 to 1867, told of the dangers of working on the Underground Railroad. When a young boy, he lived with the one hailed as "Black Moses" in her Auburn home. Eighty-two years of age in 1939 when corresponding with Conrad, Bowley could still bring to mind his aunt's thrilling stories.[4]

Another vivid recollection of Tubman's power as a storyteller comes to us from Vivian Carter Mason, the civil rights activist and educator who became the third president of the National Council of Negro Women in 1950. Born in 1900, Mason was the daughter of the Reverend George Carter and his wife Florence, onetime residents of Auburn. When the National Council was putting together *The Historical Cookbook of the American Negro* in 1958, Mason contributed a recipe for "Cornbread Harriet Tubman," said to be Aunt Harriet's favorite dish, along with a delightful account of having heard the "brave and dauntless woman [who] revitalized the meaning of freedom" tell of her exploits.

> As a child I could not realize what a wonderful privilege it was to have known the famed freedom fighter, Harriet Tubman. Many the time "Aunt Harriet," as we called her, would tramp through the ice, snow and bitter cold of the northern winters from her home on the outskirts to our snug house in Auburn, New York, to sit before the huge kitchen range and warm her thin body before the glowing coals.
>
> My mother, Florence, and my father, The Reverend George Carter, loved and revered Harriet Tubman and taught their children to do the same. She would draw us to her side and while we made ourselves comfortable with old pillows on the floor, tell hair-raising stories of her escape from slavery and subsequent returns to the plantation to bring over four hundred men and women to freedom as the chief "conductor" of the underground railroad. As she talked, her head thrown back and eyes closed, we were in the woods with her tramping at night through stony creeks where the water was cold, hiding in the bush during the day and glad for a piece of cornbread washed down by the water of a hidden spring. We shivered as we heard the sound of horses' hoofs, fearing the men searching the woods and highways for black Harriet and her runaways. That they never caught up with her was always the triumphant ending of a fearful and frightening recital of days full of danger and suffering.

Then mother would call us to dinner, and as the lamps cast a bright light on the huge kitchen table, with the steaming bowls of rice soup and the crisp cornbread piled high, it was not hard to imagine that in the darkness outside someone was still searching for Harriet and would take us too.[5]

With the passing away of individuals who had heard "Aunt Harriet" tell her own story, and with the weakening of the oral tradition over time, text-based accounts of Tubman's life began to appear. Part of the difficulty in probing memories about Tubman is that by the time written testimonials to her greatness began to appear in profusion, the legend and the lady—that is, the iconic symbol and the historical person—were intertwined. This is especially true of the information passed down about Harriet's experiences prior to her escape from Maryland in 1849. Nevertheless, authors who write accounts of Tubman's life for young readers highlight the first decades of her life, hoping, perhaps, that children will find cause to be inspired by their young heroine's triumph over adversity in spite of her hardships.

Our historical knowledge about children's experiences within America's so-called peculiar institution is limited. Frederick Bailey (Frederick Douglass), whose first two decades were spent under "the whip and the lash" on Maryland's Eastern Shore in Talbot County, not far from where Harriet grew up in Dorchester County, told of his childhood experiences and struggles in several autobiographical works.[6] Harriet A. Jacobs revealed the injustices visited on a young female slave in her *Incidents in the Life of a Slave Girl*.[7] While numerous ex-slave narratives touch on childhood experiences, few of them were written with the intent of chronicling childhood as such. Secondary literature focuses, for the most part, on adults, and until recent decades primarily on African and African American men who bore slavery's yoke. Since the interpretive lens of gender has been employed, historians have given greater attention to the theme of "Black Women and Slavery."[8] Scholarly attention to the lives of children in the slave quarters of the antebellum South did not flourish until the 1990s. Written accounts of Harriet's childhood and experiences as a young woman began to appear, however, long before there was any special interest in the interior or exterior lives of slaves who were both young and female.

Until Tubman sat down with Sarah Bradford after the Civil War to tell something of her story as background for Bradford's biographical sketch of her, published in 1869, interest in the childhood of the woman who became "Black Moses" lagged behind stories about her Underground Railroad heroics and Civil War experiences. Benjamin Drew's brief mention of Harriet Tubman in his book *A North-Side View of Slavery*, based on Drew's encounter with her while visiting St. Catharines in 1855, has Tubman telling the white journalist and abolitionist: "I grew up like a neglected weed,—ignorant of liberty, having no experience of it. Then I was not happy or contented: every time I saw a white man I was afraid of being carried away. I had two sisters carried away in a chain-gang,—one of them left two children."[9] Apart from this one reference to Tubman's life story prior to her escape, nothing else about Tubman's early years appeared in print for public consumption until 1863, when the Boston-based newspaper *Commonwealth*, edited by Franklin B. Sanborn, carried a three-column-long story under the title "Harriet Tubman."

Sanborn told his readers that his black heroine had been given the birth name Araminta when born "as near as she can remember, in 1820 or in 1821" in Dorchester County, Maryland. He reported that she was the daughter of Benjamin Ross and Harriet Greene (Green) and that both of her parents were enslaved. Sanborn claimed that Araminta was the granddaughter of a "native African" without "a drop of white blood in her veins."[10]

Recent scholarship suggests that Harriet actually had eight siblings (four brothers and four sisters). Kate Clifford Larson discovered that Anthony Thompson paid a midwife two dollars in mid-March 1822 to aid Harriet "Rit" Green in childbirth. Larson believes that "this could be a fortuitous record of Tubman's birth," suggesting that she was born in late February or early March 1822.[11] We may never know Araminta's exact birth date, but it is not far-fetched to imagine, along with the painter Jacob Lawrence, that a bright star shown on the night of the birth of Black Moses. Lawrence's powerfully evocative "Harriet, Harriet, Born a Slave" (see Plate 1) brings to mind cradle scenes of the baby Jesus and his parents.

Thompson's farm was located south of Madison in the Parsons Creek district of Dorchester County. This means that Tubman was not born in the Bucktown area on property owned by Edward Brodess, as so many children's books have stated. As to the claim that Tubman was the granddaughter of a "native African," usually thought to be of Asante origin, recent biographers entertain the possibility that Modesty, Tubman's grand-mother, or perhaps another grandparent may have originated from West Africa, specifically from the region now known as Ghana, but definitive proof has not been found.[12]

At six, according to Sanborn's article, Harriet was taken from her mother and removed ten miles away to learn the weaver's trade in a white household, that of James Cook. She was so ill at ease in this new environment that she refused a favorite drink: "I was as fond of milk as any young shote [young pig]. But all the time I was there I stuck to it, dat I didn't drink sweet milk."[13] Harriet became ill and was temporarily returned to her mother. Though she was brought back to work for the Cook family when her health improved, she refused to learn weaving and hated her mistress. Sanborn did not mention an especially onerous task young Harriet had to perform while hired out—wading in cold water during winter to check on muskrat traps, even when she was sick with the measles.

Sanborn did tell the public in 1863 about the incident when Harriet, "after she entered her teens [and] was hired out as a field hand," received an injury that had long-lasting consequences. Readers of the *Commonwealth* article learned that an overseer, attempting to whip a slave who had left his work and gone to a crossroads store, threw a two-pound weight at the runaway. It missed and struck Harriet "a stunning blow on the head." She, "among others," had sought to intervene between overseer and slave.[14]

This "blow to the head" incident has been a primary strand in the Tubman story as recapitulated and illustrated for children. A popular book written by David A. Adler and illustrated by Samuel Byrd graphically depicts Harriet almost being killed (Figure 1). Harriet, said to be thirteen or perhaps fifteen, refuses to help tie up the runaway Jim (a name not given in the primary sources), is hit on the head, falls to the ground, and, bleeding from a long gash, is carried to the slave quarters. Her mother fears for her life.[15]

Tubman's sleeping spells and seizures dramatize the "Minty" books; illustrators frequently depict Tubman having one of her sleeping spells. Approximately eight years before her death in 1913, Tubman revealed details of the trauma she had experienced as a teenager. An interviewer reported her as saying: "I had a shoulder shawl' ob de mistis' ober my haid an' when I got to do sto' I was shamed to go in, an' said [saw] de' oberseer raisin' up to throw an iron weight at one ob de slaves an' dat wuz de las' I knew . . . broke my skull and cut a piece ob dat shawl clean off and druv it into my haid. Dey carried me to de house all bleedin an' faintin. I had no baid, no place to lie down on at all, an' dey lay me on de seat ob de loom, an' I stayed dere all dat day an' nex.'"[16]

Sanborn's sketch continued with an account of how Harriet worked "for five or six years" for John T. Stewart, first in the house but later hiring her time out, earning enough in one year to purchase a span of oxen for forty dollars. She drove oxen, carted, and ploughed in the fields. She also worked for her father, Ben Ross, a timber inspector, cutting and hauling logs. Tubman books written for children often include an illustration of Harriet at work in the woods (Figure 2), underscoring the theme that she became unusually strong physically, a characteristic that would become useful when she served as an Underground Railroad conductor.[17]

Sanborn's biographical profile did not include several stories about Tubman's younger years that have become basic components in the "Black Moses" legend. From sources published much later, the public learned that Harriet had to break flax, an unpleasant task for a child. She was whipped at age five for failing to keep a baby quiet, and she ran away at seven to escape punishment after taking a lump of sugar. Harriet hid out in a pigpen, where she had to compete with the swine for food, an incident depicted for young readers by the illustrator Rick Cooley in *Harriet Finds a Way*, written by Dolores Ready (Figure 3).

In retelling and illustrating these stories, the authors and artists under-score the cruelty of slavery, of course, but they also create a character that their young readers should admire. Harriet suffered much, but by sur-viving and not being broken psychologically, she triumphed. It is an old paradigm: The hero has many tribulations but, in the end, survives and ultimately overcomes all persecutors.

"Somewhere about 1844," Sanborn wrote, Harriet, then known as Minty Ross, married a free black man named John Tubman "but had no children."[18] Sanborn gave no further information about this mar-riage. Sarah Bradford, Tubman's biographer in 1869, cast John Tubman in an unfavorable light, writing that he ridiculed Harriet, calling her "a fool, and said she was like old Cudjo, who when a joke went round, never laughed till half an hour after everybody else got through."[19] Little is

In 1835, Harriet came between a master and a slave who was running away. The master threw a metal weight at the runaway. It hit Harriet instead and almost killed her.

1. Harriet hit with metal weight. Illustration by Samuel Byrd. From David A. Adler, *A Picture Book of Harriet Tubman* (New York: Scholastic, 1994). Text copyright © 1992 by David A. Adler. Illustrations copyright © 1992 by Samuel Byrd.

2. Harriet chopping wood. Illustration by Karen Ritz, From Jeri Ferris and Karen Ritz, *Go Free or Die: A Story about Harriet Tubman* (Minneapolis: Carolrhoda Books, a division of Lerner Publishing Group, 1988). Text copyright © 1988 by Jeri Ferris. Illustrations copyright © by Carolrhoda Books, Inc.

3. Pigpen. Illustration by Rick
Cooley. From Dolores Ready,
Harriet Finds a Way (Minneapolis:
Winston Press, 1978).

known about Tubman's first husband. Larson speculates that John Tubman must have loved his wife, given the "great cost" entailed in marrying
an enslaved woman whose children would inherit her status.[20]

During the two years prior to her escape, Harriet went to work for
Anthony Thompson, the son of her master's guardian, Anthony Thompson, the elder. The younger Thompson died in 1849. Fearing that her
family was to be broken up, Harriet, resolving not to be sold, "walked
away one night alone."[21] In light of the life-altering importance of Tubman's decision to run away, Sanborn's brief mention of her escape is
striking.

Most secondary sources place Tubman's flight from the South that was
her Egypt sometime in 1849 (see Plate 2). No confirming documentation
accompanies these accounts, though recently historians have called attention to a runaway notice found in a Maryland newspaper that would suggest late fall as the time of Harriet's break for freedom. Placed by Eliza
Ann Brodess, it refers to Tubman as Minty and describes her as "about
27 years . . . of a chestnut color, fine looking, and about 5 feet high."[22]
This advertisement, dated October 3, 1849 (Figure 4), also asked for the
return of Tubman's brothers "Harry, aged about 19 years" and "Ben, aged
about 25 years" who with Minty are said to have escaped on Monday, September 17, 1849. Given the inclusion of Ben and Harry (actually Henry),
the notice no doubt pertains to the first attempt Harriet made to escape.
She had been unable to convince her brothers to go on, and all three

THREE HUNDRED DOLLARS REWARD.

RANAWAY from the subscriber on Monday the 17th ult., three negroes, named as follows: HARRY, aged about 19 years, has on one side of his neck a wen, just under the ear, he is of a dark chestnut color, about 5 feet 8 or 9 inches hight; BEN, aged aged about 25 years, is very quick to speak when spoken to, he is of a chestnut color, about six feet high; MINTY, aged about 27 years, is of a chestnut color, fine looking, and about 5 feet high. One hundred dollars reward will be given for each of the above named negroes, if taken out of the State, and $50 each if taken in the State. They must be lodged in Baltimore, Easton or Cambridge Jail, in Maryland.

ELIZA ANN BRODESS,
Near Bucktown, Dorchester county, Md.
Oct. 3d, 1849.

☞The Delaware Gazette will please copy the above three weeks, and charge this office.

4. Reward notice from *Cambridge [Md.] Democrat*, October 3, 1849. From Kate Clifford Larson, *Bound for the Promised Land: Harriet Tubman, Portrait of an American Hero* (New York: Ballantine Books, 2004). Courtesy James Meredith.

runaways returned. Sometime thereafter, perhaps within a period of two weeks or so, Tubman made good her escape.

Historians remain unsure of Tubman's exact escape route. A white woman, possibly a Quaker, helped her at one point. Harriet gave her a bed quilt as a gesture of appreciation. When she finally crossed into Pennsylvania and stepped onto free soil, Tubman paused to savor the moment. Sarah Bradford reported that Tubman told her, "When I found I had crossed dat line, I looked at my hands to see if I was de same pusson. There was such a glory ober ebery ting; de sun came like gold through the trees, and ober the fields, and I felt like I was in Heaben."[23]

The remaining sections of the *Commonwealth* article concern Tubman's Underground Railroad years, association with John Brown, and wartime service, themes discussed in subsequent chapters. The *Freedom's Record* of March 1865, another Boston-based publication, essentially repeated the foregoing information about Tubman's pre-escape life, drawing heavily on Sanborn's story. The article's author, Edna Dow Cheney, a white, New England–based reformer and suffragist, reinforced Sanborn's notion that Harriet Tubman's story had the "power to shake the nation that was long deaf to her cries"[24] by writing that Tubman was "probably the most remarkable woman of this age."[25] Cheney offered no new details about Tubman's life when she was known as "Minty."

The American public, such as it was interested at all, had to wait another four years for more information about Tubman's experiences while held as a slave. Sarah Bradford's little book titled *Scenes in the Life of Harriet Tubman* came out in 1869. Bradford, a white woman then living in Geneva, New York, had written a handful of stories for children, but her Tubman biography was directed toward adults in a money-raising effort. Bradford devoted approximately nine pages to Harriet's childhood and pre-escape experiences, introducing readers to the dusting episode (Harriet is whipped for not dusting a piano to Miss Susan's satisfaction) and the story of Harriet falling asleep while rocking a sick child and again being whipped. Readers also learned of Harriet's prayer that the Lord convert her "owner" or kill him and of the dream in which she envisions a line beyond which "were green fields, and lovely flowers, and beautiful white ladies."[26]

Bradford published a revised biography of Tubman in 1886 with a new title: *Harriet, The Moses of Her People*. Bradford's second book devotes approximately a dozen pages to Harriet's life prior to the time she decided to escape. The narrative opens with "a little girl of perhaps thirteen years of age" sitting atop a rail fence. She appears to be dazed, even dull or half-witted. It is Harriet, the future "Moses of Her People," who is recovering from the blow of that heavy weight. Though Bradford provides more editorial commentary on Tubman's youthful experiences, notably on her religious temperament—her dreams and visions—in this second biography, the elements of the earlier *Scenes* are present: the story about dusting, the one concerning Harriet acting as a child's nurse when she was but a child herself, Harriet's prayer that the Lord convert her master or kill him, and so on. Nothing substantial is added to the narrative core about Tubman's pre-1849 experiences found in the *Moses* volume.[27] Bradford may have been dissatisfied with the paucity of stories pertaining to Tubman's "Minty" years, for the second edition of *Moses*, published in 1901, has an appendix that added the story about young Harriet taking a lump of sugar, running away to escape a whipping, and then having to fight with little pigs for potato peelings because she was so hungry.[28]

Scores of books now exist about Harriet Tubman written especially for children. Some of them concentrate almost exclusively on Harriet's early years when she was known as Araminta or Minty. Others carry the story forward to celebrate her as the famous "Black Moses" of the Underground Railroad. Still others include accounts of her as a Civil War nurse, spy, and scout. Most authors who wrote for the juvenile-literature market relied heavily on the Bradford books, especially Bradford's second, or 1886, biography of Tubman. Some writers have made use of Earl Conrad's biography of Tubman that was published in 1943. A close examination of Conrad's treatment of Harriet's pre-escape life reveals that, in spite of his extensive research into primary sources and contacts with people who had known Tubman, additional information about Harriet Tubman's childhood was difficult to come by.[29] This should not surprise us. Until recently, historians have not concerned themselves with the special difficulties of writing about children who grew up in the context of a slave society.

Nevertheless, many authors have written about Harriet Tubman with young readers as their audience. Tubman is the subject of more children's books than any other African American historical figure, including Frederick Douglass and Sojourner Truth, her well-known contemporaries. In another time, prior to the demands on publishers generated by debates about race and gender since the 1960s, young people might have

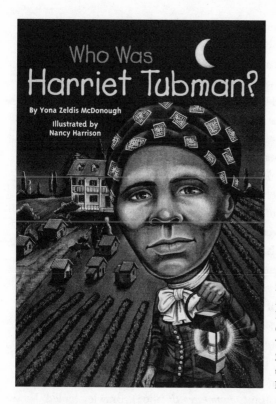

5. Book cover. From Yona Zeldis McDonough, *Who Was Harriet Tubman?* illustrated by Nancy Harrison (New York: Grosset and Dunlap, 2002). Text copyright © 2002 by Yona Zeldis McDonough. Illustrations copyright © 2002 by Nancy Harrison.

read of Booker T. Washington, George Washington Carver, or, perhaps, Frederick Douglass. Harriet Tubman, beginning in the 1960s, supplanted these personalities in popularity in the field of juvenile literature. The books attempted to answer the question posed on the cover of one written by Yona Zeldis McDonough and illustrated by Nancy Harrison: "Who Was Harriet Tubman?" (Figure 5).

The earliest sketch of Tubman's life written specifically for children may well be that penned in 1912 by the African American author Leila Amos Pendleton. A public-school teacher, Pendleton founded the Alpha Charity Club of Anacostia and the Social Purity Club of Washington, D.C. Pendleton wrote her primer on African and African American history "as a sort of 'family story' to the colored children of America."[30] She directed her book to girls and boys from twelve to fourteen with the hope that they would grow up to dedicate themselves to the improvement of "the race." Her profile of Tubman, placed between sketches of Sojourner Truth and Frances Ellen Watkins Harper, noted that her heroine still lived (February 1912). Pendleton offered no information on

Tubman's childhood or anything on Tubman's wartime experiences other than to say that her heroine had been a nurse, spy, and scout in the Union Army. The profile, brief as it is, mentions a few episodes from Tubman's career as an Underground Railroad conductor and then draws attention to "Aunt Harriet" — "said to be nearly one hundred years old" — as a benefactor of "her race" by establishing a home for the homeless in Auburn.[31] Though younger readers would have discovered only a meager amount of information about Tubman's long life in the Pendleton book, it served as a foundational stone in the educational effort to have the black youth of America improve themselves by emulating "Aunt Harriet."

In the decades following Tubman's death in 1913, white authors writing for younger readers expressed little interest in the woman hailed as "The Moses of Her People." It was left to black authors to distill and codify the Tubman legend. Some who did wrote sketches of Tubman that could be read by adults and passed on to children in the home. Benjamin Griffith Brawley, then dean of Morehouse College in Atlanta, devoted twelve pages to Tubman in his *Women of Achievement* (1919), a publication written for the Fireside Schools program of the Woman's American Baptist Home Mission Society. Brawley drew his information from Bradford's *Harriet, the Moses of Her People* (1886) and Sanborn's article about Tubman that appeared in the Boston *Commonwealth* (1863). Brawley hailed Tubman as the "greatest of all the heroines of anti-slavery," a strong-spirited character with a rock-solid confidence in God.[32] Though he offered no new information about Tubman, except for noting the tablet unveiled in her honor in Auburn in 1914, Brawley hailed Tubman as a role model for African American youth.

The same may be said of Elizabeth Ross Haynes, author of *Unsung Heroes*, a collection of biographical sketches published in 1921. Tubman's profile follows that of Booker T. Washington and precedes one about Alexander S. Pushkin. Haynes does not inform her readers of the sources she used, but the content strongly suggests that she consulted Bradford's 1886 biography. Haynes sought to enliven historical material with fictional elements. She created dialogue for her characters and background context for the reader. Haynes refrains from direct hortatory statements about the need for young people to use Tubman as a role model, but the lessons are there nevertheless. Of the seventeen "unsung heroes," two others are female historical figures: Sojourner Truth and Phillis Wheatley.[33]

Though what was being published in the 1920s was not written explicitly to develop the reading skills of children or provide them with "juvenile literature," in the sense this term is understood today, the Tubman profiles were clearly designed to encourage young people to live lives of usefulness. Hallie Q. Brown, author of *Homespun Heroines and Other Women of Distinction* (1926), said of her book, which contained a chapter on Tubman as well as sketches of less-well-known black women of merit such as Martha Payne, mother of Daniel A. Payne, the religious and educational leader who became the first president of Wilberforce University, and Sarah Allen, wife of Richard Allen, the first bishop of the African Methodist Episcopal church: "Our chief object of these introductory sentences is to secure for this book the interest of our youth, that they may have instructive light on the struggles endured and the obstacles overcome by our pioneer women. It has been prepared with the hope that they will read it and derive fresh strength and courage from its records to stimulate and cause them to cleave more tenaciously to the truth and to battle more heroically for the right."[34] Brown was serving as the honorary president of the National Association of Colored Women at the time she published *Homespun Heroines*. Her tribute to Tubman begins: "When America writes her history without hatred and prejudice she will place high in the galaxy of fame the name of a woman as remarkable as the French heroine, Joan of Arc, a woman who had not even the poor advantages of the peasant maid of Domremy, but was born under the galling yoke of slavery with a long score of cruelty. Her service to her race and country are without parallel in like achievements by any member of her sex in the history of the world."[35] Brown, as did earlier architects of the Tubman-as-role-model tradition, drew heavily on the Bradford material.

Except for the occasional inclusion of Tubman in books written to inspire African American youth, the woman once called "the greatest heroine" of her age failed to be of much interest to mainstream publishers. Then, in 1932, Harcourt, Brace and Company published *The Railroad to Freedom*, written by Hildegarde Hoyt Swift, a white woman from Auburn, New York. Swift's father had taught at the Auburn-based Presbyterian-owned theological seminary. "In the town where I grew up there lived a colored woman named Harriet Tubman," Swift recalled. "As a girl I was much interested in the story of her escape from slavery, and I often wondered why it was not written down so that other boys and girls might read it."[36] Though Swift made an effort to incorporate as much factual material about Tubman as she could glean from Bradford's two books and selected secondary sources, her own Tubman portrayal was essentially fictional. "This is a story," Swift informs the reader, "not a biography, but it is based on authentic history."[37]

The Railroad to Freedom received a generally favorable review in the *Journal of Negro History*, then the nation's most important outlet for scholarly articles on African American history. Rayford W. Logan commented in his review: "This work not only makes available in readable form the story of a remarkable woman but also serves as a corrective to the sentimental idylls of slavery that are becoming all too numerous." Logan was willing to forgive Swift her tendency to "glorify Harriet," for he felt that there was much in her fictional account of Tubman's life that was "applicable today." Logan also saw in Swift's book something of value to whites as well as blacks and recommended *The Railroad to Freedom* to a wide readership: "It is to be hoped that as many of the race of the heroine as of the author will not let pass this opportunity of learning to love one of the great women of all times."[38] No writer followed Swift's lead during the 1940s in using Tubman as the inspiration of a book written for children, but two important works appeared in the 1950s, one by Dorothy Sterling and the other by Ann Petry.

Dorothy Sterling wrote *Freedom Train: The Story of Harriet Tubman*, published in 1954 by Doubleday (Figure 6).[39] Dedicated to her daughter "so that she may know the story of a great American woman," Sterling's version of the Tubman myth drew on the Bradford biographies, an adult-oriented novel about Tubman written by Anne Parrish that was published in 1948, of which more will be said later, and the books written by Swift and Earl Conrad. Sterling's book has been published several times in the Scholastic Biography series for young readers.[40] Sterling thought of *Freedom Train* as her "living work" and used it as a springboard to publish five additional books about African American history for young people. A self-trained historian, with experience as a researcher for *Life* and for the Federal Writers' Project in the 1930s and 1940s, Sterling participated in early civil-rights activism on behalf of the Scottsboro black youth accused of raping a white woman. She gravitated toward left-wing politics and became interested in the history of African Americans written by radical authors such as the communist-oriented historian Herbert

6. Dust-jacket photograph. From Dorothy Sterling, *Freedom Train: The Story of Harriet Tubman*, illustrated by Ernest Chrichlow (New York: Scholastic Book Services, 1954). Photograph by Ross Photos.

Aptheker.[41] Someone suggested that Sterling write about Harriet Tubman and thereby fulfill her desire to empower girls and promote civil rights. Sterling reflected years later: "You can't believe what an unknown figure she was—in the white community, not in the black of course. I would never heard of her if I hadn't been reading the left-wing press."[42]

Ann Petry's *Harriet Tubman: Conductor on the Underground Railroad* came out a year after Sterling's *Freedom Train*. Petry's father, Peter Lane, was one of a small number of African Americans living in Old Saybrook, Massachusetts, where he opened the village's first pharmacy in 1901. Ann Lane (Ann Petry) became a licensed pharmacist but had a passion for writing and in 1938 moved to Harlem, where she was employed by the *New York Amsterdam News* in its advertising department and then as a writer for the *Harlem People's Voice*. She wrote about the injustices experienced by African Americans, especially by black women. Her book *The Street* (1946) sold over a million copies and was translated into Arabic, Dutch, German, and Swedish. Among Petry's other books for young readers was her *Tituba of Salem Village*. She said that her motivation for writing about Tubman arose from her concern that "the majority of text-books used in high schools do not give an accurate picture of the history of slavery in the United States."[43] Like Sterling, Petry acknowledged that she had not heard of Tubman before she decided to write about her.

Petry's *Harriet Tubman*, which has been reprinted numerous times, offers a useful checkpoint on how the Tubman myth had evolved by the 1950s. There are twenty-one chapters. Chapters 1–5 concern life in "The Quarter," Harriet's "First Years," experiences when "Six Years Old," "Hired Out," and "Flight." Chapters 6–19 deal with Tubman's heroic service as a conductor on the Underground Railroad, and chapters 20–22 concern, respectively, "The Lecture Platform," "With the Union Army," and "The Last Years." Julia Mickenberg argues that Petry, like Sterling, used the Tubman story to present antiracist and "civil-rights" ideas in a format that would simultaneously teach a more progressive interpretation of American history and underscore the fundamental values of the Constitution and the Declaration of Independence. Mickenberg calls this task of juvenile biography "civic education."[44] One wonders why so few writers, black or white, used Tubman as the centerpiece of their books for children during the heyday of the Civil Rights Movement. Compounding the problem, children, even African American youth in the public schools, rarely encountered Tubman in any of their textbooks.

The scarcity of new books on Tubman changed as Americans wrestled with the educational implications of the urban crisis in the 1960s when one black ghetto after another erupted in anger. In an effort to make restitution for the omission of the African American presence in the "shaping of America" story, writers now invoked the memory of Harriet Tubman more readily than in earlier generations. She became an all-comprehending symbol, bridging the racial divide. This compensatory and socializing function reshaped her into a national icon. She was no longer only to be seen as an inspiration for black youth. Curiously, however, attempts to resurrect Tubman in the national or public memory in those forums where children are influenced most did not send writers to the primary sources. Few questioned the inherited myth.

The latter half of the 1960s witnessed the publication of a shelf of books about Tubman produced for the youth of America. Books by Ann McGovern (1965; Figure 7), Frances T. Humphreville (1967), Sam and Beryl Epstein (1968), and Gertrude Hecker Winders (1969), to note but a few examples, took the basic threads of the Tubman myth and embel-

7. Book cover. From Anne McGovern, *Runaway Slave: The Story of Harriet Tubman*, illustrations by R. M. Powers (New York: Scholastic Book Services, 1965).

lished them with illustrations and fictional dialogue.[45] None of these authors raised questions about the Tubman myth first codified by Sarah Bradford and then enhanced by subsequent writers whose books can be categorized as juvenile literature. Corinth Books had republished Bradford's *Moses* (the 1886 volume) in 1961, making this version more readily available to writers intent on finding a black heroine whose life story could speak to the social and cultural demands of the turbulent 1960s.[46]

Amid calls for "black power" and increasing concern about the political consequences of the national debate about race, Tubman came to mind when the authors and editors put together collections of stories about American "greats." Collier Books published Henrietta Buckmaster's *Women Who Shaped History* in 1966. Here America's youth could read about Tubman in the company of Dorothea Dix, Prudence Crandall, Elizabeth Cady Stanton, Elizabeth Blackwell, and Mary Baker Eddy.[47] In 1967, Johanna Johnston told young readers about Tubman's special bravery in the context of fifteen profiles of "great" African American figures, ranging from Crispus Attucks to Martin Luther King Jr. Only three of Johnston's exemplars of bravery are female: Tubman, Mary McLeod Bethune, and Marian Anderson.[48] Senator Margaret Chase Smith and

H. Paul Jeffers had an all-female cast in their book *Gallant Women*, published in 1968. Senator Smith hailed Tubman "as the epitome of physical courage as well as moral dedication."[49] Tubman's story is told in a chapter that also deals with Harriet Beecher Stowe and Clara Barton. Althea Gibson, the tennis player, and Tubman are the only African Americans among the dozen women profiled. Tubman takes her place among such well-known white women as Susan B. Anthony, Amelia Earhart, and Eleanor Roosevelt.

Books were not the only means Tubman admirers used to reach America's youth during the 1960s. In 1966, *Golden Legacy*, an illustrated history magazine in comic format, devoted an issue to Harriet Tubman. Published and edited by Bertram A. Fitzgerald Jr., the *Golden Legacy* issue had endorsements from the New York City Board of Education, the National Association for the Advancement of Colored People (NAACP), the Association for the Study of Negro Life and History, and Benjamin Quarles, the prominent African American historian then teaching at Morgan State. The Tubman issue belonged to a set that included comics about Toussaint L'Ouverture, Crispus Attucks, Benjamin Banneker, and Matthew Henson. In a note to readers, Fitzgerald said, "The intention of our publication is to implant pride and self-esteem in black youth while dispelling myths in others."[50] Born in 1932 in Harlem, Fitzgerald grew up on a literary diet that included the Classic Illustrated series of comic books, but he felt that illustrated versions of books such as *Uncle Tom's Cabin* disparaged African Americans such as himself and saw the *Golden Legacy* series of Black History Comic Books as an instrument to remedy this (see Plate 3).[51]

More Tubman books for the juvenile literature market appeared during the 1970s. Some of them were designed for use by elementary school-age children with rudimentary reading skills.[52] Others, replete with engaging illustrations, could be used by parents to read aloud to preschoolers. Most of these books for children contained explicit pedagogical and moral lessons. For example, Ann Donegan Johnson's book about Tubman stressed the value of helping.[53] Additional books in the Value Tales series taught about such important personal characteristics as determination (Helen Keller), respect (Abraham Lincoln), and creativity (Thomas Edison).

The celebration of the bicentennial of the American Revolution in 1976 included a tidal wave of books that sought to define the essential components of the national heritage. Some of these publications began as attempts by local communities to articulate their understanding of the bicentennial in a fashion more enduring than a confetti parade. The chairman of the Bicentennial Commission of Elkhart, Indiana, asked the Notre Dame historian Jay P. Dolan to edit a series of essays that had appeared in the *Elkhart Truth* under the theme, "'76 That's the Spirit." All of Indiana's schools and libraries were to receive a copy of the commemorative volume as a gift. Benjamin Quarles, whose path-breaking book *Black Abolitionists* (1969) helped spark the black studies emphasis and filled a void in the historiography of the abolitionist movement, wrote the chapter on Tubman.[54] Quarles argued that reflecting on Harriet Tubman was especially needful at a time of national commemoration because "she embodied the great affirmations that marked the birth of the Republic."[55] None other than the Harvard historian Henry Steele Commager, an influential voice for decades in conversations about how to best define the American character, wrote the epilogue to this Midwestern community's desire to foster respect among young people for people who embodied the spirit of the American Revolution.

In the 1980s, authors portrayed Tubman as an American freedom fighter who, like the biblical Moses, led her people out of bondage into the Promised Land where the torch of freedom burns.[56] *Cobblestone*, a history magazine for young people, devoted an entire issue to Tubman and the Underground Railroad in 1981. The authors Peg Mims and Walter Olesky, at the end of their essay titled "The Woman Called Moses," urged this moral lesson on young historians: "Harriet Tubman's task is not finished. Her life stands as a challenge for all of us to follow, and her instructions are simple: dare to stand alone, dare to have a firm purpose, and dare to have your purpose known."[57] One author retold the story of Tubman to educate children about "the rainbow of humanity" that makes the United States beautiful and strong.[58] By the end of the 1980s, Tubman, more so than any other African American woman, including Sojourner Truth, had become the representative African American when collections of sketches about American "greats" were compiled.[59] She also began to be included in books written for children that drew examples of role models from around the world. In 1989, Judy Carlson's book *Harriet Tubman: Call to Freedom* appeared in a series that included short biographies on John F. Kennedy and Abraham Lincoln, who were already American icons, and Sally Ride, a living icon for having "shot for the stars" in the American space program. But the series also contained

8. Book cover. From Judith Bentley, *Harriet Tubman*, (New York: Franklin Watts, 1990). Copyright © 1990 by Judith Bentley. Jacket photograph courtesy Photo Researchers/Tom McHugh.

biographies of Christopher Columbus, "Intrepid Marine," and Mikhail Gorbachev, "Soviet Innovator."[60]

The decade of the 1990s opened with publishers continuing to swell the number of books written to persuade American youth that Tubman should be thought of as a national hero of the first rank. At least fourteen books devoted to Tubman or containing chapters about her appeared in the first three years of the decade alone. Judith Bentley wrote an often read children's book featuring the oil painting of Tubman done by Robert Pius in the 1950s on its cover (Figure 8).[61]

Judged by our knowledge of Tubman today, *Harriet Tubman: Antislavery Activist*, written by Marian W. Taylor and published in 1991, stands out as an attempt to portray the woman behind the myth. The book belonged to the Black Americans of Achievement series, the general editor of which was Nathan Irvin Huggins, then director of the W. E. B. Du Bois Institute for Afro-American Research at Harvard University. Coretta Scott King contributed an introductory essay titled "On Achievement," in which she discussed the meaning of "excellence" and stressed that each of the men and women profiled in the series had been "a tribute to the spirit of our democratic ideals and the system in which they have flourished."[62] At a time when educators were under pressure to enrich the learning experience with multicultural content, Tubman proved to be the ideal candidate for inclusion.

In 1991, AESOP Enterprises of Indianapolis produced a booklet titled *Harriet Tubman: Stand and Deliver*, with an accompanying audiotape, and marketed it to churches, homes, and schools. Potential purchasers were told that by purchasing the book and accompanying audiotape they would successfully infuse multicultural history into their respective learning environments. By obtaining AESOP's Multi-Cultural Heroes and Sheroes Series, according to the company's president, Reed S. Armstead, educators would enable children to understand that the winner in life is not necessarily the person who is the strongest or the swiftest, but that, following the example of Harriet Tubman, any child can be "our next Hero or Shero" if he or she focused on "the steady development of character."[63]

During the 1990s, some of America's most respected historians seemed ready to give Tubman her due, to recognize, as Coretta Scott King framed the question, Tubman's achievements. Henry Steele Commager wrote the introductory essay to Megan McClard's *Harriet Tubman: Slavery and the Underground Railroad*, one of ten books in the History of the Civil War series. Commager attempted to justify Tubman's inclusion in the series by making a comparison with her historical contemporaries. "It is often said," the Harvard historian wrote, "that the most influential woman of the Civil War era was Harriet Beecher Stowe, the author of *Uncle Tom's Cabin*. Tubman's contributions, while more direct, were no less important."[64]

Just as interest in Tubman appeared to be advancing at an exponential rate in the early 1990s, the controversy over multiculturalism, brewing already in the 1980s, boiled over. Historians, educators, politicians, and pundits of varied persuasions debated the merits of rewriting the textbooks students used in America's public school system. Conservatives, and some liberals, expressed alarm over the degree to which educators had embraced multiculturalism by rewriting American history curriculums to better reflect the racial and ethnic diversity of the nation. Identity politics, not good history, so the bill of particulars read, drove this revisionist movement. To critics of the multicultural emphasis, the new orthodoxy born of the social turbulence of the late twentieth century threatened the core American myth of having a common history and a shared system of values. Racial multiculturalists, including outspoken proponents of what was being called Afrocentric history, came under heavy criticism from conservative defenders of the Anglo-American tradition that previously held sway in American public education.

Liberals, too, weighed in on the debate. While celebrating racial diversity, they feared cultural fragmentation.[65] The prominent historian Carl Degler warned that "the national slogan of E Pluribus Unum [was] in danger of being transformed into 'Out of One, Many.'"[66] Arthur M. Schlesinger Jr., the Pulitzer Prize–winning historian who had been a special adviser to President Kennedy and belonged to the executive council of the *Journal of Negro History*, wrote an extended critique of radical multiculturalism under the title *The Disuniting of America* in which he complained, "The attack on the common American identity is the culmination of the cult of ethnicity."[67] Schlesinger, fearful of cultural and ethnic separatism, counseled, "Our schools and colleges have a responsibility to teach history for its own sake — as part of the intellectual equipment of civilized persons — and not to degrade history by allowing its contents to be dictated by pressure groups, whether political, economic, religious or ethnic."[68] He acknowledged the need for a "due appreciation of the splendid diversity of the nation," but he called for a renewed commitment to the value of a shared American identity.

Schlesinger and the other critics of radical multiculturalism attempted to press for a common history. But how should that "common history" be told? New York and California, with their large and diverse populations, had struggled, with mixed results, to redefine curricula in keeping with the demands of the multiculturalists. Was it possible, some educators wondered, to reach consensus at the national level about what students should be taught about the American past? In 1992, the National Endowment for the Humanities and the U.S. Department of Education awarded a grant of $1.75 million to work on developing a curriculum guide for the country's vast public school system. The end product proved to be a 271-page document titled *National Standards for United States History*.[69]

Though the guide aimed high enough — "Knowledge of history is the precondition of political intelligence. Without history, a society shares no common memory of where it has been [or] what its core values are" — it fell on rocky shoals. Conservatives faulted it for redefining the curriculum at the expense of traditionally honored components, notables in America's pantheon such as Thomas Alva Edison and the Wright brothers. Lynne Cheney, then head of the National Endowment of the Humanities, faulted the *National Standards* report for embracing "a warped view of American history." She listed a number of its errors of excess, evidence of the report's "politically correct" selection process. Cheney complained that Harriet Tubman was cited six times in the guide, while Lincoln's Gettysburg Address was mentioned but once.[70]

It is not necessary here to follow all the twists and turns of the culture wars that broke out in the wake of the national-standards controversy. A closer look at references to Harriet Tubman during these debates about what should be taught to students in primary and secondary schools, however, demonstrates just how strongly Tubman had become the iconic embodiment of African American history—"politically correct" on two counts: race and gender. While Tubman enthusiasts were quick to defend her inclusion in the *National Standards* report, John Elson's judgment, rendered in a *Time* magazine essay on the controversy, is worth considering: "One problem, however, is that *National Standards* is so insistent on resurrecting neglected voices that it becomes guilty of what might be called disproportionate revisionism."[71]

Tubman's reputation does not seem to have been harmed by the invocation of her name during the textbook wars. Publications about her continued to appear in the ensuing years at an astonishing rate.[72] The preschool population, the so-called early readers, began to have Tubman picture books written just for them. One of the most popular was by Alan Schroeder and illustrated by Jerry Pinkney, the artist who had been commissioned in 1978 to create the first postage stamp honoring Harriet Tubman for the U.S. Postal Service's "Black Heritage Series." Titled *Minty*, a derivative of Araminta, Harriet Tubman's "cradle name," the book deals only with her childhood (Figure 9).[73] One reviewer said of it, "This fictionalized account of the early life of the woman who became known as the conductor of the Underground Railroad is based on facts gleaned from the 1869 biography . . . *Harriet Tubman: The Moses of Her People* [by Sarah H. Bradford]. Quick action and dialogue create a taut story, although it is illustration that shapes the characters. Pinkney's well-crafted watercolors portray a highly idealized young Harriet (as well as parents and extended family)."[74]

Public interest in Tubman survived the ideological conflict over multi-

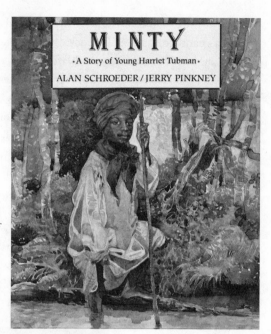

9. Book cover. From Alan Schroeder, *Minty: A Story of Young Harriet Tubman*, illustrations by Jerry Pinkney (New York: Dial Books for Young Readers, Penguin, 1996). Text copyright © 1996 by Alan Schroeder. Illustrations copyright © 1996 by Jerry Pinkney.

10. Book cover. From Monica Kulling, *Escape North: The Story of Harriet Tubman*, illustrations by Teresa Flavin (New York: Random House, 2000). Text copyright © 2000 by Monica Kulling. Illustrations copyright © 2000 by Teresa Flavin.

cultural education stronger than ever. Harriet Tubman's star continued to rise in the second millennium. A book about "girls who rocked the world" included Tubman.[75] Tubman, along with Frederick Douglass and Sojourner Truth, received biographical treatment in a "Famous Figures of the Civil War Era" series.[76] Publications about Tubman appeared directed at younger and younger readers.[77] The "Let Freedom Ring" series of books for young readers included a biography of Tubman, along with biographies of Abraham Lincoln, Jefferson Davis, Robert E. Lee, Sojourner Truth, and Ulysses S. Grant.[78] A "Step into Reading" book by Monica Kulling, with eye-catching illustrations by Teresa Flavin, used her story for grades two to three (Figure 10).[79] Tubman books intended for America's youth continue to be published at the rate of two to three per year and now total more than one hundred.

Books are not the only source for learning about "Minty." Today, the Internet offers young people easy access to information about Tubman.[80] Teachers have posted lesson plans on the theme of Harriet Tubman as a conductor on the Underground Railroad, some designed for children as young as the kindergarten level.[81] At one school in California, second graders and third graders learned about Harriet Tubman before attending the play *Freedom Train*. The children also wrote imaginary letters to Harriet Tubman and posted them on the Internet.[82] They designed charts of events in her life, acting out some of them, made time lines, and were inspired to design a freedom quilt using different patterns of wallpaper after looking at the illustrations in Faith Ringgold's *Aunt Harriet's Underground Railroad in the Sky*, one of the most popular and imaginatively designed of the dozens of books about Tubman now sold for young readers (see Plate 4).[83]

Elsewhere, young people, either as a class assignment or simply out of personal interest, have written poems and stories, drawn pictures, designed crossword puzzles, and mapped Tubman's escape route from Bucktown, Maryland, to Philadelphia. They have watched puppet shows and attended plays about Tubman with their classmates, applauding Tubman re-enactors. Children have viewed videos in which they accompany Moses on one of her heroic missions, as does Brittany, depicted as an African American girl, an avid reader and eager student, in the production *Brittany Meets Harriet Tubman*.[84] Today's schoolchildren sing songs associated with Tubman, design stamps to honor her, and in myriad other ways demonstrate that there is no shortage of exposure at present to information about the woman who once described herself as "growing like a weed" in the old slave South.

Some of these children who are so saturated with Tubman lore may even attend a public school named in honor of their heroine. Examples include Harriet Tubman School (formerly the Adolph Meyer School) in the Orleans Parish school district of Algiers, Louisiana, and Harriet Tubman Elementary in Baltimore.It is entirely possible, given the products available, that a young girl attending Harriet Tubman School in Algiers could hear about her heroine in class, then go home and act out Tubman's daring escapades with a historical adventure set, action figures included.[85] If she were persistent and interested enough, the young Tubman fan could start a collection of Tubman paraphernalia: a Tubman doll, T-shirt, coloring book, keychain, coffee mug, engineer's cap, postage stamp, videos, posters, and so on.

What might children absorb from the substantial resources available to them by the opening of the twenty-first century about the woman once excluded from American history textbooks? One example that speaks to a young person's understanding of who Harriet Tubman was and why she is important comes from the Alphabet Superhighway, a website launched under the sponsorship of the U.S. Department of Education's READ*WRITE*NOW! Initiative. Julia McCue, a fifth grader at James Eldredge Elementary School in East Greenwich, Rhode Island, wrote a poem about Harriet Tubman and shared it with other children in *Cyberzine*, an electronic journal on the Alphabet Superhighway.

Harriet Tubman

Baby girl Harriet was born a slave in 1820,
To old Rita and Ben who had no money.
Edward Brodas [*sic*] their owner and master,
Worked them and beat them to go faster.
At seven she was sent off to a new mother,
Who beat her so badly she ran to her brother.
At eleven she plowed cotton fields and with the men cut wood,
All the while dreaming of freedom if she could.
At night in whispery voices she heard,
About places in the North where you'd be as free as a bird.
It would take days and weeks of walking at night,
Hiding and praying and containing her fright.

The Underground Railroad, so it said,
Helped runaway slaves reach Canada ahead.
The station masters were people who cared,
They used their homes as stations for those who dared.
A conductor was [a] volunteer who went south,
To lead a group north by word of mouth.
Walking at night they followed the North Star,
Praying to God to lead them so far.
Harriet's husband John Tubman was not a slave,
He laughed at her dream and told her to behave.
As she was about to be moved farther south and sold,
She took the Underground Railroad and never told.
The Bucktown Station house was her salvation,
She hid in attics by day and found conservation.
Finally arriving in Pennsylvania, the free state,
She found a job cleaning and the suffering did abate.
She worked hard and made her home in the North,
And went back to the South to bring her family forth.
After leading great number of slaves to liberty,
she had the name, the name Moses, for her work in delivery.
She freed over three hundred slaves, all told,
And never let a passenger lose their hold.
During the Civil War in 1861,
She helped southern soldiers to freedom each and every one.
By April, 1865, the war was ended,
Slavery was no longer legally defended.
Living in Auburn, New York, where she helped the poor,
Harriet died at ninety, never wanting more.[86]

Young Julia's poem reveals the essential components of the Tubman myth as it had evolved, in its most elemental strands, by the beginning of the twenty-first century.

America's lack of historical interest in Harriet Tubman, as reflected in the scarcity of books written for children about her until the past quarter-century or so, was one cycle in the pattern of cultural amnesia and remembering that typifies what Michael Kammen has termed the "mystic chords of memory." The revival of interest in Tubman by publishers of books in the field of juvenile literature since the 1960s exemplifies another phase. In the search for a usable past suitable for addressing the demands of multicultural education, writers rediscovered how malleable an icon Harriet Tubman could be. Few of the popularizers made an effort to look for the historical Tubman behind the myth—or, more to the point, to sort out fact from fiction in the Tubman saga itself. Though Tubman survived the culture wars about what young people should know about the past, she remained a child's heroine, allocated to the juvenile-literature section of libraries.

When children become adults, they tend to "put away childish things," to borrow the language of Saint Paul. They outgrow the stories told to them when young. More to the point, they no longer find these stories particularly useful in dealing with their personal, social, and political needs. As long as Harriet Tubman was rendered primarily as "Minty," a character in books for children, adults did not need to take her story seriously. Few adults ventured into the juvenile-literature section of their local public libraries, except to find something to read to children. However, the "Minty" that children learned about, the little girl enslaved in Maryland, grew up to become the "Moses of Her People," thereby taking on another symbolic life, one that challenged the institutions that had held young Harriet captive.

CHAPTER TWO

"MOSES THE DELIVERER"

Harriet Tubman had been self-liberated for approximately six years when Benjamin Drew encountered her living in Canada West "under the paw of the British Lion"—to borrow her own words. In the years since her escape, she had been conducting a stealth campaign against the cruel institution under which she had grown up "like a neglected weed." Not yet widely known in abolitionist circles, and certainly not a fixture in the American pantheon of heroes, Harriet kept her own counsel and restricted her contacts to a few trusted friends of the fugitive, black and white, who, formally and informally, supported what was already being called the Underground Railroad. Indeed, it was to operatives of this clandestine network that she first presented herself as a beneficiary of helpers along the way and a willing soldier in her own right. If we are to understand the primal strands of the Tubman as "Black Moses" symbol, we must examine the earliest efforts to portray her as the liberator of her people. This will lead to a more detailed examination of the tension between historical evidence and myth in key elements of the Tubman as Moses representation, especially with regard to questions about how many she delivered out of slavery's prison and how many times she braved recapture or worse by going back into the slave South. Today Tubman is the most widely recognized symbol of the Underground Railroad. To understand how this has come to be, we turn first to the origins of the Tubman as Black Moses tradition.

African Americans, slave and free, and the handful of whites involved in the Underground Railroad who aided Tubman thought of her as Black Moses long before the general public heard of her. It would not have served their interests or been of assistance to Tubman had they revealed details regarding the numbers she liberated, the means she used, or the paths she trod. In short, the years between 1849, when Tubman escaped, and the summer of 1855, when Drew meets her in St. Catharines, are the hidden years, cloaked in secrecy because of the risks she took. During this period, the seeds of the Tubman as Moses legend germinated in the slave quarters as potential escapees waited nervously for the woman who would lead them in the direction of the North Star. Franklin B. Sanborn wrote in 1863, "By reason of her frequent visits there [the slave South], always carrying away some of the oppressed, she got among her people the name of 'Moses,' which it seems she still retains."[1]

Americans are now as likely to think of Tubman as "Moses" as they are to believe Abraham Lincoln to be the "Great Emancipator" or to celebrate George Washington as the "Father of His Country." It is highly unlikely that this book about Tubman's place in the American memory would have merited writing had Tubman not taken that first step back onto slavery's ground to free others after she had already liberated herself. Other symbolic representations and utilizations of Harriet Tubman, such as "General Tubman" or "Mother Tubman," depend on the "Moses the Deliverer" representation. By likening this poor, illiterate woman, once enslaved but now free, to the biblical character Moses, creators of the larger-than-life Tubman image drew on powerful and deep-rooted religious and cultural memories. No other name from the Bible, with the possible exception of Jesus, carried such weight in the African American collective memory than did that of Moses, the Hebrew liberator of Levitic extraction. White Christianity also honored Moses as the greatest of Old Testament heroes.

Tubman apparently welcomed being thought of as a modern-day Moses. Rosa Belle Holt interviewed her in the 1890s and reported: "Harriet was known among her people as 'Moses,' and in conversation she says: 'I felt like Moses. De Lord tole me to do dis. I said, 'O Lord, I can't—don't ask me—take somebody else.' Den I could hear de Lord answer, 'It's you I want, Harriet Tubman'—jess as clar I heard him speak—an' den I'd go agen down South an' bring up my brudders and sisters.'"[2] Tubman's decision to heed the Lord's call is all the more awe-inspiring because she began her rescue missions under threat of the recently enacted Fugitive Slave Bill of 1850, a federal measure that alarmed and enraged the abolitionist community (see Figure 11).

By putting her liberty and her life in peril to redeem others, Harriet Tubman came to be numbered among the select few whom other people

11. Anti-Fugitive Slave Law Convention, Cazenovia, New York, August 22, 1850. Courtesy Madison County Historical Society, Oneida, New York.

acknowledged as one of "the great ones," no matter her race, gender, or social class. She earned the respect and esteem of her contemporaries and of countless thousands born after her death because she dared do what many of us do not have the courage or the faith to do: put the welfare of others before our own welfare. Tubman's self-sacrificial labors on the Underground Railroad tap into emotionally powerful cultural memories of the savior hero. Little wonder that her nineteenth-century admirers compared Tubman to Grace Darling, the English lighthouse keeper's daughter who, in attempting to rescue the survivors of the stranded *Forfarshire*, risked her own life.[3]

The earliest extant documentary information regarding Tubman's work as a conductor on the Underground Railroad comes from a letter written on December 29, 1854, by Thomas Garrett, the Wilmington, Delaware, Underground Railroad station master (Figure 12). It predates Drew's interview with Harriet at St. Catharines. Garrett, a Quaker engaged in the iron and tool business, had been actively assisting runaways since 1830.[4] He customarily forwarded freedom seekers north to Philadelphia, where the African American agent William Still (Figure 13), head of Philadelphia's Vigilance Committee, took charge of their care. Garrett's letter to J. Miller McKim, corresponding secretary or general manager of the Pennsylvania Anti-Slavery Society, did not reach the general public until 1872, when Still reproduced it in a massive accounting of the Underground Railroad.[5] Nevertheless, the letter is evidence that Tubman was known to a handful of Underground Railroad operatives years before she became publicly celebrated as "Black Moses." Garrett wrote: "We made arrangements last night, and sent away Harriet Tubman, with six men and one woman to Allen Agnew's to be forwarded across the country to the city. Harriet, and one of the men had worn their shoes off their feet, and I gave them two dollars to help fit them out, and directed a carriage to be hired at my expense, to take them out, but do not know the expense."[6] In a testimonial letter written in June 1868 to Sarah Bradford, who would become the most widely quoted architect of the Tubman myth, Garrett confirmed that Harriet had been well known in southeastern Pennsylvania, a hotbed of Underground Railroad activity because of the presence of members of the Society of Friends, and that she had been "respected by all true abolitionists."[7]

While it is likely that Still, Garrett, and others involved in aiding Tubman, such as the Allen Agnew mentioned earlier, talked among them-

12. Thomas Garrett. Courtesy Historical Society of Delaware, Wilmington.

13. William Still. From frontispiece to William Still, *The Underground Railroad* (Philadelphia: Porter and Coates, 1872).

14. Franklin B. Sanborn, 1860. From Franklin B. Sanborn, *Recollections of Seventy Years* (Boston: Gorham Press, 1909), vol. 1, facing 188.

selves about her exploits, general public knowledge of her forays into the land of the enemy below the Mason–Dixon Line must have been scant before 1856, when Drew's volume appeared. Even then, Drew did not disclose—indeed, may not have been aware of—the number of return trips Tubman had made into slavery's domain or of the number of individuals she rescued. Though Drew's inclusion of Tubman's brief testimony in his 1856 publication may well be the earliest notice of her intended for public consumption, it appeared without comment or explanation. Readers of Drew's volume ignorant of other knowledge of Tubman's achievements would have had meager justification to hail her as the liberator of her people.

Franklin B. Sanborn (Figure 14), a young white abolitionist and schoolteacher at home among New England's literary elite, first introduced Tubman as "Moses" to the American public, thus beginning the campaign for wider awareness of her mighty deeds. The Civil War was in full blaze when the tribute "Harriet Tubman" appeared in July 1863 in the *Commonwealth*, a Boston-based abolitionist newspaper that Sanborn edited. Unlike the brief interview with Tubman done by Drew, Sanborn's article (nearly a full three columns and on the front page) was written with the specific intention of introducing Harriet Tubman to the public as a heroic figure of the day. Sanborn's opening lines place her in the context of a new paradigm of American history, centering on those who struggled to rid themselves of slavery's yoke. A white abolitionist in need of a black hero to confirm the validity of his reform commitments, Sanborn rhapsodized:

> It was said long ago that the true romance of America, was not in the fortunes of the Indian, where Cooper sought it, nor in the New England character where Judd found it, nor in the social contrasts of Virginia planters, as Thackeray imagined, but in the story of the fugitive slaves. The observation is as true now as it was before War with swift, gigantic hand, sketched the vast shadows and dashed in the high lights in which Romance loves to lurk and flash forth. But the stage is enlarged on which these dramas are played, the whole world now sit as spectators, and the desperation or the magnanimity of a poor black woman has power to shake the nation that so long was deaf to her cries. We write of one of these heroines, of whom our slave annals are full, — a woman whose career is as extraordinary as the most famous of her sex can show.[8]

This is a stunning passage. Sanborn uses Tubman to make the case that American history should be rewritten so that peoples of African descent take their rightful place in the canonical pages of whom and what is worth remembering at all. Sanborn was at least a century ahead of his time in arguing that the life story of "a poor black woman" was as important to the public's understanding of "we the people" as were the mythic sagas of the Puritans, Virginia's planter aristocracy, or James Fenimore Cooper's Leatherstocking characters.

According to William Wells Brown, the Buffalo-based author and Underground Railroad operative, Tubman was a fixture at abolitionist gatherings before the Civil War. In Brown's book *The Rising Son; or the Antecedents and Advancements of the Colored Race*, published in 1874, we find this passage: "For eight or ten years previous to the breaking out of the Rebellion, all who frequented antislavery conventions, lectures, picnics, and fairs could not fail to have seen a black woman of medium size, upper front teeth gone, smiling countenance, attired in coarse, but neat apparel, with an old-fashioned reticule or bag suspended by her side, and who, on taking her seat, would at once drop off into a sound sleep."[9]

At some of these abolitionist meetings, Tubman spoke from the stage. On July 4, 1859, for example, Thomas Wentworth Higginson introduced her to attendees at the Massachusetts Anti-Slavery Meeting, held in Framingham, as "a conductor on the Underground Railroad." According to a report of the convention in the *Liberator*, Higginson told the excited crowd: "She came here from a place in the slave States; she came by land, and had been here a reasonable time. (Laughter) At the South, she was called 'Moses'—after that ancient leader, who took men and women into the Promised Land. (Applause)."[10] When Tubman spoke, she captivated her hearers with a recounting of her trials and tribulations while enslaved, of how she escaped, and of her Underground Railroad work. In response, the abolitionists took up a collection to support her.

On August 1, 1859, at an African American celebration of the anniversary of West Indian emancipation, Tubman spoke again, this time in Boston. Introduced as "Miss Harriet Garrison" to cloak her identity, Black Moses denounced the American colonization movement, a scheme to remove African Americans to Liberia in West Africa. Tubman told of a man who planted onions and garlic to get more milk from his cows. The butter would not sell. He tried sowing clover to sweeten it, but the wind spread the garlic and onion seed all over the fields where his cows grazed. "Just so," Tubman was reported to have said, "the white people had got the 'nigger' here to do their drudgery, and now they were trying to root 'em out and send 'em to Africa. . . . They can't do it; we're rooted here, and they can't pull us up."[11] By 1859, if not a year or two earlier, Tubman had become a celebrity, someone whom the abolitionists, black and white, welcomed onto the platform as a symbol of the self-liberated.

Tubman was not the seasoned public speaker that Sojourner Truth became as she traveled the nation testifying, but Black Moses could tell her own story effectively and powerfully before small audiences. Higginson wrote of Tubman in 1859, "She is jet black and cannot read or write, only talk, besides acting."[12] An eyewitness present on July 4, 1859, when Tubman spoke at Framingham, reported that after Higginson introduced her, "'Moses,' the deliverer, then stood up before the audience, who greeted her with enthusiastic cheers. She spoke briefly, telling the story of her sufferings as a slave, her escape, and her achievements on the Underground Railroad, in a style of quaint simplicity, which excited the most profound interest in her hearers." Feeling incapable of capturing Tubman's inimitable style and oratorical power, this author simply urged others "to take the earliest opportunity to see and hear her."[13] Writing in about 1905, Emma Paddock Telford affirmed that, even in her old age, Tubman excelled at telling her own story: "As a raconteur, Harriet herself has few equals and the story of her life taken from her own lips as I have so often heard it, enriched by the picturesque Southern dialect and embellished by the eloquent gesture peculiarly her own, gives a unique picture of the ante-bellum days and the stirring events which followed."[14]

Unlike other black female activists in antebellum America, such as Frances Ellen Watkins Harper, the poet and writer of fiction, Tubman could not wield the pen against the abomination of slavery. But like other black female "doers of the word," to borrow a phrase from the title of Carla Peterson's provocative and insightful analysis of nineteenth-century black female speakers and writers, Tubman bravely stepped into a zone of marginality when she came forward on the stage to speak in those abolitionist assemblies dominated by white men. This self-marginalization, or liminality, as Peterson argues, was a racialized and gendered betwixt and between that simultaneously threatened the black female activists and empowered them.[15] Tubman, like Sojourner Truth, entered this liminal public space armed only with her voice—she could not write, only testify, telling her story over and over again. As Tubman's fame increased among abolitionists and their allies, word of her deeds preceded her. Audiences expected her to tell them of her travails while enslaved and of her triumphs since running to freedom. In her case, deeds (the doing) preceded and authenticated the words (the telling).

Boston and its vicinity served as the epicenter of Garrisonian abolitionism. When Tubman visited Boston, she met many of the veteran abolitionists, as well as leading white intellectuals, writers, and reformers. Perhaps a more apt interpretation of the evidence is to say that they were introduced to her, for it seems as if New England men and women of accomplishment were eager to meet the woman whose abolitionism was more than words. Though unable to read the torrent of publications coming from Garrison's pen or influence the debate through the written word, Tubman had persuasive power of her own. She was, to use an expression already popular in the 1850s, a "genuine article." The educated white reformers of Boston and environs would remember their first encounter with "Moses" for the rest of their lives.

These abolitionists were instrumental in molding the Tubman as Black Moses tradition, helping to popularize stories told in the slave communities of Maryland's Eastern Shore and kept alive in the fugitive colonies in Canada. With access to the printed word, they, like Sanborn, could influence the opinions of others who had never heard of the exceptional and compelling odyssey of Araminta Ross, known in her adult years as Harriet Tubman (Figure 15). The African American author and abolitionist William Wells Brown thought her story extraordinary: "How strange! This woman—one of the most ordinary looking of her race; unlettered, no idea of geography, asleep half of the time" yet able to pilot the freedom-hungry from the interior of the slave states all the way to Canada.[16] New England reformers were even more captivated by the appearance in their midst of Black Moses. Brown recalled, "Moses had no education, yet the most refined person would listen for hours while she related the intensely interesting incidents of her life, told in the simplest manner, but always seasoned with good sense."[17]

One of those so entranced was Thomas Wentworth Higginson, the radical abolitionist and Unitarian clergyman who commanded black troops (the First South Carolina Volunteers) during the Civil War. Higginson, who was also a member of "the Secret Six" who aided John Brown, moved freely in sophisticated circles in Boston and met many famous people. However, when writing at the end of the nineteenth century of contemporaries who most impressed him, the old abolitionist warrior said, "It had been my privilege to live in the best society all my life—namely, that of abolitionists and fugitive slaves. I had seen the most eminent persons of the age: several men on whose heads tens of thousands of dollars had been set; a black woman [Harriet Tubman], who, after escaping from slavery herself, had gone back secretly eight times into the jaws of death to bring out persons she had never seen; and a white man, who, after assisting away fugitives by the thousand, had twice been stripped of every dollar of his property in fines, and when taunted by the court, had mildly said, 'Friend, if thee knows any poor fugitive in need of breakfast, send him to Thomas Garrett's door,' I had known these; but I had not known the Browns."[18]

No sector of American society, other than African Americans, enslaved and free, who had personal contact with Tubman or heard of her exploits and passed on lore of her, usually by oral means, was more responsible for creating the legend of "Black Moses" than these white abolitionists and reformers, many of them embodiments—or, at least, heirs—of "the New England character" to which Sanborn referred in his 1863 tribute

15. Harriet Tubman. From Franklin B. Sanborn, *Recollections of Seventy Years* (Boston: Gorham Press, 1909), vol. 1, facing 188.

to Tubman. They needed a usable symbol to fuel their abolitionist campaign; they created it by embracing Tubman as the representative of all the oppressed who chose to run to freedom knowing that the decision was a life or death one.

Disparate ethnic and cultural groups have claimed that their "story" is central to the American character. Sanborn seems to have recognized this in 1863, when, ironically, Yankee and Reb fought to the death over whose traditional way of life and definition of the core American myth would prevail. Would it be "the New England character, where Judd found it" or "in the social contrasts of the Virginia planters, as Thackeray imagined"? The ancestral regional myths of a Yankee North and a Cavalier South that emerged before the Civil War have been enshrined in folkways and cultural stereotypes ever since.[19] Because of the erasure of African and African American history, not just of the enslaved but also of the free, it is all the more striking that Sanborn should suggest that Harriet Tubman, this "Black Moses," epitomized the most fundamental thread in the American national tapestry.

Perhaps Sanborn was easily drawn to the Moses motif because at the time he put pen to paper the nation as a whole was wrestling with the question of the meaning of "we the people" as enshrined in the country's charter documents. The war was on, and hopes of a quick and relatively bloodless settlement had faded. President Abraham Lincoln's reluctance to declare the conflict a freedom war troubled many abolitionists, black and white. Lydia M. Child, whose books and essays dealing with the evils of slavery led admirers to hail her as "the first woman of the Republic," despaired as the war ground on without direction or higher purpose. Child's biographer says that she took heart by quoting Harriet Tubman, whose "uncouth utterance" Child thought was "wiser than the plans of politicians." In a letter dated January 21, 1862, and written to the Quaker poet and abolitionist John Greenleaf Whittier, Child captured this Tubman remark: "Dey may send de flower ob dair young men down South, to die ob de fever in de summer, and de agoo in de winter. . . . Dey may send dem one year, two year, tree year, till dey tired ob sendin, or till dey use up all de young men. All no use! God's ahead ob massa Linkum. God won't let massa Linkum beat de South till he do de right thing."[20]

Though fostered in the slave quarters, preserved in the African American oral tradition, and transmitted to the larger American public by literate "friends of the slave" in the North, Tubman herself essentially created the "Black Moses" myth. As Tubman moved about in the company of fellow fugitives, whether en route to the Promised Land, be it some place of refuge in the Northern states or in that distant country called Canada, she told her story, a narrative she reinforced and elaborated on during her long, post–Civil War life. In the free black communities where she found help and in the homes and assembly halls of the abolitionists, she told her story. When she journeyed to abolitionist centers like Boston, there given an audience by women and men who were trying to shape public opinion, she told her story. When seeking funds to establish a home for herself and her aged parents in Auburn, New York, in the late 1850s, she told her story. When acting as a nurse, spy, and scout during the Civil War, she told her story. When asked by friends eager to help establish her claim to government compensation for her wartime service, she told her story. When asked by Sarah Bradford, Tubman's most famous interlocutor, about constructing a small biography to sell to the public and thereby offset the mortgage on the Auburn property, Tubman told her story. Even when attending women's suffrage meetings during her later years, Tubman told thrilling tales of her exploits as a conductor on the Underground Railroad.

Charlotte Forten, an African American educator from Philadelphia, witnessed Tubman's extraordinary storytelling gift when she visited Beaufort, South Carolina, on a sunny Saturday in January 1863. As she had done in the abolitionist circles of New England before the Civil War, Tubman regaled her listeners with stories such as the one about a man named Joe (Josiah Bailey) for whom the authorities had posted a reward of one thousand five hundred dollars. Tubman had escorted him along the Underground Railroad as far as the Suspension Bridge at Niagara Falls (Figure 16). Tubman told Forten that Joe showed no interest in the spectacle of the cascading river, remaining moody and silent. Not until she said, "Now we are in Can[ada]," did he erupt in shouts and glad song. When he touched free soil, Tubman recollected, Joe shouted "as if he were crazy." Forten wrote in her diary, "How exciting it was to hear her tell the story. And to hear her sing the very scraps of jubilant hymns that he sang. She said the ladies crowded around them, and some laughed and some cried. My own eyes were full as I listened to her—the heroic woman!"[21]

The story of Joe illustrates the manner in which Tubman herself cultivated and shaped the "Black Moses" myth. She had a stock of dramatic

16. Suspension Bridge used by Tubman connecting the United States and Canada as it looked circa 1863. From F. H. Johnson, *Guide to Niagara Falls and its Scenery* (Philadelphia: George W. Childs, 1863).

vignettes about the formerly hidden years that she delivered orally to willing listeners. Some of these auditors, like Forten and Bradford, put her stories down on paper, attempting as best they could to capture both content and idiom. Tubman's use of orature to define herself in keeping with other people's perceptions of her as "Black Moses" should not surprise us, for Tubman's African ancestors as well as her African American kin in the slave quarters used oral methods to position themselves in a hostile world.

Many of the creators and custodians of the Tubman myth never had the opportunity to meet her or hear her talk so powerfully of oppression and deliverance. Before the summer of 1858, when Tubman began to appear in public and speak at abolitionist meetings, few outside of "the sheltered and intimate parlors of abolition's elite, or the homes of her fellow fugitives in Canada and elsewhere,"[22] to borrow Kate Larson's apt phrasing, witnessed firsthand Tubman's extraordinary ability to dramatize her experiences. Though Tubman excelled at these performances, she was dependent on others, mostly admirers in abolitionist circles, to get her story out.

The American public, as far as it cared at all, first came to know Harriet Tubman because her admirers and publicists hailed her as the deliverer of her people via the Underground Railroad, an institution with its own mythic tradition and romance. Thomas Garrett wrote to William Still in 1857, "It would be a sorrowful act if such a hero as she, should be lost from the Underground Railroad."²³ With rare exceptions, such as the notices that the Reverend Jermain Loguen placed in Syracuse newspapers advertising his home as a place of refuge, conductors and station masters did not publicly reveal details about their dangerous work while actively engaged in helping fugitives.²⁴ After the passage of the Thirteenth Amendment freeing the enslaved, Tubman did disclose some details about how she operated, with the knowledge that her story was going to be published for the whole world to read, if it so desired. While the "peculiar institution" still thrived, she kept her counsel, and we obtain only a sketchy picture of her missions from surviving documentary sources created before the Civil War began.

A few antebellum primary documents pertaining to Tubman's modus operandi as a conductor do survive. One such evidentiary piece exists in the Rochester Ladies' Anti-Slavery Society papers at the William L. Clements Library of the University of Michigan. Dated November 29, 1856, the letter is a brief note directed to the attention of allies in Rochester, New York. W. E. Abbott was then serving as treasurer of the Syracuse Fugitive Aid Society. Here is Abbott's letter in full:

> Mr. Porter
> Dear Sir
> The woman who accompanies the party on their way to Freedom is well known to us for her untiring devotion to the cause of the enslaved. She herself [is] an escaped bondwoman and this the second company that she has brought forth out of the land of servitude at great risk to herself. It has been our custom to forward all directly on to the Bridge. But now our funds fail us & we are obliged to send them forward to the different half way houses that are on their route.
> Yours for the Enslaved,
> W E Abbott Treasurer
> Syracuse Fugitive Aid Society²⁵

The bridge that Abbott mentions was very likely the Suspension Bridge spanning the Niagara River between the United States and Canada. Abbott's reference to this party as "the second company" Tubman escorted to freedom is interesting in light of the emphasis many legend builders have placed on the number of trips Tubman made as an Underground Railroad conductor.

Today, Tubman's name is virtually synonymous with the Underground Railroad, the first person Americans think of when discussing the topic. "Moses the Deliverer" holds first place primarily because the public believes that no other conductor, male or female, black or white, came close to matching her in total numbers saved or in the total number of trips. In spite of recent scholarly studies showing that the traditional belief that Tubman rescued three hundred individuals during nineteen trips cannot withstand serious historical scrutiny, the legendary numbers live on. Among Tubman admirers, an emotional attachment to the three hundred rescued and nineteen trips figures defies rational argument. How these numbers came to be so essential a part of Tubman lore is more than a quarrel among historians about details of the Tubman story. The numbers question illustrates the power of myth over history.

The earliest published account of Tubman's rescue missions can be found in Franklin B. Sanborn's *Commonwealth* article of 1863. Sanborn lists nine trips. According to his recollections, Tubman's first trip was to Baltimore in December 1850 to bring away "her sister [actually, a niece], and two children, who had come up from Cambridge [Maryland] in a boat, under charge of his sister's husband, a free black." The second trip, "a few months later," involved the rescue of "her brother and two other men." In the fall of 1851, Tubman went down to Dorchester County to find her husband. Though pained by his infidelity, she "did not give way to rage or grief, but collected a party of fugitives and brought them safely to Philadelphia." On her fourth trip, in December 1851, Tubman returned to the region of Maryland's Eastern Shore, where she had suffered under the slavery's yoke, and "led out a party of eleven among them her brother and his wife." This time she escorted her charges all the way to Canada West where they would be "under the paw of the British Lion," as she told the author of the *Commonwealth* essay. Her fifth trip, Sanborn claimed, occurred in the fall of 1852. This time, Tubman brought nine freedom seekers out of Maryland. In the years between 1852 and 1857, the *Commonwealth* author asserts, Tubman made but two journeys (numbers six and seven), "in consequence partly of the increased vigilance of the slaveholders, who had suffered so much by the loss of their property." Tubman's next raid (number 8) on the slaveholders' assets came in 1857

17. Illustration of twenty-eight fugitives escaping from the Eastern Shore of Maryland. From William Still, *The Underground Railroad* (Philadelphia: Porter and Coates, 1872). Courtesy Library of Congress LC/USZ62–75975.

when she brought her elderly parents out and took them to St. Catharines. Tubman's ninth and last journey took place in December 1860. This time, she rescued a party of seven; among them was the infant who had to "be drugged with opium to keep it from crying on the way" (Figure 17).[26]

In 1865, a brief article entitled "Moses" appeared in the *Freedmen's Record*, the official organ of the New England Freedmen's Aid Society, an agency established in Boston to assist emancipated blacks in the South. At the time, Tubman was living in Beaufort and supporting herself by making cakes and pies for sale. No author's byline accompanies the "Moses" sketch; historians have identified the writer as Edna Dow Cheney, a white New England abolitionist and dedicated Tubman supporter. Cheney acknowledges dependence on the earlier *Commonwealth* article and echoes Sanborn's laudatory praise of Tubman, hailing her as "probably the most remarkable woman of this age," whose reputation as "Moses the deliverer" was "universally known" among the enslaved and well earned. Cheney wrote in her "Moses" sketch that after Tubman escaped, she went back "seven or eight times" to bring others out. She provided no details about these rescue missions except about the trip in December 1860 (which Cheney calls Tubman's last trip) when "Moses" had to administer laudanum (a soporific drug) to an infant to keep it from crying and alarming the authorities. Cheney does not claim ignorance of

Tubman's other journeys. She simply says, "So various and interesting are the incidents of these journeys, that we know not how to select from them."[27]

If the early published versions of the Tubman as Moses myth written for public consumption could account for only seven to nine trips, then from where does the oft-repeated number of nineteen come? The count of nineteen first appears in Sarah Bradford's *Scenes in the Life of Harriet Tubman*, published in 1869, six years after Sanborn's *Commonwealth* piece. Because the Tubman–Bradford relationship is the focus of a subsequent chapter, suffice it to say here that Bradford put together the small 1869 volume in great haste as she was preparing to leave for Europe. Bradford interviewed Tubman and solicited information about her life from others, including Sanborn, who forwarded the sketch from the *Commonwealth*.[28] Bradford described her tribute to Tubman as a "*quixotic* attempt to make a heroine of a black woman and a slave."[29] *Scenes* was not a biography such as a contemporary historian might undertake.

On the question of how many trips Tubman made to bring others out of slavery, Bradford wrote: "She went back and forth *nineteen times*, according to the reckoning of her friends. She remembers that she went eleven times from Canada, but of the other journeys she kept no reckoning."[30] Here we have the original source of the oft-repeated figure of nineteen trips. It is striking that the number nineteen came not from Tubman but from unnamed "friends." Who were these friends? And how were they in a position to keep an accurate record of the total number of trips if Tubman herself was unable to do so? The historical record is silent about the identity of the people from whom Bradford obtained her trip count.

Perhaps sensitive to the expectations of potential readers who hoped for thrilling details pertaining to each of the purported nineteen trips, Bradford acknowledged: "It will be impossible to give any connected account of the different journeys taken by Harriet for the rescue of her people, as she herself has no idea of the dates connected with them, or of the order in which they were made."[31] By the time Bradford wrote a revised and enlarged edition of her black heroine's story, published in 1886 under the title *Harriet, the Moses of Her People*, the important qualifier specifying Tubman's anonymous friends as the source for the figure of nineteen trips had been removed. Bradford states: "After her almost superhuman efforts in making her own escape from slavery, and then returning to the South nineteen times, and bringing away with her over three hundred fugitives, she was sent by Governor Andrew of Massachusetts to the South at the beginning of the War, to act as spy and scout for our armies, and to be employed as hospital nurse when needed."[32]

Others who published early tributes to the woman who by the closing decades of the nineteenth century was living quietly in Auburn, New York, replicated Bradford's reckoning of nineteen trips. For example, Lillie B. Chace Wyman wrote an eight-and-a-half-page testimonial honoring Tubman for *New England Magazine* in 1896. Of Tubman's claim to fame, Wyman says, "No record was kept of the number [of fugitives] she thus delivered from slavery, but it is probable that it amounted to about three hundred; and she went down nineteen times to rescue these people."[33]

Bradford's *Harriet, the Moses of Her People* also influenced Wilbur H. Siebert's classic *The Underground Railroad from Slavery to Freedom*, published in 1899. Siebert was the first trained historian to attempt a history of the Underground Railroad. His portrayal of the heroic work of conductors fostered the further mythologization of what some were already calling "the liberty line." Siebert tells us that he did not have access to Bradford's 1869 volume, but he did employ Bradford's *Moses*. He classified Bradford's second Tubman book as a "personal recollection." Siebert also referenced the Wyman article from *New England Magazine*. On the numbers question, Siebert wrote: "She is said to have accomplished nineteen such trips, and emancipated over three hundred slaves."[34]

Siebert met Tubman on one occasion. He was visiting Cambridge, Massachusetts, in 1897 when she was also there and had what Siebert terms a "conversation" with her on April 8. One wishes for a transcription of that interview, for such a record might shed light on how Tubman wished to have herself presented in Siebert's impending publication. Alas, no such documentary account exists, and we are left with Siebert's recollections. The historian must not have heard the figure "nineteen" from Tubman herself, for in *The Underground Railroad from Slavery to Freedom* he only says, "*She is said to have* accomplished nineteen such trips, and emancipated over three hundred slaves."[35] As a source for this information, Siebert cites James Freeman Clarke's *Anti-Slavery Days* and a book entitled *Fugitive Slaves*, by Marion G. McDougall.[36] Clarke was a Unitarian clergyman involved in Transcendentalism as well as abolitionism. His recollections of the antislavery struggle in the United States appeared in 1884. Siebert refers to the section in which Clarke reports a story Tubman told him of once going to Baltimore and helping a cook whose children had been sold escape by successfully getting tickets on a steamer headed for Delaware.[37]

By the time of Tubman's death in 1913, the number nineteen was firmly fixed in the small number of historical works then in print concerning the history of African Americans. For example, Booker T. Washington, who went to Auburn in 1914 to speak at the dedication of a memorial plaque honoring Tubman, said in his *The Story of the Negro: The Rise of the Race from Slavery* (1909): "As a matter of fact, Harriet Tubman succeeded, in the course of nineteen different trips into the South, in bringing more than three hundred slaves from the South into the Northern States and Canada, and in no case was a fugitive under her care ever captured."[38] The 1912 *Negro Year Book and Annual Encyclopedia of the Negro*, a reference work edited by Monroe Work, included a short profile of Tubman, hailing her as "one of the most singular and famous of the Underground Railroad operators." The yearbook's compiler reckoned that Tubman had escaped in 1849 but was uncertain as to her age at the time ("between twenty and twenty-five years"). On the numbers question, Work wrote, "In nineteen trips she is said to have brought over three hundred slaves from the South into the Northern States and Canada."[39] By the time that the 1913 edition of the *Negro Year Book* appeared, Tubman had passed away, which was noted in the 1913 edition along with a repeat of the 1912 statement concerning nineteen trips and three hundred rescued. *Year Book* readers were advised to consult Bradford's *Harriet, the Moses of Her People* for additional information.[40]

It was Bradford's interpolation of what she supposedly heard from Tubman's unidentified friends that passed into the written historical record. Once Tubman died, no living soul could ask her about Bradford's story that she had made nineteen trips back into the South as an Underground Railroad conductor. Few Tubman admirers seemed to be troubled by the inconsistencies in Bradford's books. In the 1886 preface to the *Moses* volume, Bradford wrote that Tubman piloted "three or four hundred slaves to freedom."[41] However, in *Scenes*, published in 1869, Bradford told the public that Tubman should be credited with rescuing "somewhere near three hundred."[42]

The white-dominated historical establishment ignored Tubman during her life and after her death. African American authors, some of them trained historians, were content to perpetuate the Bradford-inspired notion of nineteen trips. Not until Earl Conrad began his personal quest to reintroduce Tubman to America as a genuine black heroine in the late 1930s did the question of the number of trips receive critical review. Conrad's book *Harriet Tubman*, copyrighted in 1943, was a publishing landmark and a defining moment in the evolution of the Harriet Tubman as the Moses of her People tradition. Conrad begins by acknowledging, "It has often been said, 'She made nineteen trips into the slave country,' but the meaning of this enormous enterprise has been hidden in the lack of illustration."[43] In bemoaning "the lack of illustration," Conrad was not so much concerned about a detailed accounting of each of Tubman's raids on the South's so-called property as he was with the lack of appreciation authors and their readers had for the difficulties Tubman faced when she reentered slave territory. Conrad characterized her Underground Railroad work as "small-scale guerrilla warfare," where the risk of being "hounded, harassed, jailed, and wounded," not to mention being kidnapped or killed, was high.[44] Only after introducing information about Tubman's modi operandi did he take up the question of how many trips she made.

Conrad found it impossible to date and document each of the purported nineteen trips. At one point, he appears to opt for a "conservative estimate of fifteen excursions," while at another place he seems willing to accept Bradford's count of nineteen as a matter of faith. He was passionately devoted to rescuing his subject from the dustbin of history and elevating her to a prominent place in the pantheon of American greats. He contended that it was not the total number of rescue missions made by Tubman that is important, but her "total Underground effect."[45] He underscored this shift of focus as follows: "It has been estimated that Harriet made nineteen excursions into the slave land, and most authorities have accepted this estimate. But if she had conducted only fifteen voyages, or even a dozen, her record of rescues, the moral influence upon the Abolitionists, the economic consequences in weakening the slaveholders, the increased stimulus to Negro morale in the South, and the culminating political result in intensifying the North–South contradictions, still add up to the career of an unparalleled conspirator and social fighter in any clime, in any nation, in any period of history."[46]

Confusion about the number of rescue missions persisted in spite of Conrad's reservations about blindly following Bradford's count. Consequently, late-twentieth-century references to Tubman's work as an Underground Railroad conductor are at variance. The editors of the *Black Abolitionist Papers* (1992) adopted a conservative number: "She made at least nine trips during the 1850s to lead some 180 slaves to freedom—most were relatives and friends from plantations near Cambridge [Maryland]."[47] However, the Tubman entry in *The Oxford Companion to American History* (2001) reads: "In 1850–51, she made three trips back to bring out various of her siblings and their families. As the decade went on, she made some sixteen more trips to Maryland, displaying great courage and ingenuity in assisting other slaves to escape, including in 1857, her aged parents. Estimates of the number of slaves she helped escape range from sixty to more than three hundred."[48] Many contemporary authors, perhaps aware of the problem attendant in documenting Tubman's trips, use qualifying language when writing of her rescue missions. Expressions like "as many as" and "is said to have" and "approximately" appear frequently. Some writers sidestep the historical-accuracy question altogether and adopt a reporting style, attributing the figure nineteen to other, often unnamed, sources.

Since Tubman could not read, it is unlikely she urged Bradford to correct the number nineteen, even if she, in her old age, could recollect with complete accuracy how many rescue missions she had undertaken. Perhaps it did not matter to her. Nevertheless, it has mattered to the creators of the Tubman legend. It is therefore unfortunate that they have so often relied on the unreliable and exaggerated Bradford figures instead of attempting to discover what Tubman was telling her supporters and abolitionist allies before the Civil War.

Here is a sampling of primary sources that predate Bradford and are therefore more reliable. Franklin B. Sanborn wrote to Thomas Wentworth Higginson on May 30, 1859, that he should pay a call on Tubman, then visiting in the Boston area, as she was "the woman who brought away 50 slaves in 8 journies made to Maryland."[49] Higginson wrote to his mother on June 17, 1859, that Tubman had "been back eight times secretly and brought out in all sixty slaves with her, including all her own family, besides aiding more in other ways to escape."[50] Higginson certainly had no reason to deny Tubman credit for any of her trips; he was already hailing her as "the greatest heroine of the age."[51] The *Liberator*, a Garrisonian paper sympathetic to Tubman, reported in a brief notice on July 6, 1860, that she had made eight journeys into the South.[52]

After careful consideration of multiple primary sources, Kate Clifford Larson and Jean Humez, the authors of the most reliable recent Tubman biographies, have given us a much clearer picture of Tubman's rescue missions. They agree that Bradford's notion of nineteen cannot withstand serious historical scrutiny. In reaching this conclusion, they follow in the footsteps of James A. McGowan, a Tubman admirer and author who may well be the first Tubman scholar to seriously question the Bradford-inspired tradition. The biographer of Thomas Garrett, McGowan began intensively researching Harriet Tubman nearly a quarter-century ago. Unfortunately, his conclusions did not receive wide notice, as he released them in a self-published journal that eventually expired.[53]

Larson sums up her remarkably exhaustive research on Tubman's years as an Underground Railroad conductor this way: "In total, she made approximately thirteen trips, spiriting away roughly seventy to eighty slaves, in addition to perhaps fifty or sixty more to whom she gave detailed instructions, nearly all from Dorchester and Caroline Counties in Maryland."[54] Humez, who argues that we ought to give more credence to Tubman's own statements to supporters in 1859 (such as Sanborn and Higginson) than to Bradford's numbers, writes that when all of the fragmentary and sometimes contradictory evidence is accounted for, we are brought to "ten or eleven trips, with fifty-nine to seventy fugitives brought north. Adding the last documented trip (December 1860) with its party of seven would make the grand total, by this conservative method, eleven (or twelve) trips, with sixty-six to seventy-seven rescued."[55]

Historians may yet discover new evidence pertinent to the number-of-trips question, but it is highly unlikely that anyone will be able to substantiate Bradford's claims. Larson and Humez wisely used primary sources that Bradford did not have available to her, such as the letters of Thomas Garrett and the records kept by William Still. Still and Garrett were Tubman supporters, intimately involved with her Underground Railroad work. Larson and Humez acknowledge the difficulties in sorting out the sometimes conflicting evidence. Humez tried to reconcile Sanborn's trip count that credits Tubman with having made five trips by the end of 1852 (December 1850, early 1851, fall 1851, December 1851, and fall 1852) with that given by Thomas Garrett in a letter to Eliza Wigham in which Garrett reported that Tubman had made "four successful trips to the neighborhood she had left" as of the date he wrote, December 16, 1855.[56] Sanborn wrote in his 1863 article that Tubman undertook a rescue mission in December 1851 leading out "a party of eleven among them her brother and his wife."[57] Humez decided to allow for variance in her total trip count—"eleven (or twelve) trips." Humez comments, "If we think of this [the Christmas trip] as a separate trip not included in Garret's four, we would need to increase the trip count by one, and the total number of fugitives by eleven. But I think Sanborn, writing in 1863 without Harriet Tubman there to ask, may have gotten the date wrong when remembering the Christmas rescue."[58] Kate Larson's total count of "approximately thirteen" is slightly higher than that of Humez. She enumerated one additional trip.[59]

The trip-count question is paired with the question of how many individuals Tubman rescued. In a 1907 study of economic cooperation among black Americans, edited by W. E. B. Du Bois and conducted at Atlanta University under the patronage of the Carnegie Institution, we read: "'Moses,' as Mrs. Tubman was called by her own people, was a most remarkable black woman, unlettered and very negrine, but with a great degree of intelligence and perceptive insight, amazing courage and a simple steadfastness of devotion which lifts her career into the ranks of heroism. Herself a fugitive slave, she devoted her life after her own freedom was won, to the work of aiding others to escape. First and last Harriet brought out several thousand slaves."[60] Not even Tubman's most avid admirers today claim that she rescued "several thousand." However, Orson Welles, the narrator of a made-for-television movie about Harriet Tubman, played by Cicely Tyson, claimed as much. As the 1978 film ends, Wells tells viewers that "Moses" liberated a thousand of the enslaved, but this exaggeration may have been the result of poor script writing.[61]

Sarah Bradford first introduced the number three hundred in *Scenes*, the hastily composed sketch of Tubman's life up to the year 1868. Bradford solicited recollections and testimonials from those who knew Moses before the Civil War. Thomas Garrett sent a letter, which Bradford quoted in full. Garrett apologized for not being able to "furnish so interesting an account of Harriet's labors" as he wished, for he had not been at liberty to "keep any written word of Harriet's or my own labors, except in numbering those whom I have aided." As a consequence, he could but estimate that Tubman had brought out "from 60 to 80 persons" from the Maryland region where she had been enslaved.[62] Bradford was not satisfied with this assessment and commented on Garrett's 1868 letter: "Friend Garrett probably refers here to those who passed through his hands. Harriet was obliged to come by many different routes on her different journeys, and though she never counted those whom she brought away with her, it would seem, *by the computation of others*, that there must have been somewhere near three hundred brought by her to the Northern States and Canada."[63]

In her 1886 revised and expanded account of Tubman's life, Bradford again reproduced the Garrett letter, but this time she commented that the number Harriet rescued ("by the computation of others") "must have been somewhat over three hundred brought by her to the Northern States and Canada."[64] In the intervening seventeen years, "somewhere near" had become "somewhat over." All qualifiers were dropped at another point in the 1886 volume. Of Tubman's heroic work, Bradford rhapsodized: "Then she piloted them North, traveling by night, hiding by day, scaling the mountains, fording the rivers, threading the forests, lying concealed as the pursuers passed them. She, carrying the babies, drugged with paregoric, in a basket on her arm. So she went nineteen times, and so she brought away over three hundred pieces of living and breathing 'property,' with God given souls."[65] Sanborn's 1863 article gave no summary total of the number Tubman rescued.[66] Similarly, the 1865 Cheney article on Tubman in the *Freedmen's Record*, which, as noted earlier, was based in part on the earlier *Commonwealth* piece, contains no summary total.[67] Bradford's reference to anonymous "friends" of Tubman as the source of her information frustrates any effort to corroborate the count she gives (whether near three hundred or more than three hundred).

Earl Conrad took up the question of how many of the enslaved Tubman escorted to freedom, though with less earnestness than he did with the conundrum of the number of trips she should be credited with. Conrad was of the opinion that the number rescued was in large measure a corollary of how many trips Tubman might have made. According to available sources, the largest group Tubman brought out at any one time was eleven. The other documented or dated rescues involved groups averaging six or seven individuals. It is difficult, therefore, to come up with a figure of three hundred (more or less) with as few as eleven or twelve trips. Nineteen trips would average approximately fifteen fugitives a trip.[68]

Conrad understood the dilemma confronting the historian in search of definitive answers. In the 1970 essay celebrating what he believed to be the one-hundred-fiftieth anniversary of Tubman's birth, Conrad attempted to steer readers to a more fundamental theme. He acknowledged that the so-called man in the street, regardless of race, knew little of Tubman's real achievements. "Even scholars," Conrad asserted, "have a kind of stereotyped view of her which is usually summarized in a prosaic expression such as, 'She made nineteen trips into the southland and brought to freedom more than 300 slaves.' This description of her labors and significance usually ends with some quotation from her arsenal of 'quaint' or wise or militant expressions: and that is Harriet Tubman for many or most. No description or estimate of her could be further from the truth than that customary handling of her."[69] For his own part, Conrad was content to say, "If Harriet had not absconded with about 300 slaves, as is likely, and ran off with only 200, it would still be an economic blow to the slave power worth $200,000."[70] In an effort to underscore once again the symbolic rather than the literal nature of Tubman's Underground Railroad labors, Conrad wrote of her "stimulating, as she did other hundreds, perhaps five hundred, perhaps a thousand, to escape, and contributing above all others to a State-wide panic, that we run into much larger figures, much more significant end-results, and a much more likely estimate of her real contribution."[71]

Another numbers question demonstrates the tension between Tubman the legend and Tubman the person. The Tubman legend would have us believe that Southerners promised a reward of at least twelve thousand dollars for the capture of Black Moses and perhaps as much as forty thousand dollars. Tubman spoke at the Worcester, Massachusetts, church of Thomas Wentworth Higginson in June 1859 telling her "tales of adventure." Shortly thereafter, Higginson wrote that there was "a reward of twelve thousand dollars offered for her in Maryland."[72] Sarah Bradford wrote in *Scenes* that advertisements had been posted "for the head of the woman who was constantly appearing and enticing away parties of slaves from their masters" and specifically mentioned "one reward of $12,000." However, Bradford had seen an article with a higher figure and quoted it: "'*Forty thousand dollars* was not too great a reward for the Maryland slaveholders to offer for her.'"[73] Bradford reproduced the article, actually a letter published in 1867 in the *National Anti-Slavery Standard* containing the sentence, "Forty-thousand dollars was not too great a reward for the Maryland slaveholders to offer for her." "When asked about this," Bradford wrote in 1868, "Harriet said she did not know whether it was so, but she heard them read from one paper that the reward offered was

$12,000."[74] In spite of what Tubman told her, Bradford stipulated "a reward of $40,000" in 1886 when she published her revised and enlarged edition of the Tubman biography, now called *Harriet, the Moses of Her People*.[75] Tubman's most recent biographer, Kate Larson, has concluded, "There never was a $40,000 reward for Tubman's capture, a figure that became grossly exaggerated through the retelling of her story."[76] She adds, "Though a reward notice for Tubman's capture has yet to be found, it is likely that there was one; whether it was $1,200 or $12,000, Tubman would have been a significant catch for southern bounty hunters."[77]

Defining Tubman's "real contribution," to borrow Conrad's phrase, to the Underground Railroad is made difficult by the nature of the enterprise she engaged in. Her contemporary and admirer Frederick Douglass (see Plate 5), who settled in Rochester in 1847, some two years before Tubman's escape, said of her in the tribute he sent Bradford in response to her request for reminiscences about Black Moses: "The difference between us is very marked. Most that I have done and suffered in the service of our cause has been in public, and I have received much encouragement at every step of the way. You on the other hand have labored in a private way. I have wrought in the day—you in the night."[78] Tubman's hidden history—her night service, as it were—remains largely opaque, for it was dangerous business, witnessed, as Douglass affirmed, but "by a few trembling, scared, and foot-sore bondmen and women."[79] That so much of the Tubman iconic development rests on so small a body of known fact is illustrative of the power of myth and of the socio-psychological need to create a black heroine in an American culture saturated with white male historical icons.

Tubman's odyssey strikes many as unique. Here was an unlettered black woman who risked recapture and worse by conducting multiple raids upon the slaveholding South and redeeming its living "property." Underground Railroad stories abound in references to men striking a blow for freedom; indeed, by most historians' estimates, the majority of escapees were male. The Tubman as Moses myth introduces issues of gender, and, as we shall see in a subsequent chapter, women's rights. Her advocates in the nineteenth century as well as radical feminists in more recent decades have used Tubman as a symbol in their own political struggles. Tubman enthusiasts are quick to point out that she should be honored not only because she was a brave woman, but because she embodied bravery itself. Bradford underscored this in the preface to the

1869 volume, where she invites the reader to consider the importance of her subject in comparison to other historical figures deemed "heroines": Joan of Arc, Grace Darling, and Florence Nightingale. "Not one of these women," Bradford asserted, "has shown more courage and power of endurance in facing danger and death to relieve human suffering, than has this woman in her heroic and successful endeavors to reach and save all whom she might of her oppressed and suffering race, and pilot them from the land of Bondage to the promised land of Liberty. Well has she been called 'Moses,' for she has been a leader and deliverer unto hundreds of her people."[80] The contemporary artist Paul Collins has captured this Tubman as Moses theme in a painting popular today (see Plate 6).

If the numbers questions have not solely been determinative of Tubman's fame, then why does the ritualistic "nineteen trips and three hundred slaves rescued" refrain so saturate references to Tubman? The pattern of the hero—or in this case, the heroine—demands some symbolic number. It has ever been so. According to biblical lore, "Saul slew his thousands, and David his tens of thousands." Some aspects of her work as the liberator of the enslaved will forever remain hidden, lost to the historian who tries to follow the evidentiary trail. The Tubman as "Black Moses" tradition is now so firmly fixed in the American consciousness that it will not soon be amended by scholars who point out that the counts of nineteen and three hundred originated not from Tubman but from a white woman hastily putting together a small sketch of "Moses the Deliverer" in 1868.

Every Underground Railroad conductor, regardless of how many successful missions he or she made or the number he or she rescued, had to demonstrate courage and cleverness. Tubman excelled as a tactician. Stories about her amazing ability to outwit her pursuers are base elements in forging the Tubman heroic persona, especially so in the large body of literature directed at young readers. Tubman is famous for having told audiences, as she did at a Rochester Women's Rights Convention, "I was de conductor ob de Underground Railroad for eight years, an' I can say what mos' conductors can't say—I nebber run my train off de track an' I nebber los' a passenger."[81] Some of these stories have taken on a parable-like quality. They teach moral lessons, usually having to do with the need to be brave and help others.

Talk to Tubman devotees, and they will tell you about having seen illustrated accounts of how Black Moses held a book upside down, pretending to read it to divert attention from potential captors who were examining a wanted poster describing their prey as illiterate (Figure 18).[82] Many youngsters find the story of Tubman releasing two chickens and chasing after them to befuddle her master a very clever ruse (Figure 19).[83]

Others can tell about how Tubman used a potato hole as a hiding place.[84] Many books about Tubman highlight her use of coded language of songs and spirituals to communicate with potential passengers on her railroad, such as, "Moses go down in Egypt, Till ole Pharo' let me go; Hadn't been for Adam's fall, Shouldn't hab to died at all," which she sang as a warning.[85] By changing routes and picking up her passengers on Saturday nights, Tubman increased the odds in her favor. She was also pragmatic and is said to have carried a gun to encourage the fainthearted to keep going.[86] Illustrated accounts of Tubman's life portray her toting a pistol (Figure 20).

In keeping with the classic paradigm of the powerless making a fool of the powerful, Harriet Tubman deserves her reputation as the liberator of her people. It is a heroic tale in which the "trickster"—facing overwhelming odds against surviving—wins in the end, having, as it were, the last laugh. Tubman told Sarah Bradford that she would hide in the woods with her charges and watch the white pursuers come down the road putting up advertisements for the runaways on fences and trees: "And den how we laughed. We was de fools, and *dey* was de wise men; but we wasn't fools enough to go down de high road in de broad daylight."[87]

Renewed public interest in the Underground Railroad has driven an intense research effort for approximately the last fifteen years. Investigators, some professional historians, many not, have recovered a richer and more detailed history of the Underground Railroad than existed in the early 1960s when the modern Tubman revival began. We now know that other conductors risked their lives to bring out freedom seekers by doing as Tubman did, reentering the South. Some of these conductors are said to have saved many individuals, some family members, some not.[88] According to his published narrative, *His Promised Land*, John Parker, son of a white man and an enslaved mother, rescued over four hundred from lifetime servitude. "A more fearless creature never lived," claimed the *Cincinnati Commercial Tribune* shortly after his death. "He gloried in danger. He would go boldly into the enemy's camp and filch the fugitives to freedom."[89] Stories survive of the daring rescue work of other

18. "Pretending to Read." Illustration by Steven James Petruccio. From Kate McMullan, *The Story of Harriet Tubman: Conductor of the Underground Railroad* (New York: Bantam Doubleday Dell Books for Young Readers, 1991). Illustrations copyright © 1991 by Steven James Petruccio.

19. Tubman using chickens. Illustration by Den Schofield. From Megan McClard, *Harriet Tubman: Slavery and the Underground Railroad* (Englewood Cliffs, N.J.: Silver Burdett Press, 1991). Illustrations copyright © 1991 by Den Schofield.

20. "No Turning Back." Illustration by Teresa Flavin. From Monica Kulling, *Escape North: The Story of Harriet Tubman* (New York: Random House, 2000). Text copyright © 2000 by Monica Kulling. Illustrations copyright © 2000 by Teresa Flavin.

conductors along the Ohio River, such as Calvin Fairbanks, an Oberlin College graduate, and John Fairfield, son of a slaveholding family, both of whom are credited with escorting large numbers to safety.[90] Charles L. Blockson, a key figure in the contemporary Underground Railroad renaissance, tells us that the black conductor Elijah Anderson, working out of Cleveland, "is said to have taken hundreds of fugitives to a depot in Detroit."[91]

How is it, then, that Harriet Tubman's name became so well known, with the result that she remains the dominant symbol of the Underground Railroad? Fergus Bordewich, author of the best new history of the Underground Railroad, offers this insight: "Nothing can or should diminish the story of Tubman's boldness and amazing success over a long period. However, she was by no means unique. She became perceived as unique, I think, because she was operating in the best-known theater of the URR operations, and came to the attention of the most prominent people in the abolitionist movement. In other words, I think that she got a degree of recognition, and publicity, that others did not. She also lived a lot longer, and told her story to many people."[92]

The biblical Moses did not enter the Promised Land to battle with the enemies of the Israelites who occupied it. That mantle of leadership passed on to Joshua, who went up against the fortified cities of Canaan. Tubman's story transcends the limitations of the biblical parallel of Moses. Her military service during the Civil War resonates more with the figure of Joshua than Moses. When piloting scared fugitives out of slavery's prison, Tubman is said to have carried a gun. Most white abolitionists drank deeply from the well of nonviolence; this was especially true of the Garrisonians in the Boston clique of abolitionists. Had Tubman's reputation as a liberator been forged, as was Nat Turner's, in the school of blood and violence, she might not have been embraced as the Moses of the Underground Railroad. In the wake of John Brown's attack on Harpers Ferry, some abolitionists, including Franklin B. Sanborn, architect of that early Tubman iconic representation, jettisoned older notions of nonresistance to evil and took up a philosophy of righteous violence. In their minds, the Civil War was a cleansing fire, purging out the dross of slavery. Their "Black Moses" must also be a warrior.

CHAPTER THREE

"GENERAL TUBMAN"

"I will not disarm Harriet Tubman," Mike Alewitz vowed in 2000 during a controversy ignited by his design of a mural depicting a musket-toting Harriet Tubman as Moses parting the Red Sea.[1] Intended for display on an outside wall of the headquarters of Baltimore's Associated Black Charities, the 25-by-125-foot painted mural was to be one of five honoring Tubman (Figure 21). An image of a martial Tubman displayed so prominently on the side of their building at Cathedral and Chase streets in Baltimore, where gun violence caused public concern, troubled some of the officials of Associated Black Charities, as well as other members of the community.[2] Alewitz defended his depiction of Tubman with a rifle in one hand and a lantern in the other as an expression of artistic freedom, as might be expected. He also argued that taking the gun away from Tubman would be historically inaccurate. When asked to turn the rifle into a less controversial staff, Alewitz responded, "They have an objection to Harriet Tubman with a rifle. It's like you want to see wolves in the wild— but without teeth. They can refuse the mural, and that's their right. We'll find another wall."[3]

Ironically, as the journalist Sara Rimensnyder points out, "Public parks across American are littered with larger-than-life statues of war heroes, most of them carrying guns."[4] Julianne Malveaux, the African American columnist, observed that African Americans "are woefully under represented in our nation's statuary" and commented on the controversy raised by Alewitz's mural: "Actually, there is nothing funny about this story, about society's tendency to whitewash black history, to make it warm, fuzzy, and comfortable, instead of as violent, confrontative, and resistant as it was."[5] The debate over how Tubman should be represented by Alewitz tapped into deep emotional crosscurrents. Some saw Tubman as the militant revolutionary. Others wanted to stress a less confrontational symbolic Tubman. Kat Lindsey, a Tubman reenactor, gladly posed as a model for the Harriet Tubman mural created by the artist Sam Donovan that appeared on a side of the Goldburg building in downtown Philadelphia. Donovan's and Lindsey's Tubman was a seventy-foot-tall figure holding a lantern (and not a gun) pointing toward the North Star. There was no public controversy like that in Baltimore.[6]

That a public debate should erupt over having Harriet Tubman depicted as armed and dangerous in 2000 is not altogether surprising, for Americans are not in agreement as to how she should be remembered—or, to be more precise, how the memory of her should be used as leverage by special interest groups today. Though Alewitz defended his rendering of Tubman with a musket as historically accurate, he declared, "The importance of Harriet Tubman's life lies not in the past, but in the future. At a time when African-Americans were kept as chattel, when even the abolitionist forces were riddled with the racism and bigotry of the time, Harriet Tubman and thousands of anti-slavery activists organized an effective liberation struggle which divided and conquered the forces of reaction. Their will to triumph, in the face of tremendous adversity, is an inspiration for those who struggle for social justice today."[7]

Alewitz's reading of movement or mainstream abolitionism is flawed if he means to say that a gun was symbolically representative of this philosophy. The American Antislavery Society embraced William Lloyd Garrison's doctrine of nonresistance, a form of Christian pacifism. Nonviolence was the creed of most abolitionists, black and white, until John Brown's raid on Harpers Ferry and the outbreak of the Civil War raised questions about its utility.[8] If Alewitz's interpretation of abolitionist history is suspect, what of his notion of Harriet Tubman as armed and dangerous?

Alewitz's artistic representation of Tubman as a revolutionary liberator with musket in hand draws heavily on the image of her that appeared as the frontispiece of Sarah Bradford's first book, *Scenes in the Life of Harriet Tubman*. In the introductory statement written by the Reverend Samuel Miles Hopkins of Auburn and dated December 1, 1868, we learn that "the spirited wood-cut likeness of Harriet, in her costume as scout, was furnished by the kindness of Mr. J. C. Darby of this city."[9] The woodcut shows Tubman standing and holding a rifle. Several field tents

21. "The Dreams of Harriet Tubman." Mural by Mike Alewitz, Department of Art, Central Connecticut State University, New Britain, Conn. Courtesy Mike Alewitz

stand in the background. Darby obviously meant to invoke in the viewer's mind thoughts of Tubman's service to Union forces during the Civil War. Darby had not been in the theater of war with Tubman. Perhaps Tubman described what she had worn when she was a spy and scout during the war years, or she may have put on her Civil War "uniform" for Darby to sketch from sometime after her return to Auburn. Whatever the circumstances, the martial image has long been fixed in the public mind as emblematic of Tubman as a freedom fighter. Samuel Hopkins Adams, Sarah Bradford's nephew, heard Tubman speak of the woodcut likeness of her in her scout uniform many times: "She was inordinately proud of that woodcut. Reference to it never failed to loosen her tongue."[10]

The Tubman myth became more multifaceted because of her work as a nurse, spy, and scout during the Civil War (Figure 22). Before 1862, she was primarily known as "Black Moses," once enslaved but self-liberated, who went back multiple times to bring out others. Encoded in this presentation of Harriet Tubman are ideals custodians and preservationists of the Tubman as "Black Moses" tradition wished to hold up for emulation—most significantly, the importance of personal courage or bravery. Nineteenth-century Tubman admirers had difficulty in extricating their admiration for her from conventional attitudes about the role of women in society. Women were to be passive; men, active. Gender-specific norms reserved soldier-like characteristics for males. It is therefore striking that Tubman should be referred to using language drawn from martial traditions.

Perhaps the most persistent and widely known instance of this was the appellation ascribed to her by abolitionist friends and allies who called her "General Tubman." The image of Tubman as a female military leader with a rank of a general has caused controversy. When Earl Conrad was

"GIB DE COUNTERSIGN ER I SHOOTS!"

22. Tubman as a Union scout. Illustration by James Daugherty. From Hildegarde Hoyt Swift, *The Railroad to Freedom: A Story of the Civil War* (New York: Harcourt, Brace and World, 1932). Copyright © 1960 by Hildegarde Hoyt Swift.

negotiating in 1941 with Carter G. Woodson of Associated Publishers regarding his two-hundred-fifty-page biography of Harriet, he proposed the title "I Bring You General Tubman." "I rather liked that," Conrad recalled in 1970 in an article for the *Black Scholar* written in celebration of what he believed to be the sesquicentennial of Harriet Tubman's birth. "I liked the emphasis on the military character of this woman in a time that was revolutionary and military, and I thought Phillips [actually, John Brown] had dubbed her correctly, but Dr. Woodson, a bit more conservative or perhaps more literary, asked me if it would be all right to reduce the title to simply *Harriet Tubman*. It was."[11] Conrad's "revolutionary and military" time, as we shall see in a subsequent chapter, was during the 1930s when he was involved with radical and left-wing political-action groups.

According to available sources, John Brown (Figure 23) first introduced Harriet Tubman as "General Tubman" to fellow abolitionists on one of his visits to New England when he called on the great orator Wen-

23. John Brown, from the last Boston photograph, 1859. From Franklin B. Sanborn, *Recollections of Seventy Years* (Boston: Gorham Press, 1909), vol. 1, facing 142.

dell Phillips. Lydia B. Chace Wyman, a fellow Bostonian and friend of Phillips, was present at the meeting, which she said took place in the "little reception room of Mr. Phillips' Essex Street house."[12] Phillips himself wrote of meeting Tubman in a letter, dated June 16, 1868, that he sent to Bradford as she was preparing her first sketch of Tubman's life. In that letter, which Bradford reproduced in *Scenes*, Phillips said, "The last time I ever saw John Brown was under my own roof, as he brought Harriet Tubman to me, saying, 'Mr. Phillips, I bring you one of the best and bravest persons on this continent—General Tubman, as we call her.'" Phillips added, "In my opinion there are few captains, perhaps few colonels, who have done more for the loyal cause since the war began, and few men who did before that time more for the colored race, than our fearless and most sagacious friend, Harriet."[13]

Brown and Tubman first met in St. Catharines in the spring of 1858. Tubman lived in a rented house on North Street and was a well-known figure among the fugitives who located near a local branch of the British

Methodist Episcopal church. As to Tubman's prior knowledge of Brown, Earl Conrad speculated that while "piloting her broods northward to a new life" she had heard of his abolitionist work out in Kansas and "was amazed at how an old man fought for her people."[14] Brown, in the company of the Reverend Jermain Loguen of Syracuse, had come to St. Catharines hoping to recruit freedom fighters from among the fugitives there and enlist the aid of Tubman. On April 8, 1858, Brown wrote to his son from St. Catharines, "I came on here direct with J. W. Loguen the day after you left Rochester. I am succeeding, to all appearance beyond my expectations. Harriet Tubman hooked on his whole team at once. He [Harriet] is the most of a man, naturally, that I ever met with. There is the most abundant material, and of the right quality, in this quarter, beyond all doubt."[15]

Brown's use of the masculine pronoun to refer to Harriet Tubman has caused comment. Catharine Clinton, author of a recent Tubman biography, writes: "Brown was an Old Testament patriarch, who condemned the second-class status of blacks but accepted women's subservient role." Because Brown thought of armed resistance as an attribute not likely to be found in women, he had "ignored the fact that Tubman was a woman—'transubstantiating' her into a male."[16] Though Brown's opinion that Tubman was the "most of a man, naturally," betrayed Tubman by the erasure of her gender, it enhanced her martial image. Earl Conrad turned what might be considered an insult into an accolade by saying that "John Brown was so astounded at the physical impression of this woman, together with the knowledge of her achievements, that he could only convey his regard for her by applying masculine terms to describe her."[17]

Wyman is the source of the claim that, when Brown entered the house where Tubman was staying and the two met, he shook her hand three times and said, "The first I see is General Tubman, the second is General Tubman, and the third is General Tubman."[18] Since no eyewitness record of this historic meeting on April 7, 1858, exists, and later references to it reveal little of substance, we can only guess at what Brown might have told Tubman of his plans. Wyman may have heard directly from Tubman of Tubman's first encounter with Brown, for she writes: "When John Brown bade Harriet good by, he again called her 'General' three times, and informed her that she would hear from him through Douglass. This was probably the parting which the writer once heard Harriet describe, when she stood on her doorstep and gazed after him as long as she could see him, and then watched the omnibus which he had entered till it was out of sight. They were two souls who dealt in action, but were alike moved by impulses from mystical and hidden sources."[19] Mystical is the right word, for Tubman said that before meeting Brown she had had a dream in which "the head of an old man with a long white beard" rose up out of the rocks and bushes, only to be struck down by a crowd of men. After meeting Brown, Tubman recognized the figure in her dream.[20]

On May 8, 1858, Brown was in Chatham, Canada West. Located on the Thames River about forty-five miles east of Detroit, Chatham, like St. Catharines, had a sizable body of freedom seekers who had fled the American South. Brown convened a convention for organizing a provisional government that he intended to set up after liberating the slaves. But as Edward J. Renehan Jr., author of *The Secret Six: The True Tale of the Men Who Conspired with John Brown*, has observed, there was a disappointing turnout. None of Brown's chief white supporters attended, and "Frederick Douglass and Harriet Tubman, both enthusiastically invited to participate, were also conspicuous in their absence."[21] Tubman's failure to attend Brown's organizational meeting may have been due to a mix-up in plans, as she had gone on to Toronto from St. Catharines. Tubman's absence at the Chatham enclave does not trouble those who depict her as a staunch ally of Brown. Earl Conrad argued, "If anything took precedence over her work as a conductor, it was her developing association with John Brown, and their plans for raiding the Government arsenal at Harpers Ferry at a later date."[22]

Tubman admirers believe that she did not waver in her support of the "Old Man," as Brown was already being called. She is said to have urged Brown to set July 4, 1858, as the day for the raid on Harpers Ferry. She thought it was a good time "to raise the mill."[23] Instead, Brown looked to strike about the middle of May 1858 and would have done so had it not been for Hugh Forbes, who informed Henry Wilson, a senator from Massachusetts, that something was afoot. Frederick Douglass backed out after a meeting with Brown at Chambersburg, Virginia. He judged Brown's plan to be neither prudent nor realizable.[24] Tubman, however, is said to have had "messianic beliefs" about Brown and kept her faith in him.[25]

Brown and Tubman were in Boston in late May 1859, Brown to solicit support for his proposed raid and Tubman to garner funds to aid her parents. On May 30, Franklin B. Sanborn wrote to Thomas Wentworth Higginson, "I wonder if you rec'd two letters from me about Cap. B. who has been here for three weeks and is soon to leave, having got his $2000. He is at the U.S. Hotel, and you ought to see him before he goes, for now he is to begin. Also you ought to see Harriet Tubman, the woman who brought away 50 slaves in 8 journeys made to Maryland; but perhaps you have seen her. She is the heroine of the day. She came here Friday night and is at 168 Cambridge St[reet]."[26] Brown had dinner with George Stearns at the Parker House Hotel before leaving Boston. He told Stearns, "I think it probably that we may never meet again in this world."[27] Given available sources, it appears that Brown and Tubman did not meet in Boston that spring and never crossed paths again.

The historical record is silent on Tubman's movements in the weeks preceding the attack on Harpers Ferry. Brown seems to have lost contact with her. John Brown Jr., acting as an agent of his father, went to Syracuse a few weeks before the raid to raise support for his father. While in upstate New York he received a letter from Lewis Hayden, the Boston-based abolitionist, former fugitive from Kentucky, and active participant in the rescue of Shadrach Minkins in February 1851. Hayden wrote on September 16, 1859, "I received your very kind letter, and would state that I have sent a note to Harriet requesting her to come to Boston, saying to her in the note that she must come right on, which I think she will do, and when she does come I think we will find some way to send her on. I have seen our friend at Concord [Franklin B. Sanborn]; he is a true man. I have not yet said anything to anybody except him. I do not think it is wise for me to do so. I shall, therefore, when Harriet comes, send for our Concord friend, who will attend to the matter. Have you all the hands you wish? Write soon."[28]

It is widely believed that Tubman intended to join in Brown's assault on the federal arsenal at Harpers Ferry. Had she done so on that fateful day, October 16, 1859, and therefore been killed or captured and hanged, the Harriet Tubman myth would have converged more closely with that of "The Thundering Voice of Jehovah," as John Brown has been called, than has been the case. Most secondary sources claim that illness prevented Tubman from becoming a martyr along with Brown, and she is said to have been in New Bedford, Massachusetts, as the so-called Harpers Ferry Incident unfolded.[29] Somehow Tubman got word that Brown wanted her to join him and his small army in Virginia, and with abolitionist funds she began her trip South. Tubman was in New York City when she learned that the insurrection at Harpers Ferry had begun without her; two of Brown's sons were killed, and Brown was captured.

Though many details regarding Tubman's support of John Brown remain elusive, it is clear that Brown saw in her material strong enough for the military-like mission he had set for himself and his small army of raiders. Tubman thought equally highly of John Brown. Tubman's admiration for Brown prefigured the heroic status he has held in the memory of his African American allies and black generations since the Civil War.[30] Franklin B. Sanborn, in a letter of reminiscences sent to Sarah Bradford as she was preparing her first Tubman biography, recalled a visit Tubman made to his house in Concord, Massachusetts, sometime after Brown went to the gallows. Tubman entered a room where there was a sculpture of Brown, a bust done by Edward A. Brackett. "The sight of it, which was new to her," Sanborn reported, "threw her into a sort of ecstasy of sorrow and admiration."[31] Tubman felt Brown's loss deeply. After he went to the gallows on December 2, 1859, she sought consolation among her Boston friends, including Edna Cheney. Cheney would later write that Tubman's "heart was too full, she must talk." Talk Tubman did, affirming to Cheney that she still believed that God, who had set the North Star in the heavens, gave her strength and meant her to be free.[32] Tubman would tell another supporter that John Brown had "done more in dying, than 100 men would in living."[33]

The notion that Tubman and Brown were allies in common cause became firmly entrenched in the public mind, in the United States and abroad. During a meeting to commemorate the fourth anniversary of John Brown's death held in London on December 2, 1863, the Reverend Moncure D. Conway said of Tubman, "A fugitive Negro woman came from the center of Georgia [sic] to the North. She is now known as Moses, because of the numbers of slaves she has rescued; and she, hearing some one speak of John Brown as having been hung in Virginia, said: 'We Negroes in the South never call him John Brown; we call him our Savior. He died for us.' Ah! How much truth have those lowly hearts searched out?"[34]

Like so many of the aspects of the Tubman myth, Tubman's image as "General Tubman" originated because of the abolitionist circles in which she moved, where there was need for a black iconic figure militant enough to be willing to take on the challenge of breaking slavery's stranglehold on the nation. Though the label "General Tubman" first came into the public consciousness because of her association with John Brown, today's symbolic use of Harriet Tubman as "General Tubman" is a composite construction drawing on several aspects of her personal war on slavery and injustice and not simply on her association with the leader of the attack on Harpers Ferry. Tubman may not have been one of Brown's insurgent band, but she did demonstrate a willingness to risk bodily harm by throwing herself into the fray when freedom was at stake.

The most notable instance in which Tubman actually got into a fight took place in the North. It is known as the "battle for Charles Nalle."[35] Nalle fled Virginia in 1858 after his so-called owner threatened to put him up for auction. He eventually settled in Troy, New York, working as a teamster for a lumberman and as a coachman. On the morning of Friday, April 27, 1860, U.S. Deputy Marshal John W. Holmes arrested Nalle and took him to the office of U.S. Commissioner Miles Beach at the corner of State and First streets. William Henry, a black grocer with whom Nalle boarded and a member of the local Vigilance Committee, spread the alarm. Soon, a crowd composed of abolitionists as well as pro-slavery sympathizers gathered in front of the commissioner's office. Tubman was in Troy visiting a cousin, John Hooper, and en route to Boston, where she planned to attend an antislavery meeting at the request of Gerrit Smith. On hearing of Nalle's arrest, she rushed to the commissioner's office.

Franklin B. Sanborn first gave the American public notice of Tubman's heroic participation in the battle for Charles Nalle in his *Commonwealth* article of 1863. Edna Dow Cheney mentioned the incident briefly in 1865 as an example of Tubman's habit of telling "racy stories." Cheney has Tubman shouting "her favorite motto" — "Give me liberty or give me death" — during the struggle to rescue Nalle. Cheney says of Tubman, "She is perfectly at home in such scenes; she loves action; I think she does not dislike fighting in a good cause."[36]

Sarah Bradford embellished the Nalle story based on her interviews with Tubman in 1868. Bradford places Tubman inside the building where Nalle's hearing took place. A crowd gathered outside, watching and worried that Nalle had been spirited away to a fate worse than death. Some of the would-be rescuers could see Tubman's sunbonnet in a window and said, "No, there stands 'Moses' yet, and as long as she is there, he is safe." Bradford then has Tubman sending several small boys out to cry "fire." Bells ring, and more people arrive on the scene. When the officers holding Nalle try to clear the stairs to bring him down, Tubman, pretending to be an old woman, attempts to block the way. The U.S. marshal and his men finally bring Nalle out, just as Tubman shouts from a window, "Here he comes—take him!" Bradford went on to describe how Tubman "darted down the stairs like a wild-cat" and pulled an officer off Nalle. In the ensuing struggle, she lost that sunbonnet and "her stout shoes." Even as her clothes were ripped from her, Tubman hung on to Nalle, dragging him to the river, where he tumbled into a boat. According to Bradford, Tubman followed across in a ferryboat over to Troy. Schoolchildren pointed her to a house where Nalle was being held on the third floor. With officers firing down on Nalle's rescuers, two men down and wounded, "our heroine," Bradford writes, climbed over their bodies "and with the help of others burst open the door of the room, dragged out the fugitive" and carried Nalle down the stairs. A man with a fast horse and wagon happened to be passing by. Nalle was "hurried in" and taken to Schenectady.[37]

To forestall criticism from readers to whom her description of Tubman's role in the Nalle rescue "seemed too wonderful"—that is, too fanciful—Bradford sought corroboration of the oral account Black Moses had given her. She asked the Reverend Henry Fowler to visit Troy and "ascertain the facts." Fowler interviewed Nalle's lawyer, Martin Townsend, and had intended to supply Bradford with a written report of Townsend's "rich narration," but Fowler fell ill, "stricken down by the heat of the sun" while visiting the inmates of the state prison at Auburn. Lacking verification from Fowler, Bradford turned to a newspaper account of Nalle's rescue that appeared in the *Troy Whig* on April 28, 1859. The *Whig* article does not mention Tubman by name at all, much less attribute to her a major role in rescuing Nalle, as Bradford's account does.[38] Perhaps as a way to compensate for the absence of any reference to Tubman in the newspaper account, Bradford appended a statement she had been sent by Townsend. Two paragraphs in the Townsend material speak to the question of the instrumentality of Tubman in the "battle for Charles Nalle":

> When Nalle was brought from Commissioner Beach's office into the street, Harriet Tubman, who had been standing with the excited crowd, rushed amongst the foremost to Nalle, and running one of her arms around his manacled arm, held on to him without ever loosening her hold through the more than half-hour's struggle to Judge Gould's office, and from Judge Gould's office to the dock,

where Nalle's liberation was accomplished. In the melee, she was repeatedly beaten over the head with policemen's clubs, but she never for a moment released her hold, but cheered Nalle and his friends with her voice, and struggled with the officers until they were literally worn out with their exertions, and Nalle was separated from them.

True, she had strong and earnest helpers in her struggle, some of whom had white faces as well as human hearts, and are now in Heaven. But she exposed herself to the fury of the sympathizers with slavery, without fear, and suffered their blows without flinching. Harriet crossed the river with the crowd, in the ferry-boat, and when the men who led the assault upon the door of Judge Stewart's office, were stricken down, Harriet and a number of other colored women rushed over their bodies, brought Nalle out, and putting him in the first wagon passing, started him for the West.[39]

Tubman was fond of retelling the story of the Nalle rescue in her later years. Samuel Hopkins Adams recalled that she entertained Auburn youth with the particulars of her participation, of how, for example, she herself carried Nalle out of harm's way: "I th'ow um acrost my shouldah like a bag o' meal and tote um away outen theyah." She also, according to the account given by Adams, claimed to have stolen the horse upon which Nalle made his escape, though the Bradford version in *Scenes* has it that the owner volunteered his "blood-horse."[40]

Any attempt to sort out the details of Tubman's participation in the "battle for Charles Nalle" must wrestle with the by now familiar problem of multiple and sometimes varying emphases in the sources. Bradford underscored Tubman's instrumentality. The author of the *Troy Whig* offered another interpretation of the day's events, one that is notably silent about Tubman's personal role. Bradford appended Townsend's statement without explanation as to what motivated the lawyer's desire to add his witness. Had Bradford explicitly asked him to speak to the question of Tubman's participation in the rescue? Was Townsend interested in expanding on and underscoring the martial image of "General Tubman"? Setting aside the question of who did what for whom on that fateful day in Troy, it is clear that Tubman's role in the rescue underscored the portrayal of her as a champion of freedom's cause who, when the situation demanded action, actually fought. Abolitionists celebrated

24. Charles Nalle's rescue, April 27, 1860. Site of the U.S. Commissioner's Office, corner of First and State streets, Troy, New York. Courtesy Michael Saafir.

black participation in the "battle for Charles Nalle" and called attention to blacks in "the rank and file"—"African fury is entitled to claim the greatest share in the rescue."[41] Some contemporary retellers of the story, however, make it appear as if Harriet Tubman singlehandedly won the "battle for Charles Nalle."[42] Tubman's name does not appear on the bronze plaque just off the corner at First and State streets in today's Troy (Figure 24). It reads, simply, "Here was begun April 27, 1860 the rescue of Charles Nalle, an escaped slave who had been arrested under the Fugitive Slave Act."

While the martial image of Tubman has its roots in her association with John Brown and the rescue of Charles Nalle, it grew and blossomed during the Civil War. Given the early reluctance of the federal government to allow African Americans to join in the fight to put down the Confederate rebellion, it is remarkable that Harriet Tubman, a black woman, got into the theater of war at all. After Union troops captured Port Royal Island in November 1861, plantation owners in the Sea Islands region fled, leaving thousands of so-called contraband to fend for themselves. Major-General David Hunter, whose headquarters were on Port

Royal Island, needed someone to assist with caring for the men, women, and children who were neither slave nor free. Massachusetts Governor John Andrew urged Tubman to go from Boston to Beaufort, South Carolina, which she did in the spring of 1862 on board the Union ship *Atlantic*.[43] General Hunter assigned Tubman to the headquarters of General Stevens and provided her with a document that read, in part, "Pass the bearer, Harriet Tubman . . . and give her free passage at all times, on all Government transports. . . . She has permission, as a servant of the government, to purchase such provisions from the Commissary as she may need."[44]

While in the Beaufort area, Tubman nursed the sick, contraband and soldier alike, administering her own remedies made from roots and herbs. She supported herself by selling pies, gingerbread, and root beer in the camps. She spent her own money to have a wash house built that women, former slaves, could use. Her labors on behalf of the occupants of the Beaufort contraband camp became widely known, and others engaged in educational and missionary work came to visit her. Charlotte Forten, a young teacher from one of Philadelphia's most prominent African American families, recorded in her journal on January 31, 1863: "In B[eaufort] we spent nearly all our time at Harriet Tubman's—otherwise 'Moses.' She is a wonderful woman—a real heroine. Has helped off a large number of slaves, after taking her own freedom."[45]

Sarah Bradford recorded Tubman as telling her: "I'd go to de hospital, I would, early eb'ry morning," sponging the wounded until the water was warm and "red as clar blood."[46] Tubman's nursing skills have earned her accolades as a pioneer in the medical profession. In an article published in the *Bulletin of the History of Medicine* titled, "Black Abolitionist Doctors and Healers, 1810–1885," Leslie A. Falk wrote, "Harriet Tubman (1820–1913) typifies the colored woman nurse and folk healer. She is officially referred to as a nurse and matron by many, including Surgeon-General V. K. Barnes of the Union Army and Dr. Henry K. Durant, Acting Assistant Surgeon in charge of the Beaufort, South Carolina 'Contraband Hospital' for escaped and freed slaves, who worked with her for two years."[47] Though nursing is one of the three Civil War roles Tubman is frequently credited with, she was not on the roster of army nurses— at least, insofar as Dorothea Dix, appointed "superintendent of women nurses" on June 10, 1861, by Secretary of War Edwin M. Stanton, was concerned.[48]

Before the Civil War, nursing was a male prerogative, and men such as Walt Whitman continued in that tradition when Union forces took to the battlefield. Mary E. P. Mahoney, a graduate in 1879 of the white-controlled New England Hospital for Women and Children, is said to be "the first colored woman who prepared herself for professional nursing."[49] African American women had few opportunities to enter the nursing profession until 1891, when Dr. Daniel H. Williams took the lead in founding the Provident Hospital Training School for Nurses in Chicago. Though Tubman is given credit for rendering "invaluable service in the Union Army as a spy, scout, and hospital nurse" in an early history of African Americans in the nursing profession,[50] first honor as a black professional nurse should probably go to Mahoney. Like so many of the women who ministered to the sick and dying during the Civil War, Tubman did so as a volunteer without formal training. Nevertheless, Tubman holds a place of honor as a black nursing pioneer, one of the "sisters on the front lines."[51]

In addition to being remembered for her nursing contributions, Tubman admirers honor her for her Civil War work as "spy and scout," though the two roles are not clearly distinguished. The contrabands at Beaufort first knew her as a nurse and relief worker, but Tubman's reputation as "Black Moses" went with her wherever she went. Union officers needed intelligence about the Confederates, and Tubman was put in command of a small band of scouts and river pilots, contrabands all, who knew the Beaufort area.[52] Anything Tubman might learn about enemy encampments and fortifications would be especially useful to Colonel James Montgomery (Figure 25), who commanded a black unit known as the Second South Carolina Volunteers. Brevet Brigadier-General Rufus Saxton, military governor of the Union Department of the South, sent a letter to Sarah Bradford in 1868 that summed up his recollections of Tubman's wartime service, "MY DEAR MADAME: I have just received your letter informing me that Hon. W. H. Seward, Secretary of State, would present a petition to Congress for a pension to Harriet Tubman, for services rendered in the Union Army during the late war. I can bear witness to the value of her services in South Carolina and Florida. She was employed in the hospitals and as a spy. She made many a raid inside the enemy's lines, displaying remarkable courage, zeal, and fidelity."[53] P. K. Rose, in an article appearing on the Internet at a site sponsored by the Central Intelligence Agency and titled, "The Civil War: Black American

25. Colonel James Montgomery. By permission of Kansas State Historical Society, Topeka.

Contributions to Union Intelligence," asserts: "The tactical intelligence Tubman provided to Union forces during the war was frequent, abundant, and used effectively in military operations."[54]

Though Saxton's letter spoke of "many a raid," the most famous was the foray up the Combahee River north of Port Royal to the vicinity of the Combahee Ferry (Figure 26). Tubman's reputation as "General Tubman" derives in large part from portrayals of her actions during this military advance into Confederate-held territory.[55] Tubman, at the request of General Hunter, accompanied Colonel James Montgomery and the Second South Carolina Volunteers in an effort to clear torpedoes from the river and destroy the Confederate supply line by taking out bridges and railroad tracks. On the night of June 1, 1863, the Union troops started up the river on gunboats and by the early hours of the next day were raiding riverside plantations. The raiders managed to liberate more than seven hundred individuals from Colleton and Beaufort county plantations. They clambered upon the three gunboats as if they were chariots of freedom.[56]

Tubman participated in a celebration of the successful raid held in Beaufort on June 3 and, in a dictated letter that appeared in the Boston

26. Raid of the Second South Carolina Volunteers, led by Colonel James Montgomery, among the rice plantations on the Combahee. From *Harper's Weekly*, July 4, 1863.

press, told of the plight of those whom she had helped liberate: "Most of those coming from the mainland are very destitute, almost naked. I am trying to find places for those able to work, and provide for them as best I can, so as to lighten the burden on the Government as much as possible, while at the same time they learn to respect themselves by earning their own living."[57] Long after the Confederates had surrendered and slavery's dungeon doors were flung open, Tubman continued to retell of the glorious June back in 1863 when she, as the author Samuel Hopkins Adams, grandnephew of Sarah Bradford, remembers her saying in the late 1870s, "fit on de Calm-bee Rivah . . . up de creeks an' in de wide ma'shes. Alligathas longah'n a pine plank. Turkles big as a do.'"[58]

Ignoring the fact that Tubman carried no military rank, accompanied Montgomery's forces but did not command them, and was called "general" only in the figurative sense, claims have been made that she is "America's Most Unsung Civil War General" and "the U.S. Army's First Woman General." In 1993, during a Black History Month celebration at Fort Meade, Maryland, Captain Rosa Gaines asserted that Tubman, as "the U.S. Army's First Woman General," got "upwards of 100,000 young Black men to join the Army and Navy."[59] The author Helene Smith contended: "Men who worked under the guidance of Aramenta [*sic*] respectfully called her 'General'—recognizing that she truly had, 'superior or chief rank and extended command'—Webster's definition of the term, 'general.'"[60] By this reasoning, which confuses ascribed status with formal rank, one is a "general" by acting as if one holds the title. Nothing in the documentary evidence suggests that Montgomery's soldiers deferred to Tubman in the place of their commanding officer. Smith made the claim that "Aramenta (also known as Harriet Tubman) carried out the only military campaign in the history of America in which a woman planned and led 300 men in a dangerous amphibious maneuver—a record she holds to this day."[61] The notion that Tubman, not Montgomery, commanded the Combahee foray has lodged itself at the core of the "General Tubman" myth, so much so that the Smithsonian Institution saw fit to honor Harriet Tubman in 1982 as "the only woman in American History to plan and lead a military raid."[62]

The Smithsonian accolade has not gone uncontested—at least, if we are to believe proponents of having women assume strategic or combat positions in the American military. Writing in 1990 in the context of the debate within the U.S. defense establishment about assigning women combat duties, C. Kay Larson argued that it is important to remember "Bonny Yank and Ginny Reb" of the Civil War era because "their past successes are linked to our potential future ones, as their activities legitimize ours."[63] Larson estimated that "thousands" of women served as soldiers during the Civil War, some disguised as men, and claims to have identified forty-one who "served in or worked for the military." She gives most prominence to Anna Ella Carroll, calling her a "'superwoman' example of women's participation in the war effort."[64] Larson believed that Carroll presented a plan to the Lincoln administration on November 30, 1861, that successfully argued for a campaign up the Tennessee River in place of a planned Mississippi expedition. While Carroll may be said to have helped "plan" the Union move up the Tennessee River to capture Fort Henry, no claim is made that she actually participated in the military campaign.[65] Larson does cite a woman who fought, the wife (unnamed) of a Colonel Turchin of the Nineteenth Illinois. Supposedly, she led his regiment into battle after he became seriously ill.[66] While it might be argued that Carroll planned but did not lead a military raid and Colonel Turchin's wife fought and led but did not actually plan battlefield tactics, whereas Tubman did both in the raid up the Combahee, if we take the

Smithsonian's description of her roles literally, the entire debate of who deserves "first honor" turns on semantics. In profiling Tubman's military career, Larson skirts the question of who commanded whom by saying, "Montgomery and Tubman led 150 black troops in a raid up the Combahee River."[67]

Earl Conrad devoted an entire chapter to the "Campaign on the Combahee" in his 1943 book-length biography of Tubman. He argued that Tubman "formulated" the Combahee strategy and that in the raid "it was Montgomery who was the auxiliary leader."[68] This differed from the assessment Bradford recorded after hearing Tubman talk of the offensive: "She said she would go if Col. Montgomery was to be appointed commander of the expedition. . . . Accordingly, Col. Montgomery was appointed to the command, and Harriet, with several men under her, the principal of whom was J. Plowden . . . accompanied the expedition."[69] Conrad drew his conclusion in large part from the journalistic report that came from the pen of a correspondent for the *Wisconsin State Journal*, stationed in the Department of the South.[70] This was the same report that was picked up by Franklin B. Sanborn's *Commonwealth* and published on July 10, 1863. In Conrad's reprinting of the article written for the *Wisconsin State Journal*, he drew attention (by italicizing) to three specific claims regarding Tubman's agency in the Combahee raid: (1) "Col. Montgomery and his gallant band of 300 black soldiers, *under the guidance of a black woman*, dashed into the enemy's country"; (2) "The Colonel was followed by a speech from the black woman, *who led the raid and under whose inspiration it was originated and conducted*"; and (3) "*Many and many times she has penetrated the enemy's lines and discovered their situation and condition, and escaped without injury*, but not without extreme hazard."[71] Though Conrad was willing to accept the Wisconsin journalist's characterization of Tubman's role in the raid on the night and morning of June 2, he contradicted the correspondent's reckoning of "300 black soldiers" as participating by stating that the black troops numbered "about 150" in three of what the slaves called "Lincoln's gun-boats."

Whatever the numbers of troops involved, Tubman felt that they should receive some of the credit for "taking and bringing away seven hundred and fifty-six" contrabands. In the dictated letter sent to Franklin B. Sanborn, dated June 30, 1863, and taken down at Beaufort, Tubman says, "You have without doubt, seen a full account of the expedition I refer to. Don't you think we colored people are entitled to some of the credit for that exploit, under the lead of the brave Colonel Montgomery?"[72] If we credit this excerpt from the dictated letter, which Conrad quotes but does not draw attention to, Tubman herself acknowledged that Montgomery commanded the raid up the Combahee River.

The distinction between commanding a raiding party in the capacity of a scout—indeed, the leader of a small company of scouts, including several who were known to be very familiar with the Combahee river region—and commanding an official military company seems to have been lost on Conrad. Needing to drum up interest in his forthcoming biography of Tubman, which he was intending to call "I Bring You General Tubman," Conrad penned an article for *Negro Digest* that appeared in December 1940 under the title, "General Tubman on the Combahee." After citing the Wisconsin journalist's tribute, as it was published in the *Commonwealth*, and making mention of Tubman's legendary work on behalf of the Underground Railroad, Conrad says, "But the Combahee raid is significant as the *only* military engagement in American history wherein a woman, black or white, *led*."[73]

As with other aspects of the life story of Harriet Tubman, variant interpretations of her as "General Tubman" arise out of the challenge of getting to the facts behind the legend. Accounts of her exploits during the Civil War appeared at a time when she was already being hailed as "Moses," a heroic figure whose fame preceded her to the battlefield, and emendations to the myth, made many years later, are read back into its formative period. What many Tubman enthusiasts have cited as primary evidence turns out on close inspection to be material compromised by efforts to eulogize Tubman.

During her later years, Tubman loved to tell of her Civil War adventures. A good case in point is her story about having served Colonel Robert Gould Shaw his last meal before the assault by the Fifty-fourth Massachusetts on Fort Wagner. Earl Conrad's source for this story was Hildegarde Hoyt Swift, the author of *The Railroad to Freedom: A Story of the Civil War*, a book published in 1932 and reviewed as especially suitable for young readers. Though Swift's book is a fictionalized account of her heroine's life, she talked with several individuals who had known Tubman, including two of Tubman's nieces who lived in Auburn, and made use of the Bradford material.[74] Swift has Tubman appearing at Colonel Higginson's headquarters prior to the attack on Fort Wagner and boldly entering, whereupon she says to the colonel: "Culnul Higginson, will you obcept ob dis brace o' ducks, which I done bring fo' you f'om de Comba-hee Ribber?"[75] Swift gives no source for this story, though Conrad says Swift had based it on hearing an account from Tubman herself. In 1939, Swift wrote to Conrad, "She always stoutly maintained that she fed Col. Shaw his last meal etc. and that she was present at this time."[76]

The Reverend James E. Mason, secretary of Livingston College, the African Methodist Episcopal Zion church school at Salisbury, North Carolina, also knew about Tubman's association with Shaw. At the first annual "homecoming" celebration held in Auburn on October 14, 1920, he spoke of the "Soldier Spirit of Harriet Tubman." His speech overflows with martial imagery, praising both Tubman and the black soldiers who fought and died in the Civil War. Mason called Tubman "a modern Ama-zon" and patriot of the highest order. "She cooked," he asserted, "the last meal of Colonel Shaw ere the gray dawn of the morning" when the Fifty-fourth Massachusetts stormed the red ramparts of Fort Wagner.[77]

Tubman is associated with the "Glory" story of the Fifty-fourth Mas-sachusetts in yet another way. Secondary accounts of her life regularly tell of her witnessing the Fort Wagner battle. When a source is cited for this aspect of the Tubman story, the historian Albert Bushnell Hart is brought to the witness stand. Hart, to his credit, broke rank with the establishment white historians of his day who were ignoring Tubman by including a reference to her in his study *Slavery and Abolition* (1906). Hart met Tubman in Boston and had been impressed with her ability to paint unforgettable word pictures. He wrote, "Her extraordinary power of statement was illustrated in her description of a battle in the Civil War: 'And then we saw the lightening, and that was the guns; and then we heard the thunder, and that was the big guns; and then we heard the rain falling, and that was the drops of blood falling; and when we came to get in the crops, it was dead men that we reaped."[78] Hart did not specify which battle Tubman described.

Other authors, including Conrad, have assumed that the picturesque account derived from Tubman's witnessing the carnage that resulted as the Union troops attacked Fort Wagner. Booker T. Washington, how-ever, understood Hart to be saying that Tubman's remarks placed her at Gettysburg in the summer of 1863. In *The Story of the Negro: The Rise of the Race from Slavery*, published in 1909, Washington wrote: "This same natural gift of expression, which is frequently possessed by some of the rude and unlettered people of my race, has been frequently noted by other persons. A typical example of this is Harriet Tubman's description of the Battle of Gettysburg, which Prof. Albert Bushnell Hart has noted in his 'History of Slavery and Abolition.' He heard this description from Harriet Tubman's own lips as she was describing some of her experiences during the Civil War."[79] Despite some confusion in secondary sources as to which battle Tubman's poetic words describe, she has long been popularly associated with the Fort Wagner story.[80] Perhaps this is why an artist's rendition of the battle hung for many years in a room of the restored Tubman home in Auburn, New York, set up as the bedroom in which Black Moses supposedly died.

In February 1865, Tubman asked for a leave of absence so she could return to Auburn to visit her elderly parents. In transit home, she stopped in Washington, D.C., to see Secretary of State William Seward, who earlier had authorized her appointment as "Nurse or Matron at the Colored Hospital in Ft. Monroe, VA." Tubman pressed her claim for monetary compensation for her wartime service, a matter that would concern her for the next quarter-century. Tubman's long struggle for a military pension was as much about official recognition as it was about money. In the post–Civil War decades, members of the old Grand Army of the Republic wore their uniforms with pride in a fraternity of honor; Tubman's fight was to be counted as one of these veterans. In an affidavit filed in 1898 as part of her request for a pension, Tubman states: "My claim against the U.S. is for three years service as nurse and cook in hospitals, and as commander of several (eight or nine) as scouts during the late war of the Rebellion under directions and orders of Edwin M. Stanton, Secretary of War, and of several Generals. I claim for my services above named the sum of eighteen hundred dollars."[81]

Tubman came home to Auburn in October 1865, weary and still suffering the ill effects of being assaulted by a white train conductor in New Jersey. Tubman had insisted that she was eligible to sit where she liked on a half-fare ticket because of her government service. She put up a good fight but was eventually thrown into the smoking car, according to one source, or the baggage car, as Sarah Bradford has it. In the melee, Tubman's shoulder was injured, and several of her ribs may have been broken. Still, she had sufficient spirit to tell the conductor, as Martha Coffin Wright reported in a letter dated November 7, 1865, that "he was a copperhead scoundrel" and that "she didn't thank anybody to call her [a] colored person—She would be called black or Negro—she was as proud of being a black woman as he was of being white."[82] News of Tubman's rough treatment and her bold response spread among her friends, and before long the train incident was attached to the litany of heroic stories about her. When Frances Ellen Watkins Harper, the African American author and suffragist, spoke before a women's rights convention in New York City in 1866, she invoked the name of Tubman:

> We have a woman in our country who has received the name of "Moses," not by lying about it, but by acting it out (applause)—a woman who has gone down into the Egypt of slavery and brought out hundreds of our people into liberty. The last time I saw that woman, her hands were swollen. That woman who had led one of Montgomery's most successful expeditions, who was brave enough and secretive enough to act as a scout for the American army, had her hands all swollen from a conflict with a brutal conductor, who undertook to eject her from her place. That woman, whose courage and bravery won a recognition from our army and from every black man in the land, is excluded from every thoroughfare of travel.[83]

Tubman's return to Auburn signaled a new chapter in her life. Her Underground Railroad days and wartime service had ended. She was in ill health and nearly destitute. Her friends began a campaign to obtain compensation for her for her war work. This would be a test of whether or not the nation was ready to honor her for the self-sacrificial labors she had rendered and a test of whether or not her fame as "Black Moses" could be translated into hard currency. William Henry Seward took it upon himself to press the case for Tubman's Civil War pension and enlisted the aid of several of Tubman's Auburn admirers.

Charles P. Wood, an Auburn banker who had been active in recruiting and equipping soldiers from the area and providing relief for families who had lost loved ones during the long conflict, assumed the task of documenting Tubman's wartime service. He interviewed her and sketched out a nine-page manuscript that made use of the various official papers Tubman had retained. Wood recorded, "During the service of more than three years, Harriet states that she received from the Gov't only two hundred dollars ($200) of pay. This was paid her at or near Beaufort, and with the characteristic indifference to self—she immediately devoted that sum to the erection of a wash-house, in which she spent a portion of her time in teaching the freed women to do washing—to aid in supporting themselves instead of depending wholly on Gov't aid."[84]

Seward passed on the Wood report to Congressman Clinton MacDougall, the former Gettysburg general. But Tubman's petition drowned in a flood of requests for compensation. As Earl Conrad wrote, "It was Reconstruction, when thousands of bills went before Congress. There was a mad rush; there was debate upon fundamental questions like Negro rights, woman's rights, State's rights, pensions for white men. What chance had a black woman, even the famous Harriet Tubman in a wordy rush like that."[85] Further efforts were made to obtain relief for Tubman by her friends and admirers, such as William Lloyd Garrison and Edna B. Dow Cheney, but Washington officials responded with silence or outright denial. Conrad had an explanation: "The Southern Congressmen, sitting with the Northerners on the pension committees, regarded as quixotic the war claims of a black woman."[86] America's political leaders were not ready to ascribe veteran status to Tubman or recognize her soldier-like achievements.

In 1881, Tubman's white friends presented her case again during the forty-third session of Congress, with equally disappointing results. The Committee on War Claims of the House of Representatives recommended "appropriating the sum of $2,000 for services rendered by her to the Union Army as scout, nurse, and spy,"[87] but nothing came of this. In 1887, Tubman made an effort to revive her claim by asking that her supporting documents be returned to her.

Tubman's second husband, Nelson Davis, died on October 14, 1888. This opened the way for Tubman to receive a modest amount of financial relief as a widow of a veteran under the Dependent Pension Act of 1890. Tubman applied on July 24, 1890. Bureaucrats within the pension bureau must have questioned Tubman's eligibility, for on November 28, 1892, she placed her mark (an "x") on a general affidavit swearing to the fact that she had been married to John Tubman, "a colored man who died, or was killed, at or near Cambridge[,] Dorchester Co[unty], Md. on or about September 30, 1867." And further, as her affidavit stated, "That late husband, the soldier Nelson Davis, had not previously married."[88] A complicating factor in Tubman's petition was the fact that Nelson Davis had mustered using the name Nelson Charles. When the pension bureau was satisfied that Nelson Davis was the same man who served in the 8th United States Colored Infantry Regiment, it granted Tubman a widow's pension of eight dollars a month, but this was not until October 1895. Later that month, Tubman was given five hundred dollars as retroactive compensation for the five years her widow's claim had been pending.[89]

Tubman's friends and supporters, unhappy with the widow's mite given the aging veteran of the freedom cause, continued to push for compensation for her own service to the federal government. The Honorable Sereno E. Payne, representing the twenty-eighth district, introduced a bill in 1897 to have Congress grant Tubman a pension of $25 a month for her wartime service as a nurse in the union army. To support the cause, thirty Auburn citizens and Tubman supporters, including William Henry Seward Jr., a partner in the legal firm of Underwood, Storke and Seward, signed a petition dated March 1, 1898, and sent it to Payne, stating:

> We write to you in behalf of our old colored friend, Harriet Tubman Davis, in the hope that you may be able to get Congress to do something for her in the line of a pension or other form of relief. General MacDougall informs us that while a member of the House, he had introduced a bill giving her relief, which passed the House but did not pass the Senate. We who are interested in her (and there are many more of them in Auburn) would be greatly gratified if you would take up this affair, have a proper bill drawn, and endeavor to have it passed by Congress.[90]

Once again, the case had to be made. Wood's earlier brief was resurrected and included as documentary evidence. New affidavits were taken, including one from Tubman. She appeared before an Auburn notary public on January 1, 1898, and stated:

> I am about 75 years of age. I was born and reared in Dorchester Co., Md. My maiden name was Araminta Ross. Sometime prior to the late War of the Rebellion I married John Tubman who died in the state of Maryland on the 30th day of September 1867. I married Nelson Davis, a soldier of the late war on the 18th day of March 1869 at Auburn, N.Y. I furnished the original papers in my claim to one Charles P. Wood, then of Auburn, N.Y., who died several years ago. Said Wood made copies of said original papers which are hereunto annexed. I was informed by said Wood that he sent the original

papers to one James Barrett an attorney on 41/2 Street, Washington, D.C., and I was told by the wife of said Barrett that she handed the original papers to the Hon. C. D. MacDougall then a member of the House of Representatives.[91]

Longstanding friends and admirers of Tubman from Auburn, Syracuse, New York City, and Boston appended a note to the affidavit imploring Payne to revive the failed petition asking for $1,800 for wartime services as "scout, nurse, and spy."[92]

Tubman's claim started in the House of Representatives. The House Committee on Invalid Pensions (Report 4774) recommended that the beneficiary, "Harriet T. Davis, of Auburn, N.Y.," be awarded an increase from eight dollars to twenty-five dollars per month in recognition of her service as an army nurse, though mention is also made of her duties as a "cook in hospital, and spy."[93] The bill, now known as "A Bill Granting an Increase of Pension to Harriet Tubman Davis," was reported back during the Fifty-fifth Congress with the recommendation that it pass. When the Committee on Pensions of the Senate, to whom H.R. 4982 (the bill to grant a pension to Harriet Tubman Davis) had been referred, reported out, signs of disagreement appeared. The Senate's Committee on Pensions feared setting a precedent and reduced the House's recommendation of twenty-five dollars to twenty dollars a month and set aside the question of awarding Tubman veteran status:

> The papers in this case show that a claim for this woman was once presented to the House of Representatives and referred to the Committee on War Claims. Manifestly, that would be the better way to reimburse her for her alleged services to the Government, but her advanced years and necessitous condition lead your committee to give the matter consideration. There is, however, a strong objection to the bill in its present form. The number of nurses on the pension roll at a rate higher than $12 a month is very few indeed, and there are no valid reasons why this claimant should receive a pension of $25 per month as a nurse, thus opening a new avenue for pension increases. She is now drawing pension at the rate of $8 per month as the widow of a soldier, and in view of her personal services to the Government, Congress is amply justified in increasing that pension.[94]

27. Susie King Taylor. Frontispiece to Susie King Taylor, *Reminiscences of My Life in Camp with the 33rd U.S. Colored Troops, Late 1st South Carolina Volunteers* (Boston: Susie King Taylor, 1902).

The amended bill went back to the House, was signed by the Speaker, and then forwarded to the executive branch. President William McKinley signed it on February 28, 1899. Tubman had approximately fourteen years yet to live. In summary, Tubman ended up receiving eight dollars per month as a veteran's widow and twelve dollars a month for her services as a wartime nurse, plus the compensatory lump sum of about five hundred dollars in October 1895. It is important to note that Tubman's pension as a nurse was not a military pension but a special pension granted former nurses who served during the Civil War. Susie King Taylor (Figure 27), whose nursing activities are often compared to those of Tubman, did not receive a pension because she had not been classified as an Army nurse.[95]

Proponents who want the U.S. government to do right by Tubman have resurrected the pension matter periodically over the years. In October 2003, Senator Hillary Rodham Clinton announced that she had been successful in obtaining $11,750 from the government, "the sum which compensates for the widow's pension withheld from Harriet Tubman between January 1899 and her death in 1913, adjusted from 1913 to the present day."[96] The money, earmarked for "the descendants of Harriet Tubman," was to go toward restoration of the Tubman-related sites in Auburn. It was unclear whose faulty thinking resulted in the notion that Harriet Tubman, childless as far as we know, had "descendants." However, the press reported the payout under banners such as, "Government Stiffs Tubman," and some Tubman enthusiasts railed at the paltry sum. An editorialist for the Syracuse *Post-Standard* claimed that Tubman was "shortchanged about $840 at her death in 1913. Compound the interest over the intervening 90 years and you get not $11,750, but more like $855,000."[97]

The compensatory pension measure passed in 2003 struck Tubman scholars as based on faulty history. Senator Clinton reportedly learned of the pay-inequity issue during a visit to the Albany Free School from elementary-school students who were learning about Tubman.[98] In point of fact, Tubman was not due twenty-five dollars a month. Her pension of twenty dollars a month, as noted earlier, was the result of a compromise reached after the Senate modified the House resolution and included the eight-dollar-a-month compensation for her as a the widow of a veteran. Senator Clinton's bill to award any monies gained in 2003 to "Tubman descendants" was most curious. None of the press reports that described how the $11,750 had been calculated were factually correct. Most conflated Tubman's war widow's claim with her request for compensation as a Civil War nurse.[99] More important, Clinton's legislative measure ignored the fact that Tubman had been given approximately five hundred dollars as retroactive compensation for the five years that her widow's claim had been pending and confused the widow's pension with her claim for compensation as a nurse. Setting aside the thorny matter of how politicians construe or misconstrue history, a fair reading of the pension issue leads to the conclusion that the U.S. government made amends on Tubman's claims for compensation as a veteran's widow and for her nursing work. She did not receive a veteran's pension because she has never been awarded official veteran status for her service, intermittent as it was, as a scout and spy for the Union army.

Had the Tubman case gone to the Committee on War Claims, as it had during the Forty-third Congress, then America's elected representatives would have had to wrestle with the thorny question of granting Tubman veteran status.[100] Tubman herself took pride in her wartime service and regarded herself as a member of the Grand Army of the Republic. So did many of her friends and admirers, and when she died, they granted her military honors. However, official guardians of the roll of military veterans have not numbered her among those who deserve formal veteran status. Emblematic of present-day attempts to rewrite the record books to make amends for past slights, the Honorable Edolphus Towns of New York introduced legislation on the floor of the House of Representatives on July 19, 2000, to grant Harriet Tubman Davis veteran status posthumously. Other Tubman enthusiasts have campaigned to obtain the Congressional Medal of Honor for their heroine.[101] As of this writing, neither effort has been successful. Tubman is, however, included in the company of spies featured in the International Spy Museum in Washington, D.C., along with the entertainer Josephine Baker, who spied for France.[102]

More so than any of Tubman's early biographers, Earl Conrad built up the image of "General Tubman" to complement that of "Black Moses." Conrad prided himself on discovering the Wood manuscript and wrote in many places that Tubman ought to rank as one of America's military heroes. Were Conrad alive today to participate in the debate over whether or not Tubman ought to be awarded veteran status, one suspects his voice would join that of Edolphus Towns. Nevertheless, in a letter written to Samuel Hopkins Adams dated March 11, 1940, Conrad offered a perspective on Tubman's wartime years that may be the balanced one that will stand the test of historical scrutiny when all of the evidence is evaluated. Conrad told Adams:

> You'll be interested to know that I've just unearthed the Charles P. Wood manuscript. As I suspected it is the best account of Harriet's war service. It was on file in the House of Representatives in connection with pension material there—in her pension file. It was a valuable find. It verifies that Harriet was virtually in charge of the intelligence service of the Department of the South. And in another document, this one dictated by Harriet, she refers to herself as "commander of several men (about eight or nine) as scouts during the late war of the rebellion." Harriet's indifference to routine procedures, to red tape, to regulations, etc., meant that she was not a commissioned soldier, and her connections with the service were therefore irregular—which caused her much difficulty later when

she sought compensation from the government—but the Wood manuscript clears up these matters.[103]

Harriet Tubman's courage has never been questioned. A chorus of voices sings her praises in this regard. She put herself at risk for the sake of others, be it as a guide for frightened freedom seekers, as a nurse caring for sick contrabands and the battlefield wounded, or ministering her folk remedies in the Florida swamps in spite of infectious diseases to which she herself had no immunity. Yet the controversy about the Alewitz mural referred to in the opening paragraphs of this chapter has struck a nerve in our contemporary culture, with its divided conscience on the question of carrying guns.

Some would disarm Tubman; others are in need of a symbol of a militant African American woman, a twenty-first-century "General Tubman." Take away Tubman's gun, so the argument goes, and you have defaced a powerful symbol. Though there is evidence that Tubman bore firearms, there is no report of her actually firing a weapon at anyone. On at least one occasion, she took out the gun she carried and used it to intimidate those who lost their nerve and the will to press on. Several authors have speculated that her pistol had no bullets. But the empty-gun thesis cannot be verified in the primary sources. Had the citizens of Baltimore, especially those troubled by Alewitz's proposed mural of Tubman holding a rifle, gone back to the frontispiece in the 1869 Bradford biography that has powerfully shaped the public's image of Tubman, they would have encountered Tubman the armed scout (Figure 28). Still, the argument may be made by some that a marked difference exists between a military encampment and the public space of one of America's leading cities. An outside observer of the controversy in Baltimore, bemused by a debate that is more about how Americans today ought to treat each other than about the "real" Tubman, might point out an irony of some importance. Tubman may have carried a gun during the Civil War, but, as with the pistol she toted when a conductor on the Underground Railroad, there is no record that she ever injured anyone, Confederate or otherwise.

Tubman's Civil War experiences are now important sources for her multidimensional symbolic usefulness. She is honored for her willingness to go into battle for the cause of freedom, as well as for her role as caregiver. She is simultaneously remembered as "General Tubman"

HARRIET TUBMAN.

28. Harriet Tubman in her Civil War scout's uniform. Woodcut likeness by J. C. Darby, Auburn, New York. Frontispiece to Sarah H. Bradford, *Scenes in the Life of Harriet Tubman* (Auburn, N.Y.: W. J. Moses, 1869).

and "nurse, spy, and scout." This compounding factor makes her a more complex symbol and, thereby, more appealing to a diverse constituency today. Tubman admirers with contrasting political views and agendas can extract useful inspirational capital by highlighting one or more of the multiple facets of Tubman's Civil War years. This makes her a complex and more all-comprehending historical figure in the contemporary public debate about national character and identity than, for example, John Brown. Most Americans think of Brown as the one-dimensional angry man of 1859. Taken separately, none of Tubman's Civil War symbolic constructions might have had enough strength to persist for long on its own. Others matched her contributions as a nurse, and her spying did not result in military intelligence significant enough to influence the outcome of the Civil War. Collectively, however, the embodiment of these roles in one person is significant, considering how powerfully the Tubman as Moses symbol has become. The symbolic Tubman is Moses the Deliverer, but she is a Moses who, unlike the biblical Moses, makes it to the Promised Land and then returns to spy out the land of the enemy, and when the final battle erupts, she is there to give material and spiritual solace to those in need.

CHAPTER FOUR

SARAH BRADFORD'S HARRIET TUBMAN

According to the *Freedmen's Record* article that appeared in 1865, Tubman hoped that when the Civil War was over, she might have the opportunity to become literate. Then she would "write her own life." "It is the strong desire of her friends," Edna Cheney affirmed, "that she should tell her story in her own way at some future time." Though Tubman would live nearly another half-century, entering into the post–Civil War and Auburn period in her mid-forties (Figure 29), she is not known either to have taken the opportunity to become literate or to have been provided with the means to do so. The blow to the head Tubman received at about thirteen may have been the root cause of her illiteracy. According to Cheney's sketch, "The trouble in her head prevents her from applying closely to a book."[1]

Frederick Douglass discovered that by putting words on paper he could define himself for posterity. Tubman's place in the American memory is largely the result of having her story written down by others. While alive, she could shape and influence the public's perception of her by telling her own narrative. Even in her declining years, a few pilgrims found their way to Auburn, New York, and sat transfixed as the woman long known as Black Moses but now called Aunt Harriet told tales of her heroic exploits. However, after 1913 Tubman's voice fell silent. The public—at least, that segment that wanted to recover the life and legacy of Black Moses—turned to the writings about her created and controlled by others. The problem of listening for Tubman's voice is still with us, as it must ever be, but it is now possible to recognize and examine the phenomenon of the mediated Tubman. By focusing our attention on one of the principal creators of the Tubman myth, we equip ourselves to sort out fact and fic-

29. Harriet Tubman, studio photograph, Auburn, circa 1865. Courtesy Library of Congress, LC/USZ62–7816.

tion in the strands of public memory about this larger-than-life historical figure.

Though several dictated letters survive, nothing written by Tubman's own hand exists.[2] Nevertheless, many Americans think they know the authentic Harriet Tubman because of two books written by Sarah Hopkins Bradford. Bradford's first book, *Scenes in the Life of Harriet Tubman*, appeared in 1869. The printer W. J. Moses published it in Auburn, New York. A slim volume of approximately twenty-seven thousand words, 132 pages in length and small enough to slip into a vest pocket, Bradford's *Scenes* served as the principal textual source for information about Harriet Tubman for more than a quarter-century.[3] *Commonwealth* promoted sales of the Bradford sketch of Tubman in a January 9, 1869, notice: "Mrs. Sarah H. Bradford, of Geneva, N.Y., has made quite an interesting memoir of this devoted woman, which has been published in neat book-form, and the proceeds of the sales of which go to her support, she being now very old and quite infirm."[4]

In 1886, Bradford put out a revised and enlarged version of *Scenes* under a new title, *Harriet, the Moses of Her People*. George R. Lockwood and Son published it in New York City. Longer by some two thousand seven hundred words, 149 pages in length, and larger in format, the 1886 book supplanted the earlier volume.[5] Two additional printings appeared during Tubman's lifetime, the first in 1897, again by Lockwood and Son, and the second in 1901 (with a new appendix), this time by J. J. Little of New York City.[6] Original copies of *Scenes in the Life of Harriet Tubman* are now valuable commodities among dealers in antiquarian materials, going for as much as six thousand dollars. *Harriet, the Moses of Her People* rarely appears for sale in the 1886, 1897, or 1901 printings. In contrast to the *Scenes* book, which has been republished but once, Bradford's second attempt to bring Tubman to the attention of the American public has been periodically reprinted and republished in the past half-century, but there was a seventy-five-year period (1886–1961) during which readers in pursuit of the *Moses* book had to make do with a copy of one of the editions published before Tubman's death. In 1961, Corinth Books provided the public with an inexpensive version of Bradford's 1886 *Moses*, helping to fuel the tremendous surge of interest in Tubman in succeeding decades.[7]

Sarah Elizabeth Hopkins Bradford (1818–1912) was the youngest of the seven children of the Honorable Samuel Miles Hopkins, lawyer, and the former Sarah Elizabeth Rogers. Born in what is now Livingston County, New York, Bradford moved with her parents and siblings to Geneva in Ontario County in 1832. The early 1830s was a time of intense debate about slavery in New York's "Burned-Over District." The Reverend Charles G. Finney, the great revivalist, visited Geneva in 1831 and sparked an outbreak of religious enthusiasm that had an impact on Geneva's First Presbyterian Church, with which the twenty-two-year-old Sarah united in 1836. Tubman's most important nineteenth-century public voice would remain a faithful and dedicated churchgoer her entire life, firmly rooted in the New School Presbyterian fold of American Protestantism. Bradford taught Sunday school and infused her writings with the language of piety and religious conviction.[8]

Sarah Hopkins married John Melancthon Bradford, a lawyer, on May 15, 1839. The couple had three sons and three daughters. According to a church record, John Bradford "walked out" on his wife and family in 1857 and set up a law practice in Chicago. Rumor has it that, when he left Geneva, he took the family maid with him.[9] To support herself and her large family, Sarah opened "Mrs. Bradford's School for Young Ladies and Little Girls" in her home on South Main Street. She operated this school for girls ages three to seventeen until 1869, when she and her daughters left for Europe. They remained there for eight years. After returning from Germany, Bradford lived for a number of years in Union Springs, then removed to Rochester, where she found a home during her declining years in the household of one of her daughters. Bradford died in Rochester in 1912, approximately a year before Tubman did.

Though she was instrumental in perpetuating the tradition of Harriet Tubman as "Black Moses," Bradford's own reputation suffered with the passing of time. Her papers have never been found; according to the recollections of a former neighbor, Bradford had little interest in preserving her own writings. This same neighbor described Geneva's forgotten author and historian this way: "She was of middle height with eyes of bluish grey, and a very good nose, and some pretty short curls at the side of her face. Her expression was animated. You felt that she was a woman of intelligence" (Figure 30).[10]

Julia Sill, Sarah Bradford's first cousin, spoke to the moral character of Tubman's biographer in an obituary notice: "She was a leader in all good and charitable work in the town and in everything connected with village improvement, intellectual and social. At her house were entertained

30. Sarah E. Hopkins Bradford. Photograph courtesy Geneva Historical Society, Geneva, New York.

prominent persons who came to Geneva to lecture and so forth. Her door was always open in gracious hospitality."[11]

Sarah Bradford lost two of her sons (Charles and William) in the Civil War. While the battles yet raged, she served as the secretary of Geneva's Women's Relief Corps. Though thoroughly opposed to the abomination of Christian principles that chattel servitude was, Bradford did not come to her task of codifying Tubman's story with sterling credentials in the pre–Civil War abolitionist phalanx. She had published an antislavery story in 1855 called "Poor Nina, the Fugitive," but it had limited circulation.[12] Her other publications included sketches and stories meant for the moral edification of children, short biographies of Peter the Great (1858) and Christopher Columbus (1863), Sunday school literature (*The Chosen People*, 1861), and assorted poems and inspirational songs. She sometimes wrote using a pseudonym, thereby making it more unlikely that her name was widely known in abolitionist circles before the publication in 1869 of the first Tubman biography.[13]

Given the immense impact her publication of *Uncle Tom's Cabin* had on American public opinion in the 1850s, Harriet Beecher Stowe would have brought great notoriety to her subject had she written on Tubman. However, Stowe's books subsequent to *Uncle Tom's Cabin* faltered, and she never achieved the success with any of them equal to that of her one great work. Some authors argue that Harriet Beecher Stowe's modest literary skills never found a subject equal to that of her one great abolitionist novel.[14] Stowe did turn her attention to Sojourner Truth and penned "Sojourner Truth, the Libyan Sibyl," which appeared in the *Atlantic Monthly* in April 1863.[15] Harriet Tubman's life story, with its intrinsic drama, might have provided Stowe with sufficient material for a tribute to Black Moses. Bradford herself acknowledged this, for she writes early in *Scenes*, "By the graphic pen of Mrs. Stowe, the incidents of such a life as that of the subject of this little memoir might be wrought up into a tale of thrilling interest, equaling, if not exceeding, anything in her world-renowned 'Uncle Tom's Cabin'; but the story of Harriet Tubman needs not the drapery of fiction; the bare unadorned facts are enough to stir the hearts of the friends of humanity, the friends of liberty, the lovers of their country."[16]

Perhaps it was for the best that a celebrity with Stowe's reputation left the Black Moses story to a less well-known author. Harriet Tubman is said not to have had a very high opinion of *Uncle Tom's Cabin*. According to Bradford's 1869 version of Tubman's life story, friends once asked the former slave and veteran Underground Railroad operative if she wished to see a stage version of "Life among the Lowly," as *Uncle Tom's Cabin* was subtitled. Dramatic renderings of Stowe's book, some of them highly bowdlerized, appeared in profusion before and after the Civil War. Tubman's response, as related by Bradford, was that she did not care to go to see Stowe's book played out by actors (to "go and see the sufferings of my people played") for she had lived the real thing. Bradford has her saying, "I've heard Uncle Tom's Cabin rad, and I tell you Mrs. Stowe's pen hasn't begun to paint what slavery is as I have seen it at the far South."[17] We do not know if Stowe was aware of Tubman's feelings. In any case, she left Tubman's story for others to chronicle.

Tubman moved her aging parents Benjamin Ross and Harriet Green Ross, from St. Catharines to Auburn in 1859, approximately two years after she had brought them out of Maryland. Tradition has it that Tubman's parents did not care for the cold and dreary winters in Canada and desired a warmer climate. Tubman favored central New York be-

31. Reverend Samuel Miles Hopkins, professor, Auburn Theological Seminary. From John Quincy Adams, *A History of Auburn Theological Seminary 1818–1918* (Auburn, N.Y.: Auburn Seminary Press, 1918), facing 80.

cause of the many times she passed through the region while an Underground Railroad conductor. She had friends and supporters in places such as Rochester, Syracuse, Auburn, and Peterboro. William Henry Seward, twice the Whig governor of New York and a prominent citizen of Auburn, was instrumental in helping Tubman's parents move to a small house on about seven acres of land situated in the Town of Fleming along the southern edge of Auburn. More will be said regarding the history of the Auburn property in a subsequent chapter. Here it is sufficient to point out that the Bradford–Tubman connection was made possible because both women had cause to be in Auburn.

Geneva, New York, is located approximately thirty-five miles west of Auburn. While living there and operating her school for girls, Sarah Hopkins Bradford would from time to time journey to Auburn for extended visits with her brother, the Reverend Samuel Miles Hopkins (Figure 31). Hopkins began his fifty-four-year association with the Auburn Theological Seminary in 1847, when he was appointed to teach church history. The Auburn Theological Seminary, a Presbyterian institution founded in 1818, was a bastion of moderate theology and conservative in political matters. The seminary's leaders resisted the excesses generated in the Burned-Over District. Revivalists and abolitionists alike criticized Auburn's faculty for failing to move with the reform currents that had been sweeping across the region ever since 1825, when Finney began preaching up a fire storm. Samuel Miles Hopkins rose to the rank of professor of ecclesiastical history and ancient languages. In 1866, he assumed the prestigious post of moderator of the New School Assembly. An urbane and dignified man noted for his erudition and rhetorical flour-ishes, Hopkins took a lifelong interest in Harriet Tubman and assisted his sister with promoting Tubman's story and Tubman's welfare.[18]

Bradford tells us that she personally was not as well acquainted with Tubman's story as were some others in her circle of acquaintances. Through Tubman's friends and relations in Auburn, as well as through Isabella Swift of Geneva, she learned about her subject. Isabella Swift was the former Isabella Fitzhugh. She and her husband, Commodore Jonathan Williams Swift of the U.S. Navy, belonged to Geneva's social elite. Isabella may have heard about the woman called Black Moses from her sister, Ann Carroll née Fitzhugh Smith, the wife of the abolition-ist Gerrit Smith. Tubman was a welcome guest at the Smith mansion in Peterboro, Madison County, and obtained financial aid and shelter from the extended Smith family. Greene Smith, son of Gerrit and Ann, lived in Geneva for a short period, and in 1869, Elizabeth Smith Miller, the ardent suffragist and originator of the bloomer dress, moved to Geneva with her husband, Charles Dudley Miller.[19]

We lack evidence on when and under what circumstances Bradford and Tubman first met or who first proposed the biographical project that would bring the two women together. When Bradford took up residence in Auburn for several months during the Civil War, she encountered Tub-man's aged mother at a Sunday school that Tubman's mother attended. Tubman's parents once asked Bradford to write letters for them directed to Union commanders in the South inquiring about their daughter's wel-fare.

In the introductory note to Bradford's 1869 book, the Reverend Samuel Miles Hopkins tells us that his sister wrote her "little story" about Tub-man "with the single object of furnishing some help to the subject of the memoir" whose "services and sufferings during the rebellion" had not brought her pension relief. Bradford, again according to Hopkins, wrote her tribute, about which she made no claim "whatever to literary merit," on the eve of her departure for Europe. This would have been in 1868, for Bradford was in Germany when the Harriet Tubman memoir appeared. Hopkins makes the interesting claim that his sister had modest expectations regarding the sale of *Scenes*: "Her hope was merely that the considerably numerous public already in part acquainted with Harriet's story, would furnish purchasers enough to secure a little fund for the relief of this remarkable woman. Outside that circle she did not suppose the memoir was likely to meet with much if any sale."[20]

Tubman's friends decided to publish Bradford's little tome by subscription so that the entire proceeds of potential sales might be directed to her benefit. William G. Wise, a trustee of the Cayuga County Savings Bank, coordinated the subscription campaign and, at the request of Bradford, consented to act as Tubman's financial guardian, entrusted with the task of collecting, investing, and distributing all donations for Harriet's benefit. All but four of the contributors were citizens of Auburn. Gerrit Smith of Peterboro and Wendell Phillips of Boston stand out among the non-local subscribers.[21] Smith and Phillips gave twenty-five dollars each. Smith was upstate New York's most important political abolitionist and a proven friend of a host of African American activists. Wendell Phillips, a strong ally of William Lloyd Garrison, first met Tubman when she was in Boston on one of her visits to supporters there. Bradford's *Scenes* acknowledges thirty-four subscribers to the publishing fund, with contributions ranging from five dollars to twenty-five dollars, for a total of four hundred thirty dollars. Hopkins reported that the sum was "more than sufficient to defray the entire cost of publication." He asserted that *Scenes* was being published because Tubman had not received the pension due her for her wartime service. Bradford elaborated on Tubman's need by specifying that the "little account" of Tubman's life was being published because Tubman's parents were in danger of losing their small Auburn home, toward which Tubman had been making payments before throwing herself into "the work of aiding our suffering solders," to use Bradford's phrase.[22]

Aware that white America had little interest in placing Harriet Tubman in the pantheon of venerated historical figures dominated by white men such as George Washington, Thomas Jefferson, and Daniel Boone, Sarah Bradford candidly acknowledged that some would sneer at what she called "this *quixotic attempt* to make a heroine of a black woman, and a slave." Bradford was therefore conscious of the need to inform potential readers of the efforts she had made to verify the subject matter of her book, regardless of how hastily it had been compiled. Much of interest had to be left out in the 1869 volume, Bradford declared. She had been unable to substantiate all the stories told her by Tubman and Tubman's friends and relatives.

Lacking a cache of Bradford manuscripts and research notes, we cannot say with certainty how her narrative was constructed from the evidence, written and oral, available to her. Bradford's primary source was, of course, Tubman herself, whom Bradford hailed as no less important to posterity than Joan of Arc, Grace Darling, and Florence Nightingale.[23] Just how much opportunity Bradford had to sit down with Tubman and witness firsthand her heroine's marvelous storytelling abilities is an open question. The two women did talk in Bradford's home in Geneva. Bradford's method in putting together her "little book" during 1868 was to employ small swatches of narrative text recasting Tubman's oral testimony, paraphrases of Tubman's words, and, in some cases, attempts to capture the flavor of Tubman's speech through the use of direct quotes, as when recording the hymns Black Moses sang as she sought to convey messages to potential passengers on her Underground Railroad train.

In addition to talking with Tubman herself, Bradford gathered documentary evidence. She inserted portions of an article "from a paper published nearly a year ago" about the award advertised for Tubman's recapture.[24] Bradford examined the small and well-worn packet of documents (e.g., the military passes) that Tubman had saved from her wartime service. She sent out letters of inquiry to veterans of the abolitionist movement and the Underground Railroad. Some of these responses are reproduced in full in *Scenes*, giving the publication a scrapbook-like quality. Tubman seems to have cooperated enthusiastically with her interlocutor. She later made several inquiries through third parties seeking to advance the sales of *Scenes*. For example, Tubman wanted assurance that the small book about her would be sold at antislavery fairs. Nevertheless, it is important to remember that *Scenes* is mediated history. It must be read critically. Bradford's voice and that of Tubman have to be sorted out if we are to get closer to the unmediated "Moses."

Though Sarah Bradford appears to have taken reasonable measures to make her first presentation of her black heroine to the American public as true to the facts as possible, the completed work has the hallmarks of one of those hastily written and published "bios" that appear today in the wake of an unexpected event. There is a helter-skelter quality to *Scenes*. About two-thirds of the way through the narrative, Bradford says in an aside to the reader, "The writer here finds it necessary to apologize for the very desultory and hasty manner in which this little book is written. Being herself pressed for time, in the expectation of soon leaving the country, she is obliged to pen down the material to be used in the short and interrupted interviews she can obtain with Harriet, and also to use such letters and accounts as may be sent her, as they come, without being able to work them in, in the order of time. A very material assistance is to be rendered her by the kind offer of an account of Harriet's services during the war, written by Mr. Charles P. Wood, of Auburn, and kindly copied by one of Harriet's most faithful and most efficient friends, Mrs. S. M. Hopkins, of that place."[25]

Bradford's 1869 sketch of Tubman's life is not a biography in the rigorous sense. Apart from glossing over Tubman's wartime service because Wood failed to finish his sketch in time for Bradford to use, *Scenes* lacks a methodical treatment of Tubman's life up to the opening of the Civil War. The "book" wants a controlling chronological framework and narrative voice. Less than half of the 132 pages came from the pen of Sarah Bradford. There is one long section, pages 9–47, in which Bradford attempts to sum up Tubman's escape and subsequent career as a conductor of others to freedom. Even this material is episodic and disjointed in nature. Readers desirous of information about Tubman's childhood and adolescence must have been disappointed, for there is little of Harriet's experiences up to the year 1849.

Following a brief preface introducing the subject and purpose of the book, *Scenes* (Figure 32) opens with testimonials to Tubman's character and veracity. Gerrit Smith, Wendell Phillips, and Frederick Douglass wrote to Bradford in 1868 in response to her appeal for recollections about her black heroine. The longer Bradford material, referred to earlier, ensues. It abruptly stops when a letter from Franklin B. Sanborn is inserted (on pages 53–55). Bradford then makes an editorial aside about Tubman's propensity to employ dreams and visions in dangerous situations or as portents of the future. Next comes a brief account of the rescue by Tubman of her brothers and parents. Then we find a series of insertions, starting with letters written in 1868 by Rufus B. Saxton and William Henry Seward supporting Tubman's pension request. Next come nearly a dozen of the wartime letters of introduction, passes, and

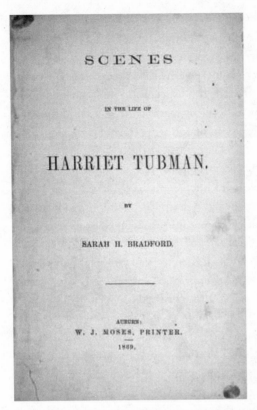

32. Title page. From Sarah H. Bradford, *Scenes in the Life of Harriet Tubman* (Auburn, N.Y.: W. J. Moses, 1869).

other military documents. Even here, Bradford made no effort to hold to a historical time line. For example, a letter from Gerrit Smith dated November 4, 1867, concerning Tubman's claim for governmental assistance is set down among the documents dating from August 1862 through July 1865. This section of *Scenes*, if "section" is indeed the right word for such loosely organized material, ends with an undated note to William Seward, then Lincoln's Secretary of State, from V. K. Barnes, Surgeon-General, providing Seward with information about the African American residents of Beaufort, South Carolina, who acted as Tubman's assistants, scouts, or pilots when she was engaged in espionage work.

Though the reader is by now only at page 71 of the 132-page-long *Scenes* book, the remainder of the volume is almost entirely made up of documents Bradford copied. First comes a letter from the Reverend Henry Fowler, another one of Harriet's sponsors in Auburn. On March 18, 1869, Fowler presided at the wedding ceremony of Tubman and Nelson Davis,

Plate 1. "Harriet, Harriet, Born a Slave," by Jacob Lawrence. From Jacob Lawrence, *Harriet and the Promised Land* (New York: Aladdin Paperbacks, 1997). First Simon and Schuster edition, 1993. Reprinted with permission of Simon and Schuster Books for Young Readers, an imprint of Simon and Schuster Children's Publishing Division, from *Harriet and the Promised Land*, by Jacob Lawrence. Copyright © 1968, 1993 Jacob Lawrence.

Plate 2. "Harriet Tubman's Escape," by Jacob Lawrence. From Ellen Harkins Wheat, *Jacob Lawrence: The Frederick Douglass and Harriet Tubman Series of 1938–40*. Hampton University Museum, Hampton, Virginia, in association with University of Washington Press (Seattle and London), 1991. Paintings and captions copyright © Hampton University Museum. Copyright © 2005 Jacob and Gwendolyn Lawrence Foundation, Seattle/Artists Rights Society (ARS), New York.

Plate 3. Comic cover, "The Saga of Harriet Tubman: 'The Moses of Her People,'" *Golden Legacy*, vol. 2 (New York: Fitzgerald Publishing Company, 1967). Copyright © 1966.

Plate 4. Book cover. Faith Ringgold, *Aunt Harriet's Underground Railroad in the Sky* (New York: Crown Publishers, 1992).

Plate 5. Frederick Douglass, included as one of the "Heroes of the Colored Race." Copy of slide courtesy Library of Congress, LC/USZC2–1720.

Plate 6. "Harriet Tubman's Underground Railroad." Copyright © Paul Collins. Courtesy Paul Collins, Collins Fine Art, Grand Rapids, Michigan.

Plate 7. Aaron Douglas's painting "Spirits Rising" (1930–31), which is also known as the Harriet Tubman and Alfred Stern mural. Oil on canvas. At the Rose Mae Withers Catchings Personal Development Complex, Bennett College, Greensboro, North Carolina. Commissioned by Alfred Stern of Chicago, son-in-law of the philanthropist Julius Rosenwald, for Bennett College. Illustration in Richard J. Powell, *Black Art: A Cultural History*, 2d ed (London: Thames and Hudson, 2002), 65, illustration 36.

Plate 8. "Harriet Tubman" (circa 1945), by William H. Johnson. Smithsonian American Art Museum, 1967.59.1146. Courtesy Smithsonian American Art Museum.

Plate 9. Harriet Tubman U.S. postage stamp, thirteen cents. First issued in 1978. In the author's collection.

the Civil War veteran. The wedding took place in Auburn's Central Presbyterian church, which was organized in 1861 as on offshoot of Auburn's Second Presbyterian church. Fowler, an abolitionist, and a group of supporters had withdrawn from Second Presbyterian after conservatives pressured Fowler's Presbyterian supervisors to demand that he cease preaching so violently against the South's "peculiar institution." One of Fowler's backers was Charles P. Wood. These Christian "come-outers" replicated a pattern common to many churchgoing abolitionists during the abolition controversy. Christians with abolitionist convictions separated themselves from impure assemblies, either voluntarily or under duress, and formed new churches and, in some instances, new denominations such as the Wesleyan Methodists and Free Presbyterians.[26] Tubman would have felt at home at Fowler's Central Presbyterian church, which initially met in rooms of the Young Men's Christian Association on Genesee Street. An edifice was built in 1869 on William Street and dedicated a year later. Fowler served as Central Presbyterian's pastor until his death in 1871. Many of Tubman's Auburn supporters, including, according to one press account, "many of the first families in the city," attended the wedding.[27]

Bradford does not speak of Tubman's wedding in *Scenes*. She had already rushed her manuscript(s) to William J. Moses, the printer, and was either in Europe or on her way there. The printer may well have had more discretion in assembling the assorted documents Bradford left with him than most readers can surmise from a casual reading of *Scenes*. Given comments Bradford made with respect to the time constraints under which she gleaned stories and materials for her project, it is not far-fetched to think of Bradford as the collector or compiler and Moses as the editor of *Scenes*. He was a trustee of Auburn's First Methodist Episcopal church and friendly to the effort to assist Harriet.

The Reverend Henry Fowler also had a keen interest in Tubman and her thrilling odyssey. He told Bradford in June 1868 that Tubman's "life forms part of the history of the country, and that it ought not to depend upon tradition to keep it in remembrance." Fowler had himself "aspired to be her historian," but "the pressure of professional claims," so he informed Bradford, prevented him from doing so. He was pleased that Sarah Bradford had become the "chosen Miriam of this African 'Moses.'"[28] Fowler's reference to Miriam, the sister of the biblical Moses, is intriguing. Miriam was a prophet in her own right and came out of Egypt with Moses, having watched over him since he was a baby in a basket (Exodus 2). When Moses married an Ethiopian woman, Miriam spoke against him, raising the question, "Is Moses the only one who can hear God?" (Numbers 12). As punishment for her jealousy, Miriam was made to suffer from leprosy, though she was later restored to health. It is surprising that Fowler should use an analogy with such a putative meaning.

Franklin B. Sanborn's Tubman sketch, copied from the Boston *Commonwealth* of 1863, follows the Fowler letter with but a transitional sentence. After the Sanborn material, we have an account of Tubman's role in the rescue of Charles Nalle. Details of the rescue of Nalle were readily available to Bradford in the public press. *Scenes* republishes the story called "Fugitive Slave Rescue in Troy" from the *Troy Whig* of April 28, 1859. Bradford had first heard the story from Tubman herself, but feeling that, to "some persons it seemed too wonderful for belief," she sought to corroborate it by seeking "the facts" from Fowler. Fowler went to Troy and interviewed the lawyer who served as Nalle's counsel during the hearing. Bradford tells her readers that she expected Fowler to write out his findings for her "little book" but that he had fallen ill from heatstroke while "engaged in some kind efforts for the prisoners at Auburn."[29] Lacking Fowler's report, Bradford had to depend on the newspaper account. Bradford prefaces her synopsis of what Tubman told her by saying that Nalle's rescue took place in the "Spring of 1860," but a few pages later, we have the article from the *Troy Whig* dated April 28, 1859. Here is yet another indication of the haste with which *Scenes* was thrown together.[30]

The body of *Scenes* ends with an appeal. Bradford addresses the reader as follows:

> This woman of whom you have been reading is poor, and partially disabled from her injuries; yet she supports cheerfully and uncomplainingly herself and her old parents, and always has several poor children in her house, who are dependent entirely upon her exertions. At present she has three of these children for whom she is providing, while their parents are working to pay back money borrowed to bring them on. She also maintains by her exertions among the good people of Auburn, two schools of freedmen at the South,

providing them teachers and sending them clothes and books. She never asks for anything for herself, but she does ask the charity of the public for "her people."[31]

To this is appended a scrap of poetry:

> For them her tears will fall,
> For them her prayers ascend;
> To them her toils and cares be given,
> Till toils and cares will end.

Bradford had written religious and sentimental verse before, so this may well have been her tribute to Tubman. Since Bradford was soon to depart for Europe, she asked that donors interested in aiding Tubman and her benevolent work send their contributions to her brother, the Reverend Samuel M. Hopkins.[32]

The remaining pages of *Scenes* consist of an appendix (pages 107–30) and the List of Subscribers to the Publishing Fund (pages 131–32). The appendix is of puzzling content and construction. Bradford tells her readers that the information was derived from conversations with Tubman. In answer to Bradford's inquiry as to the age of Tubman's mother, Black Moses related how twenty-three years earlier (1845, if we assume 1868 as the time when Bradford is interviewing Tubman) she paid a lawyer to look up the will of her mother's first master. According to Tubman as retold by Bradford, the will stipulated that Tubman's mother should serve the master's granddaughter and her offspring until "Rit," as Tubman's mother was called, became forty-five. The granddaughter died without heir or provision for Tubman's mother. Rit was kept ignorant of this turn of events and remained a slave under Southern law until Ben Ross purchased her freedom from Eliza Brodess for twenty dollars sometime before 1855.[33]

This conversational snippet gives way to a few sentences about how Tubman's parents regularly attended church services in Auburn, falling asleep almost as soon as they sat down. Bradford wondered about the fast Tubman's parents observed on Sundays. Tubman had told her that Ben Ross did not eat or drink on Good Friday and the five Fridays thereafter "for de five bleeding wounds ob Jesus," according to Tubman. Bradford asked, "But is he a Roman Catholic, Harriet?"—to which Tubman is to have responded, "On, no Misses; he does it for conscience; we was taught to do so down South. He says if he denies himself for the sufferings of his Lord an' Master, Jesus will sustain him."[34] This is important material and most logically should have been placed in the main body of *Scenes*, had there been a sustained and ordered narrative of Tubman's life and an attempt to understand how her pious parents influenced Harriet's religious character.

Dislocation is also apparent in the next appendix segment. Bradford writes about her heroine's ability to extract money from others for others. She says that after one of Harriet's "*intimations*" that her parents (then still in Maryland) were in need, she showed up at the office of a New York City gentleman (not named) and staged a sit-in, swearing not to eat or drink until she got a donation. Her potential benefactor ran a program to aid fugitive slaves but told Tubman that he could not provide the twenty dollars she wanted. Tubman fell into one of her deep sleeps, and when she woke, she discovered that she had been given sixty dollars by those who came into the office and had heard of her plight. This vignette says much about Harriet Tubman's method of operation, her persistence and faith, yet it appears in the appendix, a kind of afterthought on Bradford's part.[35]

Bradford follows this story about Tubman's resourcefulness in securing help for others with one illustrating Tubman's faithfulness. Once, when the snow lay deep and her parents were unable to leave their small home, her father was suffering from rheumatism and unable to go out to replenish the household larder. Harriet plunged through the drifts and made her way into the village of Auburn. She went to the house of one of her friends and, with great reluctance, said, "Miss Annie, could you lend me a quarter till Monday? I never asked it before." Aid came for the family. Then on Monday, to the surprise of her benefactors, Harriet showed up with the quarter, proving her self-sacrificing and trustworthy character.[36] Bradford commented, "Even now, while friends are trying to raise the means to publish this little book for her, *she* is going around with the greatest zeal and interest to raise a subscription for her Freedmen's Fair." Tubman, according to Bradford, solicited a subscription from William H. Seward for her Freedmen's Fair. Seward responded, "Harriet, you have worked for others long enough. It is time you should think of yourself. If you ask for a donation for *yourself*, I will give it to you; but I will not help you to rob yourself for others."[37]

Bradford underscores her black heroine's self-sacrificing nature and her charity for all by contending that it embraced "even the slaveholder." "It sympathizes even with Jeff. Davis, and rejoices at his departure to other lands, with some prospect of peace for the future." Jefferson Davis, former president of the Confederate States of America, did not die until 1889, so here both Bradford and Tubman were indulging in wishful thinking. Tubman's point, however, was that even the chief of sinners might be redeemed. Bradford quotes her as saying, "I tink dar's many a slaveholder'll git to Heaven. Dey don't know no better. Dey acts up to de light dey hab. You take dat sweet little child (pointing to a lonely baby), — 'pears more like an angel dan anyting else — take her down dere. Let her nebber know nothing 'bout niggers but they was made to be whipped, an' she'll grow up to use the whip on 'em jus' like de rest. No, Missus, it's because dey don't know no better."[38] Bradford uses this last vignette in *Scenes* to direct an appeal to potential readers of her tribute to Tubman. They, in "like charity," should come to the assistance of her heroine so that "the last days of her stormy and troubled life may be calm and peaceful."[39]

The foregoing representations of Tubman's selfless nature might well have been integrated into the main body of *Scenes* where Bradford compared her heroine to three of the female icons of the day. She invokes Joan of Arc, Grace Darling, and Florence Nightingale as points of comparison in the preface to *Scenes*.[40] Because post–Civil War Americans had not yet constructed a pantheon of American women worthy of heroic stature, they reached back to Europe (Figure 33). Joan of Arc (d. 1412) was the young French girl who called for the withdrawal of English troops in an effort to help King Charles VII. Like Tubman, young Joan is said to have arrived at her understanding of the will of God for her life through dreams and visions. Her claim to have heard voices led to an accusation of witchcraft and heresy, and she went before the Inquisition, though her countrymen thought her divinely inspired. So powerful was the legend of Joan of Arc that she was beatified by Pius X in 1909.

Mark Twain spent twelve years researching and two years writing the life of the French girl known by contemporaries as la Pucelle, or the Maid. Published anonymously and serialized in *Harper's Magazine*, beginning with the April 1895 issue, Twain's tribute to the visionary French village peasant is puzzling, for Twain (Samuel Langhorne Clemens) had the reputation of a religious skeptic. Thomas Howard observes: "It is an extraordinary (and baffling) literary phenomenon that Mark Twain, who

HARPER'S WEEKLY.
JOURNAL OF CIVILIZATION

Vol. XVIII.—No. 897.]   NEW YORK, SATURDAY, MARCH 7, 1874.   [WITH A SUPPLEMENT. PRICE TEN CENTS.

© 1999 HARPWEEK®

33. "Joan-of-Arc (1412?–31)," used as a symbol in the anti–"King Alcohol" campaign. *Harper's Weekly*, March 7, 1874.

was not disposed to see God at work in the melancholy affairs of men, should have been so galvanized by the life and achievement of this young woman that he devoted years of his life to this book about her."[41] Twain said, "I like Joan of Arc best of all my books." One wonders how Twain might have handled the story of Harriet Tubman, who Bradford lauded for surpassing Joan of Arc "in courage, power of endurance, in facing danger and death to relieve human suffering."[42] As far as I have been able to determine, Mark Twain ignored Harriet Tubman, never mentioning her in any of his published works.

Bradford reached again to a non-American heroine when she compared Tubman to Grace Darling (Figure 34). Darling's biographer, Jessica Mitford, writes, "Grace Darling can be precisely and anachronistically de-

34. Grace Darling
(1815–42). From North-
umberland Communi-
ties website at http://
communities.north
umberland.gov.uk/
images/008530FS.jpg.

scribed as the first media heroine."[43] Grace was the daughter of William
Darling, the keeper of a lighthouse off England's Northumberland Coast.
In September 1838, a ship went aground on a rock in the North Sea. According to the legend, Grace, then only twenty-two, took the lighthouse
coble, a short, flat-bottomed boat, and went out to the wreck. Five of the
nine survivors managed to climb into the coble and reach safety back at
the lighthouse. Victorian girls grew up aspiring to emulate this model of
feminine courage. American readers of Bradford's *Scenes* might not have
felt as passionately about Darling as did the British, but they would have
been more familiar with the legend of this English heroine than we are
today.[44]

Florence Nightingale, like Grace Darling and Joan of Arc, hailed from
Europe. Born in Florence, Italy, in 1820, and raised in England, Nightingale enjoyed an upper-class lifestyle and a classical education, laced with

a strong dose of mathematics. She claimed to have heard the voice of God in 1837 commanding her to take up some great mission. Nightingale discovered her vocation in 1849 when she went to Europe to study the hospital situation. After the Crimean War began in 1854, she volunteered to care for the sick and wounded and introduced a system for recording and reporting mortality statistics, which demonstrated that many more British soldiers died of disease as the result of poor medical care than perished in battle. In 1869, when the war was over, Nightingale founded a professional school for nursing in London and went on to pursue a distinguished career in health reform. The Royal Statistical Society made her a fellow in 1858, and in 1874 the American Statistical Association elected her to honorary membership. Biographers have told the story of Nightingale's life many times over, a task facilitated because it is so well documented. Florence Nightingale was a widely known contemporary of Tubman.[45]

Though Sarah Bradford wished to have the American public view Tubman as a more heroic figure than any of then popular female heroines, she was away in Europe when *Scenes* was published and could do little to promote its sales. It is highly unlikely that Tubman was able to exercise control over how *Scenes* was written and compiled. One wonders if the book was ever read back to her, either in whole or in part. Perhaps some of her literate friends, black and white, commented to her on portions of her life story as represented in *Scenes* and she expressed an opinion as to their accuracy, but this informal post-publication critical voice is lost to us.

Fortunately for our attempt to understand the evolution of Harriet Tubman from an unknown to an American icon, Tubman retained her gift of storytelling. She held the key to the box of memories from which others drew and from which they sought to construct written representations of her. Contemporaries vouched that Black Moses talked with conviction, her stories replete with telling detail, her imagination warm and rich. She drew verbal pictures so dramatically that her hearers were convinced of the veracity of her accounts, as if she were reliving her daring and dangerous experiences, whether as a conductor of others to freedom or as a scout for Union troops chasing Confederates along the rivers and the backwaters of the South. In a testimonial letter written in response to Bradford's appeal for confirmation of Tubman's story, Gerrit Smith wrote from Peterboro in 1868, "Of the remarkable events of her life I

CHAPTER FOUR

124

have no personal knowledge, but of the truth of them as she describes them I have no doubt. I have often listened to her, in her visits to my family, and I am confident that she is not only truthful, but that she has a rare discernment, and a deep and sublime philanthropy."[46] In a letter of endorsement intended to promote the 1886 account of Tubman's life by Bradford, Oliver Johnson, one of the few surviving veterans of the Underground Railroad days, said, "No one who listened to her could doubt her perfect truthfulness and integrity."[47]

Bradford, whether consciously or not, constructed *Scenes* in a manner that gave Tubman's own voice greater play than might have been the case had Bradford had the time to exercise greater editorial control. This will become more apparent when we analyze the second volume about Tubman that Bradford published in 1886. Here it is important to stress that Bradford's first book about Tubman is appropriately entitled "scenes" in the life of Black Moses. Its scrapbook-like construction using an assortment of primary documents captures more of the vitality and authenticity of Tubman herself than the 1886 edition. Tubman devotees today ought to begin with a close analysis of *Scenes* rather than depending on the *Moses* volume that has been so frequently reprinted.

Bradford tells us that the 1886 book, as had *Scenes*, originated because of a crisis. Harriet had need of assistance in establishing a home in Auburn for the shelter and care of elderly African Americans, whose welfare was sadly neglected by the existing white-sponsored institutions for the aged. Of her subject, Bradford wrote in the 1886 text, "Her own sands are nearly run, but she hopes, 'ere she goes home, to see this work, a hospital, well under way."[48] Black Moses would live for more than a quarter-century, and Tubman's home for the aged would not open until 1908, but Bradford could not have known this as once again she sought to stir the American conscience on behalf of a woman handicapped by illiteracy from writing her own story.

Bradford was still concerned that the reading public would reject her account of Tubman's heroic accomplishments out of hand. She again made efforts to assure potential purchasers of her book about its authenticity. Bradford claimed to have "received corroboration of every incident related to me by my heroic friend. I did this for the satisfaction of others, not for my own. No one can hear Harriet talk, and not believe every word she says. As Mr. Sanborn says of her, 'she is too *real* a person not to be true.'" Bradford asserts that she rejected some of the incidents told to her by Tubman (or perhaps about Tubman by third parties) because she "had no way of finding the persons who could speak to their truth."[49] By 1886, many of the veteran abolitionists had died or were in their declining years.

Bradford framed the 1886 book as a revision of her 1869 *Scenes*. However, *Harriet, the Moses of Her People* reaches further than one might expect for a second edition. It sculpts Tubman into a Christian saint according to Bradford's notion of what such a model should be. The Reverend Samuel M. Hopkins embraced and supported the 1886 book as he had the 1869 one. Of his sister's intent, Hopkins wrote: "The book is good literature for the black race, or the white race, and though no similar conditions may arise, to test the possibilities that are in any of them, yet the example of this poor slave woman may well stand out before them, and before all people, black or white, to show what a lofty and martyr spirit may accomplish, struggling against overwhelming obstacles."[50]

If Bradford consciously wrote for a black audience as well as a white one, as Hopkins suggested, she missed the mark. *Moses* is flawed by racist and stereotypical language and imagery. Here is how Bradford begins the biographical section of the 1886 book:

> On a hot summer's day, perhaps sixty years ago, a group of merry little darkies were rolling and tumbling in the sand in front of the large house of a Southern planter. Their shining skins gleamed in the sun, as they rolled over each other in their play, and their voices, as they chattered together, or shouted in glee, reached even to the cabins of the negro quarter, where the old people groaned in spirit, as they thought of the future of those unconscious young revelers; and their cry went up, "O, Lord, how long!" Apart from the rest of the children, on the top rail of a fence, holding tight on to the tall gate post, sat a little girl of perhaps thirteen years of age; darker than any of the others, and with a more decided *woolliness* in the hair; a pure unmitigated African. She was not so entirely in a state of nature as the rollers in the dust beneath her; but her only garment was a short woolen skirt, which was tied around her waist, and reached about to her knees. She seemed a dazed and stupid child, and as her head hung upon her breast, she looked up with dull blood-shot eyes towards her young brothers and sisters, without seeming to see

them. Bye and bye the eyes closed, and still clinging to the post, she slept.

The other children looked up and said to each other, "Look at Hatt, she's done gone off agin!" Tired of their present play ground they trooped off in another direction, but the girl slept on heavily, never losing her hold on the post, or her seat on her perch. Behold here, in the stupid little negro girl, the future deliverer of hundreds of her people; the spy, and scout of the Union armies; the devoted hospital nurse; the protector of hunted fugitives; the eloquent speaker in public meetings; the cunning eluder of pursuing man-hunters; the heaven guided pioneer through dangers seen and unseen; in short, as she has well been called, "The Moses of her People."[51]

This section illustrates how strongly Bradford took literary license with Tubman's oral accounts and repackaged them to make them palatable for readers in post–Reconstruction America, a time when racism thrived and African Americans suffered from stereotypical characterizations that offend readers of Bradford's *Moses* today.[52] Bradford's accommodation to the prevailing manner of writing about African Americans among well-meaning white authors, particularly those appealing to a popular audience, is a serious impediment to today's student of Harriet Tubman's life.

Tubman admirers also have difficulty in trying to determine what Black Moses actually told Bradford because of the editorial changes made in *Moses*. We can see this by comparing specific sections of the 1886 volume with their counterparts in the 1869 publication. In some cases, the differences are a result of Bradford's attempt in the 1886 volume to purge Tubman's speech of dialect, with inconsistent results. For example, here is a passage, frequently quoted in secondary sources today, where Harriet talks about that glorious moment when she crossed the Mason–Dixon Line. The single underscored material is common to both versions, while the crossed-out text is from *Scenes* and the double-underscored text is from *Moses*:

"I looked at my hands," she said, "to see if I was de same ~~pusson~~ <u><u>person now I was free</u></u>. ~~There~~<u><u>Dere</u></u> <u>was such a glory ober</u> ~~ebery~~ ~~ting;~~<u><u>eberything</u></u>, <u>de sun came like gold</u> ~~through the~~<u><u>trou de</u></u> <u>trees, and ober</u> ~~the~~<u><u>de</u></u> <u>fields, and I felt like I was in</u> ~~Heaben~~<u><u>heaven</u></u>."[53]

These editorial changes may seem insignificant in and of themselves, but the sum total of Bradford's revoicing of Tubman's colloquial speech is yet another example of the degree to which the 1886 text departs from the 1869 book.

Somewhat more disconcerting are passages where the differences between *Scenes* and *Moses* amount to more than an attempt by Bradford to have Tubman speak "good English." Here is an example where Bradford altered and added to the 1869 text. Bradford is attempting to give readers a sample of her heroine's use of song to communicate to those she was seeking to rescue:

Hail, oh hail, ye happy spirits,
Death no more shall make you fear,
~~No grief~~Grief nor sorrow, pain nor ~~anger (~~anguish),
Shall no more distress you ~~there~~dere.
Around ~~him~~Him are ten ~~thousan'~~thousand angels,
Always ready to ~~'bey comman.'~~obey command;
Dey are always ~~hobring~~hovering round you,
Till you reach ~~the hebbenly lan'~~de heavenly land.
Jesus, Jesus will go wid you;,
He will lead you to his throne;
He who died, has gone before you,
Trod de wine-press all alone.
He whose thunders shake creation;,
He who bids ~~the~~de planets roll;
He who rides upon the ~~temple, (~~tempest) ~~An' his,~~
And whose scepter sways de whole.
Dark; and thorny is de ~~desert, Through~~pathway,
Where de pilgrim makes his ways~~, Yet beyon';~~
But beyond dis vale of sorrow,
~~Lies~~Lie de ~~fiel's~~fields of endless days.[54]

Bradford assures her readers in *Scenes* that she was giving "these words exactly as Harriet sang them to me to a sweet and simple Methodist air."[55] Some seventeen years later in *Moses*, Bradford dropped this declaration and instead offered the following to her readers: "The air sung to these words was so wild, so full of plaintive minor strains, and unexpected quavers, that I would defy any white person to learn it, and often as I heard it, it was to me a constant surprise."[56]

In summary, what are we to make of Sarah Bradford's portrayal of Harriet Tubman? Answering this question is complicated by the fact that we have two so-called biographies of Tubman by Bradford. The differences between the two amount to more than minor editorial revisions. For example, James A. McGowan pointed out in 1994 that Bradford made "a deliberate and conscious change of the information" about the size of the reward offered for Joe Bailey, raising it five hundred dollars in the 1886 book over the amount she gave in the 1869 biography. She also inflated the number of fugitives Thomas Garrett allegedly helped from two thousand in *Scenes* to three thousand in *Moses*. In some instances, McGowan argues, Bradford told two different stories about the same incident, as is the case with her account of Tubman's first attempt to escape. In *Scenes*, Bradford tells us that Harriet tried to run away with two of her brothers after hearing that two of her sisters had been put in a chain gang to be sold off. In *Moses*, Bradford has Harriet trying to escape with three of her brothers because she had heard that she and her brothers were going to be sent far south. *Scenes* tells us that Harriet's brothers dragged her back with them; *Moses* tells us that Harriet went back voluntarily.[57]

Because of these and other inconsistencies and what he terms her "writing deficiencies," McGowan lamented the "long-range negative effect" that Bradford has had on later biographers who accepted her two books uncritically. He asked, "Was there no one else?" McGowan wondered why William Still, William Wells Brown, or, most important, Frederick Douglass did not write Tubman's first biography. "It is incomprehensible," McGowan wrote in the *Harriet Tubman Journal* in 1994, "to think that these men who felt so responsible for helping the slave, for recording and documenting the history of Black people, did not act to record the life and times of one of the greatest Black people of that age, a simple and courageous woman who walked among them. Instead, they left her history to Sarah Bradford . . . who left it a mess."[58]

While Bradford seems to have been of sincere intent and strongly sympathetic to her heroine, she could not overcome the impediments created by her own life situation; nor did she successfully surmount the challenges of writing mediated biography. Bradford assumed that there was common ground because she and her subject were "sisters in Christ." However, the middle-class white woman from Geneva, New York, and the former bondswoman from Maryland derived their sense of religious self from two contrasting, though interconnected, cultural streams. In spite of this tension, Bradford and Tubman forged a partnership both practical and self-serving. Tubman needed someone to "write up" her life, in part because she was illiterate but also because she needed money. Bradford needed Tubman to tell her the rudiments of the story of her life.

It is ironic that Bradford's attempt at fixing the story of Tubman should have resulted in so much ambiguity and uncertainty about the lady behind the legend. Jean Humez, the author of a contemporary biography of Tubman that is sensitive to the pitfalls of mediated history, reminds us that in spite of all the testimonials to Tubman's truthfulness and integrity by those who knew her, Black Moses "was a skillful strategist, who could and did present herself in a variety of disguises as the situation demanded." Humez advises that we underscore "Tubman's own agency, as both giver and withholder of truths about her life."[59] Humez, like Mc-Gowan, has taken Bradford "to task for many failings as a writer and biographer." Nevertheless, she is helpful in pointing out that, if we know "something of Bradford's own history as Tubman's accidental biographer and later self-appointed protector, we are in a good position to make critical use of the valuable oral historical material captured in the 1868 interviews" Bradford did as she rushed to get *Scenes* published.[60]

The search for the historical Tubman, the Tubman contained in and concealed by Bradford's portraits of her, is not unlike the scholarly quest for the historical Jesus. Many investigators have mined the Gospels trying to recover what Jesus actually said and did. New Testament scholarship, at least in the theologically more liberal traditions, points to the layered nature of the Gospels and posits a more primal oral narrative at the heart of the Jesus story. Searching for the historical Tubman also involves an attempt to get behind existing texts about her. Bradford's biographical renderings of Harriet Tubman are valuable resources for our understanding of the woman behind the legend. We need to read them critically, recognizing that they are constructed memories used for symbolic purposes.

CHAPTER FIVE

SAINT, SEER, AND SUFFRAGIST

In spite of the publication of Bradford's *Scenes* in 1869, Harriet Tubman, the woman who had been hailed as "the greatest heroine of her age," drifted into obscurity after the Civil War ended and the old abolitionist vanguard began to pass from the scene. At one time, Tubman's stage, her theater of operations, had been more national. She moved in abolitionist circles during a time when the reformers dreamed of liberating the enslaved as well as establishing a post-emancipation equalitarian and biracial society. Tubman surely hoped that the Thirteenth Amendment and then the Fourteenth Amendment would prove to be but down payments on the debt that white America owed black America. Though she did not take an active part in the post–Civil War efforts by educators, missionaries, and politicians who went into the South to reconstruct it, her labors in helping fugitives to escape and furthering the Union cause during the Civil War signified that she embraced the larger vision of a free and prosperous black South.

Northern politicians and their Southern counterparts shattered this hope of a new South in which black and white shared in the first fruits of the land and enjoyed democratic liberties when a devil's bargain was struck in the Hayes–Tilden election. The end of Reconstruction in 1877 drew down the curtain of hope. By this time, many of Tubman's abolitionist allies had died. Her theater of operations was now Auburn, New York, a much smaller arena than the one she had occupied up through the Civil War. Tubman had been known as "Black Moses" and "General Tubman." Three additional iconic images solidified during her Auburn years—those of saint, seer, and suffragist.

During Tubman's long Auburn period, she moved freely among some of Auburn's important white families. The wives of prominent white businessmen and professionals occasionally employed her as a domestic. Martha Coffin Wright may be the best example of a stalwart ally of Black Moses during the Auburn years. Born in 1806 of Quaker parents, Martha was expelled from her Quaker meeting in 1824 after marrying Peter Pehlham, a non-Quaker. Peter died in 1826, leaving Martha a widow with an infant child. Martha moved to Auburn, married David Wright, a young lawyer, and had six additional children. In addition to employing Tubman from time to time, Martha and her friends supported her charitable work (see Figure 35) and constructed the image of her as a saintly matriarch, a woman of deep faith who demonstrated that faith by mothering others though she had no children of her own. When they turned their energies to the cause of women's rights, the white women of Auburn who had connections to the Seneca Falls movement tried to draw on the emblematic power of Tubman as a woman of courage and deep faith, albeit a faith given over to dreams and visions, thus linking the iconic images of saint, seer, and suffragist.[1]

Sarah Bradford helped to fashion the primary lens through which the American public was now to see Tubman as a woman of great piety. In the 1886 edition of her mediated biography of Tubman, Bradford writes: "Harriet's religious character I have not yet touched upon. Brought up by parents possessed of strong faith in God, she had never known the time, I imagine, when she did not trust Him, and cling to Him, with an all-abiding confidence. She seemed ever to feel the Divine Presence near, and she talked with God 'as a man talketh with his friend.'" Then in a passage that revealed how much cultural dissonance existed between Bradford's world and that of her subject, Tubman's amanuensis acknowledged, "Hers was not the religion of a morning and evening prayer at stated times, but when she felt a need, she simply told God of it, and trusted Him to set the matter right."[2]

Bradford accepted Tubman's religious testimony as compatible with her own understanding of Christianity, but only to a degree. Schooled as she was in the norms, rituals, and beliefs of evangelical Protestantism as expressed in Presbyterian circles of the day, Bradford thought she understood Tubman's religious self. After all, the black woman of whom Bradford wrote claimed to be a Christian, not a follower of the Islamic faith or some other religious tradition thought of as "foreign" by nineteenth-century Americans. Bradford made an effort in both *Scenes* and *Moses* to

35. Some of Harriet's helpers. From left to right: unidentified woman (possibly Eliza Wright Osborne's daughter), Martha Coffin Wright, Eliza Wright Osborne (Martha's daughter), and Lucretia Mott. Courtesy Friends Historical Library of Swarthmore College, Swarthmore, Penn.

verify the stories Tubman told about her adventures as an Underground Railroad conductor. It was more difficult to find confirming evidence of Tubman's inner life, especially her dream life.

When Bradford wrote about the subjective side of Tubman's extraordinary story, she showed both admiration and suspicion. The "realness" of Tubman's frequent references to direct messages from God was not something Bradford could empirically verify. Tubman's friends and supporters from pre–Civil War abolitionist circles did provide recollections of having heard similar stories from Tubman about her chats with the Lord. Some had witnessed in her personality the same characteristic of a deep, almost mystical piety that Bradford sensed. But neither Bradford nor the other white writers who called the public's attention to Tubman were capable of determining whether or not Tubman actually heard the voice of God or dreamed the dreams she spoke of in so compelling and dramatic a fashion. These were uniquely personal experiences of the inner self.

There are sources other than the Bradford books that speak to the question of Tubman's non-white religious self—that is to say, to her affinity with African American folk traditions rooted in African traditional culture. William Wells Brown visited Canada in 1860 and talked with several ex-fugitives. They told him that they believed Tubman possessed supernatural powers. One man said, "Moses is got de charm." Brown, who would express personal skepticism bordering on disdain, for the extravagant religious styles of blacks he observed while touring the South in the post-Reconstruction era, queried his informant for more information on Tubman's unusual gift. The man replied, "De whites can't catch Moses, kase you see she's born wid de charm. De Lord has given Moses de power." Brown asserted that Tubman herself felt that she possessed "the charm" and that this conviction "nerved her up, gave her courage, and made all who followed her feel safe in her hands." African American soldiers in the camps Tubman frequented during the Civil War also saw her as religiously gifted. "These black men," Brown claimed, "would have died for this woman, for they believed that she had a charmed life."[3]

What was this "charm" or "power" that Tubman is said to have possessed? Franklin B. Sanborn, writing that seminal article for *Commonwealth* in July 1863, struggled to explain how it was that Tubman always escaped her pursuers when operating as an Underground Railroad conductor. He proposed two explanations: her "quick wit" and her "'warnings' from Heaven." "She is," the Harvard-trained New England educa-tor asserted, "the most shrewd and practical person in the world, yet she is a firm believer in omens, dreams and warnings."[4]

Sanborn cited examples of Tubman's extraordinary prescience. Knowledge of future events came to her in the realm of dreams. Before escaping, she once said, she dreamed of flying over fields, towns, and mountains "like a bird." In this out-of-body dream sequence, a fright-ened Tubman reaches "a great fence or sometimes a river" and despairs of surmounting the obstacle. Ladies, "all drest in white ober dere," reach out to Tubman and pull her across to safety. Sanborn comments, "There is nothing strange in this perhaps, but she declares that when she came North she remembered those very places, as those she had seen in her dreams, and many of the ladies who befriended her were those she had been helped by in her visions." Tubman told Sanborn that her ability to see into the future, whether as a forewarning of danger or a prelude to a more benign event, also had physical manifestations—"'pears like my heart go flutter, flutter, and den dey may say 'Peace, Peace' as much as dey likes. *I know its gwine to be war.*'" Tubman, according to the Sanborn ac-count, claimed that her extraordinary psychic powers had been inherited from her father. Benjamin Ross, his daughter vouchsafed, could predict the weather and had foretold the Mexican War. Sanborn let Tubman's reputation as seer and prophet stand without much speculation on its validity, other than to note the "singular" juxtaposition in her of prac-tical shrewdness (her "wit") and psychic ability (her use of dreams and visions).[5]

Bradford was of two minds regarding Tubman's fusion of traditional notions of Christian piety with the psychic powers associated with "the charm." She seems to have been genuinely awestruck that God had chosen so ordinary an instrument as Harriet Tubman to be "the Moses of her People." Though the two women spoke a religious language heavily freighted with Protestant symbolism and concepts common to the evan-gelical communities, North and South, this shared paradigm masked im-portant differences. Unlike the enslaved whom Tubman rescued, Brad-ford stood as an outsider to African American religious culture born in the interaction of African traditional rituals and beliefs and Southern white evangelicalism.

Bradford's ambivalence about Tubman's black religious self shows itself in both the 1869 and the 1886 biographies, but especially so in the

1886 volume. In *Scenes*, Bradford introduces the topic of Tubman's reliance on dreams and visions, her belief in direct messages from God, and her ability to foresee events by citing extracts from a letter she had solicited from Franklin B. Sanborn. Bradford comments: "Of the 'dreams and visions' mentioned in this letter, the writer might have given many wonderful instances; but it was thought best not to insert anything which, with any, might bring discredit upon the story. When these turns of somnolency come upon Harriet, she imagines that her "'pirit' leaves her body, and visits other scenes and places, not only in this world, but in the world of spirits. And her ideas of these scenes show, to say the least of it, a vividness of imagination seldom equaled in the soarings of the most cultivated minds."[6]

Then, in an attempt to establish common ground, Bradford relates how she herself had witnessed the more exotic side of Tubman's religiosity: "Not long since, the writer, on going into Harriet's room in the morning, sat down by her and began to read that wonderful and glorious description of the heavenly Jerusalem in the two last chapters of Revelations. When the reading was finished, Harriet burst into a rhapsody which perfectly amazed her hearer—telling of what she had seen in one of these visions, sights which no one could doubt had been real to her, and which no human imagination could have conceived, it would seem, unless in dream or vision. There was a wild poetry in these descriptions which seemed to border almost on inspiration, but by many they might be characterized as the ravings of insanity. All that can be said is, however, if this woman is insane, there has been a wonderful 'method in her madness.'"[7] It is striking that these two women, so different in life experiences, found inspiration in the apocalyptic visions portrayed in the Book of Revelations.

When Bradford came to the subject of Tubman's unorthodox mode of religious expression in the 1886 revision and expansion of her 1869 book, she seemed almost apologetic about Tubman's religious otherness:

> I hardly know how to approach the subject of the spiritual experiences of my sable heroine. They seem so to enter into the realm of the supernatural, that I can hardly wonder that those who never knew her are ready to throw discredit upon the story. Ridicule has been cast upon the whole tale of her adventures by the advocates of human slavery; and perhaps by those who would tell with awe-struck

countenance some tale of ghostly visitation, or spiritual manifestation, at a dimly lighted *"seance."* Had I not known so well her deeply
religious character, and her conscientious veracity, and had I not
since the war, and when she was an inmate of my own house, seen
such remarkable instances of what seemed to be her direct inter-
course with heaven, I should not dare to risk my own character for
veracity by making these things public in this manner.[8]

In an effort to give credence to her representation of Tubman's religious self, Bradford invoked character witnesses in the 1886 biography—
William H. Seward, Gerrit Smith, Wendell Phillips, Frederick Douglass,
and her brother, Samuel M. Hopkins. She quoted from a letter written in
1868 by Thomas Garrett that originally appeared in *Scenes*. Garrett had
written to Bradford: "In truth I never met with any person, of any color,
who had more confidence in the voice of God, as spoken direct to her
soul. She has frequently told me that she talked with God, and he talked
with her every day of her life, and she has declared to me that she felt no
more fear of being arrested by her former master, or any other person,
when in his immediate neighborhood, than she did in the State of New
York, or Canada, for she said she never ventured only where God sent
her, and her faith in a Supreme Power truly was great."[9]

Most nineteenth-century Christians believed in the power of prayer.
It was a form of talking to God. Fewer were so bold as to claim that God
talked back and gave them specific instructions. Tubman did. Sanborn
had written in 1863 that Tubman showed a "strange familiarity of communion" that seemed "natural" to African Americans.[10] In an article published in the *Chautauquan* in 1896 and written by Rosa Bell Holt after she
had conducted three interviews with the aged black heroine, Tubman is
quoted as saying: "I felt like Moses. De Lord tole me to do dis. I said, 'O,
Lord, I can't—don't ask me—take somebody else.' Den I could hear de
Lord answer, 'It's you I want, Harriet Tubman,'—jess as clar I heard him
speak—an' den I'd go agen down South an' bring up my brudders and sisters." Holt looked for larger-than-life historical figures against whom to
measure Tubman's significance and turned, as Bradford and many other
molders of the Tubman iconic tradition did, to the virginal French maid:
"So truly as Jeanne d'Arc believed in her visions did this brave colored
woman of the South."[11] Of Tubman's feeling that God had called her by
name and would protect her, Bradford employed an Old Testament meta-

phor: Her saintly heroine was "always conscious of an invisible pillar of cloud by day, and of fire by night."[12]

Do the Bradford biographies, heavily mediated as they are, contain an authentic skeletal spiritual autobiography of Tubman? Jean Humez believes that we must look to the 1869 biography instead of to the later one for an answer. She argues that Bradford's 1886 biography had "the effect of censoring aspects of Tubman's personality and politics," thereby making "Tubman's personality less salty and more saintly." Humez notes that the 1886 version lacks some of Tubman's witticisms, omits the story about her making a fool of her master by singing coded spirituals (originally on pages 17–18 in *Scenes*), and eliminates "all references to Tubman's racial politics," such as her dislike of Stowe's *Uncle Tom's Cabin* and her plan to pursue legal action after the incident in 1865 of racial discrimination on the train when returning from Washington, D.C. Concerning the reasons for domesticating Tubman, Humez says, "In fairness to Bradford, it seems likely that she censored Tubman's life story in the revision at least in part for fear of marring the image of a saintly African-American heroine that she was trying to construct for white readers in a post–Reconstruction era of virulent white racism."[13]

Humez offers us a useful perspective on the contrasting understandings of Tubman and Bradford with respect to the divine–human nexus: "The surviving sources strongly suggest that Tubman's view of the relationship of human beings to God was very different from Bradford's. Bradford seems to have seen God as being relatively remote and possessing two faces or aspects: the kind savior who welcomed the good into heaven, and the stern, intimidating judge who would ultimately punish evildoers. In contrast, Tubman's God emerges from the words attributed to her by her interviewers as a single figure, an approachable partner and unfailing support for those who were righting wrongs. God was her name for the source of visionary guidance for her antislavery action. Prayer enabled her to tap directly into the source of such guidance."[14] Tubman's sense of a personal God, immanent and accessible, correlates well with evidence found in many ex-slaves' accounts of their religious conversions and in the spiritual autobiographies of other African American women of the nineteenth century, such as Jarena Lee, Rebecca Jackson, and Amanda Smith.[15] Visionary experiences, an extensive dream language, a belief in an immanent and personal deity, and notions of having the "charm" have also been associated with black revolutionaries such as Nat Turner and Gabriel Prosser.[16]

Though Bradford acknowledged Tubman's other religious self, rooted in the "invisible institution" of the pre–Civil War period, when the enslaved gathered secretly to sing and pray and dance, she, like Sanborn, thought of it as peculiar to "the race." Northerners, black and white, were sometimes mystified by the folk religious culture that they encountered when attempting to aid the contrabands during the Civil War and the emancipated thereafter. Charlotte Forten, for instance, had difficulty in gaining the confidence of contrabands in the Sea Islands region. A member of a prominent Philadelphia black family, Forten resisted total immersion into the folk culture of ex-salves.[17] Tubman seems to have felt more of an affinity with the religious worldview and practices of Southern blacks. Though Tubman told Bradford that she had difficulty understanding the language of the Gullah people she met during her years as a nurse, spy, and scout in the coastal areas of South Carolina, she joined in singing their camp-meeting hymns, attended their funerals and experience meetings, and paid sufficient attention to Gullah forms of preaching and dancing to able to imitate them for Bradford years later.[18]

Bradford's portrayal of Tubman as pious Christian par excellence is a well-meaning biographical fabrication and not a clear window through which we can view Tubman's inner spiritual self. Humez describes Bradford's portrayal of Tubman "a partial, mediated spiritual autobiography, whose meaning is contested by two women who, though politically allied and sharing a respect for spiritual life, have clearly different understandings of God, and of the relationship of human and divine in history."[19] To Bradford's credit, she created space in her symbolic re-presentation of Tubman for Tubman's religious voice, a voice we hear despite the filtering device that a mediated biography inevitably becomes. Sarah Bradford may have deemphasized Tubman's black religious roots, but she fairly presented her heroine to potential readers as a deeply religious person and conveyed as best she could something of the dream world Tubman accessed without dismissing this aspect of her heroine's personality out of hand.

In contrast, Earl Conrad, Tubman's second major biographer, attempted to explain Tubman's visionary experiences away. He speculated that Tubman's dream life was somehow connected to the fits of somnolence she experienced. These sleeping attacks, as Conrad called them, were reported and in some cases witnessed by many of Tubman's friends and allies. Bradford had written of Tubman's penchant for falling asleep at odd times, even while in conversation with a potential supporter, without attributing her sleeping attacks to her head injury. Conrad made the link and looked to twentieth-century medicine for an explanation of Tubman's visions and psychic abilities. He felt that the blow to the head she that suffered could account for her narcolepsy, those bouts of deep sleep that were often accompanied by visionary experiences.[20]

Conrad sent inquiries to a number of prominent hospitals and research institutions during 1939 when he was working on the manuscript for his 1943 biography of Tubman. Typically, he began his letters by describing the incident when Harriet, at about thirteen, was struck on the head, with the result, so Conrad thought, that her skull was fractured. He wrote to authorities at the Battle Creek Sanitarium in Battle Creek, Michigan:

> From about this time on she suffered fits of somnolence, or sleeping attacks, if you call them such. She would be taken with these seizures two or three times a day, and they would last for varying short periods, perhaps a half hour or an hour. She would fall into a comatose state. Whether this was a sound sleep or semi-sleep, or whether it was varied and was either at various times, I do not know. But one of the results of the sickness was that she developed a very extensive dream life. These dreams she would relate to the people about her, and she began to present them as visions, and she gave vent to expressions of forebodings, omens, warnings and signs of this sort. She was generally disregarded, and was considered to be "touched in the head."[21]

Though Conrad acknowledged that religious-minded people of Tubman's day, including leading abolitionists, took Tubman's dream life seriously and that she regarded her visions as God-sent, he was not ready to do so. "For myself," he informed the medical experts, "not believing in the supernatural and knowing also that the measurement of the woman must finally rest upon her deeds rather than upon her visions, I have a normal layman's view about the origin and development of her dream life."[22]

Dr. W. H. Riley of the Battle Creek Sanitarium responded to Conrad's query. He began with a caveat, explaining: "It is quite impossible for a physician to make a positive diagnosis of a case that he has not had the opportunity of examining." Riley held the opinion that Tubman's symptoms—which he described as somnolence, dreams, hallucinations, and delusional ideas—might have been caused by the effects of the "trying and unpleasant life which she had as a slave" and "the injury which she received to the head." The narcolepsy, he speculated, could have been symptomatic of "hysteria"—"a real disease." As to Tubman's dream life, Riley thought that it arose during the second stage of the sleep cycle, when one is not sleeping soundly. As to Tubman's "so-called hallucinations and delusional ideas," Riley speculated that that these might be symptomatic of dementia praecox or schizophrenia, though he was reluctant to confirm such a diagnosis, lacking "a proper examination and x-rays of the head."[23] Conrad accepted Riley's suggestions that Tubman suffered from narcolepsy and that her dream life was somehow related to "her difficult past," but he balked at the notion that she might have been schizophrenic. He wrote Riley on August 14, 1939, "I think that in my letter to you I completely overstated the mystical quality in this woman and completely omitted mention that she was regarded all through her period of activity and contribution as the sanest possible person."[24] Riley responded by withdrawing his earlier suggestion that Tubman suffered from any serious mental disease.[25]

During the period when Conrad and Riley were exchanging letters, Conrad was also corresponding with Dr. Louis Casamajor of the Neurological Institute in New York City. A psychiatrist of national prominence, Casamajor was unwilling to give a diagnosis, given the paucity of data, but he doubted that Tubman's dream life was a byproduct of narcolepsy, which he termed "real sleep." "The patient," he told Conrad, "is entirely unconscious while in the attack and I have never seen one who had any dreams during this period." Casamajor suggested an alternative explanation—something he called a hysterical twilight state, which, so he claimed, may or may not be related to drowsiness and could last from a few seconds up to several weeks.[26]

In the end, Conrad excluded references to his efforts to seek an explanation for Tubman's sleeping fits and related dream life in his 1943 biography of her, though he frequently referred to his account as the "definitive" book about her. His failure to extract a convincing medical or psychological diagnosis from those whom he contacted at a half-dozen prominent hospitals and research centers may have dissuaded him.

He also had reason to refrain from probing too deeply into Tubman's psychohistory because of his desire not to present her in a fashion that would detract from the public's willingness to view her as the greatest woman in American history. He was also aware of how important religion was to black Americans, especially those who, like Tubman, drew from the wellspring of Southern folk culture. Though Conrad was himself a self-proclaimed agnostic in matters religious, it would not do to cast aspersions on Tubman's religiosity, no matter that secularists and skeptics might consider it a relic of the prescientific age. Many of Tubman's admirers, certainly many black Christians, still lived within the framework of the "ol' time religion." They would not accept a book that discredited their belief in a God who answered prayer directly, in the religious import of dreams and visions, and in periods of altered consciousness in which individuals are said to be possessed by the Holy Spirit.

Nevertheless, Conrad did not want to portray Tubman as a kind of "exotic," a racialized and stereotypical female Uncle Tom, overly pious and subject to haunts and conjure. In correspondence with Alice Brickler, who introduced herself to Conrad as the daughter of Harriet Tubman's "favorite niece," Conrad downplayed the religious factor, stating that "it was by no means the important thing" about Tubman.[27] Brickler responded, alarmed at the prospect of any portrayal of Harriet that neglected her religious core: "I may be wrong but I believe that every age, every country and every race, especially during the darkest history, has had its unusual Souls who were in touch with some mysterious central originating Force, a comprehensive stupendous Unity for which we have no adequate name. Aunt Harriet was one of those unusual souls. Her religion, her dreams or visions were so bond together that nobody, and I certainly should not attempt it, could separate them." Brickler reminded Conrad that her great-aunt had been "a member of an oppressed race" and, as such, she depended on "the inspiration of the mystic as well as sagacity." "It was her dreams which saved her life often," Brickler observed, "and it was her superhuman courage and beliefs which gave her the power to accomplish what she had undertaken." Brickler admitted that she herself was not "over-religious" and so had simply referred to Tubman as having been in communication with "a mysterious Force, a Unity"—but Tubman called it "God's voice which spoke to her in a dream and she never failed to obey the Master."[28]

Conrad responded to Brickler's attempt to reinsert an emphasis on her great-aunt's dependence on a higher spiritual power with a long letter on the dangers of doing so. To his way of thinking, attributing Tubman's brave deeds to a belief in God would detract from her greatness. "God," he lectured Brickler, "is too often given credit for achievements when human beings, who receive too little out of life, should receive such credit." Conrad, a close student of radical and left-wing politics of the Marxist-inspired labor movement during the 1930s, wanted to write the biography of an extraordinary woman who drew her inspiration from an oppressed people. If he were to interpret her achievements as the result of her trust and belief in God, he would, so he told Brickler, be writing "the biography of a Supreme Being." Writing in March 1940 during World War Two, Conrad pressed the ironies of history on Brickler: "All causes have tried to claim god was on their side. The south claimed that the bible justified slavery; and the north said that the bible justified them. Kaiser Wilhelm said, 'Gott mitt me [sic]," and now Hitler says God is with him and Chamberlain also invokes god, the church, and the bible." Then, his Marxist politics showing, the young white journalist told the black woman who had reminded him of the importance of religion to the oppressed: "God is a piece of heavy artillery, employed by the rich to keep the poor content, satisfied, unrebellious, unmoving."[29] Brickler responded to what she called Conrad's "spirited disapproval" of her opinions about the source of "the duration of Aunt Harriet's power" with a patient and charitable "I will not 'parley with thee' but I can hardly wait to read your book."[30]

The extant Conrad-Brickler correspondence does not reveal what Alice Brickler thought of Earl Conrad's treatment of religion in *Harriet Tubman* after it was published in the fall of 1943. As the absence in the book of any serious discussion of how religion, especially in its Southern and black folk manifestations, motivated Tubman demonstrates, Conrad failed to follow Brickler's counsel. Where Conrad does admit "religion" into the biography, he does so by redefining it. For example, at one point Conrad tells of young Harriet's prayer that God convert her master (Edward Brodess): "'And so,' she said, 'from Christmas until March (probably of the years 1835–36) I worked as I could, and I prayed through all the long nights—I groaned and prayed for old master. Oh Lord, convert master! Oh Lord, change that man's heart.'" Conrad comments: "Her prayer at that time is one of the most revealing in the annals of religion, or more correctly, in the history of practical revolutionary thinking."[31] When Tubman prays in Conrad's book, it is a political act, and when she dreams, it is in the figurative sense, not as one gifted with unusual psychic powers. About the most that Conrad could say about Tubman was that she acquired the "*applied* religion" common to Nat Turner, Denmark Vesey, Cato, and the other black revolutionaries of antebellum America. Her salvation was to be in the emancipation of her people and not, Conrad implies, at the hand of God.[32]

What Conrad missed and Bradford sought to domesticate belongs to the prophetic and visionary strand within African American religion sometimes associated with the belief that certain individuals are born with unusual seer-like powers. Nat Turner, for example, was said to have been born with the caul, a sign of extraordinary religious abilities.[33] Whether we are talking about Tubman's "spiritual gift of protective foresight," to use Humez's apt phrase, or the many expressions of trust and belief in God that are attributed to her, Harriet Tubman cannot be understood in a holistic way if, like Conrad, we dismiss the subject of religion or rob Tubman of her core spirituality.

Understanding Tubman's spiritual self is complicated by the blurring of two representations of her: seer and saint. The saintly image invokes notions of someone with a deep trust in God who is credited with living a pious life dedicated to helping others. This was Bradford's iconic use of the Tubman image. Other authors emphasize Tubman's psychic powers, such as foreseeing the future or having the mental ability to keep danger away. These are seer-like skills. James A. McGowan is one of the few Tubman scholars to consider the question of Tubman's psychic abilities seriously. He argues that the first public manifestation of Tubman's psychic abilities most likely occurred in the fall of 1848, after Tubman was hit on the head by that two-pound weight, a blow that, according to Bradford, broke Tubman's skull. McGowan wrote in 1995:

> The onset of Harriet Tubman's psychic life parallels that of other well-known, contemporary, psychics. For example, like Peter Hurkos, the Dutch psychometrist, Harriet Tubman's psychic experiences began to manifest after she received a severe blow on the head from which she almost died. Parapsychological records are replete with similar cases in which individuals began experiencing and

manifesting psychic awareness after head injuries, some after being struck by lightening, others after undergoing prolonged periods of intense fever.[34]

McGowan believed that the psychic powers attributed to Tubman are an important aspect of her life and cites Sanborn's comment, which appeared in the *Springfield Republican*, that no biography about her should be written that does not mention them.[35] As to the analogy Sarah Bradford and dozens of others have drawn between Tubman and Joan of Arc, McGowan says: "Writers are mistaken in their belief that this resemblance to Joan of Arc was that, like Joan of Arc, Harriet Tubman led men into battle. The resemblance is that, like Joan of Arc, Harriet Tubman *heard voices* and had *visions*." He also points out that many nineteenth-century Americans trafficked in spiritualism, including Harriet Beecher Stowe and Abraham Lincoln. Spiritualists were especially active in up-state New York's old Burned-Over District.[36]

Tubman did not distinguish between seer and saint. She seems to have believed that her trust in the Lord enabled her to meet all of life's exigencies with a confident foreknowledge of how things would turn out, a habit that others found impressive, or uncanny, as the case may be. Bradford tells of having once gone to see Tubman in Auburn to deliver supplies to her. Tubman was already very old, but her house, "always neat and comfortable," with a small parlor that was "nicely and rather prettily furnished," sheltered some of those whom Tubman was providing for, despite her age and poverty (Figure 36). Bradford recounted this surprise call on Tubman in 1901 when a new edition of her 1886 biography was published. "The lame, the halt, and the blind, the bruised and crippled little children, and one crazy woman, were all brought in to see me," Bradford reported, "and 'the blind woman' (she seemed to have no other name), a very old woman who had been in Harriet's care for eighteen years, was led into the room—an interesting and pathetic group." When Bradford was about to depart, Tubman accompanied her as far as her carriage and was given the provisions. Tubman, or "Aunt Harriet," as she was being called, turned to one of her dependents and, according to Bradford's recollections, asked, "What did you say to me dis mornin'? You said, 'We hadn't got noting' to eat in de house,' and what did I say to you? I said, 'I've got a rich Father!'" Bradford editorialized: "Nothing [that] comes to this remarkable woman ever surprises her. She says very little in

36. Photograph of Harriet Tubman and seven dependents, circa 1887. From left to right: Harriet Tubman, Gertie Davis (adopted daughter), Nelson Davis, Lee Cheney, "Pop" Alexander, Walter Green, "Blind" Aunty (Sarah) Parker, and grandniece Dora Stewart. Florence Woolsey Hazzard Papers, 1819–1976. Collection number 2516. Division of Rare and Manuscript Collections, 2B Carl A. Kroch Library, Cornell University, Ithaca, New York. Courtesy Division of Rare and Manuscript Collections, Cornell University Library.

the way of thanks, except to the Giver of all good. How the knowledge comes to her no one can tell, but she seems always to know when help is coming, and she is generally on hand to receive it, though it is never for herself she wants it, but only for those under her care."[37]

Tubman is said to have had little concern for material goods, except as they might be of use to those she cared for. When her larder of supplies dwindled, she would make the rounds of her white friends in Auburn seeking donations. Armed with dignity and perseverance, she asked for help on behalf of those she cared for without sham humility. Emma Paddock Telford said in a tribute to Tubman written in 1914, "While Harriet never begged for herself, the cause of the needy at once sent her out with a basket on her arm to the kitchen of her friends, and this without a shadow of hesitancy. She always took thankfully, but never effusively, whatever was given her. 'I tell de Lawd what I needs,' she used to say, 'an he provides.'"[38]

Tubman's reputed seer-like ability to know in advance of some time-bound event failed her on one occasion. Aunt Harriet was flimflammed. In October 1873, two black men called on John Stewart, one of Harriet Tubman's brothers. Stewart, a teamster at D. M. Osborne and Company, lived near the old tollgate house of the Auburn–Fleming Plank Road Company, not far from his sister. The strangers told Stewart that they knew of an ex-slave who had brought a trunk of gold pieces, totaling nearly five thousand dollars, to the vicinity of Auburn from South Carolina. The ex-slave, so they said, wanted to exchange the gold pieces for greenbacks because he did not trust whites. Stewart suggested that they visit his sister, as she might be able to raise the money from her white friends. Harriet gave the strangers lodging and then sought to borrow two thousand dollars from Charles P. Wood of the Auburn Savings Bank and several other white supporters. Help eventually came, but not from Tubman's circle of friends. Auburn residents knew Anthony Shimer as the "tramp millionaire." He operated a jewelry business at the corner of State and Genesee streets and bought and sold real estate. He also owned the Casey Opera House, which he filled with a collection of miscellaneous items—Shimer's treasure but junk to others. Always on the lookout for a fast profit, Shimer obtained two thousand dollars in cash from the First National Bank.

On the afternoon of October 1, 1873, Shimer; Tubman and her husband, Nelson Davis; John Stewart; Charles O' Brien, a cashier at First

National Bank; and one of the swindlers, who called himself Johnson, went in search of the man with the gold. At Smith's Corners (now Poplar Ridge) south of Auburn, the party of six registered at a tavern. Then Tubman and Johnson set out to meet the "gold man." They found him and his trunk near some woods. The "gold man" claimed he had forgotten the key, and he and Johnson left Harriet alone. Tubman became frightened, "thinking," as she later said, "of the stories about ghosts haunting buried treasures." A cow roaming the woods startled her. When the "gold man" returned, he chloroformed, bound, and gagged Tubman and took the greenbacks. She managed to roll and crawl back to the tavern. Tubman was then taken to the Slocum Howard home in Sherwood, where she recovered. Shimer lost his money. The flimflam men escaped. Tubman was embarrassed. None of her psychic powers had prevented her victimization in what was to become known as the "gold swindle."[39]

Nevertheless, accounts of this episode cast no aspersions on Tubman's saintly character. She is said to have been motivated not by personal greed but by a desire to obtain funds to create a Home for the Aged and Indigent Negroes (Figure 37). She was apparently operating a care facility on a modest scale by this time, probably in the brick residence on the smaller parcel, but she may already have been thinking about obtaining more land and a larger building.

Tubman's saintly character, her reputation for altruism, and her close relationship with God has been an enduring part of her legacy. Authors writing in the field of Christian literature hold her up as the model of someone who trusted God implicitly, an ordinary person who was willing to sacrifice everything for others. She has been canonized in some circles as a Christian saint and role model to the dispirited and the doubting.[40] Secular authors—that is to say, authors without a specifically religious agenda or audience in mind—have likewise invoked Tubman to motivate readers, especially young readers, to be brave, to care for others, and to be true to their values.[41]

The iconic image of Tubman as gifted with extraordinary psychic abilities has had its own proponents.[42] Anthony Shafton refers to Tubman's psychic gift as prophetic dreaming. He cites the story of her calm reaction to the announcement of the Emancipation Proclamation in 1863, saying that she had foreseen the moment and had celebrated in her own way three years earlier. Shafton advises that we distinguish between the psychic and the spiritual in light of the plethora of self-proclaimed

37. The Harriet Tubman Home for the Aged, circa 1908. From James E. Mason and E. U. A. Brooks, *Tribute to Harriet Tubman, the Modern Amazon*, pamphlet,1915, Earl Conrad Collection, Norman F. Bourke Memorial Library, Cayuga Community College, Auburn, New York.

psychics, celebrity and otherwise, in business today. He attempts to link Tubman's gift with the African American tradition of believing in dreams and visions, which he claims is rooted in the African practice of divination.[43] Tubman's dream life has marketing potential today. A website promoting Robert Moss's "Dream School Course in Active Dreaming" seeks clients by invoking the name of Tubman as one of the great dreamers in human history who can inspire others.[44]

Tubman's symbolic visibility and usefulness as Black Moses and General Tubman weakened during her long Auburn period. In the post–Reconstruction years, with so many of her abolitionist and Underground Railroad allies gone from the scene, most Americans had little interest in the black freedom fighter of old. Bradford's 1886 revised biography muted Tubman's more radical self and presented her primarily as a woman of deep Christian piety, albeit one given to dreams and visions. The spiritualization of the Tubman symbol tended to divorce it from the political questions of the day. What utility did Black Moses or General Tubman have for a nation dominated by the consensus, North and South, that African Americans should accommodate to Jim Crow? There was, however, one cause for which Tubman could still be invoked, one movement for which she could serve as symbol and inspiration.

Perhaps the most popular image today of Tubman to come out of her post–Civil War years is that of her as an American suffragist and, by extension, women's rights activist. Tubman's gender has become a highly negotiable commodity in contemporary feminist politics, but the symbolic use of her as a woman who battled against the restrictions placed on women in her day is complicated by the factor of race. Some black feminists have resented what they consider to be the misappropriation of Tubman by white feminists. These overlapping and sometimes conflicting symbolic uses of Tubman can be better understood if we examine how she was related to the nineteenth-century suffrage movement.

The New York State Woman Suffrage Association met in Rochester, New York, on November 18, 1896, to hold its twenty-eighth annual meeting. The suffrage color of yellow dominated the YMCA where the women assembled. Palms and an American flag adorned the rostrum. According to a report in Rochester's *Democrat and Chronicle*:

> Certainly the most picturesque, if not the most interesting incident of the afternoon's meeting was the appearance on the rostrum of Susan B. Anthony, the veteran worker of political emancipation for women, leading by the hand an old colored woman. Miss Anthony introduced her as Mrs. Harriet Tubman, a faithful worker for the emancipation of her race, who had reason to revere President Lincoln. The old woman was once a slave, and as she stood before the assemblage in her cheap black gown and coat, and big black straw bonnet without adornment, her hand held in Miss Anthony's, she impressed one with the venerable dignity of her appearance. Her face was very black, with her race characteristics, but through it all there shows an honesty and true benevolence of purpose which commanded respect. She bowed modestly as Miss Anthony presented her, and when she commenced to speak, her voice low and tremulous at first, rose gradually as she warmed to her subject, till it was plainly heard throughout the hall.[45]

If this press report is a full and accurate account of the proceedings that day, Tubman did not make a suffrage speech. Instead, at the invitation of Anthony (Figure 38), she told about her escape from slavery, of her adventures as an Underground Railroad conductor, and of how she had

38. Susan B. Anthony (bottom left), among "Representative Women" of the suffrage and women's rights movement. Courtesy Library of Congress, LC/DIG-ppmsca-08978.

39. Carrie Chapman Catt. Courtesy Library of Congress, LC/USZ62-109793.

ministered to the wounded during the Civil War. Of Tubman's situation in 1896, the journalist said: "The old woman, who can neither read nor write, has still a mission, which is the moral advancement of her race. She makes her home in Auburn, but depends on the kindness of friends to assist her, by a dollar now and then, or a bed, or a meal, as she travels from place to place."[46]

Ignoring the fact that Tubman did not speak about suffrage, Conrad interpreted Tubman's presence at the Rochester meeting as a high-water mark in the long struggle for women's rights. In an article published in 1940, he said that when Anthony led Tubman to the rostrum on that November day in 1896, it was "a moment of significant history in suffrage annals, for here in simultaneous appearance was the greatest white woman in national history and the most important black woman of all time."[47] Conrad's effort to uncover Tubman's connections to the suffrage campaign—and, by extension, to the women's rights movement of the nineteenth century—proved more difficult than he had anticipated. The problem of where to place Tubman in the annals of great suffragists surfaced in correspondence Conrad had with Carrie Chapman Catt (Figure 39) in 1939. Catt had devoted herself to developing the Iowa Woman Suffrage Association until succeeding Susan B. Anthony in 1900 as president of National American Woman Suffrage Association.

The National American Woman Suffrage Association (NAWSA), founded in 1890, united two rival groups that been in conflict since 1869 when the American Equal Rights Association (AERA) split. Abolitionists and advocates of enhancing the political rights of women had established the AERA in 1866 to push for political rights for blacks and women. In the struggle over the passage of the Fifteenth Amendment, some of the organization's strategists decided to focus on suffrage for black men, believing that it was the "Negro's Hour." The old abolition–feminist alliance broke apart. Lucy Stone led the majority of the suffragists into the Boston-based American Woman Suffrage Association (AWSA). Elizabeth Cady Stanton and Susan B. Anthony refused to support the Fifteenth Amendment, since it applied to black men only, and formed the National Woman Suffrage Association (NWSA), which was dedicated to women's suffrage alone. These feminists, writes Wendy Hammand Venet, "would narrow their focus to white, middle-class issues, leaving aside their earlier altruistic rhetoric about justice and equality for all and their plans to reform the whole of American society."[48] When Carrie Chapman Catt assumed Susan B. Anthony's mantle of leadership of the reunited organization in 1900, Harriet Tubman was already in her declining years.

Operating under the assumption that Tubman had played an important role in the suffrage and women's rights movements, Conrad wrote to Catt in 1939 asking for her recollections. Catt responded, "I was rather amazed at your letter for, so far as I can recall, I never heard of Harriet Tubman. That does not prove that she was not a great woman."[49] Catt did remember that Sojourner Truth, "a very pious woman," spoke at the old Women's Rights conventions. She told Conrad that she had checked the *History of Woman Suffrage* and had not found Tubman's name in the index.[50] She did not know about Bradford's books about Tubman. On June 8, 1939, Catt wrote to Conrad, "What you tell me is very interesting, but I do not think you have quite evidence enough to show her great importance in the movement when, in the whole record of the campaigns of her day, there seems to be no mention of her."[51] Conrad persisted, informing Catt that Oswald Garrison Villard recalled that Tubman had spoken on the same platform in the women's rights campaign as had his mother.[52]

Then in August, Conrad made a discovery that he thought proved that Tubman belonged in the suffragist hall of fame. He had just found Susan B. Anthony's copy of Bradford's *Harriet, the Moses of Her People* in the rare books division of the Library of Congress. It contained the following inscription:

> This most wonderful woman—Harriet Tubman—is still alive. I saw her but the other day at the beautiful home of Eliza Wright Osborne, the daughter of Martha C. Wright, in company with Elizabeth Smith Miller, the only daughter of Gerrit Smith, Miss Emily Howland, Rev. Anna K. Shaw, and Mrs. Ella [Ellen] Wright Garrison, the daughter of Martha C. Wright and the wife of Wm. Lloyd Garrison, Jr. All of us were visiting at the Osbornes, a real love feast of the few that are left and here came Harriet Tubman. Susan B. Anthony, 17 Madison Street, Rochester, N.Y., Jan. 1, 1903.[53]

Conrad was elated, but Catt was not yet convinced. She responded by telling Conrad that in "strict truth" she had never heard of Tubman and did not think that "she had much, if anything, to do with the woman suffrage movement." As to the gathering in Auburn referred to in Anthony's note, Catt said: "This party at Mrs. Osborne's home, I should say, was held in memory of the earlier period when all of them had been workers. They had all been interested in the Underground Railway movement. I think their connection with Mrs. Tubman was through that enterprise and they probably invited her to the Women's Rights meetings and she came, but I do not think she did anything in particular."[54]

Conrad was not ready to let go of his belief that Tubman deserved a place of honor in any memorialization of the women's rights movement. He informed Catt that Alice Stone Blackwell remembered Tubman stopping in at the offices of the *Woman's Journal*, launched by Stone in 1870, on one of her trips to Boston.[55] Catt replied that, yes, it was possible that Tubman had been more connected to the American wing (Lucy Stone's AWSA) than with Anthony's NWSA.[56] Catt, sounding irritated, responded to Conrad by asking that he leave out her name in any publication he intended about Tubman's relationship to the women's rights movement, "because, to tell the truth, I had never heard of Harriet Tubman when you first wrote me." Catt told Conrad that she and Anthony had once gone on a trip together to the South. They had talked about the Underground Railroad and of the "early days," but Anthony had not mentioned Tubman. Catt summed up:

Harriet Tubman undoubtedly agreed with the proposition of the women to gain the vote, but her idea was far away from that as an aim. She did not assist the suffragists or the woman suffrage movement at any time. It was they who were attempting to assist her. That much I know from the nature of things and to make Harriet Tubman a leader in the woman suffrage movement and in all other good movements is quite wrong. There was no leadership on the part of the colored people at that time and there is very little even now. I have not the slightest doubt that she did good things and I hope you can get a good deal of information about her, but do not try to make her what she was not.[57]

Conrad was stunned. He lectured Catt about having so categorically "dismissed a remarkable woman, together with a whole people."[58] Catt held to her conviction that Tubman had not played a key role in the old women's rights organizations and that her presence at the home of Elizabeth Wright Osborne in Auburn did not signify "any leadership on her part." Then, as a way of closing off the conversation with Conrad about the merits of the case, Catt wrote, "I do not wish to be understood as opposed to the fame of Harriet Tubman. I only say that I am not yet convinced."[59]

Conrad's attempt to evoke strong recollections of Tubman from the descendants and ideological heirs of activists in the suffrage and feminist movements went poorly. Lucy E. Anthony, niece of Susan B. Anthony, told him, "Harriet Tubman is just a name to me which I just remember Aunt Susan's mentioning from time to time."[60] Alice Stone Blackwell did remember Tubman coming into the Boston headquarters of the *Woman's Journal* in Boston. Her memory, however, did not substantiate what Conrad wanted (and had conveyed to Catt). "I think her connection with my mother," wrote Blackwell, "had probably been along anti-Slavery, rather than Woman Suffrage lines."[61] Conrad had earlier admitted to Blackwell, "I have heard from Carrie Chapman Catt, Harriet Stanton Blatch and others, but none of these has been able to add very much to my understanding of her [Tubman's] suffrage contribution."[62]

Despite these difficulties in obtaining confirmation of his belief that Harriet Tubman had been an important figure in the suffrage movement from veterans of the cause, Conrad proceeded to portray Tubman in that light. He sought to enlist the aid of Eleanor Roosevelt and wrote to her:

"Harriet's story is the story of American womanhood from bondage to suffrage, as well as the story of the emancipation of her own race."[63] Yet in the book-length biography of Tubman that was finally published in 1943, Conrad depicts Tubman as having a supporting and not central role. Catt seems to have dissuaded Conrad from making too much of Tubman's alleged suffragist contributions. On April 2, 1940, he wrote to Catt:

> In closing, for the time being, I would say again that we must not judge Harriet as a suffragist, but as a woman of the war. Harriet was essentially a revolutionist. As a revolutionist I believe that she had no other American woman equal. The suffragists were revolutionaries too, and Susan Anthony's periodical, "The Revolution," was correctly named. But Harriet knew that type of activity which we call work in the Underground; she had at least ten years of this type of activity in the Underground Railroad. That was a tremendous movement and to be the symbol of it is to have a place in American history.[64]

In the 1943 biography, Conrad tells of the breakup of the old AERA, but he acknowledges that no definitive answer can be given to the question of where Tubman stood in the dispute. He was sure of one thing: Despite Anthony's serious error in separating the suffrage cause from that of black rights, Tubman "did not doubt the essential, the honest, the great Susan B. Anthony."[65] Conrad may well have had in mind something that Tubman told Anne Fitzhugh Miller, granddaughter of Gerrit Smith and a feminist in her own right, during a visit Miller made to Tubman in 1911.[66] James B. Clarke, an African American student from Cornell University who was promoting a building fund for the Harriet Tubman Home for the Aged, recorded Tubman's response to a comment Miller made about once seeing Tubman at a suffrage convention in Rochester. "Yes," said Tubman, "I belonged to Miss Sus'n B. Antony's 'sociation." Miller had come on behalf of the Geneva Political Equality Club to see the legend living in the little house south of Auburn. What ensued, insofar as Clarke accurately recorded it, was an interchange that reflected both Miller's attempt to capitalize on Tubman's fame for her organization, as well as Tubman's attempt to cooperate, and yet maintain something of her own voice. Miller begins by telling Tubman:

I should like to enroll you as a life member of our Geneva Club. Our motto is Lincoln's declaration: "I go for all sharing the privileges of the government who assist in bearing its burdens, by no means excluding women." You certainly have assisted in bearing the burden. Do you really believe that women should vote?"

Aunt Harriet paused a moment as if surprised at this question, then quietly replied, "I suffered enough to believe it."

When Miss Miller asked her full name she answered in solemnly measured tones, "Harriet Tubman Davis."

"Shall I write it with or without Mrs.?"

"Anyway you like, jus' so you git der *Tubman*," the old woman responded.

Clarke appended an editorial note to this interchange between the elderly black woman and the young white feminist: "Aunt Harriet proved by this answer that she is a good suffragette and an independent, self-assertive woman."[67]

The iconic identification of Tubman with feminist issues, variously defined, has been one of the most enduring aspects of the symbolic use of the Tubman life. It began, as we have observed, when the white suffragists tried to claim her as one of their own in her declining years. At least one contemporary author has argued that Tubman was instrumental in the founding of the women's rights campaign. Tubman is said to have helped drive white middle-class women in the 1840s to "face reality" and fight for their rights.[68] This assertion ignores the fact that Tubman did not escape from Maryland and slavery until 1849 and did not appear on any public platform where the issue of women's rights was being debated until many years later.

Another point of contention arises as to whether or not white feminists ought to be appropriating historical black figures for symbolic purposes. The African American author Alice Childress has commented on this tendency: "Harriet Tubman and Sojourner Truth spoke out for the rights of all people. Look at Sojourner Truth's speech, 'Ain't I a Woman?' She wasn't invited to the suffragist meeting as a speaker. Neither was Harriet Tubman. They used to attend the meetings and talk from the floor. Now they are quoting them as if they were invited as speakers. They spoke from the audience."[69] Tubman did not, as Childress would have us believe, always "talk from the floor." She was on occasion invited

I Sell the Shadow to Support the Substance.
SOJOURNER TRUTH.

40. Sojourner Truth, "I Sell the Shadow to Support the Substance." Courtesy Library of Congress, LC/DIG-ppmsca-08978.

to the rostrum. Nevertheless, Childress has a point. White suffragists have been willing to employ Tubman as an emblem, to extract capital, as it were, from the legendary conductor of the Underground Railroad. Yet, as the historian Rosalyn Terborg-Penn has pointed out, African American women often found themselves put in subsidiary roles by white suffragist leaders during the long struggle for equality at the polls.[70] This seems to have been the case with Tubman. When Anthony took her in hand and escorted her to the stage at that Rochester convention, it was a symbolic gesture, not a substantive step forward in giving black women a voice in organizational leadership.

Sojourner Truth (Figure 40), more so than Harriet Tubman, has become the principal icon of feminist reconstructions of the place black women occupied in the struggle for the rights of women. Carrie Chapman Catt informed Conrad that she had never heard of Harriet Tubman. But of Truth, Catt wrote in 1939, "There was a colored woman, who went by the name of Sojourner Truth, who was quite immortalized by the things said about her and the same should have been true about Harriet Tubman if she was as important as you tell me."[71] No aspect of Truth's life has become more of a staple in discourse about issues of gender today than the speech she is reported to have given at a women's rights convention in Akron, Ohio, in 1851.

The speech, in which Truth is alleged to have confronted those at the assembly who attempted to prevent a black woman from speaking with the question "Ain't I a Woman?" does not appear in the 1850 edition of the *Narrative of Sojourner Truth*, for which Olive Gilbert was the amanuensis.[72] The historians Carleton Mabee and Susan Mabee Newhouse have demonstrated persuasively that Frances D. Gage, the presiding officer of the convention, writing some twelve years after the Akron meeting, was most responsible for what has been inaccurately attributed to Truth. After a detailed examination of the Akron convention and the speech, Mabee and Newhouse concluded, "Unless evidence to the contrary turns up, we have to regard Gage's account of Truth's asking the 'Ar'n't I woman?' question as folklore, like the story of George Washington and the cherry tree. It may be suitable for telling to children, but not for serious understanding of Sojourner Truth and her times."[73]

Folklore, especially when it is useful in political struggles, does not yield easily to fact. The symbolic use of the image of a strong black woman turning the tide at that Akron convention, overcoming both racism and sexism and having her say, continues as if Truth had in fact asked the famous question. For example, the illustrated history based on the documentary film by Ken Burns and Paul Barnes about the women's rights crusade, *Not for Ourselves Alone*, published in 1999, includes a sidebar containing an image of Truth under the caption "Ain't I a Woman?" The text reads as if Carleton Mabee and Susan Mabee Newhouse, Nel Painter, and other demythologizers of the Akron legend had not been consulted.[74] Equally puzzling are those instances where authors, knowing of the revisionist scholarship, have elected to hang on to the legend. Deborah Gray White wrote a well-received scholarly examination of female slaves in the plantation South, first published in 1985 under the title *Ar'n't I a Woman?* It opened with Truth taking the podium at the Akron women's rights convention and, during her speech, asking the question that became her signature.[75] Thirteen years later, in an essay written for a revised edition of her book, White acknowledged that "aspects of the mythology's dismantling have been disquieting. Most unsettling perhaps is the documented revelation that Sojourner Truth did not stand before the 1851 Akron, Ohio, Woman's Rights convention and ask the penetrating question "Ar'nt I a Woman?" Nevertheless, White begins the revised edition of her book by using the old story, explaining, "If I were writing *Ar'n't I a Woman?* today I would still use that discredited speech as theoretical grounding, but I would also use the significant body of new work on difference and black female consciousness."[76] Old myths die hard, especially those that can be parlayed into political capital.

Tubman and Truth have been, as Boyd B. Stutler told Earl Conrad back in 1939, "curiously jumbled" in the American memory.[77] Both suffered under slavery; both were female, black, and illiterate, and reputedly expressed a "simple faith." Both worked as nurses among the contrabands during and after the Civil War. Most significant for our purposes, both women were subjects of mediated biographies. Olive Gilbert portrayed Truth in 1850 as an "aging child of nature," rooted in a preindustrial and prescientific worldview.[78] Sarah Bradford forged the iconic image of Tubman as the God-sent deliverer of her people in *Scenes*. Bradford's *Moses* muted the earlier portrayal of a radical agent of freedom by overlaying an image of the extraordinarily pious Tubman. Tubman and Truth had other commonalities, including a propensity for visionary experiences and skill in the use of orature. Both are said to have "grounded gendered black power in the vitality of the working woman."[79] Nell Irvin Painter, author of a richly textured and insightful analysis of Truth the person and Truth the symbol, said in 1994 in an essay dealing with the intersection of memory and history: "For a century or more the two most famous nineteenth-century black women were both untutored ex-slaves: Harriet Tubman and Sojourner Truth. Until just now, at least, the naive, rather than the educated persona seems to have better facilitated black women's entry into American memory."[80]

Nevertheless, it is hard to understand why Tubman and Truth, arguably "the two most famous African-American women of the nineteenth century,"[81] as Painter reminds us, have been so frequently conflated. Some of the differences between them are striking; others are trivial by comparison. Truth, as Carla Peterson reminds us, moved across the land relatively disconnected from active participation in black communities. Her loneliness sometimes drove her into the company of marginal white religious groups. She seemed to be in a constant search for a home place.[82] Tubman, though she was often on the move, operated out of a black refuge in Canada and, after the Civil War, made her home in Auburn.

It may or may not be significant that Harriet Tubman asked for and wore the bloomer dress as a spy and scout during the Civil War while Sojourner Truth is said to have disparaged this symbol of women's liberation as too costume-like. Painter has called attention to more substantive ways these "contrasting figures" differed, despite the frequency with which many people "confused the two because both lived in an era shadowed by human bondage." Painter writes: "New York was Truth's Egypt; Tubman's was in Maryland, these respective places marking each woman with a regional identity that Truth, at least, later came very much to prize. Born in about 1797, Truth was a generation older than Tubman, born in about 1821."[83]

There are other contrasts. Surely no one who saw Truth and Tubman in person could have mistaken one for the other. Truth was almost a foot taller than Tubman, who barely reached five foot in height. Truth went on to extensive public speaking after the publication of Gilbert's narrative of her life. Tubman was less conspicuous on the national stage after the appearance of Bradford's first biography about her. Tubman's post–Civil War life was more private and more localized than that of Truth, who made many appearances on the public platform on behalf of women's rights and equality for African Americans until the 1870s, when she did less traveling. "Harriet Tubman," Painter writes, "spoke up occasionally at antislavery meetings, and the drama of her actions lent weight to her words. But she could not sustain appearance after appearance."[84]

It was Truth and not Tubman, as is commonly thought, who went to the White House to see President Abraham Lincoln. Indeed, the two women differed in their assessment of Lincoln. Tubman criticized Lincoln for not readily allowing for the enlistment of black troops and for the disparity in pay that black soldiers received. Truth campaigned for Lincoln and the Republican ticket prior to the 1864 election. Truth and Tubman are said to have been great friends; perhaps they were. But the available evidence suggests that they met but once, in Boston in August 1864, at which time Truth may have counseled Tubman to have more faith in Lincoln.[85] Truth, in the company of the white abolitionist Lucy Colman, had a brief audience with Lincoln on October 29, 1864. Lincoln signed Truth's autograph book. William Lloyd Garrison's *Liberator* published Truth's recollection of the meeting in the White House: "I am proud to say that I never was treated with more kindness and cordiality than I was by the great and good man Abraham Lincoln, by the grace of God President of the United States for four years more."[86]

Sojourner Truth died in 1883. Tubman lived another thirty years. Though often ill and lacking the means to travel the country, the aging veteran was still being invoked as a symbol of the crusade for African American rights. In 1896, she attended the inaugural meeting of the National Association of Colored Women in Washington, D.C., and inspired the founders of what was to become the nation's most important black women's organization. Tubman, as Dorothy Sterling has said, was at that moment "the embodiment of black women's capacity to struggle." Sterling gives us a stirring word portrait of what happened when Harriet Tubman came to the front of the assembly. "'The audience rose as one person and greeted her with the waving of handkerchiefs and the clapping of hands,' an observer reported. During the emotional session, Mother Harriet, the oldest member of the convention, was asked to introduce the 'baby of the association,' the infant son of Ida B. Wells. Many who witnessed the meeting of the aging heroine of the antislavery wars and the youthful antilynching crusader perceived it as a moment in which a torch was passed from one strong bearer to another."[87] Rosetta Sprague, the only daughter of Frederick Douglass; Ellen Craft, daughter of William and Ellen Craft, who were famous for having run a thousand miles to freedom; Frances Ellen Harper, the veteran abolitionist and suffragist; Fanny Jackson Coppin, principal of the Institute for Colored Youth in Philadelphia; and Charlotte Forten Grimké, who had taught contrabands during the Port Royal Experiment, represented the older generation of freedom activists. Mary Church Terrell, educator and first president of the National Association of Colored Women; Ida B. Wells, the crusading journalist; and Margaret Murray Washington, named president of the National Federation of Colored Women's Clubs belonged to the vanguard of the younger generation. All were names to be reckoned with. But, according to Paula Giddings in her book *When and Where I Enter*, it was "the grand old woman, who had led more than three hundred slaves to freedom, had been a Union spy, and had been active in women's organizations after the war [who] stole the show."[88]

Although Tubman's contributions to the suffrage and women's rights movements were more symbolic than substantial, a recognition of this most likely will not deflate her currency as an icon now or in the future.

41. National Association of Colored Women, founding meeting, July 1896. From Booker T. Washington, Norman Barton Wood, and Fannie Barrier Williams, *A New Negro for a New Century* (Chicago: Chicago American Publishing House, ca. 1900).

Feminist and women's groups of varied political orientations continue to employ Tubman as emblematic of their own struggles for equity and justice, and as long as America falls short of these goals, the symbolic use of Harriet Tubman remains important. Carleton Mabee and Susan Mabee Newhouse argued that Sojourner Truth challenged the white feminists of her day and their opponents to believe that "slave women, black women, poor women, [and] uneducated women, these less favored women, could shed their accustomed passivity, rise up to take their rights, and join more favored women to become a power in the land."[89] In word and deed, as Carla Peterson effectively argues, Truth debunked white notions of female inferiority embedded in the nineteenth-century "cult of true womanhood whereby [quoting Truth] 'dat man ober dar say dat womin needs to be helped into carriages, and lifted ober ditches.'"[90]

The same can be said of Harriet Tubman, though it is difficult to sort out which of her symbolic representations is being appealed to when her name is invoked today, sometimes in the company of Truth, sometimes in her own right. Tubman has been seer to some, saint to others, and suffragist to yet another group of admirers. One thing is certain. In her own way, she embodied strength and courage, breaking through the gender constrictions of her day. Even as she lay dying, Harriet Tubman proved to be an inspiration to women.

Mary B. Talbert, president of the Empire State Colored Women's Association, proclaimed shortly after Tubman's death that "the last star in that wonderful galaxy of noble pioneer Negro womanhood has fallen—Phillis Wheatley, Sojourner Truth, Frances Ellen Watkins Harper, Fanny Jackson Coppin, Harriet Tubman!" Talbert's paean of praise continued with the prediction that Tubman's star would continue to rise long after her mortal remains were committed to the grave: "It may be that no costly marble shall announce to generations following the final resting place of Harriet Tubman, but her life will shine on, brighter and brighter until the perfect day—and even we may hear some voice in heaven blessing God that she has lived." Then, in an effort to draw encouragement for the present moment from the past, Talbert quoted some of Tubman's parting words when she lay dying: "Tell the women to stand together for God will never forsake us."[91]

CHAPTER SIX

THE APOTHEOSIS OF "AUNT HARRIET"

By the 1890s, if not earlier, Harriet Tubman had become a relic, honored by a few but neglected by the many. M. A. Majors, M.D., published a tribute to African American womanhood in 1893 with the title *Noted Negro Women: Their Triumphs and Activities* and under the imprimatur of this quote: "A race, no less than a nation, is prosperous in proportion to the intelligence of its women."[1] Majors provided laudatory sketches of nearly three hundred women, including Phillis Wheately, the New England poet; Edmonia Lewis, the sculptress; Amanda Smith, the traveling evangelist; and Ida B. Wells, the journalist and antilynching crusader. Sojourner Truth is included, but not Harriet Tubman. Majors treats scores of now obscure individuals, such as Maria Becraft, Eliza Moxley, and Madame Wetzel, but not Harriet Tubman, hailed by those who knew her during the Civil War era as "the greatest heroine of the age."

Why didn't Majors include Tubman in his extensive roster of "noted Negro women"? She was yet alive, though her arena of influence was now largely limited to Auburn and an occasional symbolic appearance among admirers outside upstate New York. She may have been viewed as a relic of the old days. Celebrating her or commemorating her legacy would invoke memories of the pain (and shame) of slavery. As a consequence, writers intent on shaping attitudes in the black public sphere looked elsewhere for inspiration.

Rosa Bell Holt belonged to the small company of Tubman admirers who attempted to alert the public to the importance of the old woman in Auburn who provided a link to that noble chapter in American history when the fight for and about black rights consumed a nation. Holt visited with Tubman three times, the last occasion being an interview with her at the home of a mutual friend a month before Holt's article "A Heroine in Ebony" appeared in the Woman's Council Table section of the popular magazine *Chautauquan* in July 1896.[2] Holt reminded her readers that few of the champions of liberty from the Civil War years remained alive. But Harriet Tubman kept on keeping on. The memory of "what she did for her own people in the days of the Rebellion should be treasured and handed down from one generation to another." At one time, Holt argued, a host of prominent figures in the black freedom struggle could have vouched for Tubman's brave deeds and faithful service, notables such as Frederick Douglass, William H. Seward, William Lloyd Garrison, and Oliver Johnson. Their voices had been silenced by the hand of death, and now the woman they so admired was living in a "very plain home" that she had turned into an asylum for "the poor people of her own color." Her husband was dead. She had no children. The government had never adequately recognized her for her sacrificial service during the war years, "with shot falling all about her."[3]

As the physical and temporal husk that had encased Harriet Tubman's indomitable soul broke down, word went out that the famed Black Moses was dying. Her dying and her death are important lodestars in the long chronicle of Tubman's memorialization. Her material self expired on March 10, 1913. Her death—her physical death—served to resurrect her in the memory of the living. We witness some of this revitalization of the Tubman as Moses myth in the funeral and memorial events held in her honor in 1913 and in the placement of a memorial plaque on the Cayuga County Court House in 1914. The twentieth-century apotheosis of Harriet Tubman is rooted in her dying.

Harriet Tubman died on the tenth day of March in the thirteenth year of the twentieth century. In the year of her passing, Robert Hayden, the future poet, was born in Detroit, and Lionel Hampton, jazz musician extraordinary, first saw the light of day in Louisville, Kentucky. Booker T. Washington, said to be America's most powerful black leader, was at war with the radical element of the NAACP. A black group of mail clerks organized the National Alliance of Postal Workers, the National Negro Retail Merchant's Association came into being, and black collegiate women created a sorority known as Alpha Kappa Alpha. The price of cotton plummeted in the South. President Woodrow Wilson, whose inaugural ceremony coincided with Tubman's funeral almost to the day, signed an executive order mandating the segregation of black employees in federal rest rooms and eating facilities. Oswald Garrison Villard, grandson of

William Lloyd Garrison and one of the founders of the NAACP, asked Wilson to set up a National Race Commission to study the status of the African Americans. Wilson refused. In the face of hostility toward racial justice at the highest levels, James Weldon Johnson summoned up the nerve to publish his poem "Fifty Years," celebrating the anniversary of the Emancipation Proclamation.

Tubman outlived most of those who fought for freedom in the crusade against America's primal sin of slavery. The abolitionist phalanx was gone by 1913, having succumbed to the rigors of old age and death long before the one whom they knew as Black Moses took to her bed and quietly slipped away. Many of Tubman's compatriots in the freedom cause died in the 1870s, figures such as Thomas Garrett (d. 1871), William H. Seward (d. 1872), Jermain Loguen (d. 1872), Gerrit Smith (d. 1874), and William Lloyd Garrison (d. 1879). Sojourner Truth passed away in 1883 in Battle Creek, Michigan, at about eighty-six, though she had often claimed to be over one hundred.[4] Frederick Douglass, born in 1818, lived until 1895, battling against racial stereotypes and racial discrimination, the twin relics of slavery, almost to the end. William Still, Tubman's friend and supporter from the heyday of the Underground Railroad, survived until 1902. Elizabeth Cady Stanton passed away in 1902, and Susan B. Anthony died in 1906. During the last decade of her life, and perhaps for more years than that, Harriet Tubman must have felt like many of the very old who find their circle of friends and neighbors dwindling year by year until they are alone with their memories. Then death comes, and the living must find some way to ritualize the passing of the ancients and memorialize them so that succeeding generations appreciate who they were and what they symbolized.

Tubman's passage into the archives of the American public memory actually began prior to her physical death. Some authors wrote of her using the past tense while she was yet alive and living quietly in Auburn. The historian Albert Bushnell Hart first comments on Sojourner Truth in his volume *Slavery and Abolition*, published in 1906, and then says: "A similar character was the heroic Harriet Tubman."[5] Hart managed to write Tubman into his narrative (albeit briefly) and thus broke the silence other white historians cast over her accomplishments, but he did so by drawing down the curtain on her life seven years before her death. It is therefore not surprising that an article that appeared on June 25, 1911, in the *World* under the title "Moses of Her Race Ending Her Life in Home

She Founded" should state, "Probably few of the present generation have heard of the existence of this forgotten old former slave." A dispatch sent from Auburn "a few days ago" reported that the woman whom they once called the "Moses of her people" had so deteriorated in health that she had entered the home she founded for "dependent colored women and orphans." "Now," wrote the *World* reporter, "with the weight of almost a hundred years on her shoulders, she seeks rest during her few remaining years." Though Tubman was more likely closer to ninety than one hundred when she died, the reporter correctly noted that the passage of so many years had worn her down. When the reporter had visited her "some years ago," Tubman was no longer able to tell her own story with the drama and vividness that were once her hallmark. "Thru these beautiful June days she sits on the porch and dozes as she sat and dozed four-score years ago on a fence rail on the plantation of her master. What she thinks, no one knows, for her days of talking intelligently have passed."[6]

The author of the *World* article may well have been Frank C. Drake, a newspaperman who also worked for the *New York Herald*. In 1907, he went to Auburn and visited with Tubman. His account of that visit with the aging black heroine appeared as "The Moses of Her People" in the Sunday edition of the *Herald* on September 22, 1907, under the subtitle, "Amazing Life Work of Harriet Tubman. A Story Stranger Than Fiction. After 80 Years of Devotion She Lives to Lament That She Can Do No More Than Plan." Drake, as others had done before him, recapitulated the glory days of Tubman, when she was hailed as the "Black Moses" of the Underground Railroad who also served bravely the cause of freedom during the Civil War. Then, as Drake observed, Tubman returned "unobtrusively to her homely life in Auburn, where, after 80 years of service to her people and to the cause of human justice, she is closing her life in poverty." The irony of her situation did not escape Tubman, for, as Drake tells us, "It was not plaintively, but rather with a flash of scorn in her eyes, that she remarked to this writer last week, 'You wouldn't think dat after I served de flock so faithfully I should come to want in its folds.'" Tubman directed Drake's attention to the apple orchard on her Auburn property. "Do you like apples?" she asked the reporter, who assured her that he did. "Did you ever plant any apple trees?" the old freedom fighter inquired. The white journalist confessed that he had not, to which Tubman replied, "No, but somebody else planted 'em. I liked apples when I was young, and

I said, 'Some day I'll plant apples myself for other young folks to eat, and I guess I done it.'" Next, as Drake tells us, "This heroine of her race," who in seeking to establish "an industrial home for the deserving of her race" despite being in the "midnight of her own life," broke into song. "Throwing back her furrowed face, into a wild melody, beating the time with her hands upon her knees and gleefully swaying to and fro," she summoned up a refrain from a song sung by former slaves as they celebrated the fall of their oppressors:

> Dar's cider an' brandy in de cellar,
> An' de darkies dey'll hab some;
> Mus' be now de kingdom's comin'
> An' de year ob Ju-bi-lum![7]

How Harriet Tubman understood her "flock" is not clear from Drake's account of his visit with her. Was she mindful only of the African American community she had served so faithfully in Auburn for nearly fifty years, or was she thinking more generally of the allies for humanity who, like her, had once enlisted in the crusade for black rights? Perhaps she meant to stir the conscience of America as a whole, to remind it that the cause of freedom for which she had sacrificed so much was still wanting faithful laborers in God's vineyard. As for herself, she had accomplished her purpose; she had planted the seeds. Others must come along, reap the harvest, and carry on.

Illiteracy prevented Harriet Tubman from shaping how future generations should remember her by writing a memoir during her declining years, as General Ulysses S. Grant did before his death in 1885 and reformers such as Samuel J. May, Frederick Douglass, and Elizabeth Cady Stanton did prior to exiting life's theater. Tubman did speak about her place in history to the handful of admirers who sought her out in those last years of near-obscurity. In these interviews, she may have been attempting to shape how she would be remembered, summoning up memories—good and bad. She spoke yet again of the hardships of slavery, of the risks she took rescuing others, and of the sacrifices she made working with Union troops and contraband survivors of slavery's domain.

James B. Clarke's tribute to Harriet Tubman, published in 1911, is one of the most revealing of the surviving printed accounts of an interview done with Tubman once she became so feeble that she was moved into the Home for the Aged she had established in Auburn. A British subject from the West Indies, having been born in 1888 at Saint Vincent, Clarke was a student at Cornell University (Class of 1912) when he journeyed to Auburn to sit at the feet of the venerable Moses of Her People. An associate of Cornell's *Cosmopolitan Student*, he had already made a name for himself by writing "Race Prejudice at Cornell." The occasion for his protest had been the exclusion of African American coeds from Sage Hall, a women's dormitory. Clarke, whose father was an Anglican clergyman, had at one time thought of entering a Roman Catholic seminary.[8] He had been active in soliciting funds to help Harriet Tubman found the modest home for the elderly in Auburn where she resided (at the time of the interview) with "four or five" other old women.

Clarke found his heroine furrowed of brow. Her hands appeared to have lost their old-time vigor, but her mind remained "astonishingly fresh and active." In spite of her advanced age (Clarke thought her to be nearly one hundred), Tubman was not "ready to be *oslerized*." She demonstrated that by coming downstairs to breakfast on the day of Clarke's visit and by eating heartily (spring chicken with rice, pie, cheese, and "other good things"). She resented the notion that her nurse or one of the other women present should feed her. Though no longer able to "keep house" and entertain her friends as she had done in her own house "by the road" (the brick house), Tubman retained enough presence of mind to tell Clarke about the medal sent to her by Queen Victoria and displayed the "ready wit" for which she was famous.

As if to ensure that Clarke would remind the American public of her exploits of old, Black Moses told her student visitor from Cornell about how she had assisted in the liberation of hundreds of slaves during the Civil War and brought them to the headquarters of the federal army at Beaufort, South Carolina. Once again, "this centenarian Amazon," as Clarke calls her, sang the song she had sung to comfort "the motley throng of frightened black Israelites" facing the federal gunboats. Clapping her hands and stamping her feet on the floor, her withered arm accentuating the refrain, Harriet Tubman chanted:

> Come along, come along, and don't be fool,'
> Uncle Sam rich enough to sen' us all to school;
> Come along, come along, don't be alarm,'
> Uncle Sam rich enough to give us all a farm.[9]

Clearly in awe of the woman he was interviewing, young Clarke summed up his impressions with the words: "Her life has been one long 'word of consolation' and inspiration to her people."[10]

Clarke, though a British citizen, was fully cognizant that the American government had not fulfilled all of its promises to Harriet Tubman's "people." He ended his sketch on a melancholy note. Tubman's days were numbered. "Her song," Clarke wrote in 1911, "is well-nigh ended." Soon her voice would be stilled. And yet, Clarke held out the vision of Tubman's soul "marching on" like the soul of John Brown, "him whom she calls her dearest friend." Who were the custodians of Tubman's memory meant to be? Clarke invoked the racial imperative: "For Harriet Tubman's soul—the spirit of progress, the determination to rise above the weight of oppression and injustice and breathe the free air of opportunity—is deeply rooted in the people for whom she has lived and worked."[11]

Though Clark's observation that African Americans' aspirations for freedom and justice, as modeled in the life and work of Harriet Tubman, ran deep and true, it is not altogether certain that this translated into support for Tubman in her declining years. Robert W. Taylor, the financial secretary of the Tuskegee Institute, made seven annual visits to Auburn beginning in the mid-1890s to raise funds for Booker T. Washington's school in Alabama. He customarily paid a call on Tubman at her house off South Avenue. In 1901, he found her greatly in need. She was caring for "two friendless old women and two homeless orphans" and burdened with a mortgage of one thousand seven hundred dollars on the twenty-five-acre property that she wished to transform into her dreamed-for Home for Aged Colored Men and Women. According to Taylor, who published his appeal on Tubman's behalf in 1901 as *Harriet Tubman: The Heroine in Ebony*, "The hand of affliction has rested heavily upon her for more than a year."[12] Taylor found that Tubman no longer traveled and that many of the white friends to whom she appealed for aid had "crossed the bar." He thought that Tubman had been forgotten and, in her destitution, was becoming "dependent almost entirely on what may be handed her by occasional callers and the scant earnings of her brother, several years her senior."[13] Taylor came away from his last courtesy call on Tubman impressed with how strongly she was "bowed down with infirmity." Her "gait," Taylor said of his black heroine, "is unsteady, her eye is dim; the sun of her life ere long must set."[14]

One senses subdued anger in Taylor's portrayal of Tubman's situation as the twentieth century dawned. Here was a sad irony. Taylor's black heroine—"She stands without a parallel in history,—solitary, majestic, sunkissed"—was close to becoming one of those elderly and indigent African Americans for whom she attempted to provide shelter and aid. In an effort to drum up support for the one who had been hailed as Black Moses, Taylor wrote a laudatory sketch of her life, with a brief introduction by Booker T. Washington, the Wizard of Tuskegee. Washington underscored Taylor's appeal by hailing Tubman as one of the "brave champions of human liberty who sounded the death-knell of American slavery." Washington argued that Tubman was "a character of whom any race might be proud," but he made it clear that Taylor's pamphlet was meant to be of special service to "the race" Tubman represented. Taylor had sent out an earlier appeal on behalf of Tubman, vetted through "several colored newspapers," and received a mere seventy-seven dollars. He hoped that his 1901 pamphlet would make each reader "a missionary for the cause of Harriet Tubman."[15]

It is not exactly clear when Tubman's infirmities of body and purse became so burdensome that she no longer left Auburn. As late as 1897, she made a trip to New England, for on April 8 of that year Tubman met with Wilbur H. Siebert in Boston. Siebert was conducting research for *The Underground Railroad from Slavery to Freedom*, published in 1899 (Figure 42).[16] Siebert found Tubman "very poor" and "subject to the infirmities of old age, infirmities increased in her case by the effects of ill treatment in slavery."[17]

This representation of an aged and penurious Tubman is also apparent in a sketch written by Lillie B. Chace Wyman and published in 1896 in the *New England Magazine*. Wyman reported that Tubman was "very poor," dependent on the charity of her few remaining friends. One of Tubman's benefactors and admirers had written to Wyman, "She would have died long ago but for her indomitable courage and will."[18]

Harriet Tubman's death was more process than event. The slow but inevitable journey she took from being independent, proud never to have to resort to begging for herself, to that of a semi-invalid wrapped in a shawl (Figure 43) and having her meals prepared for her by others must have been infuriating.

When her physical powers declined to a point at which she could no longer adequately care for herself, the woman whom Sarah Bradford credited with piloting hundreds to freedom and serving as a nurse,

42. Harriet Tubman, "The Moses of Her People." From Wilbur H. Siebert, *The Underground Railroad from Slavery to Freedom* (New York: Macmillan, 1899).

43. Harriet Tubman in old age, group photo, circa 1913. Courtesy Cayuga County Historian's Office, Auburn, New York.

spy, and scout during the Civil War turned to others for help. According to a newspaper article dated June 3, 1911, "Harriet Tubman, the aged negress, known as the 'Moses of her people,' was last Thursday taken to the Harriet Tubman home, penniless, to end her days."[19] She joined three other black women at the home, all under the care of Frances Richardson, a nurse who had been trained at the Douglass hospital in Philadelphia. The Reverend Charles A. Smith, a retired clergyman who had served in the famous Massachusetts Fifty-fourth Regiment, was the chaplain of the Tubman home. His wife served as matron. The Reverend E. U. A. Brooks of the African Methodist Episcopal Zion church in Auburn functioned as the home's secretary and financial agent. Tubman's last will and testament, which she endorsed with an "x," is dated the November 18, 1912.[20] During the last year of her life, Tubman was almost totally bedridden, unable to get up except for a few minutes each day.

On March 10, 1913, someone in Auburn informed the *New York Tribune* (probably by telegram) that "Harriet Tubman, a negro woman, 95 years old, who is said to have been a friend of Abraham Lincoln and Secretary of State, William H. Seward, and to have been associated with John Brown in Anti-Slavery work, is dying here of pneumonia." The alert did not appear until Tuesday, March 11.[21] By then, Tubman was dead.

Black Moses died of a pulmonary infection, which she had battled for more than a year, on the evening of March 10, 1913. In the afternoon of that day, a Monday, Dr. G. B. Mack and Martha Ridgeway, a hired nurse from Elmira, New York, who had been engaged the previous October, concluded that death was imminent. Harriet asked for her friends. Reverend Smith was summoned, as was Reverend Brooks. Eliza E. Peterson, a Women's Christian Temperance Union officer responsible for temperance work among blacks who had come to Auburn from Texarkana, Texas, to see Tubman, was invited to join the small band that now gathered in a death watch around Aunt Harriet's bed. Tubman, as was her nature, took charge and is reported to have directed the final service held on her behalf. Joining Reverend Smith and his wife, nurse Ridgeway, Eliza Peterson, and, one assumes, Dr. Mack in the prayer circle was William H. Stewart, Harriet's nephew, and his son, Charles Stewart. Aunt Harriet united in the singing between coughing spells and received the sacrament. Then she directed her attention to the two clergymen present: "Give my love to all the churches." Another severe coughing spell. When she had recovered, Tubman laid a blessing on those present. In a thick voice, she quoted the biblical passage: "I go away to prepare a place for you, and where I am ye may be also."[22] Afterward she lapsed into unconsciousness. Death was pronounced at 8:30 P.M.[23] As Earl Conrad wrote in 1943, "Perhaps the most astonishing thing of all in the life of Harriet Tubman was the *strength* with which she died."[24]

Auburn's newspapers carried lengthy articles on Tubman in the days succeeding her death, as did some of the regional press, such as Syracuse's *Post-Standard*.[25] But the *New York Times*, which heretofore had neglected any mention of Tubman, did not print her obituary until Friday, March 14, 1913. Two brief paragraphs noted her passing, tucked into the Social Notes section on an inside page between the obituary of a Brooklyn man, described as "a capitalist and a contractor," who built Manhattan's Forty-ninth Street sewer and the Coney Island railroad, and the obituary of Edmund O. Beers, a Civil War veteran who had been sheriff of Chemung County.[26]

For a detailed rendering of the events that transpired following Aunt Harriet's death, we must turn to the local press. It is there that we can best understand how her funeral and the subsequent memorial service reveal something of the conflicted state of mind Americans were in not only about the woman herself but about the social and racial issues of the time. Both the *Auburn Citizen* and the *Auburn Daily Advertiser* provided the public with summaries of Tubman's extraordinary life, wrestling with such disputed points as how old she was at the time of her death,[27] as well as chronicling her funeral on March 14, 1913. A writer for the *Auburn Daily Advertiser* underscored the importance of giving the public a full accounting of Tubman's life and death: "There is not a woman in the United States today whose career can be compared with that of the old slave."[28]

The Reverend C. A. Smith and Reverend Brooks took charge of making the funeral arrangements. Tubman left instructions for how they were to proceed. Once details of the funeral service had been agreed on, they were reported in the Auburn press. Denominational officials were notified, and members of the Board of Trustees and the Board of Women Managers of the Harriet Tubman Home made plans to attend. Two of Tubman's grandnieces, Alida Stewart and Eva Stewart, who had been in Washington, D. C., for the inauguration ceremonies of Woodrow Wilson as the twenty-eighth president of the United States, got word by telegram of "Aunt Harriet's" death and made plans to return to Auburn. Mary

Talbot of Buffalo, president of the Empire State Federation of Colored Women's Clubs, which had given one hundred forty-one dollars toward the support of "Aunt Harriet" during her final illness, sent word that she would be present at the funeral. The press was still voicing uncertainty about Tubman's age at the time of her passing. Some informants gave it as ninety-eight, though there was speculation that Tubman was "nearer 110 years."[29]

In the midst of a frenzy of preparations for the funeral, Booker T. Washington, whom the *Auburn Citizen* characterized as "the leader of the negro race," sent a telegram. He would not attend, but of Tubman he said, "She was a picturesque, heroic character, not unlike some of the heroic figures described in the Bible. After devoting almost three score and ten years to the service of her race, she has at length fallen asleep. Her life is an inspiration to all."[30]

Friday, March 13, 1913, dawned cold and gray. Harriet Tubman's body lay in state at the Harriet Tubman Home. The private service attended by family, the surviving residents of the home (six women), and invited guests, which was scheduled for 11:00 A.M., did not begin until 11:30 A.M. because of the late arrival of out-of-towners. Several hundred "colored residents" of Auburn attended, according to a report in the *Auburn Citizen*, which, if accurate, accounted for a significant percentage of Auburn's African American population.[31]

The private service included the reading of biblical texts appropriate for the dead from Job, Psalms, and Ecclesiastes. Reverend Brooks delivered a short eulogy on the life of "Aunt Harriet," and the young people's choir from Auburn's African Methodist Episcopal Zion church sang "Arise My Soul, Arise." Then all joined in with "There Is a Fountain Filled with Blood," an old standard in the Zion tradition. The service closed with a prayer offered by Tubman's old friend, Reverend Smith, chaplain of the home. He had seen action in the attack on Fort Wagner during the Civil War. Tubman, assigned by Colonel Montgomery to care for the victims, ministered to the wounded Smith. Now he returned the favor, but he was overcome with grief and was quoted by the Auburn press as saying, "I don't care to remain as chaplain of the Harriet Tubman Home any longer. My mother is gone. I learned to call her mother on the battlefields in Maryland and Virginia. I will feel eternally lonesome. She used to call my wife, the matron of the home, her Good Samaritan. My wife feels the loss more than she can explain."[32]

Sometime after the close of the private service, Tubman's body was removed to the African Methodist Episcopal Zion church on Parker Street, Auburn's only African American congregation. The open casket, draped with an American flag and surrounded by floral decorations, was placed near the pulpit. The female managers of the Harriet Tubman Home acted as a guard of honor. Tubman's body was clothed in a black dress and waist. A medal, most likely the one sent to her at the request of Queen Victoria, had been pinned to her waist. Tubman's hand held a crucifix, a gift of the late Father Mulheron. According to the report sent to Syracuse's *Post-Standard* by its branch office in Auburn, "More than 1000 persons sought admission to the church, but half that number had to be satisfied with a view of the body, as the Parker street house of worship can accommodate only 500."[33] Those unable to get into the church to pay their respects stood outside.

The service at the church, scheduled to begin at 3:00 P.M., was remarkably devoid of specifically African-based cultural symbols or rituals, as might have been expected from the declaration in the *New York Tribune* that the deceased was "an ex-slave of pure Ashantee negro blood."[34] The makeup of the participants in the principal funeral service, unlike that of the earlier, more private prayer service conducted in the morning, signaled how strongly Harriet Tubman had served as a bridge between Auburn's black and white communities. In the convergence of black and white at the funeral, and about a year later at the dedication of the memorial tablet, representatives of the two sides of America's racial divide, a chasm of significant width in 1913, found common ground in honoring Black Moses. That some of the white speakers at and commentators on the funeral were unable to see Tubman as anything more than a heroine of "her race" signaled how difficult the journey to racial parity was going to be. That some of the African American speakers and commentators echoed the notion that Tubman belonged to the "race," a proprietary icon, is hardly surprising. What is striking, and therefore worthy of our attention in underscoring the malleability of the Tubman myth, is that the Black Moses as American Patriot theme is embedded in the eulogistic remarks. The Tubman as American Patriot refrain sounded even more strongly in the post-funeral dedication ceremony in 1914.

The funeral service included readings from Scripture by the Reverend R. F. Fisher of Ithaca (Psalm 19) and the Reverend J. M. Morse of Oneida (Corinthians 15:1). The Reverend E. S. Bailey of Syracuse offered a prayer. All were ministers of the African Methodist Episcopal Zion denomination; their presence demonstrated that old Zion, which prides itself, then and now, on being the Freedom Church to which such stalwarts as Frederick Douglass, Sojourner Truth, and Harriet Tubman belonged, would provide the requisite ecclesiastical blessing to the funeral rituals. But Tubman had not been narrowly parochial in denominational matters and apparently felt at home among all liberty-loving Christians, regardless of their color or creed. On occasion, she worshiped at predominantly white churches.[35] In keeping with Tubman's interracial and interdenominational spirit, a white quartet from Auburn's Central Presbyterian church sang "The Sands of Time Are Sinking" at the funeral.

Then the eulogies began. Auburn's mayor was in Albany on business, so John P. Jaeckel, president of Auburn's Common Council, spoke for the city's white establishment. "No one of our fellow citizens of late years," Jaeckel asserted, "has conferred greater distinction upon us than has she." Jaeckel told of how he had known "Aunt Harriet" since he was a small boy. He and his chums had been in awe of her, thinking of her "as sort of supernatural being," her tales of her adventures firing their imaginations. Jaeckel, as would other speakers, black and white, in years to come, urged the youth of the day to use Tubman as a role model. He drew particular attention to Tubman's deep religious character. "In this workaday world filled with its activities," Jaeckel lamented, "what a contrast we find between the average person's life filled with petty vanities, as compared with the unselfish life of our good sister, filled with sympathy and devotion to her people."[36] The quartet from Central Presbyterian offered another selection, "Good Night, I'm Going Home."

Afterward, Mary B. Talbert spoke. Talbert, whose home was in Buffalo, was the leading voice of the black women's club movement in New York State and chair of the executive committee of the National Federation of Woman's Clubs. Talbert had called on Tubman only a month earlier and had been inspired by her faith and fortitude. The bedridden icon of black womanhood told Talbert of the "sweet spirit" present in the Harriet Tubman Home. The aged one's voice was feeble, so the younger woman bent over to hear Tubman ask that her guest express the invalid's appreciation for the care she was being given. As Talbert arose to go, Black Moses grasped her hand firmly and whispered, "I've been fixing a long time for my journey and now I'm almost home. God has shown me the Golden Chariot, and a voice spoke to me and said, 'Arouse, awake!

Sleep no longer, Jesus does all things well.'" There was a moment of hesitation. Then Tubman, who had once graced the platform of suffragist conventions and was a charter member of the black women's club movement, said to Talbert: "Tell the women to stand together for God will never forsake us." On leaving, Talbert shook Tubman's wrinkled and bony hand to say goodbye. The ancient one smiled and said, "I am at peace with God and with all mankind." After Talbert spoke, Reverend J. C. Roberts of Binghamton made a few remarks. He was followed by a solo from Mrs. George Parker, a local woman whom Tubman had favored, and then Reverend Brooks, pastor of Auburn's branch of black Methodism, gave a précis of Tubman's life, reinvoking Tubman's last words, "Give my love to all the churches," and making the dubious claim that President Abraham Lincoln had sought her counsel on various occasions.[37]

The pulpit was then given over to Bishop G. L. Blackwell of Philadelphia. Blackwell served as president of the Board of Trustees of the Tubman Home. He delivered the funeral sermon, at some inconvenience, he said. The "inconvenience," as Blackwell informed those present, was that his attendance at the funeral forced him to bow out of the honor of introducing Colonel Theodore Roosevelt, the former president, to the largest black congregation of Philadelphia. Despite the disappointment of being called away from Philadelphia, Blackwell was quick to claim Black Moses for the Zionite connection. "The African Methodist Episcopal Zion church," Bishop Blackwell declared, "feels honored for having had 'Aunt Harriet' as a communicant in its ranks for many years." Most of Blackwell's remarks fell into the mold of typical Protestant funeral homilies of the day, replete with admonitions about the certainty of death for all and the need to prepare for eternity. "Generation after generation," Blackwell intoned, "has risen up only to place the keys of the tomb in his [death's] proud and conquering hand, while we are but mourners following in the funeral train, soon to meet the fate of all succeeding generations." Not until the latter half of his funeral oration, did Blackwell turn to the deceased. Of this "fallen heroine and loving patriot," he said, "If the colored race grew up a generation of women as resolute as Aunt Harriet, the future of the race would be secure." He closed with a ringing peroration linking Tubman with the greats of the past and urging his people forward: "Then live on Aunt Harriet amid the enchanted beauties of celestial light. Walk over the plains of grandeur and visit the mansions of your long line of comrades who with you in the thickets of the fight for human liberty proved true. Tell Bishop Germain [Jermain] W. Loguen, Frederick Douglass, Gerrit Smith, William L. Garrison, John Brown, Wendell Phillips, Oliver H. Johnson, William H. Seward, Sec. of State, Phillips Brooks—tell them that 'the fight is on' for mental, moral, and spiritual emancipation."[38] One cannot escape the observation that Blackwell's litany of heroic progenitors included none of the names Talbert had held up for honor.

Following Blackwell's sermon, Reverend J. W. Brown of Rochester offered a set of resolutions, as did Mrs. Harry T. Johnson, secretary of the Board of Lady Managers of the Harriet Tubman Home. The resolutions applauded the deceased's "valuable service to her race before, during, and since the war" and affirmed her giving of the Home for the Aged and Indigent over to the management of the Western New York Conference of the African Methodist Episcopal Zion church.[39]

At the conclusion of the church service, the Women's Auxiliary of the Charles E. Stewart Post of the Grand Army of the Republic (GAR), in partnership with the Charles E. Stewart Relief Corps, conducted a ceremony of last rites with a semi-military character. Federal authorities may have been remiss in recognizing Tubman's contributions to the military during the Civil War, but Harriet Tubman is said to have taken great pride in her GAR affiliation and the women of the Stewart Post auxiliary expressly requested that the American flag be draped over the casket.

Tubman's body was placed in a sturdy oak outer casket and interred in lot 439 of the West Lawn, section C, Fort Hill Cemetery (Figure 44). Brew's Funeral Home of Auburn took care of the arrangements.[40] A brief committal service took place at the gravesite, and the group of mourners retired from the cemetery. Fort Hill Cemetery, according to a recently published photographic retrospective, had been planned "as a park, a nature preserve, and a repository of monumental sculpture during the era when mourning was raised to an art form."[41] Opened in 1851, the cemetery takes advantage of a strikingly beautiful natural setting of Native American mound-builder origin. Once the seat of the Cayuga people and thought to be the birthplace of Chief Logan, the cemetery grounds contain the graves of Auburn's notables, including William H. Seward and many of the prominent white families who aided Harriet Tubman after she settled in Auburn.

Tubman's final resting place lacked a marker until the Harriet Tubman Club of New York City and the Empire State Federation of Women's

44. Harriet Tubman's burial. The quality of the original photograph is poor, but this is an important illustration that shows the casket, among other things, at the graveside ceremony in 1913. Gladys Bryant (marked by an "x"), Tubman's grandniece, was present as a young girl. From Bessie Cooper Noble, *Ain't Sleep, Ain't Gone: A Tribute to Harriet Tubman* (Fayetteville, N.Y.: Manlius Publishing, 1978).

Clubs dedicated the Harriet Tubman memorial monument on July 5, 1917. In 1937, a granite stone four feet high, courtesy of the Empire State Federation of Women's Clubs, replaced it. Eighty of the clubwomen motored up from Ithaca, where they were holding their annual conference to honor Tubman as one of their own. Two of Tubman's grandnieces, Gladys Stewart Bryant of Auburn and Thelma Thompson of Ithaca, ceremoniously unveiled the new monument. Bryant had been present on that cold and gray day in March 1913 when Tubman's mortal remains were placed in the ground at Fort Hill. She remembered little of the event when interviewed about it many years later. A photograph taken of the funeral shows her as a young girl standing near the front of the crowd.[42]

The funeral and burial of Harriet Tubman gave participants an opportunity to sing the praises of a woman whom most Americans had forgotten or had never come to know. She was a relic of another age, a heroic time when the national struggle over slavery could be sketched out in stark contrasts of good against evil. There are no Tubman papers as such, no anthologies of collected writings, few documents to query, interpret, and quarrel about, as students and scholars do with the monumental Douglass literary corpus. Once Tubman's voice was stilled by death, the living had only their memories of her to sustain them. After 1913, the Harriet Tubman myth fell into the hands of anyone who cared enough to remember her. It could be shaped and reshaped at will, depending on the needs of the rememberer and the changing historical context. When disputes about the accuracy of this or that detail arose, none could consult the oracle herself.

The malleability of the Tubman myth showed in the post-funeral effort by Auburnites and others to memorialize Black Moses. The funeral had been largely a local affair, attended by relatives, old friends, church and denominational representatives, a significant proportion of Auburn's African American community, and a few spokesmen for the city's ruling establishment. No nationally prominent figure, white or black, was present. Were it not for extensive coverage in the local press, we would not be able to reconstruct today a detailed accounting of the funeral events of March 13. Though it is not clear precisely where the initiative originated, Auburn's leaders busied themselves with plans for a post-burial memorial service to which the whole nation would be invited.

To give tangible expression of their desire that Tubman be remembered by future generations, Auburn's city fathers commissioned a memorial tablet. They sought out Allen G. Newman, said to be the "best known of the younger sculptors of New York City."[43] Newman's catalog of achievements included the Triumph of Peace monument in Atlanta's Piedmont Park, erected by the Gate City Guard to commemorate the end of the Civil War. To give the dedication ceremony national significance, memorial planners invited Booker T. Washington to give the principal address. Auburn and the nation had about a year to get ready for the grand event. It was scheduled for early June 1914.

As June approached, the Auburn press reported on the progress of the community's effort to suitably memorialize "Aunt Harriet." In the May 25, 1914, edition of the *Advertiser-Journal*, William Donald Mitchell gave a detailed report on Newman's tablet. Cast in one piece of United States standard bronze (90 percent pure copper and 10 percent tin and zinc), it measured four feet high and two feet, five inches, wide. Extended corners, an arched top, and a raised border decorated with bead and reel ornament augmented its rectangular shape. "The City of Auburn," Mitchell told the public, "will, of course, in the years to come, have many beautiful works of art in sculptural marble and bronze, but there will be none which will tell a story of greater self-sacrifice and greater heroism than the story told in this Tubman tablet relief; a story of an obscure member of the negro race inspired to deeds of patriotism and love for her fellow men—and this story, now set forth in this table of imperishable bronze, forms an inspiring 'page in bronze' of American history which will still exist, when the granite walls of the building on which it is placed have crumbled into dust."[44] On Friday, June 5, the *Advertiser-Journal* announced that the tablet had arrived, shipped to Auburn from the John Williams foundry of New York City.

With the pace of pre-memorial events picking up, tributes to Tubman began to appear in the press from those unable to be present at the forthcoming ceremonial unveiling. The Reverend James E. Mason, one of the original incorporators of the Tubman Home, posted a most revealing memoir of Black Moses. He had first met Tubman nearly thirty-five years earlier, when the Genesee Annual Conference of the Zion Methodists convened at its branch congregation in Auburn, then on Washington Street. The love feast or communion ritual was in progress when Mason arrived; hymns drifted out the open windows. "I entered," Mason recalled in 1914, "and was seated near the altar, facing the audience. Singing, soul stirring and reviving, continued. Seated four pews from the front, on my right, was a woman with shoulders somewhat stooped, and head bent forward. She had a broad forehead, piercing eyes, thin lips and strong, masculine features." At this point, Mason had no idea who the woman was, though it appears that he had heard of the legendary Black Moses. Mason's tribute continues: "At the close of a thrilling selection she arose and commenced to speak in a hesitating voice. I understood her impediment resulted from a violent blow, which broke her skull, when a child. In a shrill voice she commenced to give testimony to God's goodness and long suffering. Soon she was shouting, and so were others also. She possessed such endurance, vitality and magnetism, that I inquired and was informed it was Harriet Tubman—the 'Underground Railroad Moses.'" Then, reaching for a suitable analogy from the past, Mason invoked a female biblical character. "Here was a modern Priscilla, a prophetess, telling out of the fullness of her heart God's revelations to her in the secret of His presence. Service ended, I greeted her. She said 'are you saved?' I gave an affirmative reply. She remarked: 'Glory to God,' and shouted again."[45] After rehearsing Tubman's mighty labors on behalf of

45. Booker T. Washington, circa 1890–1910. Courtesy Library of Congress, LC/USZ62–36291

the oppressed, Mason asked rhetorically, "When can the Afro-American pay the debt of gratitude they owe their heroine? This Joan of Arc; this modern Amazon?"[46]

If there was any single African American to which the organizers of Auburn's Tubman memorial celebration could turn for an answer, it was Booker T. Washington (Figure 45). On the eve of the Great Migration, when a great mass of black Southern labor stirred itself in reaction to white racism and in response to the need for industrial workers in the North due to the outbreak of World War One, Booker T. Washington was still preaching the Tuskegee philosophy that had garnered support for his school from white elites and black conservatives and downplaying the importance of the fight for political and social equality. Washington's accommodationist agenda, as outlined in his famous Atlanta Exposition speech in 1895, angered W. E. B. Du Bois and the other radicals who participated in the Niagara Movement, which claimed philosophical kinship to the pre–Civil War abolitionists. Born in the spring of 1856 (as with Tubman, there is uncertainty as to the exact date of Washington's birth), Washington was near the end of his career, his power and influence waning.[47] He would die at the campus of his beloved Tuskegee Institute (which he founded in 1883) in 1915, about a year after he responded to Auburn's call to deliver the keynote speech at the tablet's unveiling. Washington had been in Auburn on one previous occasion. In March 1911, he spoke at a mass meeting of African American men in Auburn's Burtis Auditorium, the site of the planned unveiling.[48]

Never one to miss an opportunity to promote Tuskegee Institute, which in 1914 had over two thousand students, Washington or his agents struck an agreement with the organizers of the memorial event, the Auburn Business Men's Association and the Cayuga County Historical Society, that any receipts gleaned from the sale of the souvenir program above and beyond production costs should be split between Washington's school and the Harriet Tubman Home.[49] Purchasers of the program received a twelve-page pamphlet entitled *Souvenir Harriet Tubman Memorial*.[50] Its cover features a quote on "Success" from the Wizard of Tuskegee, whose autobiography, *Up from Slavery*, published in 1901, had been influential in shaping white America's attitude toward black Americans: "I have learned that success is to be measured, not so much by the position that one has reached in life, as by the obstacles which he has overcome while trying to succeed." One page of the souvenir program described the Harriet Tubman Home's status as of 1914. Written by Superintendent E. U. A. Brooks, the sketch appealed to "some kind friend or friends" of "Aunt Harriet," whom Brooks described as "an honored guest at the Home from May 19, 1911, until her death on March 10, 1913," might be so moved as "to manifest his or their reverence for the deceased heroine in a very tangible manner" by helping to reduce the eight-hundred-dollar debt on the property still owed the Cayuga County Savings Bank. Two pages are devoted to Tuskegee Institute and Booker T. Washington. One of these features a halftone of Tompkins Hall from Tuskegee's campus and a picture of Dr. Washington, accompanied by a biographical profile promoting him as a "writer, and speaker on racial and educational subjects." The second of the pages gives a brief history of the Tuskegee Normal and Industrial Institute, noting that, "from its foundation to date over 9,000 men and women have gone out from the school and are now doing good work as teachers and industrial workers." The rest of the printed program consists of a halftone of the memorial tablet, the "Order of Exercises," a roster of the organizing committee, the committee on tickets and programs, names of the ushers, and a list of the contributors to the fund to defray the cost of the tablet.

In looking over the list of contributors, one is struck by the diversity of those who gave to the memorial fund. Auburn's major employers, including International Harvester, are represented, as are civic officials such as John P. Jaeckel, the former mayor. The community's fraternal and social groups did their share, including the Central Rebekah Lodge, No. 305, International Order of Odd Fellows, and the Stewart Relief Corps., No. 11. Dr. and Mrs. E. U. A. Brooks contributed, as did William Freemen, a descendant of the first African American settler when the hamlet that became the village and city of Auburn was known as Hardenbergh's Corners. Some of the wealthiest gave, as did some of the poorest. Veterans of the reform causes with which Harriet Tubman was identified, such as Emily Howland and Emma Paddock Telford, subscribed, as did the Young Ladies' Class of Central Presbyterian church and the Owasco Chapter of the Daughters of the American Revolution. Despite this community-wide effort to underwrite the cost of the bronze tablet, a deficit remained, and according to an editorial that appeared in the *Auburn Citizen* on June 10, organizers would have to charge a small admission fee to the unveiling ceremony, two days hence. The editorialist reminded the public of how Tubman had persevered in times of need, trudging from place to place seeking alms to maintain her home for the elderly and indigent.[51] Fortunately, Washington had agreed to speak without personal compensation, and other program participants did the same.

On Thursday, June 11, Mayor Charles W. Brister directed that the flag be displayed on all municipal buildings and asked loyal citizens to follow suit. "If the stars and stripes could float from every home in Auburn," the major urged, "we believe that it would inspire patriots and demonstrate that we are not forgetful of those who suffered so much for the cause of freedom and were willing to die that we might have one country and one flag."[52] Had a visitor to Auburn unfamiliar with Harriet Tubman's wartime service causally perused the issue of the *Auburn Citizen* in which Brister's appeal appeared, he or she might be forgiven the impression that the mayor was commenting in reference to one of Auburn's well-known white Civil War veterans, such as the dashing soldier of fortune Myles Keogh (1840–76), who fought in several Civil War battles and whose grave at Fort Hill Cemetery is marked by an imposing nine-foot-tall tombstone.[53]

On Friday, June 12, 1914, Booker T. Washington arrived in Auburn by train at 5:25 in the afternoon. Auburn's civic leaders met him at the

46. Emily Howland (1827–1929), present at Tubman's memorial service. Courtesy Friends Historical Library of Swarthmore College, Swarthmore, Penn.

station and escorted him to Major Aiken's home on Owasco Road for dinner. According to a reporter for the *Auburn Citizen*, the Wizard of Tuskegee was as impressive a figure as he had been when he last visited Auburn in 1911, though he appeared a "trifle older." [54] Shortly before 8:00 P.M., Washington was whisked to the Burtis Auditorium, where a large crowd had assembled, filling the entire floor of the auditorium as well as the boxes. Emily Howland (1827–1929; Figure 46), born of Quaker parentage at Sherwood (Cayuga County) and a longtime friend of Tubman, occupied one of the boxes. The Howland home had been an important stop on the Underground Railroad in Cayuga County.

According to a report in the *Auburn Citizen* the following Saturday, "A large number of colored people from various portions of the state were present to pay tribute to the woman who braved so many dangers and underwent untold hardships in bringing about their freedom. A section of the theater was reserved for them and they filled it completely." [55] Does this signify segregated seating? As the eight o'clock hour approached, Olmstead's Orchestra and the Auburn Festival Chorus took their places on stage, along with other participants in the "Order of Exercises."

Olmstead's Orchestra opened the evening's program with the Adelle

Selection. Then Lenna J. Brooks, soloist, and the festival chorus led the assembly in the singing of Julia Ward Howe's famous "Battle Hymn of the Republic," with the audience joining in on the refrain. Reverend John Quincy Adams offered a prayer. Adams had been present in Charleston, Virginia, when authorities had hanged John Brown. At the time of Tubman's funeral fourteen months earlier, Adams, then living in Harrisburg, Pennsylvania, sent a letter to the Auburn papers expressing his deep sorrow at her death. Her passing reminded him of the great martyrs of the Civil War: "When I think of Lincoln and John Brown as a boy standing one hundred yards off and saw Stevens and Hazlett hanged at Charleston, Va., how can I forget the sainted Aunt Harriet?" "Not only the colored but the good whites, many of them," Adams vouchsafed, "helped her in her efforts at all times. Mrs. Adam's uncle, John W. Jones of Elmira, New York, was associated with her and others in the Underground System. He told us very much of Aunt Harriet's great work."[56] Auburn's Festival Chorus followed the prayer with a rendition of the stirring hymn "Jerusalem, the Golden."

Now came the most dramatic moment of the unveiling program. The Honorable E. Clarence Aiken stepped to the podium and said, "There have been very few monuments erected to slaves and very few to the memory of Negroes and I believe but one to a Negro woman and a slave, but Auburn is erecting this tablet." The lights in the house dimmed. Alice H. Lucas stepped forward. The tablet (see Figure 47) occupied center stage, set against a backdrop of paper mache designed in the shape of a seashell and surrounded by red, white, and blue lights. Tubman's grandniece approached the tablet and drew back the flag that had covered it. There was a moment of hushed silence as the interracial audience took in the picture. "In the light of the colored electric bulbs," reported the *Auburn Citizen*, "the effect was most pleasing."[57] With "epigraphic conciseness," as the *Advertiser-Journal* said, "the noble achievements" of Harriet Tubman were summed up in the inscription on the tablet:

IN MEMORY OF
HARRIET TUBMAN
BORN A SLAVE IN MARYLAND ABOUT 1821
DIED IN AUBURN, N.Y., MARCH 10TH, 1913
CALLED THE "MOSES" OF HER PEOPLE
DURING THE CIVIL WAR, WITH RARE

COURAGE, SHE LED OVER THREE HUNDRED
NEGROES UP FROM SLAVERY TO FREEDOM
AND RENDERED INVALUABLE SERVICE
AS NURSE AND SPY.
WITH IMPLICIT TRUST IN GOD
SHE BRAVED EVERY DANGER AND
OVERCAME EVERY OBSTACLE, WITHAL
SHE POSSESSED EXTRAORDINARY
FORESIGHT AND JUDGMENT SO THAT
SHE TRUTHFULLY SAID
"ON MY UNDERGROUND RAILROAD
I NEBBER RUN MY TRAIN OFF DE TRACK
AND I NEBBER LOS' A PASSENGER."
THIS TABLET IS ERECTED
BY THE CITIZENS OF AUBURN
1914

Once the auditorium lights came back on, Mayor Brister stepped forward to receive the memorial tablet on behalf of the City of Auburn: "In accepting this table we reaffirm in a public way our belief that in the fullness of time character shall be measured by its true standard irrespective of its origin or its surroundings. . . . Measured by such a standard, the woman whose memory is today honored and perpetuated must be ranked with the great characters of history. . . . Not because the subject of this memorial was a woman, nor because she was black, is this tribute tendered, but rather to commemorate the inherent greatness of her character."[58]

Mayor Brister's remarks bestowed on Tubman the honor of belonging to everyone—she was to be thought of as an American patriot, bridging divides of race and gender. As if to underscore this, the Festival Chorus followed the mayor's acceptance of the tablet with Eichberg's patriotic hymn "To Thee O Country." Then Mary B. Talbert gave a sketch of Tubman's life and work. She spoke for the "colored women" of the country and in so doing attempted to reclaim Tubman as "the great heroine of my race."[59]

This dialectic over the ownership of Tubman as symbol played itself out once again when Booker T. Washington, the principal speaker of the evening, came to the podium following the next musical interlude, a ren-

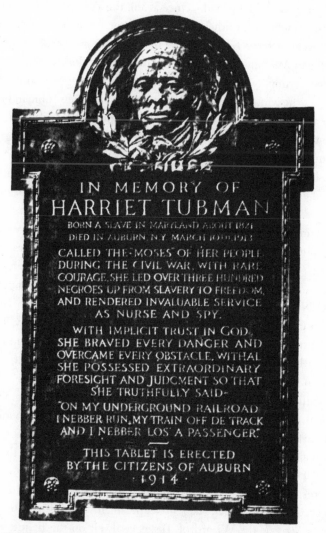

IN MEMORY OF
HARRIET TUBMAN
BORN A SLAVE IN MARYLAND ABOUT 1821
DIED IN AUBURN N.Y. MARCH 10TH 1913

CALLED THE "MOSES" OF HER PEOPLE
DURING THE CIVIL WAR, WITH RARE
COURAGE SHE LED OVER THREE HUNDRED
NEGROES UP FROM SLAVERY TO FREEDOM,
AND RENDERED INVALUABLE SERVICE
AS NURSE AND SPY.

WITH IMPLICIT TRUST IN GOD
SHE BRAVED EVERY DANGER AND
OVERCAME EVERY OBSTACLE, WITHAL
SHE POSSESSED EXTRAORDINARY
FORESIGHT AND JUDGMENT SO THAT
SHE TRUTHFULLY SAID —

"ON MY UNDERGROUND RAILROAD
I NEBBER RUN MY TRAIN OFF DE TRACK
AND I NEBBER LOS' A PASSENGER."

THIS TABLET IS ERECTED
BY THE CITIZENS OF AUBURN
·1914·

47. Tubman memorial plaque, Cayuga County Court House. Photograph by the author.

dition of Mendelssohn's "He, Watching over Israel." "Harriet Tubman," Washington intoned, "was a unique and great character of which any race and any age should be proud." Once again, the Wizard of Tuskegee was demonstrating how adroitly he could maneuver through America's entangling thicket of race. To underscore the bridging quality of memorializing Tubman, Washington elaborated: "In the ten millions of black people scattered throughout this country, there are many great souls, heroic souls, that the white race does not know about. Harriet Tubman brought these two races nearer together and made it possible for the white race to know the black race to place a different estimate upon it. In too many sections of our country, the white man knows the criminal Negro, but he knows little about the law-abiding Negro; he knows much of the worst types of our race, he does not know enough of the best types of our race."

Washington spoke for about an hour. Unlike Talbert, he devoted little of his address to the details of Tubman's life, telling his hearers, "These you know better than I." He opened with complimentary remarks about Auburn ("Indeed, she was not without honor in her own home") and upstate New York, which had given the nation, in addition to Tubman, William H. Seward, Frederick Douglass, and Susan B. Anthony. Then in what must have been an especially touching moment, the acknowledged leader of black America turned his attention to an elderly white woman sitting in one of the auditorium boxes—Emily Howland—"a woman," Washington averred, "who, through her generosity and interest in all that concerns my race, has endeared herself to this and future generations." With the formalities of thanking his hosts completed, Washington turned to the major theme of his speech, satisfying the question, "Was the heroic work of Harriet Tubman worthwhile?"

In responding to the question he posed, Washington drew on a familiar discourse. As he had done personally in his autobiography *Up from Slavery*, the Wizard of Tuskegee dwelt on the themes of self-responsibility, progress, and racial uplift. African Americans had climbed the mountain of opportunity, despite tremendous obstacles. The race now numbered more than 10 million and, through hard work and mutual support had accumulated 20 million acres of land. Blacks had built and paid for 600,000 houses; owned and operated 10,000 grocery, dry goods, and shoe stores; 400 drug stores; and over 60 banks. "Progress in these directions," Washington argued, "will indicate that the work of Harriet

Tubman was not in vain." When Washington turned to the question of education, he took up a subject especially dear to him. When freedom came, he claimed, only 3 percent of the African American population could read or write. In 1914, "by the official records, it is shown that 69 percent of the American Negro can both read and write."

As Washington approached the end of his address, he invoked the legacy of Tubman and the old phalanx of antislavery fighters. They had, he contended, freed two races. African Americans had been liberated from the yoke of slavery; whites America had been liberated from a fratricidal conflict. Washington was, paradoxically, optimistic and cautious. Of the existing state of race relations in the part of the nation where nine out ten African Americans lived, he asserted: "There never was a period in the history of the country when, all things considered, there were so many evidences of racial friendship and cooperation as exist in the South today." Having said this, Washington went on to challenge those who had gathered to honor Tubman. The battle was not over. There still was work do. In the face of problems, whether local or national, Americans should look to Harriet Tubman for inspiration: "From this humble and comparatively ignorant black woman we can all, white and black, glean a lesson which will strengthen us, broaden us, and make us of more service to our community, to our race, and to our nation." [60]

At the conclusion of Washington's remarks, Mrs. Harry A. Tidd, soloist, and the Auburn Festival Chorus sang Stephen Foster's "Way Down upon the Swanee River," replete with the racialist language about "darkies" and cheerful images of plantation life (banjo and bees a-humming) among "de old folks at home," a stereotype that historians would routinely debunk in another half-century and Tubman herself contradicted, as any of the survivors of the "peculiar institution" might have. The unveiling program closed with a benediction, offered by Reverend Brooks, and music by Olmstead's orchestra. Some days later, the tablet was fixed to the front of the Cayuga County Courthouse, where it can be seen today. One wonders if it still elucidates from passersby something of the purpose set for it by its sponsors: "It will teach generations that success in its true sense is a spiritual nature—and in thinking of this woman's monument many a person, white as well as black, will realize that the unselfish life is the genuine life to lead." [61]

Emma Paddock Telford lived in Auburn and had known "Aunt Harriet" well for many years. In her tribute, published as an open letter to the

48. Woman's group at graveside. From *Tribute to Harriet Tubman: The Modern Amazon* (Auburn, N.Y.: Auburn Business Men's Association, 1914).

community, Telford acknowledged that Tubman's physical self "sleeps today on our green hillside" in Fort Hill (Figure 48). "But the wonderful spirit that animated it, brave, invincible, like that of her old friend, John Brown, 'still goes marching on,' deathless in its influence and one of the 'immortals.'"[62]

Had the apotheosis of Harriet Tubman fostered in the funeral and memorial events made amends for the long period when most of America seemed to have forgotten the woman and her contributions to the patriot cause of securing liberty for all? Despite the undercurrent of racialist language flowing through some of the sentiments expressed when the funeral took place, and later at the unveiling of the memorial tablet, there was a new and encouraging development in the communal process of shaping the national memory of Tubman. She was being hailed as an American patriot, an icon bridging the chasms of gender and race. Did this portend admittance into the pantheon of American "greats"—into the hall of fame occupied by historical figures such as Abraham Lincoln and Thomas Jefferson? The American memory is capricious, at best, and arbitrary, inconstant, and contrary at worst, jealous of its prerogatives. Harriet Tubman's apotheosis, as we shall see, was fragile and momentary.

CHAPTER SEVEN

EARL CONRAD AND THE BOOK
THAT ALMOST WASN'T

In December 1939, Cyril Briggs, editor of the Crusader News Agency (CNA), trumpeted a forthcoming book about Harriet Tubman. He urged the two hundred fifty black newspapers his agency served to subscribe to it in serial form: "We confidently predict that this thrilling biography by Earl Conrad will be thunder on the literary horizon. Conrad's story of Harriet Tubman revives a magnificent and heroic period in the history of the Negro people. It will grip and thrill your readers! It will set them agog! It will win you readers!" Of the author of the proposed *I Bring You General Tubman*, Briggs said, "CNA believes that this is the first time in American literary history that a white writer has treated the Negro without making the subject exotic, without patronizing, but handling the theme, indeed in the manner to which 'the greatest woman in the nation's history,' as he called her, is entitled." Briggs predicted that Conrad's book would "probably stand as the definitive life of Harriet Tubman as long as the Negro people remember their leaders" and announced that Conrad's "monumental work" would be published in book form in 1940.[1]

In June 1939, Briggs had carried an appeal from Conrad for "leads on historical material" about Tubman, whom Conrad then described as "historically the foremost woman in the nation's history."[2] Now that the book was imminent, or so he thought, Briggs enthusiastically endorsed it and put the following question to the black editors of America: "Is Harriet the greatest woman in American history as Conrad declares her to be? The Negro people, through CNA and the papers it serves, will have the first opportunity of passing upon this question. Conrad's work will be published in book form during 1940. Meantime, we offer you this opportunity to bring it first to our people and thereby win the plaudits of your readers and recruit new readers."[3]

Briggs and the million and a half black readers whom he claimed the CNA reached through the black press had to wait three more years for the publication of Earl Conrad's book-length biography of Harriet Tubman.[4] When *Harriet Tubman* appeared in the autumn of 1943, Conrad's dedicatory note was both an exorcism and an expression of gratitude. To his wife, Alyse, the crusading journalist and newspaperman said: "This is the book that you helped me to do,—the one that the white publishers would not issue. That is because this is of the people that the white rulers are slow to free. But free them they must or conflicts like the present will go on until this matter is settled right."[5] Then only thirty-one, Earl Conrad had devoted more than five years to rescuing Harriet Tubman from the dustbin of history and positioning her in an honored place in the American memory. In the process, he discovered how deeply rooted racism's roots were. His tribute to Tubman, the first serious attempt to reconstruct her life based on primary sources as well as an exhaustive probing of stories about her since the publication of Sarah Bradford's biographical sketches, remained the most reliable source for Tubman enthusiasts for more than six decades. Subsequent writings about Tubman invariably drew on Conrad's book. Readers in search of the "authentic" Tubman have often turned to Conrad's constructed Tubman as "definitive," but his iconic Tubman was, like Bradford's, a construction for the times in which the book appeared.

When trying to sell his manuscript to skeptical editors and publishing outlets, Conrad often said that he was writing the "definitive" biography of Harriet Tubman. In 1963, twenty years after *Harriet Tubman* appeared in print under the auspices of the Associated Publishers of Washington, D.C., the publishing arm of the Association for the Study of Negro Life and History, Conrad attempted to get the book reissued by saying, "*Harriet Tubman* is the standard definitive biography of that woman. It has been a steady seller since its publication twenty years ago. It has never been sold in general book stores nor has it been a paperback. In the interracial area it is regarded as an important book, as Harriet is the outstanding woman of color in American history and is usually equated with Joan of Arc."[6] Three years later, still trying to draw attention to his Tubman book, Conrad wrote to a friend, "'Harriet Tubman' has been selling steadily since it was published 23 years ago: has sold

8,500 copies. Very well reviewed upon its appareance [*sic*], as the attached list notes. About five juvenile novels have been based—without credit to me—on this book. It is much beloved by the Negroes. They never refer to any of my other civil rights book [*sic*] as much as to this."[7] And in 1969, when America's streets echoed to cries of "Black Power!" Conrad wrote to his friend Paul Eriksson about doing a reprint: "This book [the reprint] would have to be bought and used by the black studies programs from coast to coast. It is the definitive book. There is no other. Many many books about H. Tubman, including six or seven juveniles, have been based on this book, and all the books which carry chapters on Tubman, get their information from this book: though nobody has written to me mentioning the use of the book. Most recent users of the book were Senator [George R.] Metcalf whose McGraw Hill Book on Profiles of Blacks, had a chapter on Tubman, also a couple of these hurried quickie type books, choefly [*sic*] written by blacks now, have purloined from this one. I don't mind. I would like to see the big permanent book, which has to last as long as thefe [*sic*] is a black-white question, get into the general stores."[8]

Paul Eriksson released a paperback edition of *Harriet Tubman* in 1969 (Figure 49).[9] Conrad wrote an introductory "Author's Note," in which he took pleasure in the prospect of having his rendering of the Harriet Tubman story inspire new generations. But he also recalled the painful struggle he went through to get the original version out to the American public. "It is a long time since I did the research on the life of Harriet Tubman; I began it thirty-five years ago and finished it thirty years ago. I recollect the fidelity with which I examined virtually every book published in the previous century, seeking the name of Harriet Tubman, and light on the times she lived through and helped create. In about 1940 or 1941, after that half-decade of re-living the previous century through the heart and deeds and life of a black woman, I was ready to publish the book to which I now write this later note. Alas, I happened onto a period of hard times for the literature of blackness. Nearly all of the New York City publishers saw and turned down this story."[10] Conrad acknowledged that a profusion of books and articles about Tubman had appeared by the 1970s, many of them based on his research and interpretation, a sign that the "political hush about the black-white question," so dominant when he was trying to market his original manuscript, had ended. The dedication to the Eriksson edition is, simply, "To My Wife, Alyse."

49. Book cover to paperback edition of Earl Conrad's *Harriet Tubman* (New York: Paul S. Eriks-son, 1969 [1943]).

It was left to Alyse Conrad to write the foreword to her husband's book when Associated Publishers released its own paperback edition in 1990, now under the title *General Harriet Tubman*.[11] Earl Conrad died on January 17, 1986, in La Jolla, California, survived by his wife and intellectual partner of nearly fifty years and their one son, Michael Earl Conrad. Anna Alyse Conrad, the former Anna Alyse Abrams of New York City who had married the impoverished but impassioned newspaperman in 1938, told readers as the last decade of the twentieth century began:

> The book was written in a period when blacks could not easily speak for themselves, when the stranglehold of the white power structure almost or quite measurabley [*sic*] stifled black spokesmanship and made it inevitable for an Abolitinist-type [*sic*] white spokesmanship to emerge. Earl Conrad was that kind of spokesman and Dr. Martin Luther King put it succintly [*sic*] in his book *Where Do We Go from Here: Chaos or Community*, when he wrote: "When the Negro (his designation at the time) was completely an underdog, he needed

white spokesmen. Liberals played their parts in this period exceedingly well. In assault after assault, they led the intellectual revolt against racism, and took the initiative in founding the civil rights organizations. But now that the Negro has rejected his role as the underdog, he has become more assertive in his search for identity and group solidarity: he wants to speak for himself."[12]

By the 1990s, African American authors of diverse political persuasions had indeed found their own voices, and it was left to Conrad's wife to attest to the contributions her husband had made during the previous five decades to "the black struggle." She cited some of the many books Conrad had penned about "the black condition," not mentioning the scores of articles and newspaper pieces he contributed on the same theme, and then quoted a line from her husband's unpublished autobiography about how central Harriet Tubman was to his life's work. "I became convinced," Earl Conrad said, "that the source of the essential historical America was in the black and white dilemma and that here I could find myself a modern Abolitionist. Free the black man and help free my country from it [sic] incubus of slavery and bigotry. Who to write about? Through what character could such a story be told." He found that character," Alyse Conrad recalled, "in Harriet Tubman."[13]

Who was this self-described "modern Abolitionist"? Despite the plea his wife made in 1989 as Conrad's biography of Tubman was being prepared for republication, Earl Conrad is not much known by contemporary students of American history, except as the name attached to the Harriet Tubman book. Yet he was the author of twenty-five books. He was also a widely published journalist and newspaper columnist, essayist, and progressive social reformer who knew or had contact with many of the important African American activists and writers who fought against the incubus of racism from the late 1930s into the civil-rights era (Figure 50). The following is an analysis of his struggle to place Harriet Tubman in the American pantheon of historical figures worth remembering. Conrad's *Harriet Tubman* is a mediated Tubman, no less than Sarah Bradford's two biographical treatments of her were. Conrad could no more free himself from the context of his times and the convolutions on race that were then current than Sarah Bradford could from hers. That Cyril Briggs and other voices prominent in African American communities felt that Earl Conrad succeeded in depicting Harriet Tubman heroically con-

50. Earl Conrad. Photograph by Lotte Jacobs. From the dust jacket of Earl Conrad, *The Governor and the Lady* (New York: G. P. Putnam's Sons, 1960).

firms Alyse Conrad's conviction that her husband had found in Tubman the character through whom he could contribute to the breaking down of the fortress of American racism.

In 1954, when Doubleday was preparing to release his eighth book, *Gulf Stream North*, Conrad drafted a promotional biographical sketch. It began: "I was born December 17, 1912, in Auburn, New York. From the age of five or six through my adolescence I rode over the town and countryside with my father, a cattle dealer, and watched him make innumerable horse trades. My recollections of him and that Auburn childhood resulted in the story, 'Horse Trader,' published in 1953, just a few months after my father died. Harriet Tubman, a Negro woman heroine of the Civil War, spent her declining days in Auburn, and it happened that I wrote a story of her life (spending five years on the research) and this became my first published book in 1943."[14] In correspondence written in 1939 when Conrad was immersed in the Tubman research, he maintained that he had not chosen the topic simply because of his Auburn roots. To Elmer A. Carter, a fellow native of Auburn who had become editor of *Opportunity*, Conrad wrote: "It happens that I come from Auburn, N.Y., myself, although my interest in Harriet arises out of my interest in history and in the colored people in particular, and it was here in New York that I became interested in Harriet rather than in my home town."[15] In July 1939, Conrad told Hildegarde Hoyt Swift, who also grew up in the community where Tubman lived for more than half a century, "Although I too come from Auburn, New York, I approached the subject of Harriet through channels other than that of having lived in the same town in which she also lived. My interest in the Abolition movement led me around to Mrs. Tubman."[16] Swift, the former Hildegarde Hoyt and the daughter of Professor A. S. Hoyt of the faculty of the Auburn Theological Seminary, had written a fictionalized account of the life and adventures of Harriet Tubman published as *The Railroad to Freedom* by Harcourt, Brace and World in 1932.[17] Conrad privately told a friend that Swift's book was nothing more than a "slapdash thriller," not a scholarly job.[18]

Though Conrad downplayed the notion that his Auburn connection influenced his choice of Harriet Tubman as the means by which he could help advance the cause of black liberation, his ties to the upstate New York community need to be explored, both as a way of better understanding Conrad himself but also as a means of probing how the book of which he was immensely proud came into being. "Earl Conrad" was born Earl Cohen, the son of Eli and Minnie Cohen. Though Earl Cohen chose to Anglicize his name when he began his career as a professional journalist, he does not seem to have hidden the fact that he was, as his wife informed readers of the foreword of the 1990 publication *General Harriet Tubman*, "reared in the Judaic tradition."[19] Indeed, Conrad's identity as a Jewish journalist and writer during a period in which Jewish liberals and African American activists forged an alliance is noteworthy. Alyse Conrad said of her husband in 1989, "As a victim himself of anti-Semitism he had early understood the struggle that would have to be made to achieve the kind of society [equitable for black people] he envisioned." Conrad's wife also claimed that when he was very young, Earl Cohen "often saw [Harriet Tubman] sitting on her verandah, an old woman wearing the white shawl that Queen Victoria gave her."[20] One wonders how this could be so, since Conrad was born in 1912, but a year before Tubman's death.

Earl Cohen grew up in a boisterous and spirited household. Minnie Cohen, his mother, handled the family finances and in-house grocery store, while her husband, Eli, went about Auburn with a horse-drawn grocery wagon. His passion, and his weakness, was for dealing in horseflesh. In *Horse Trader: The Story of a Real David Harum*, published in 1953 shortly after the death of Eli Cohen, Earl Conrad profiled the Cohens of Auburn. Earl had nine siblings and had to struggle to carve out his own personal identity. Though he admired his mother's ability to hold the large family together and make most of the important decisions, young Earl enjoyed riding around with his father delivering groceries.[21] Earl attended the public schools of Auburn and went to high school for four years, but he did not graduate.

Sometime in his early years, Conrad discovered what he would later call his "gift of wordiness."[22] "I knew from a very early age," he said in 1954, "that I wanted to write and I recall attempting a neighborhood newspaper at the age of twelve."[23] Only one edition appeared. At fourteen, Earl Cohen became a high-school reporter for the Auburn *Citizen-Advertiser*. Between seventeen and twenty, the future biographer of Harriet Tubman engaged in what he would later refer to as his "tramp newspaper days."[24] He worked on at least ten different newspapers in New York State and New England.

A diary kept by Tubman's future biographer that was written during his tramp newspaper days when he lived in New Bedford, Massachusetts, reveals aspects of his outlook on life prior to deciding that he should become a modern-day abolitionist. The youthful Conrad described himself as a "futalist [*sic*]" for whom "an even tenor prevailing where there is no belief in God may yet be a life not lived in vain." He celebrated the seventh anniversary of Prohibition by getting "totally drunk" but resolved to quit drinking and reestablish self-discipline and self-rule under the axiom "Knowledge Is Power." Emblematic of his better self, the youthful journalist promised that he would answer his mother's letters—in Yiddish.[25]

Conrad has declared that his discovery of the black–white dilemma of America came as a result of his travels during his apprenticeship days as a reporter and editor. "Wherever I went in those tramp newspaper days, I noticed the second class citizenship of our colored citizens, and in 1932, while visiting in the South I became interested in their lives."[26] In the autumn of 1934, in the midst of the Great Depression, Conrad went to live in New York City. Of his early years there he told Harkless Bowley, a nephew of Harriet Tubman with whom he corresponded in 1940 during the research phase of the Tubman book, "Soon after I arrived in New York I became a trade union organizer. For a long while I organized truck drivers on the waterfront; and it was here that I established my first contacts with Negroes. I found that most of the people who interested me were the Negro porters and truck drivers, and I found myself calling upon them in Harlem. I soon became convinced that the Negro people are the most important single national group in America, and that they always have been: that they have been since about 1700 anyway."[27] In his spare time, Conrad studied the history of Africans in America and "took a class or two" from a black teacher in Harlem. But labor organizing had taken its toll: "My health was weakening from too much running about." So Conrad decided to resume writing. "I looked over the various Negro figures," he told Bowley, "and I came to the conclusion that Harriet was the greatest and one about whom, for her stature, the least was known. I believed that through presenting Harriet I could show also the contribution of the Negro people."[28]

Like many American writers and journalists during the Great Depression, Conrad found that the economic downturn severely undercut his opportunities to earn a gainful living, so he took a position with the Federal Writers' Project, working on a history of New York with a stipend of $21.00 a week. While Conrad disliked being dependent on the federal government, he needed the stopgap income and joined other struggling writers on the picket line in front of the Port Authority building to protest an effort to cut back on the Writers' Project. From the history of New York project, Conrad went on to join a group assigned to write a history of America, to be called *News of the Nation*. While working on these projects, Conrad wrote a novel about newspaper work and submitted it in a contest sponsored by a publisher for the best book written by an author employed with the Federal Writers' Project. The African American author Richard Wright, whose fame would be secured by the publication in 1945 of his autobiography, *Black Boy*, took the prize with a collection of short stories titled *Uncle Tom's Children* (1938).[29] In a gesture that drew Conrad closer to the emerging coterie of left-oriented African American creative personalities based in Harlem, he went to Richard Wright and congratulated him. "You did a much better book," Conrad recalled saying, "on a more basic question." Conrad thought Wright was surprised that another writer should come to him and commend his work as superior to his own submission in the competition. Conrad held the opinion that Wright was "the best product . . . nationally" of the Federal Writers' Project.[30]

51. Book cover (dust jacket, with misspelling of Hildegarde). From Hildegarde Hoyt Swift, *The Railroad to Freedom: A Story of the Civil War*, illustrations by James Daugherty (New York: Harcourt, Brace and World, 1932). Copyright © 1960 by Hildegarde Hoyt Swift.

Conrad launched his research campaign in earnest in 1938 after having searched for publications about Harriet Tubman. There was little to inform him, for apart from the two books by Bradford, American writers had for the most part ignored her or been so dependent on Bradford that they offered no new information or interpretations. Occasional tributes had appeared in African American–sponsored publications of limited circulation since Tubman's apotheosis in 1913.[31] From time to time, the white press did give notice to Tubman, as was the case with an article by Katharine Rose Foster published in a Baltimore paper on April 21, 1924, under the title, "A Moses in War-Time Maryland: Harriet Tubman Led Many Slaves through the Lines to Freedom." Foster began her essay by acknowledging that "few people" any longer knew of Tubman's Underground Railroad work on the Eastern Shore of Maryland.[32] More influential because it appeared in 1932 in novelized book form under the imprimatur of a major American publisher, *The Railroad to Freedom: A Story of the Civil War*, by Hildegarde Hoyt Swift (Figure 51), caused Conrad to reflect on what his own purposes were in concentrating so much of his time and energy on the black woman historians of the American experience had chosen to forget.

As noted earlier, Swift (1890–1977) was a former Auburnian; the family home had been at 15 Seminary Avenue. Like Conrad, she eventually moved to New York City and took up the craft of writing. Her first book, *The Railroad to Freedom*, belongs to the category of juvenile literature. Dedicated "To the Courageous Young," and illustrated with drawings by James Daugherty, Swift's book runs to more than three hundred fifty pages in a five-by-seven-inch format. Highly fictionalized, her version of Tubman's life begins in 1831 and draws to a close with the end of the Civil War and Harriet's return to Auburn. Swift tells her readers in the introduction: "In the town where I grew up there lived a colored woman named Harriet Tubman. As a girl I was much interested in the story of her escape from slavery, and I often wondered why it was not written down so that other boys and girls might read it."[33] As to the question of what kind of narrative she was inviting readers to consider, Swift wrote: "This is a story, not a biography, but it is based on authentic history. I shall be very happy if it succeeds in bringing back to reality even a fraction of the courage, vitality and unselfish devotion of this heroic woman."[34] Though Swift received help from two of Tubman's nieces who still lived in Auburn, Mrs. Carroll J. Johnson and Mrs. Frank E. Northrup, and consulted scrapbooks held by Helen Garrett of Wilmington, Delaware, granddaughter of the Quaker stalwart Thomas Garrett, Tubman's compatriot in Underground Railroad work, she depended in large part on the Bradford volumes.

Rayford W. Logan reviewed *The Railroad to Freedom* in the April 1933 issue of the *Journal of Negro History*, the country's oldest scholarly journal dedicated to the preservation of accurate information about the accomplishments of African Americans. Logan praised Swift's book. Given the paucity of publications about Tubman then available, Logan was willing to overlook those instances where Swift took liberties with the historical record—or, to be more precise, created fictional episodes and dialogue. Swift's tendency to "glorify Harriet" troubled Logan somewhat, but he attributed this excess to Swift's enthusiasm for her heroine and her desire to show herself "in sympathy for the Negro race as a whole." Logan felt that Swift had successfully offered a corrective to "the sentimental idylls of slavery that are becoming all too numerous."[35] A professor of history at Howard University, Logan knew how strongly the view of slavery as a benevolent institution dominated American history textbooks of the day. The Southern historian Ulrich B. Phillips had codified the notion that slavery was a benign patriarchal institution in 1918 with his book *American Negro Slavery*. Phillips's portrayal of American slavery as mild but inefficient dominated academic interpretations for three decades, if not longer.[36]

Though Swift's book had been written for young readers, Conrad needed to account for it, especially in light of the favorable review in the *Journal of Negro History*.[37] He wrote to Swift in the summer of 1939 to ask if she knew where the manuscripts, notes, and letters of Sarah Bradford were and complimented her on helping to revive the public's interest in Tubman. Nevertheless, he had reservations and wrote to Swift, "Your novel seems to be equal proportions of fact and fiction." Conrad posed several questions in an attempt to determine where the line between fact and fiction had been drawn. For example, he queried Swift about the section in *The Railroad to Freedom* where Swift has Tubman feeding Colonel Shaw his last meal before the assault on Fort Wagner and then witnessing the fatal assault.[38] Swift wrote back on September 8, 1939, from Ireland, where she was vacationing, "You are naturally right in saying that 'The Railroad' is fiction and it takes liberties which documented biography cannot take." As to Conrad's specific question, Swift said: "She always stoutly maintained that she fed Col. Shaw his last meal etc. and that she was present at this time. It may of course have been only the vivid imagination of a vivid personality, but she was reliable in other respects and knowing the irregular nature of warfare in those days, the presence of camp-followers at times of extreme danger, etc. etc., is highly possible."[39]

In 1933, Sarah N. Cleghorn published *The True Ballad of Harriet Tubman*, a twelve-page poetic tribute. A Vermont woman who admired Tubman, Cleghorn may have talked with some of the same individuals Swift did, for she says that "Harriet Tubman's achievements, of which this Ballad consists, have been verified by persons who heard them from her own lips."[40] Though privately published, Cleghorn's paean to the "glorious" Tubman circulated enough so that it was known to several of the individuals to whom Conrad wrote when making his initial research inquiries. Eleanor Roosevelt wrote in her column "My Day" on January 6, 1940: "Another friend sent me: 'The True Ballad of the Glorious Harriet Tubman,' by Sarah N. Cleghorn. It should be read aloud, for it gives a wonderful picture of a time which I am thankful to say is past for all of us in this country." When gathering his research papers for preservation, Earl Conrad attached a typewritten note to a clipping of Roosevelt's "My Day" column. It reads: "I wrote to Mrs. Roosevelt a couple times about Harriet. Sarah N. Cleghorn said that a friend of hers sent on 'The Ballad.' I think Mrs. Roosevelt's comment is that of an ostrich burying its head in the sand. That time is not past for any of us. Some day it will rare up as it did once before."[41]

Apart from Cleghorn and Swift and one or two others, white authors writing for mainstream audiences ignored Harriet Tubman during the Great Depression, as they had done since her death in 1913. Eleanor Sickels did include a chapter about her, a fictionalized account replete with dialect and accounts of "brave deeds and clever disguises and hairbreadth escapes," in a collection subtitled "True Stories of American Woman, 1608–1865," which Viking Press published in 1935. The "Go Down, Moses" chapter on Tubman in *In Calico and Crinoline*, like Swift's book, focuses on Tubman's Underground Railroad period and targeted younger readers.[42]

While America's establishment publishers, with the exception of Viking, ignored Harriet Tubman, interest in her was being cultivated by left-wing organizations, specifically ones connected with the radical labor movement. Elizabeth Lawson wrote about Tubman for the *Daily Worker* on February 19, 1938, about which Conrad commented in the collection of his papers: "This copy was given to me by Mr. Lawrence Levy who had a dramatic bit on Harriet on the radio once. He had clipped it from the *Daily Worker*. Like most newspaper stories on Harriet this too revealed chiefly specific incidents in her life; that is, it is not interpreted; not critical, not related to her times. But better than other newspaper stories."[43] Conrad's own interest in leftist politics had intensified by 1938. Aware of the inroads that communist organizers had made among segments of the African American population, wooing several prominent writers and intellectuals, not to mention the famous, multitalented singer and dramatist Paul Robeson, Conrad, whose personal politics were strongly pro-labor, attempted to reach African American sources through communist outlets. On May 16, 1939, *New Masses* carried an appeal from Conrad in its "Between Ourselves" column: "I am writing the biography of that great American woman, Harriet Tubman, and I am in quest of letters, information, anecdotes, incidents and so forth, concerning her life and contribution. I should like to hear, in particular, from the descendants of Abolitionists, from the estates of Garrison, Colonel Higginson, Thomas Garrett, Gerrit Smith, any and all operators of the Underground Railroad, and descendants of any officers of the Union Army who may have been associated with her when she served as a soldier, spy, and nurse in South Carolina and Virginia."[44]

Conrad first entertained the idea of writing a book about Tubman in the popular mode of fictionalized history, for that genre offered the possibility of a larger readership than a standard biography and, therefore, more of a financial return. With much of his manuscript still to write, Conrad began the long and arduous quest for a publisher in the fall of 1939. He seemed uncertain about how to present his work-in-progress to potential mainstream publishers. In October, he wrote to the editor of Viking Press, which had published Swift's book, that the style of his proposed book about Tubman was going to be "novelized biography— but distinctly biography."[45] A month earlier, however, he had written the editor of the Boston-based Houghton, Mifflin Company: "A small biography, very inadequate, was written about her several generations ago; a few years ago a juvenile novel, 'The Railroad to Freedom,' based on her life, was written by Hildegard [sic] Hoyt Swift, but a definitive work is still to be done, and that is the job on which I have been engaged for the past year."[46]

Conrad may have been steered away from doing a fictionalized account of Tubman's life because of correspondence he had with Leonard Ehrlich, author of God's Angry Man, a novel about John Brown published in 1932.[47] Conrad asked Ehrlich about the passage in God's Angry Man that describes the incident where young Harriet was struck on the head by a heavy object: "An enraged overseer had thrown it; brooding, she waited three years to kill him with a knife." Conrad told Ehrlich, "I have never been able to learn that Harriet killed her overseer, or planned to."[48] Ehrlich wrote back that he was uncertain where he had first encountered this version of the episode and suggested that Conrad check the "standard works on Brown, such as Sanborn and Villard," which Ehrlich had consulted. He then expressed grave reservations about doing fictionalized biography: "If you find no reference [to] the particular episode I suggested then I think you can safely take it for granted that it is not historically accurate. I regret more and more that I yielded to that kind of thing—fictionally I think it is justified, but on another level it is not good, simply unfair and confusing for the reader. I suppose it is all part of the dilemma facing historical novelists; personally I think the historical novel is rather a bastard form, and I want no further part in it!"[49]

Once Conrad decided that he would write a documented standard biography, he threw himself into the research task, attempting to uncover primary sources, written and oral. Though struggling to support a wife (and after 1941, a young son) on a meager income, Conrad pursued the Tubman book relentlessly, often without regard for his own health. When the book finally came out in the fall of 1943, Conrad revealed something of the stress that the Tubman project had brought him in an interview for the *Daily Worker*. "His life became a series of rejection slips. The postman was his nemesis," the reporter wrote, adding, "Earl Conrad is a thin young man with a sensitive face and tense mannerisms. He's the type with drive and when he gets into a piece of work that captures his heart, there's no sleep on his agenda, practically."[50]

Conrad wanted to get the story right, a journalist's vocational obligation, but his task was made all the more weighty because he saw himself as a modern-day abolitionist. Writing about why he wanted to write the definitive biography of Tubman, Conrad said:

> Like other white Americans I had to do something about a condition. I think it has bothered me as much as it has Negroes. I had to do something, say something, fight someone about this thing. I chose to write about Harriet Tubman—one of the great women of all history—because I saw in her a symbol of the Negro suffering and greatness. Not because I was interested exclusively in Harriet, did I write this biography-history, but because I saw in her an instrument for carrying the story of the rise of the Negro, saw in her a force still capable of wielding a blow for the Negro peoples' rights. Somehow I felt that I—if I had to do it alone—must do something, however little, to help expiate the crime which white, ruling class America has visited upon one generation after another of the people of color for three centuries. I think it is only a little thing—this story of a great liberator. It isn't going to push over Jimcro [*sic*]. But if enough Negroes and enough whites, do some one little thing—whether it is to extend the right bit of courtesy at the right moment, whether it is to correct some kid's misstatement—or some adult's—or go to an

anti-lynch [*sic*] meeting—in any case, do something, maybe we can, together, kick over that damned wall.[51]

Sarah Bradford had been motivated by a desire to assist a poor black woman who had made many sacrifices for others, something Bradford's Christian values validated. Conrad hoped to help expiate America's primal sin of racism (the "Blot on America," to use his phrase). His approach to the task of restoring Tubman to her rightful place in the pantheon of American personalities worth remembering reflected the secular and radical politics of the late Depression era and the early years of World War Two.

Conrad cast a wide net in an effort to gather as much information about Tubman as he could, for he was convinced that the Bradford biographies about her, while useful, were inadequate. He read everything previously published about Tubman that he could get his hands on, advertised widely in the black press and other outlets for information about her, wrote to many black leaders and historians asking for leads, and returned to Auburn to interview anyone who might have known her. As he learned about living descendants of Tubman and any of the abolitionists and suffragists who had known her, he wrote to them seeking assistance. Some of Conrad's letters of inquiry strike a reader today as oddly misdirected. For example, he wrote to Father Divine asking for information about Tubman and underscored how his book could be useful in combating racial discrimination. Father Divine's response was that he did not recognize the category of race.[52]

Alice L. Brickler of Wilberforce, Ohio, who introduced herself to Conrad in a July 19, 1939, letter as "the daughter of Harriet Tubman's favorite niece," proved especially helpful. At first Brickler hesitated, for she did not feel she had much to offer Conrad that he had not already learned, but he assured her that anything she might tell him would be useful, because it was, in his words, "difficult to unearth anything really new" about Brickler's great-aunt.[53] Brickler joined in the task enthusiastically, for she enjoyed Conrad's letters; they gave her the opportunity, so she told him, "to shake the ancestral tree."[54] She soon embraced his project as hers. At one point during their interchange of letters, Brickler sent Conrad a card, writing on it: "Who is Hildegarde Hoyt Swift *&* how dare she steal our 'thunder' by writing 'Railroad to Freedom' (Life of Renowned H.T.)"[55] By the time World War Two began in early September 1939, after Nazi Germany invaded Poland, Brickler felt comfortable enough with Conrad to tell him of intimate family matters, especially of her love for her ten-year-old son Alex II, of her three-year-old daughter named Allice Harriet Mignon, and of how her husband [Alexander J. Dumas Brickler], "a descendant of the great Alexandre Dumas," had become "very interested in our written tête-à-tête." Brickler added, "And I hope Mrs. Conrad has also."[56] After young Alex was "struck and run over" by a speeding automobile while showing off a "little gasoline car" he had built as a birthday surprise for his father, Alice Brickler wrote Conrad an emotion-filled letter as if he were her close friend or spiritual adviser. When he was having trouble finding a publisher, she offered words of encouragement.[57]

Conrad also established a closeknit relationship with another family informant: Harkless Bowley of Baltimore. Bowley responded on January 4, 1939, to Conrad's initial letter of inquiry by telling Conrad: "Yes I remember Grandfather Benjamin and Grand Mother Ritty Ross very well. I can see Grandfather now walking the floor praising the Lord. They were living with Aunt Harriet when we came back from Canada."[58] Harkless's Aunt Harriet had helped his parents and two older siblings escape from Baltimore after his father, John Bowley, brought the family there from the Eastern Shore because the sale of his mother threatened to break up the family. Tubman escorted the Bowleys to Canada, where they lived until they returned with her to Auburn. Harkless was born in Chatham, Canada West, in 1858. The parents eventually returned to Maryland, but Harkless, as he told Conrad, "was left with Aunt Harriet [and] stayed with her quite awhile." In a thirteen-page handwritten letter dated August 8, 1939, Harkless Bowley, who said he would be eighty-two on December 18, 1939, complained of being "forgetful now." He told Conrad, "I am so glad that you have taken upon yourself to write the history of this great woman."[59]

Once Conrad had gained Bowley's confidence, the two men exchanged personal information. Though he complained about the drawbacks of old age, the aches and pains, and the forgetfulness, Bowley did his best to answer Conrad's detailed questions. In turn, the twenty-eight-year-old crusading white journalist revealed something of his personal situation, writing on March 11, 1940: "Well, I am married, I have a very fine wife who is thirty years old, and has worked with me on the Harriet Tubman research just as much as I have myself. She also is as much an active worker for the Negro people as I am regarded to be. . . . There isn't really much to me, or much to say. I am regarded as an intellectual. I've traveled about a bit. I don't like New York City. I have many close friends, most of whom are Negro. I have quite a time making a living as do most people and like most people I'd like a spot out in the country where it's peaceful—but where is there such a place? I don't like the present war and I hope we do not go abroad to fight any more of Britain's battles."[60] The young white journalist promised to send his elderly black confidant a picture of himself. In the last surviving letter from Bowley to Conrad, who had taken to addressing Bowley as "My dear Friend Bowley," Bowley again expressed his pleasure that someone had taken up the task of writing a biography of his aunt and wished the young journalist "much success." "I would like to see the Book when you finished it. I don't know whether I will be living or not. I have been very, very sick since I heard from you."[61]

Conrad's attempt to glean information from another individual who claimed "Aunt Harriet" as a relative did not go as well as did his contacts with Brickler and Bowley. Eva S. Northrup of Philadelphia responded to one of Conrad's letters on April 1, 1940, with questions of her own. She wanted Conrad to send her a "rough copy" of material he had already written, demanded to know what "arrangements" he intended to make with her for any information she might provide him about her aunt, asking, "Also what percentage of the royalty for the sale of your book?" Above all, Northrup wanted to inform Conrad that "Mrs. Brickler is of no relation, neither by blood or through marriage, whatsoever to my Aunt." "I have," said Northrup, "already put her down in History as an imposture [sic]. She has no rightful claim to give out information or to claim credit for an[y] information that she might give." Northrup offered Conrad the opportunity to come to Philadelphia to meet with her, but she wanted him to "bare in mind that Mrs. Brickler is in no way shape or manner a Kin of Harriet Tubman. Neither she nor her parents." Then, as if the point had not been sufficiently made, Northrup once more dismissed Alice Brickler from the select company of surviving "direct descendants," of which, she asserted, there were only seven in 1940: "I would appreciate very much if you would be cautious about using her information. Since she is not rightfully a Kin she is eliminated from sharing any honors."[62]

Taken aback by the tone and content of Northrup's letter, Conrad attempted to mollify his Philadelphia contact in a three-page, single-spaced reply. He pointed out that it was not customary for biographers to compensate their sources, and if he did ever make any money on the book, he intended to donate as much as he could to "organizations which I believe are advancing Negro interests." He noted that he had already received assistance from at least two hundred sources and that the place to recognize them would be in the acknowledgments section of his Tubman book. As to Northrup's demand for compensation, Conrad said, "I can well understand that you are poor: so am I, as I shall indicate in a moment. I only wish I could help you, and each Negro in America. Indeed, that is why I am writing the story of Harriet: I believe that through presenting the facts of her life, the white people of America can learn to understand better the Negro. . . . For a long time I thought of writing a story that would show the rise of the Negro as a nation within the American nation, and I felt that if I could prove Negro contribution and leadership, if I could vindicate the Negro past, I might be making my best contribution for the Negro generally. That is still how I feel." As to his own situation, Tubman's biographer said, "I have not made a dime from my work, and I think it is very possible this work may never earn much money. I have spent several years gathering information, have spent hundreds of dollars in various expenses attached to the research. Indeed, throughout this period my wife and I have lived in a small one-room apartment. My wife has supported me while I worked on this, and I have been and am now a case of malnutrition as a result of these labors. That is why I have been unable to come to see you. I have had no means for making the trip, and that is why I tried to draw you out via [a] letter." Then, to underscore once more how burdened he was, Conrad informed Northrup: "I am having the greatest difficulty in trying to interest a publisher in the product. They do not wish to handle a Negro subject, and I, though white, am experiencing Jim Crow with this as much as any Negro might in searching for a job."[63] Conrad made no mention in his response to the allegations made by Northrup about Brickler.

Conrad corresponded with or interviewed other individuals who claimed to be kin to Harriet Tubman, had firsthand knowledge about her, or were the recipients of oral traditions. Some correspondents had little to offer. For example, George S. Schuyler, the prominent black lawyer who grew up in Syracuse, had but one memory to pass on to Conrad: "My first knowledge of Aunt Harriet came from my mother and maternal grandmother who told me of her exploits. One vivid recollection is a story about Harriet having to hide fugitives in a manure pile with straws in their mouths to enable them to breathe. This may have been merely a tale, yet it profoundly impressed me not only with the woman's ingenuity but with the hardships of 'following the north star.'"[64]

Much more could be said about Conrad's research methods, the intensity and thoroughness with which he pursued leads, some of them provided voluntarily by strangers who somehow heard of his project, and the care that he took to cross-check stories told him. Sorting the wheat from the chaff of the Tubman legend tested all of Conrad's investigative skills. But the harder challenge was still ahead. In mid-1939, the young journalist, without a book to his name, attempted to break through the wall of silence that existed about Tubman in the publishing establishment. While yet on the research trail and with little to show potential publishers except a biographical article of about 3,700 words, versions of which became his prospectus, Conrad began the arduous task of convincing others that Harriet Tubman deserved to have her story told — and by him. The angry tone of what Conrad sent out is illustrated by the opening two sentences of his seventeen-page prospectus: "Of all the crimes of neglect performed by the world's historians, biographers and educators, perhaps the most flagrant is the deliberate suppression of the record of the life and contribution of Harriet Tubman, Negro woman Abolitionist. The amazing thing is that she is historically the foremost woman leader and personality in the land."[65] Conrad disclosed how he intended to present Tubman to the world more succinctly in a comment made to Helen Sellers Garrett, the granddaughter of Thomas Garrett, in a letter written on June 16, 1939: "I expect to treat Harriet Tubman as a neglected or deliberately suppressed Joan of Arc."[66]

Conrad engaged the literary agent Stanford Greenburger to assist in marketing his project to potential publishers. On February 3, 1940, after months of effort, Conrad wrote to Angus Cameron, the New York City-based editor of Little, Brown, that he had sold his manuscript to Pathway Press and was "free to go on." "General Tubman, in its finished state," said Conrad, "was turned down by four houses so I brought it back to Pathway Press where I had a standing offer. This a Negro firm, prepared, to do the book up nicely, and while it won't get off to any big bang like Forrest Wilson's life of Harriet Beecher Stowe, my book will be pushed year in and year out and might come in—I believe it will come in—like the tortoise. Pathway is re-issuing 'The Life and Times of Frederick Douglass' in two more weeks, and production of my book will begin directly thereafter. I got a $150 advance."[67] Richard B. Moore, founder and executive director of the Harlem-based Frederick Douglass Historical and Cultural League, started Pathway Press. According to a flyer dated June 26, 1939, that carried the imprimatur of the International Workers Order, Harriet Tubman Lodge 943, Moore was an authority on black history and abolition who planned to speak about the life and work of Harriet Tubman at a meeting of the lodge.[68] Pathway Press failed to publish Conrad's Tubman manuscript.

Conrad's enthusiasm was premature on another count. He and A. M. Wendell Malliet, president of Wendell Malliet and Company, a black publishing firm based in Harlem, had a falling out. Malliet had offered Conrad up to five hundred dollars to cover advance expenses while he finished the Tubman manuscript. Conrad wrote to Malliet on February 7, 1940, to express reservations about the firm's distribution apparatus and concern that Malliet "had become engulfed in the vanity publishing arrangement."[69] Malliet, who was reluctant to work with Conrad's agent and did not want to sign an Author's League Contract, responded by releasing Conrad from any "agreement to keep us informed of any developments regarding the MS."[70]

Conrad seems to have taken this rejection in stride, for he was still hoping to place his Tubman book with a major publisher. He was already thinking of other projects. He wanted to write a history on the theme of "Leaders of Abolition" that would contain personality treatments of about twenty of the movement's major figures, such as Harriet Beecher Stowe, Frederick Douglass, Wendell Phillips, Gerrit Smith, Thomas Wentworth Higginson, and, of course, Harriet Tubman.[71] He was also dreaming up a major new endeavor—a large-scale novel of the trilogy type. And the protagonist? "I have in mind an American Jean-Christophe, a figure who will be a combination of the mythical John Henry, the great critic Frederick Douglass, a physical Joe Louis and a cultural Paul Robeson," he informed C. Angus Cameron. Why such a figure to center an epic and thoroughly American novel on? Conrad had an answer: "I am sure that the Negro is the born critic of the environment; that criticism is his heritage. I have hung around Harlem too long not to know this truth. I have been with the radicals, with the status quo, with rich and poor—but I know that I have found a desideratum of literary potentiality." His hero was already taking shape in his mind: "This character will be a romantic character, a swashbuckling figure to whom all doors are open, and upon whom all experiences befall, all of the experiences that may befall a Negro. . . . The name of my character probably will be 'John Henry Douglass.'"[72] Neither the composite tribute to abolitionist figures nor the grand trilogy materialized, nor did the popular history of the suffrage movement that Conrad wanted to write because the "six-huge, forbidding tomes" then available as the official history of the women's campaign for the right to vote were inaccessible to most readers.[73] Conrad also proposed a fictional work of approximately 35,000 words to the Willis N. Bugbee Company of Syracuse that would be called "Red Jacket of the Finger Lakes" and draw on his familiarity with upstate New York's Native American folklore and history.[74]

By the end of 1940, Conrad was desperate. He needed a payoff for his heavy investment of time and money in researching the Tubman story. In December of that year he approached the editor of *Coronet* with the hope that the magazine might publish his Brown–Tubman material in light of the public's interest in the release of the Hollywood film *Santa Fe Trail*, an Errol Flynn western done in black and white in which Jeb Stuart, acted by Flynn, pursues John Brown, played by Raymond Massey. Ronald Reagan, the future president, played the role of General George Armstrong Custer.[75]

While Conrad was contemplating new projects, editors at the presses to which he had sent the Tubman proposal and examples of chapters were writing their rejection letters. A typical response was that of Ira Rich Kent of Houghton Mifflin, who told Conrad: "The great Negress was a grand person, but this life of hers suffers in our opinion from certain over-writing, and we do not feel that we could undertake book publication successfully."[76] Quincy Howe, an editor at Simon and Schuster, was blunt: "We have read the manuscript of the life of General Tubman, as far as you have gone with it, and the outline. It is an original biography all right, almost in fact, a freak subject."[77]

Though he disclaimed concern about competition, in June 1940 Conrad heard from Carter G. Woodson, founder and director of the Association for the Study of Negro Life and History and editor of the organization's publishing arm, Associated Publishers, that Sterling Brown of Howard University, the poet whose collection *Southern Road* (1932) drew extensively on African American folklore and vernacular language, was also writing a biography of Tubman.[78] Conrad responded, "I'm glad Brown is doing such a work; there should be, there will be a half dozen or more studies of Tubman before the last word is said upon her; and the more the merrier; for it will all react to the credit of Harriet and all that she stands for."[79]

Still, Conrad had reason to worry. His friend Angus Cameron had bad news: "The reports I have obtained on the manuscript all seem to feel that there's still a good deal of repetition in the material and that there is quite a ring of eulogy rather than objectivity in the tone of the writing. I must say that I have to agree with the former point and to a degree with the latter. I think I mentioned before that I felt this, indicating at the time that some of the eulogistic atmosphere of the sources employed by you had got into the manuscript. I also feel that the sections dealing with the early life of General Tubman are extremely repetitious. This may be due to the fact that the actual material is scarce on her early life."[80] Harold Strauss of Alfred A. Knopf added to the torrent of rejections on November 28, 1940, writing: "We have given your book several readings and we are unable to see how we can obtain a sufficient sale to warrant our making you a publication offer. The market for books on topics of this kind is limited to begin with, and furthermore your book suffers somewhat from the inflation of the factual material beyond reasonable bounds."[81]

In the face of mounting evidence that his book-length treatment of Tubman's life was having difficulty getting past the gatekeepers of white America's publishing houses, Conrad decided to mount a campaign to create public interest in Tubman. He wrote an advance publicity brief called "Some Facts about Harriet Tubman" that appeared in the January 1940 edition of the Crusader News Agency's newssheet. The brief sought to promote serialization of "I Bring You General Tubman" with hyperbolic statements such as this: "When the final word is said about Negro leaders in American history, and indeed, in world history, it is possible, it is almost *certain* that Harriet Tubman will head the list."[82] Conrad also placed a short article titled "John Brown Called Harriet Tubman 'Most of a Man'" in *Friday*, which claimed to be "the weekly magazine that dares to tell the truth." The article called attention to the achievements of African American women, particularly in the trade-union and labor movements. The lead editorial in the May 29, 1940 issue, written by D. S. Gilmore, president of the magazine, called for defending democracy by defending it internationally and at home. Conrad pointed out: "The poll tax keeps the colored women millions from voting, and their fight to live free is still on. The semi-slavery of the American Negro woman constitutes a major challenge to democracy."[83]

Conrad's strategy of trying to promote his Tubman manuscript by publishing parts of it ahead of having a contract might seem self-defeating. But he was convinced that selling Tubman to the public was a political task that had to be done. In April 1940, he told Elmer A. Carter, the *Opportunity* editor: "The reason I am releasing material to magazines is that I am having difficulty landing a publishing house, and magazine publication may help. From *Harper's* I learn, 'This is a bit [of] strong meat for us, in spite of *Native Son*.' Quite an admission of fear of using pro-Negro material. The editor at Little-Brown is vastly interested in the subject—if I will only treat Harriet as a person with 'hallucinations'! Bobbs-Merrill's southern-born Mr. Lambert Davis fears that 'it is a difficult job to sell a woman to the public and tell her story at the same time'—or could that be his real reason? Other reactions have been similar in their evasiveness and insofar as they reveal editorial notions about Negro material."[84] *Opportunity*, the official journal of the National Urban League, would itself decline to publish Conrad on Tubman. Managing Editor Edward Lawson examined chapters and then responded to Conrad with an evasive "they do not seem to fit in with [*Opportunity's*] scheme of things at the present time."[85]

Negro World Digest proved to be more amenable. A Chicago-based African American publication edited by John H. Johnson, the *Digest* published two excerpts from Conrad's book, said to be "forthcoming," one summarizing Tubman's exploits as a "great leader" and the other dealing with the Combahee raid.[86] *Crisis* also published a portion of Conrad's book-in-progress, a short article about Tubman's role in the rescue of Charles Nalle.[87] In the journal's annual review of books published by black authors, Arthur B. Spingarn noted some of the landmark publications of 1940, including books by Sterling Brown (*Poems in This Generation*); Allison Davis with John Dollard (*Children in Bondage*), W. E. B. Du Bois (*Dusk at Dawn*); E. Franklin Frazier (*Negro Youth at the Crossways*); Robert Hayden (*Heart-Shape in the Dust*); Langston Hughes (*The Big Sea*); James Weldon Johnson (*The Book of Negro Spirituals*); Rayford W. Logan (*The Attitude of the Southern White Press toward Negro Suffrage, 1932–1940*); Claude McKay (*Harlem: Negro Metropolis*); Mary Church

Terrell (*A Colored Woman in a White World*), and Richard Wright (*Native Son*, as well as a reissue of *Uncle Tom's Children*).[88] While not proof of a new open-door policy for books about black themes, the 1940 list should have encouraged Conrad. Still, the rejection letters kept coming. At least two other small pieces appeared prior to the release of Conrad's book in late 1943.[89]

Conrad went through 1941 without placing his manuscript with a publisher. He told Arthur B. Spingarn in March that the Negro Publishing Society, which Conrad described as "a newly forming publishing firm," was going to publish the Tubman book in the fall.[90] The firm failed to materialize, and Conrad continued the wait while the postman brought more letters of rejection. Helen Lincoln of Reynal and Hitchcock gave his manuscript a sympathetic reading and told Conrad that she had wanted to "go all out for" publication, but after reading what he had sent her, she concluded: "Your presentation is so scholarly that the dramatic figure of Harriet failed to take shape for me. There is so much repetition, so much conjecture, so much 'ten years later such-and-such would be happening,' and so little of Harriet herself as the dramatic and magnificent personality she was."[91] Lincoln suggested that Conrad approach a university press. He did that in May 1941, telling a representative of the University of North Carolina Press that his manuscript was completed and that Richard Wright was reading a copy and interested in dramatizing it for Broadway. Describing himself "as a lecturer and expert on Negro history" who was "known to the NAACP, the National Negro Congress, the labor movement, etc.," Conrad tried to gain entry to the press by saying that if the book were popularly priced, he thought he could arrange for the sale of 1,500 copies.[92]

Though he had no offer in hand for publication of his manuscript, Conrad was already thinking of where to deposit the primary and secondary sources he had gathered and was continuing to gather. He approached L. D. Reddick with the hope that his Tubman materials could be sold to the New York Public Library for its Schomburg Collection, but Reddick was unable to sell the idea to library officials. Conrad also tried to interest Arthur Spingarn, a well-known African American collector. He wrote to Spingarn on March 24, 1941, "I suppose I ought to make a gift of it to the Harlem Library but the long stretch of working on the book has drained me and I'm interested in realizing something for it. I don't have the proper quarters for hanging onto it myself, nor any desire to."[93]

Spingarn declined: "Thank you for your offering your Tubman collection but it does not come within the scope of my collections."[94] Conrad eventually donated the bulk of his Harriet Tubman research naterials, about 3,500 items, to the New York Public Library's Schomburg Collection of Negro Literature and History, now called the Schomburg Center for Research in Black Culture and located at 515 Malcolm X Boulevard in Harlem.[95] Conrad retained many items, particularly those related to his struggle to get published, and later included them with his personal papers, a large photograph collection, memorabilia, and oil paintings (his hobby was painting) that are now part of the Earl Conrad Collection in the Norman F. Bourke Memorial Library at Cayuga Community College in Auburn, New York.[96]

Japan's attack on Pearl Harbor on December 7, 1941, dramatically altered the mood of America. Resources of all kinds now had to be directed to supporting the war effort. Publishers began to rethink their listings. W. W. Norton and Company informed Conrad in January 1942 that there had been interest in his Tubman manuscript, but now the public's preoccupation with World War Two increased the risk of publishing the book.[97] In May, Conrad heard from Richard J. Walsh, president of the John Day Company. Walsh informed him that Pearl Buck had read the Tubman manuscript "with much interest" and referred it to his publishing house. Still, the answer was no.[98] And so it went throughout the first half of 1942.

Then the struggling journalist-turned-historian received a morale boost, and in a fashion not likely to have impressed conservative white editors. The National Education Department of the International Workers Order decided to publish and widely circulate a poem dedicated to Paul Robeson written by Conrad, who is described on the cover of the publication as the "Author of Forthcoming Story of Harriet Tubman." The poem, sold at five cents a copy, takes its title from the first stanza: "I heard a Black Man sing last night, I heard the thunder roar. I heard a man, a towering man: And I never can hear more." Conrad mentions Tubman in the sixth stanza: "John Brown was there and Tubman too, And Frederick Douglass great. The Civil War and what is more, the future of our State."[99] Conrad was pleased but somewhat puzzled by the interest in his poem, writing to Roy Wilkins, then the editor of *Crisis*, on April 1, 1942: "The International Workers Order was kind enough to take an interest in my ballad and they are pushing it very heavily. The first edition of

52. Cover of Earl Conrad, *Harriet Tubman: Negro Soldier and Abolitionist* (New York: International Publishers, 1942).

2,000 was sold out in four days and a second printing of 5,000 will begin tomorrow. I think it rather amusing in a way. I've struggled with Tubman so long and the going has been tough: then along comes a few stanzas of verse—and I have a feeling it will go sky-high. If you can find space in one of your early numbers for a review of the ballad, I'd greatly appreciate it."[100] Paul Robeson, whose radical politics on questions of race and labor, as well as his affiliation with the Communist Party, had marked him as a troublemaker in conservative circles, was himself a great admirer of Tubman, drew inspiration from her courage, and held her up as a role model throughout the 1940s and 1950s when he was at the center of the controversies about what being an American meant.[101]

International Publishers also assisted Conrad in 1942 with the publication of a booklet of about fifty pages called *Harriet Tubman: Negro Soldier and Abolitionist* (Figure 52).[102] Part of the series "On Afro-American History and Freedom," which included publications by W. E. B. Du Bois, Herbert Aptheker, Philip S. Foner, Kwame Nkrumah, and the communist councilman from Harlem, Benjamin J. Davis, Conrad's portrayal of

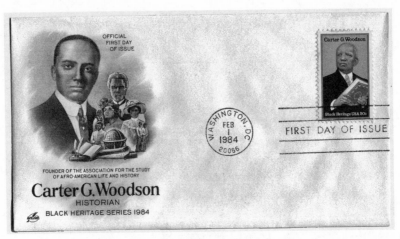

53. Carter G. Woodson stamp, Official First Day of Issue. In the author's collection.

Tubman as the archetypal freedom fighter kept company with a radical group of authors and subjects. The booklet about Tubman, at eighteen cents a copy, came out in an initial printing of ten thousand copies. It was in circulation for a long time, going into a fourth printing in 1968. Conrad had made a down payment on his pledge to use the Tubman story as leverage in the struggle to defeat American racism, but the short booklet was not a large enough canvas on which to portray Harriet Tubman on the grand scale that his still unpublished book-length manuscript, which at one time ran to over five hundred typed pages, did.

No white-controlled publishing firm wanted to take a risk on a book about a black woman whom Conrad himself had described as little known and that was written by a young journalist—unpublished in the book field, who had been moving in radical labor and political circles, and who saw himself as a neo-abolitionist. Then, on July 8, 1942, Carter Woodson sent Earl Conrad a contract for a book to be titled—not "I Bring You General Tubman" but simply *Harriet Tubman*.[103] It was Woodson (Figure 53), it will be remembered, who had warned Conrad back in January 1940 that he would have difficulty finding a publisher for his Tubman manuscript. Now Woodson's own Associated Publishers of Washington, D.C., would ensure that Harriet Tubman's story, "The one that the white publishers would not issue," as the dedicatory note to the book that came out in the fall of 1943 says, would be heard again.

Woodson had persuaded Conrad to change the title of his manuscript from "I Bring You General Tubman" to simply "Harriet Tubman." The black historian and publisher had reservations about "stretching things to call Harriet Tubman 'General.'"[104] *Harriet Tubman* finally became available in late 1943. It ran to 248 pages and cost three dollars and twenty-five cents. Reviewers were generally sympathetic to it. Arthur E. Burke of *Crisis* called the book "a story of action" that brought to life "the Moses of her people," a great humanitarian who symbolized the fight for freedom "more accurately than most of her contemporaries."[105] Sidney L. Jackson of the *New York Tribune*, with the American war effort in mind, wrote: "Mr. Conrad's writing is vigorous and poetic. Occasionally crude, it rises to admirable hights [*sic*] at times, particularly in the description of some of the more dramatic events in his heroine's career. If he starts off with a chip on his shoulder, one can hardly blame him. His book deserves a wide audience, first of all among those who take the four freedoms seriously."[106] Eugene Gordon, writing for the *Worker*, praised Conrad for having "a Marxist understanding of why and how things happen to men and women and children in a society" and for painting his subject with bold strokes as a freedom fighter.[107] Ben Burns of the *Chicago Defender* described Conrad as a fine researcher but not a skilled writer: "His is a weighty tome, too often dull and dreary when the subject calls for a brilliant and dramatic treatment."[108] Burns thought that Howard Fast, author of a biography on Thomas Paine, would have done a better job. However, Langston Hughes, a writer of great talent and one of the leading voices of the Harlem Renaissance, judged *Harriet Tubman* "a wonderful book."[109] Congressman Adam Clayton Powell said in the *People's Voice*: "It is to be hoped that every one of us will have this volume in our home. It is further hoped that such a volume will be included in the school systems of our country as a required reading."[110] The columnist Walter Winchell wrote: "Orchids to Earl Conrad for his magnificent book, 'Harriet Tubman.' It is about history's greatest Negro woman. Conrad's book will outlast its author and all the book's readers for he has chosen to tell the definitive story of one of America's two or three foremost women."[111]

If we are to judge by how frequently subsequent retellers of the Tubman story have depended on Conrad's *Harriet Tubman*, then the book that almost never got published has fulfilled Winchell's prediction. Associated Publishers' clothbound edition sold steadily. Carter Woodson's *Negro History Bulletin* reported in 1943: "The most popular book now sold by the Associated Publishers is *Harriet Tubman*, by Earl Conrad.

For more than a month the sales of this book have topped all others."[112] Some thirty years after its publication, Conrad proudly claimed that his Tubman book "won [him] the respect of the black community: that community which I have always regarded as the most important in the United States."[113] Conrad published twenty-four more books after his Tubman book. The crusading journalist kept to the theme of race and civil rights in many of them, such as *News of the Nation* (co-authored in 1944), *Jim Crow America* (1947), *Scottsboro Boy* (with Haywood Patterson, 1950), *The Public School Scandal* (1951), *Rock Bottom* (1953), *Gulf Stream North* (1954), *Mr. Seward for the Defense* (1956), *The Invention of the Negro* (1966), and *Everything and Nothing: The Dorothy Dandridge Story* (with Dorothy Dandridge, 1970).[114]

Conrad donated a copy of his 1943 Tubman book to the community-college library in his hometown of Auburn and inscribed it: "Harriet Tubman is without doubt the greatest woman in American history."[115] His book had been a biography written in the heroic fashion of the "great lives" of social revolutionaries. More hagiography than critical analysis, Conrad's book suffers from an excess of superlatives. It has the ring of a laudatory portrait written to atone for the racial sins of white America. Nevertheless, Conrad's Harriet Tubman paean should be viewed as an important benchmark in the historical process of positioning Tubman more prominently and publicly in the American memory. The young boy who grew up in Auburn early discovered that he had the gift of wordiness. He used that gift for nearly four decades as journalist, newspaper columnist, radio broadcaster, public speaker, novelist, poet, dramatist, social activist, biographer, short-story writer, and, toward the end of his life, painter and autobiographer. He died in La Jolla, California, on January 17, 1986, of complications of a lymphoma.

CHAPTER EIGHT

"SPIRITS RISING"

In 1930–31, while Conrad was struggling to make his mark as a writer, Aaron Douglas (Figure 54), the Harlem Renaissance artist, painted a powerfully evocative mural that he called "Spirits Rising" (see Plate 7). Also known as the Harriet Tubman mural and the Alfred Stern mural, the oil-on-canvas fresco appeared in public space at Bennett College for Women in Greensboro, North Carolina, a four-year liberal-arts school founded for African American women in 1873. Alfred Stern of Chicago, the son-in-law of the famous philanthropist Julius Rosenwald, had commissioned the painting. Douglas, who found inspiration in African art, was then in his mid-thirties and a key figure of the New Negro Movement, sometimes called the "Harlem Renaissance." Known as the "Dean of African American Painters," Douglas said of his mural: "I used Harriet Tubman to idealize a superior type of Negro womanhood. . . . I depict her as a heroic leader breaking the shackles of bondage and pressing on toward a new day."[1] "Spirits Rising" foreshadowed a revival of interest in Tubman that increased in intensity decade by decade after World War Two.

On June 3, 1944, less than a year after the publication of Earl Conrad's benchmark biography, the ss *Harriet Tubman*, a 4,380-ton Liberty Ship, slid into Casco Bay off South Portland, Maine. Initially planned as a small affair, the christening and launching of the ss *Harriet Tubman*, the first ship constructed for the Maritime Commission in honor of an African American woman, turned into a pro-war rally and a highly symbolic occasion. The event signaled the opening of a new chapter in the history of Tubman's canonization as an American heroine. She was being honored in a public way, her name attached to an American ship that would aid in the fight to defeat America's enemies in World War Two.

54. Portrait of Aaron Douglas, by P. H. Polk, Photographer. From Booker T. Washington Papers. Courtesy Library of Congress, LC/DIG-ppmsca-05117.

Eleanor Roosevelt, who could not be present, sent a message that was read during the ceremony: "This is a fitting honor for a distinguished woman. This Liberty Ship will carry war materials to our fighting men in all parts of the world where they will be used in defense of those principles that Mrs. Tubman sought to establish and which American women now, regardless of race, color or creed are determined to see through to victory. I wish for the National Council of Negro Women and the members of Mrs. Tubman's family success in this important undertaking."[2] Mary McLeod Bethune, president of the National Negro Council of Negro Women, organized in 1935, led the effort to honor Tubman by having a Liberty Ship named after her. Because of illness, Bethune did not attend the launching party, but nearly one hundred black Americans did, including, according to one newspaper report, fifteen individuals who claimed to be kin of Tubman. Mrs. Eva S. Northrup, one of Tubman's grandnieces, stood in for Bethune and christened the ship with the traditional bottle of champagne (Figure 55). The ss *Harriet Tubman* was only the second Liberty Ship to be named after an African American. One of 2,700 Liberty Ships built, the ss *Harriet Tubman* spent its wartime service moving cargo in the European theater. Sold for scrap after the

55. Christening the Liberty Ship ss *Harriet Tubman*, June 3, 1944. Photograph from the National Archives, Washington, D.C.

war, the ship's logs and plates were donated to the Harriet Tubman Home in Auburn in 1973.[3]

Bethune's National Council of Negro Women used the launching of the ss *Harriet Tubman* to inaugurate a national war-bond drive to raise two million dollars, the approximate cost of the ship. The clubwomen endorsed a flyer that promoted the bond campaign with references to Earl Conrad's recent book and his claim that "Harriet Tubman will be remembered as one of the greatest heroines in American history." Conrad was present that June day and must have felt partially vindicated for having spent five hard years trying to bring Tubman's story to the American public. He spoke as the "biographer of Harriet Tubman" during the ceremonies and no doubt agreed with the sentiment expressed by Jeannetta Welch Brown, executive secretary of the National Council for Negro Women, who said, "It has been a long time since the name of Harriet Tubman, one of America's immortals, has been used widely in this land. But she is back with us. The progressive nature of the war is shown by what here is symbolized."[4]

In the post–World War Two decades, African Americans fought to dismantle the racial barriers that tarnished the democracy many of them fought to protect in the trenches. Then came the Civil Rights Movement and, in turn, the birth of radical Black Nationalist ideologies. Authors who intended to write about Tubman now had less difficulty than Conrad did in being published. Harriet Tubman was indeed "back with" the American public. By the end of the twentieth century, her popularity had grown exponentially. She was being celebrated in almost every medium of human expression, including art, dance, drama, film, literature, music, poetry, and sculpture. Scores of books had been published about her. The symbolic power of her life story was being used to sell products, promote causes of one kind or another, and represent a vision of a more racially pluralistic and gender equitable America to the world abroad.

Harbingers of this revival of interest in the symbolic Tubman actually appeared while Conrad was struggling to get his book published. On April 23, 1940, Claude A. Barnett, director of the Associated Negro Press, wrote to Conrad, "Last week while in New York City, I had the privilege of seeing some remarkable sketches of the life of Harriet Tubman. They were the work of an 18-year-old boy, Jacob Lawrence, a protégé of Dr. Alain Locke at Howard University."[5] Conrad likely visited New York City's Museum of Modern Art to see Lawrence's thirty-one-panel tribute to Tubman. The young artist's eclectic style and his signature use of a palette of bright primary colors impressed critics and invoked elements of Impressionism and Cubism. Lawrence (Figure 56) turned to a paintbrush to educate America about the woman about whom his elders spoke in Harlem's black community.[6] Lawrence's Tubman mural was as much a breakthrough event in efforts to canonize Tubman in American culture as the publication of Conrad's book.

Jacob Lawrence grew up in Harlem. There he came under the influence of Alain Locke, a major figure in the black cultural revival known as the Harlem Renaissance. Lawrence studied at the Works Progress Administration–sponsored Harlem Art Workshops from 1932 to 1937 and then at the American Artists School in New York City from 1937 to 1939. The young painter's interest in the narrative use of art revealed itself first in a series on Toussaint L'Ouverture, the Haitian liberator. Then he turned to Harriet Tubman for inspiration and sought to capture the essence of the "Black Moses" myth in tempera. In comments published in 1991, Lawrence reflected on Tubman's place in the American memory: "Harriet Tubman's story is one of the great American sagas. We hear

56. Jacob Lawrence. Courtesy Library of Congress, LC/USZ62-114410.

about Molly Pitcher, about Betsy Ross. . . . The black woman has never been included in American history."[7]

Like Lawrence, the African American artist William Johnson created a visual reminder in the 1940s of the importance of Tubman. Born in 1901 in Florence, South Carolina, Johnson moved to New York City in 1918. He was there to witness the Great Migration and the cultural flowering of the Harlem Renaissance. For more than a decade, Johnson lived in Europe, but in 1938, he and his Danish wife (the textile artist Holcha Krake) returned to the United States, and in 1939 they settled in Harlem. After Krake's death in 1941, Johnson returned to South Carolina. About 1945, he began a series of works celebrating key figures in African American history. His portrayal of Harriet Tubman, an oil on paperboard, shows the dramatic use of primary colors that distinguishes his style (see Plate 8). When Johnson left for Denmark in 1946, he was already showing signs of the mental illness from which he never did recover. He died in 1970, having been hospitalized for twenty-three years.

Unlike Lawrence and Johnson, Frederic Jean Thalinger, the St. Louis-based sculptor (1915–65), chose three-dimensional art forms to honor Tubman. Unfortunately, his powerfully evocative sculpture of Tubman, done in wood (Figure 57), did not get the public attention and acclaim that it deserved.

Revitalization of the Tubman myth in text form began with fictionalized accounts in the 1940s and 1950s that drew heavily on Sarah Bradford's mediated Tubman. Anne Parrish's *A Clouded Star* was the first post–World War Two publication about Tubman to appear in book-length format. Published in 1948 by Harper and Brothers, *A Clouded Star* is fictionalized biography. Parrish had already written eleven novels, including *The Perennial Bachelor* (1925), for which she won the Harper Prize, when she decided to write about Tubman. Parrish (1888–1957) was born in Colorado Springs, Colorado, but grew up in Claymount, Delaware. She claimed that she had heard stories about Tubman from her great-grandmother who purportedly lived in a house in Philadelphia where runaways often hid and from several individuals who came from the Eastern Shore of Maryland and worked in her mother's household. Parrish acknowledged having made use of the Tubman-related books by Sarah Bradford, Hildegarde Hoyt Swift, and Henrietta Buckmaster. Buckmaster was author of the highly respected *Let My People Go: The Story of the Underground Railroad and the Growth of the Abolition Movement*, first published in 1941.[8] Curiously, Parrish makes no mention of having consulted the Conrad book. Well known for her "novels of character" and books for children, Parrish wrote *A Clouded Star* in a highly fictionalized manner, creating dialogue and characters. Both plot and content center on one journey in which Tubman brings nine individuals out of slavery and escorts them to Canada and freedom. Parrish's book makes no claim to historical accuracy. *A Clouded Star* is an early example of the fictionalized Tubman, a Tubman who has escaped from the constraints of historical fact and moves freely in the imagination of the author.[9]

In a sharp and extensive critique of Parrish's fictive life of Tubman, James McGowan observed, "Reading *A Clouded Star*, one cannot help but feel that Miss Parrish was influenced by the writings of the Southern historian Ulrich B. Philips, whose 1918 study, *American Negro Slavery*, put forth the views that slavery was basically a benign institution, civilizing a race of people—the Negro—who were inferior and, therefore best suited

57. Frederic Jean Thalinger's sculpture of Tubman. Photograph courtesy Library of Congress, LC/USZ62–54858.

for slavery."[10] McGowan concluded that Parrish's book replicated the romantic racialism found in Harriet Beecher Stowe's *Uncle Tom's Cabin*, where Uncle Tom is depicted as docile and intensely religious. "*A Clouded Star*," McGowan wrote, "is not a book about Harriet Tubman. It is, first of all, Anne Parrish's apology for slavery! It is also a not-so-subtle attempt to demean the character of a great black historical figure."[11]

At first look, McGowan's criticism of the Parrish book may seem overwrought. *A Clouded Star* is a work of fiction, despite Parrish's claim to have consulted a small cache of historical documents, letters, and such. Novelists exercise greater creative license than historians do. This caveat aside, we can understand why Parrish's work of fiction troubled McGowan. At a time when most Americans knew little about the real Harriet Tubman, in spite of the publication in 1943 of Conrad's book, the general public was not able to discern fact and fancy in novelized treatments of Tubman's life. Tubman was being popularized in the post–World War Two era in a highly bowdlerized fashion. Parrish, if we follow McGowan's argument, constructed her iconic image of Tubman in a manner that fit with the racial stereotypes of African Americans still held by segments of white America in the 1940s. As noted in chapter 1, dealing with the evolution of Tubman's reputation in the field of children's literature, the 1950s witnessed the publication of Dorothy Sterling's *Freedom Train* (1954) and Ann Petry's *Harriet Tubman* (1955). These middle-class African American authors sought to educate young readers about the heroic stature of Tubman and thereby dispel America's distorted image of black women and blacks in general.

In 1950, a Catholic nun by the name of Mary Eusebius, drawing on her master's thesis, published an article on Tubman in the *Journal of Negro Education*. She prefaced her essay by saying, "The story that I am about to tell is not new. It is, however, one that has been forgotten. Yet it is a story that should be remembered."[12] Tubman was not much remembered in a public way during the 1950s. Except for an occasional invocation of her name, civil-rights activists did not hold up Harriet Tubman as the symbol of their movement. An examination of Martin Luther King Jr.'s published works suggests that the great civil-rights leader did not use Tubman's name to mobilize grass-roots Southern blacks. When Rosa Parks, the Alabama seamstress who became an icon of the modern Civil Rights Movement, died in 2005, Henry Louis Gates Jr. hailed her as "the Harriet Tubman of our time." Here was another indication of the enduring symbolic power of Tubman. She had become the new paragon by which to measure others.

No professional historian of the 1950s took up the challenge of piecing together Tubman's life story. The same can be said of the following decade. The popularization of Tubman took place outside of academe, largely in the field of juvenile literature and fiction.

The publication in 1965 of Ann McGovern's picture book *Runaway Slave: The Story of Harriet Tubman* by Scholastic Book Services, after nearly a decade with no new books about Tubman, signaled a new wave of interest in her.[13] Written and illustrated for young children, the McGovern book came out in the year when King and John Lewis of the Student Nonviolent Coordinating Committee led the famous march from Selma to Montgomery, Alabama. The year 1965 also witnessed the riots in Watts and urban unrest in Chicago and Philadelphia. The publication of *The Autobiography of Malcolm X* in 1965 came at a time when Black Nationalist ideas were capturing the minds of many young blacks. The Civil Rights Act of 1964 was in place, but the mood in African American communities had changed from hopeful optimism to cynicism. The Black Power Movement, inspired by the fiery rhetoric of activists such as H. Rap Brown and Stokley Carmichael, swept through the streets of black America. While newspapers across the nation carried reports of violent conflict between protestors and the police, King sharpened his critique of the American power structure by expanding his civil-rights agenda to include an open housing march in Chicago in 1966 and then, a year later, by announcing that he opposed the Vietnam War. An assassin silenced King's prophetic voice on April 4, 1968. Rioting erupted in 125 U.S. cities.

In the wake of this rending of the American social fabric, calls went out to reexamine America's past with new honesty. Henceforth, the "black experience," variously defined, was to receive greater consideration in school systems across the country, ranging from elementary-school textbooks to college and university classrooms. Writers and publishers scrambled to find African American historical figures more in keeping with the mood of the post-civil-rights era than earlier icons such as George Washington Carver and Booker T. Washington. Though professional historians produced scores of books dealing with the African American experience, none of them took on the challenge of extending the public's knowledge of Tubman's life much beyond what could be found in Bradford and Conrad. The task of popularizing Tubman during the next two decades fell to the authors of books for children and fictional works and to creative minds that brought Tubman to public attention in mediums other than the printed page.

As critics of the epic *Gone With the Wind* and the flawed cinematic classic *The Birth of a Nation* acknowledge, the American public learns much of its history in the movie theater or sitting in front of the television. Popular culture feeds on celluloid images; the record of Hollywood's depiction of blacks has drawn sharp criticism. With the exception of pioneering black filmmakers such as Oscar Micheaux, Hollywood masters of the big screen ignored Tubman. Micheaux formed his film company in 1918 and made films for over thirty years. His heroes were Booker T. Washington and W. E. B. Du Bois, and he drew inspiration from the writings of black authors such as Charles Chesnutt and Paul Laurence Dunbar. Micheaux did not make a film about Tubman. He did draw on words attributed to Tubman when writing some of his scripts.[14]

It was not until 1963 that white producers put money into a project to resurrect Harriet Tubman for a mass audience. CBS-TV presented *The Life of Harriet Tubman* in its American history series. Done in black and white, the 16 millimeter film ran for nearly an hour and featured Ruby Dee, Brock Peters, Ossie Davis, and the venerable Ethel Waters. Narrated by Van Heflin, the production drew an anemic public response.[15] Nearly fifteen years were to pass before another major effort was made to use television to tell of Tubman. I remember my own reaction on viewing *A Woman Called Moses* when it first was shown on the Syracuse, New York, NBC-TV affiliate in December 1978. I had visited the Tubman Home in Auburn on several occasions since arriving three years earlier to teach in the African American Studies Program at Syracuse University. I knew something about Tubman's life, though I was not anticipating an in-depth study of her place in the American memory. I found *A Woman Called Moses* intriguing, but Cicely Tyson, the actress who played Black Moses, did not remind me of Harriet Tubman—Sojourner Truth, perhaps, but not the short (some have called her "petite") woman who braved the slave catchers (Figure 58). One wonders how much research went into preparing the film. John Getz, the actor who played the role of Robert T. Stewart, the white man to whom Tubman had been hired out at the time she made her run to freedom, told one of Stewart's descendants that *A Woman Called Moses* was done "quick as biscuits."[16]

58. Cicely Tyson, actress, as Tubman in *A Woman Called Moses*. Movie still from 1978. In the author's collection.

I knew Tyson from her role as Jane Pitman in *The Autobiography of Miss Jane Pitman*, which had appeared as a television miniseries in 1974. Tyson had won an Emmy for her portrayal of an American slave woman who survived past the age of one hundred twenty. Tyson signed on to portray Tubman with CBS-TV initially, but the network dropped the project. NBC-TV agreed to take on the project but then failed to commit its resources fully until the success of the television adaptation of Alex Haley's book *Roots*. Production of *A Woman Called Moses* began in January 1978. In preparation for her role, Tyson visited Auburn. The actress was given a key to the city and made an honorary citizen. She visited the church on Parker Street and was quoted as saying, "While sitting in the corner beneath the picture of Harriet Tubman, I imagined that she was here and all the people sitting here represented all those slaves she was able to assist to freedom." Then, as so many Tubman enthusiasts have done, Tyson offered a personal testimony to the power of the Tubman myth. She, like the woman she was about to portray, believed in divine providence. The story of Harriet Tubman, Tyson told the press, came to her "in the strangest manner." While struggling to come to terms with the death of her mother, the actress received a call from an assistant telling her of the script for *A Woman Called Moses* written by Lonnie Elder III, the scriptwriter for the film *Sounder*. The *Moses* script closely followed the book *A Woman Called Moses*, by Marcy Heidish, a middle-class white woman who was educated at Vassar and a native of Manhattan.[17]

Newsweek magazine hailed the movie Tyson starred in and Orson Welles narrated as "one of the most moving evocations of the black experience."[18] The reaction of some in the Auburn community was not so positive. Several of the women who claimed to be descendants of Tubman's siblings found Tyson's portrayal of their "Aunt Harriet" disappointing—capturing little of the deep religiosity of the real woman called Moses. Their criticisms of the film, which was produced by Ike Jones and Michael Jaffe, are echoed in reservations about the book that the film was based on voiced most forcibly by James A. McGowan, editor of the *Harriet Tubman Journal*. McGowan was at work on a book with the tentative title, "Harriet Tubman: Facts and Fiction," in the mid-1990s. He thought that Tyson "was probably more concerned with simply portraying Harriet Tubman than she was with a historically accurate portrayal of Harriet Tubman." McGowan believed that Tyson owed the public, especially African American viewers of *A Woman Called Moses*, an admission that the television version of Tubman's life was not identical to the book that had inspired the actress to take the film project to the producer Ike Jones in the first place.[19]

McGowan found Heidish's book highly disturbing. Published in 1976 by Houghton Mifflin, *A Woman Called Moses* was Heidish's first novel (Figure 59). McGowan faulted her for poor research and for the arrogance of thinking that Harriet Tubman would, as Heidish claimed, "come through her typewriter and speak to *her*."[20] McGowan rejected Heidish's portrayal of Tubman as a woman who used foul language and had sexual relationships with other slaves. McGowan was not alone in thinking that Heidish had gone too far in "imagining Harriet Tubman getting drunk, swimming in the nude with John Tubman, having sex with him before marriage, speaking of 'angels without tits,' being beaten on by John Tubman, and on and on and on." He cited a phone conversation that he had with the Reverend Guthrie Carter, director of the Harriet Tubman Home

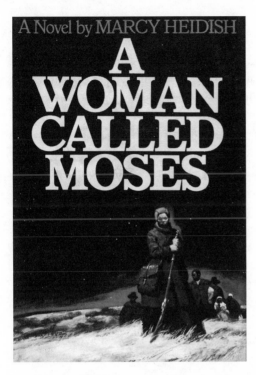

A Novel by MARCY HEIDISH

A WOMAN CALLED MOSES

59. Book cover. From Marcy Heidish, *A Woman Called Moses* (Boston: Houghton Mifflin,1976).

in Auburn. Carter, according to McGowan, said, "She [Marcy Heidish] made it seem as if Harriet Tubman was a whore." McGowan angrily denounced Heidish's book as a "deliberate distortion."[21] Though the Tyson portrayal of Tubman in the made-for-television drama censored those parts of the Heidish book that McGowan and Carter found so offensive, the controversy that *A Woman Called Moses* stirred up in some circles revealed that the place that Tubman held in the American memory was still highly contested territory.

Near the end of the Tyson portrayal of Tubman, Orson Welles, who provides the narrator's voice for the film, asserts that Harriet assisted more than three thousand (yes, three thousand) individuals to escape slavery. Xenon Entertainment distributed a home video version of *A Woman Called Moses* in 1992. Promotional text on the package made the claim that Harriet Ross Tubman had been the "founder of the Underground Railroad."[22] Both assertions are, of course, patently untrue, yet they illustrate how powerful the Tubman myth has been. Because many Americans so readily identified Tubman with the enterprise popularly known as the Underground Railroad, she took center stage in the wake of the passage of National Freedom Trail legislation in 1990. *Flight to Freedom*, subtitled "The Underground Railroad," appeared in 1995 featuring Harriet Tubman, with narration by Cicely Tyson, further cementing the notion that Tubman epitomized the Underground Railroad like no one else, black or white.[23]

Given the plethora of films and videos available dealing in whole or in part with Tubman that were available to the American viewing public already conditioned to getting history through the medium of the television, few citizens of the republic alive as the twentieth century drew to a close could justifiably say that they had never had an opportunity to learn about the woman called Moses. Tubman on film had come a long way since the early 1960s, when only a few dedicated teachers used filmstrips and 33 rpm records to tell Tubman's story in the classroom.[24]

Still, the Tubman memory train had moved slowly in venues where the paying public elected to spend its time and dollars. The African American playwright Alice Childress wrote a play about Tubman in 1975, but as of 1990 it had not been professionally produced.[25] The first major and well-publicized dramatic rendition of the Tubman myth took place on March 1, 1985, in Norfolk, Virginia, in operatic form. Thea Musgrave, a native of Scotland, composed and directed *Harriet, the Woman Called Moses* under a joint commission of the Virginia Opera Association and the Royal Opera House of London. On March 3, 1985, two hundred radio stations broadcast a second performance of Musgrave's libretto on Tubman, which the composer admitted was "freely based" on the life of her heroine.[26]

Musgrave, with operas about Simon Bolivar, the South American revolutionary liberator, and Mary Queen of Scots already to her credit, straightforwardly acknowledged that she merged myth and history in her creative and heroic depictions of historic figures whose lives have assumed epic, even archetypal stature. As a youngster growing up in Edinburgh, she had heard Paul Robeson sing spirituals such as "Go Down Moses" and "Swing Low, Sweet Chariot," songs traditionally associated with the woman called Moses and the yearning for freedom in the African American slave quarters. Musgrave viewed Tubman's story as "a moving example of the age-old conflict between good and evil." "Harriet," Musgrave asserted, "is every woman who dared to defy injustice and tyranny; she is Joan of Arc, she is Susan B. Anthony, she is Anne Frank, she is Mother Teresa."[27]

American playwrights offered numerous interpretations of Tubman on stages large and small all across the country in the last decade of the twentieth century and the early years of the twenty-first century. Debbie Allen played Tubman in the bio-drama *Harriet's Return*, written by Karen Jones Meadows, at the Kennedy Center in Washington, D.C., in 2001. A reviewer said in the *Washington Post* that the Tubman portrayed in the play "is a simple woman, unexceptional but curious, smart and tough. In short, she has all the makings of the classic American hero." "This Tubman," said the critic, "is almost certainly more appealingly spunky and less rough-edged than the actual woman, but the play is unambiguously molded as an inspirational tale."[28]

Most dramatic re-presentations of the Tubman myth have been unambiguously inspirational. For example, Voices from the Earth, a not-for-profit theater-arts company in Thomas, West Virginia, showcased *General Moses*, based on a script written by Ilene Evans. The play opens with Moses (Harriet Tubman) rousing from a deep sleep, singing the traditional spirituals. Her character quickly takes on transhistorical symbolic meaning. Evans acknowledged that she hoped to reach audiences on a deep, emotional level:

> This program of General Moses was inspired by the myth of Prometheus. Prometheus brought the gift of fire and light to humans. Prometheus led people out of the darkness and into the light, against what appeared to be the will of the gods. The gods were the "powers that be" at that time. He endured the possibility of eternal punishment for his faith in humanity. Prometheus did not regret his sacrifice. Harriet is one of the many Prometheus figures for my people. She lights the way for my struggle to stay free. I continue to be free. I continue to be inspired and strengthened by her love for her own and all people. She served humanity and God in action and deeds not in words alone. If you want to know what I believe, look at what I do. Walk your talk.[29]

Carolyn Gage's *Harriet Tubman Visits a Therapist*, a play that appeared in 1999 in New York City's Off-Off-Broadway Original Short Play Festival, employed the Tubman myth more radically and more dangerously. Described as "a lesbian-feminist playwright, author, and activist," Gage has Tubman, suffering from spells of narcolepsy, being sent by her owner Edward Brodess to see a therapist to see if she is going to run away. The therapist, played by a light-skinned African American actress, is depicted as sleeping with Brodess and tries to get Harriet to stay.[30]

Stage productions about Tubman are now quite common. In addition, more than a half dozen reenactors have established themselves in touring "one-woman" shows telling adults and children about the Tubman epic. Gwendolyn Briley-Strand's performance, which she calls *Harriet: The Chosen One*, has been one of the most heavily booked shows, especially in the month of February (Black History Month) and the month of March (Women's History Month). Briley-Strand takes her audiences, including one at the White House in 1992, on one of Tubman's journeys to rescue others. Incidentally, Briley-Strand also travels the country impersonating Sojourner Truth and Rosa Parks, women who, like Tubman, now have a permanent place in America's collective memory book. It has not always been so. There was a time when playwrights despaired of finding an audience and public space in which to share their interpretations of the Tubman myth.

The African American writer Robert Hayden was known as "the Poet of Detroit." During the 1930s, he read poetry at rallies on behalf of black workers who were seeking fair treatment from the United Auto Workers. Hayden wrote the three-act play *Go Down Moses* using dialect and celebrating the black liberation struggle within the framework of a leftist and populist aesthetic. *Go Down Moses* was performed once—in 1937 by the Paul Robeson Players of Detroit's Second Baptist church. Hayden, according to an entry in his journal, thought of taking up the Moses project again in 1946 and recasting it as an epic drama. He died in 1980. The Moses typescript was found in his desk. It had never been produced.[31]

Where Robert Hayden failed, the playwright May Miller succeeded. A pioneer in the black drama movement of the World War One period and a faculty member at Howard University, Miller, in cooperation with Willis Richardson, published *Negro History in Thirteen Plays* in 1934. One of her plays centered on Tubman. In an interview with Oprah Winfrey many years later, Miller said, "I know and understand that I am where I am because of the bridges that I crossed over to get here. Sojourner Truth was a bridge. Harriet Tubman was a bridge. Ida B. Wells was a bridge. Madame C. J. Walker was a bridge. Fannie Lou Hamer was a bridge. Every day that I'm out there I see myself as a resurrection of those women. I feel very strongly about black womanhood."[32] Miller's play about Tubman takes place in Maryland and sets Tubman's courage and heroism against the betrayal of the slave community by a mulatto house servant. May Miller's play about Tubman never made it into the nation's mainstream theaters.

Dramatic tributes to Tubman are common now in many American communities. When I attended Susan Kander's *She Never Lost a Passenger* in Syracuse in 2002, a production of the Syracuse Opera Company in cooperation with the Onondaga Historical Association, I was struck by how faithfully the short opera captured the essence of the "Black Moses" myth. William Still is there as a supporting member of the cast, as are the Quaker stalwarts Thomas and Sarah Garrett.[33] But the star is clearly Tubman-the-brave, who at one point sings, "Freedom is a hard bought thing" while taking a gun from her pocket and threatening the faint-hearted whose weakness might result in the capture of a party of freedom seekers.[34] I found the play refreshingly uplifting but was left to wonder if the Tubman romantic myth had not become so overpowering that historians might never be able to successfully raise questions about it. Archetypal histories resist demythologizing. Scholarly concerns about historical accuracy and contravening nuances of interpretation do not fare well in the shadow of an icon. I began to wonder how the public would perceive Tubman-the-heroic if evidence should be unearthed that she did indeed lose a passenger.

Musicians have joined company with artists, authors, filmmakers, and playwrights in fostering the Tubman revival. The notion that the enslaved sang paeans of praise for the woman who carried off Southern so-called property and brought them across the threshold of freedom is a staple in the Tubman myth. According to one contemporary source, "Some folklorists suggest that slaves originally sung, Swing Low, Sweet Chariot as a literal plea for Harriet Tubman to swing into the deep South and lead them to freedom. The 'chariot' in the song may have been inserted to mask the reference to Tubman, one of the most successful conductors on the Underground Railroad."[35] There is no primary evidence for this, though such pious fictions continue to thrive. In more recent times, Tubman has attracted the attention of folk singers and social critics such as Woody Guthrie, Pete Seeger, and Holly Near. Guthrie's song, composed in the 1940s and popularized by Seeger, has these lines:

> I helped a field hand make a run for freedom
> When my fifteenth year was rolling round

And the guard he caught him in a little store
In a little slavery village town
The boss made a grab to catch the field hand
I jumped in and blocked the door
The boss he hit me with a two pound scale iron
And I went black down on the floor
On a bundle of rags in our log cabin
My mother she ministered unto my needs
It was here I swore I'd give my life blood
Just to turn my people free.[36]

In the 1970s and 1980s, Holly Near, among other musical artists, popularized a Tubman tribute written by the young African American poet Walter Robinson. His lyrics drew deeply from the well of communal memory and echo Margaret Walker's poem, "Harriet Tubman," published in 1944:

One night I dreamed I was in slavery
'Bout 1850 was the time
Sorrow was the only sign
Nothing around to ease my mind.
Out of the night appeared a lady
Leading a distant Pilgrim band
"First mate" she yelled, pointing her hand.
"Make room aboard for this young woman"

Chorus: Singing come on up, I got a lifeline
Come on up to this train of mine (2 x)

She said her name was Harriet Tubman
And she drove for the underground railroad
Hundreds of miles we traveled onward
Gathering slaves from town to town
Seeking every lost and found
Setting those free that once were bound
Somehow my heart was growing weaker
I fell by the wayside's sinking sand
Firmly did this lady stand
She lifted me up and took my hand

Who are these children dressed in red
They must be the ones that Moses led

Chorus:

She said her name was Harriet Tubman
and she drove for the underground railroad.[37]

Instrumentalists have complemented the chorus of poets and praise singers with their own tributes to Tubman. For example, a hard rock-jazz band from Manhattan, formed in 1966, took the name "Harriet Tubman 'I Am A Man.'" A band calling itself the Long Ryders Two did a cut called "Harriet Tubman's Gonna Carry Me Home." Wynton Marsalis, the celebrated trumpeter, included a tribute to Tubman on his album *Thick in the South: Soul Gestures in Southern Blues, Volume 1*.[38]

Creative talents who paint and sculpt, like their counterparts in the performing arts, have been inspired by the life and legacy of Harriet Tubman. Elizabeth Catlett of Howard University and, later, the National Autonomous University of Mexico created a woodcut on woven paper honoring Tubman that is powerful in its simplicity. Earlier, Margaret Taylor Goss Burroughs used watercolors to portray Tubman. Many other artists have used canvas and clay to put their mark on the Tubman myth. The oil painting done of Tubman by Robert Pius in 1950 is now much in demand among collectors of Tubman memorabilia. Visual representations of Tubman multiplied in company with the public's fascination with the Underground Railroad, especially after the passage by congress of the National Freedom Trail Act of 1990. Copies of Alex Porter's prints "A River Crossing" and "A Passage to Freedom" have found a ready market.

Tubman's image has become so prevalent now that it can be seen in public spaces across the nation, including parts of the old Confederacy. Teenagers in the Urban Arts Training Program used a wall of the Harriet Tubman Elementary School in New Orleans on which to create a six-by-twelve-foot tile mural honoring the namesake of the school. Tubman is depicted, as the *New Orleans Times-Picayune* reported, adorned in bright hues, floating atop a giant open book, and reaching down to blacks who have broken free from their shackles. According to the newspaper, working on the mural taught the teenagers pride and the work ethic.[39] The students in New Orleans's Urban Arts Training Program, who were paid

60. Harriet Tubman monument, Boston. Photograph courtesy Gregory Matthews.

a minimum wage for the time they worked on the mural, apparently faced none of the controversy that Mike Alewitz encountered with his proposed mural of a musket-toting Black Moses for that wall in Baltimore.

The Frederick Douglass monument was dedicated in Rochester in 1899, four years after the death of "the Lion who wrote history."[40] It was the first public sculpture erected in the United States to honor an African American. A century elapsed before any American community awarded Tubman a similar tribute. Boston had no memorials honoring women on city-owned land until 1999, when Fern Cunningham's seven-by-ten foot bronze sculpture "Step on Board" was installed (Figure 60).[41] It is situated at the entrance to Harriet Tubman Park, a small piece of real estate at the intersection of Columbus Avenue and Pembroke Street in Boston's South End. The sculpture shows Tubman, Bible in hand, looking toward Heaven. She beckons five adult figures, including one cradling an infant, to follow her to freedom. Cunningham, an art teacher at the Park School in Boston, accepted the commission to do the Tubman sculpture, conscious of how this choice to use public space critiqued the tradition to honor, in the main, white male historical figures. By fashioning the bronze tribute to Tubman, Cunningham wanted to raise a question at the heart of the American dilemma: "Who is a hero?"[42]

Statues commemorating Tubman in civic space are still few in number, though this is likely to change as public officials catch up with the growing interest in Tubman by their constituents in communities where the Tubman renaissance is most intense. Corporations and private individuals have commissioned artists to create monumental art honoring Tubman. Such is the case with Jane DeDecker's figurative bronze sculpture of Tubman leading a child that was commissioned by United Development and installed in Arizona in 1995. The Colorado sculptor gave one of her limited-edition, life-size bronze Tubman statues to Brenau University in Gainesville, Georgia, in 1997.[43] This was the first instance of an institution, public or private, in the part of the United States once known as the Old South to honor Tubman in so visible a fashion. In 1993, Battle Creek, Michigan, residents witnessed the unveiling of a silicon bronze sculpture done by Ed Dwight of Denver. The Underground Railroad sculpture in Linear Park—twenty-eight feet long and fourteen feet high—includes a figure of Harriet Tubman.[44]

Perhaps we will know for certain that Tubman has been accorded her due when she takes her place among the notables in the statue and art collection located in the Rotunda of the U.S. Capitol in Washington, D.C. Jennifer Luciano, a Loyola University student who served as a congressional intern, wrote a bill to honor Tubman in this way when she worked in the office of U.S. Representative Danny Davis (D–Ill.). The measure received support from Senator Hillary Rodham Clinton and was introduced in the House of Representatives on June 20, 2001, but as of this writing it has not emerged from Congress.[45]

Randall Robinson begins his influential *The Debt: What America Owes to Blacks* with recollections of a visit he made to the U.S. Capitol Rotunda. As he stood gazing up at Constantino Brumidi's monumental fresco, painted in 1864, Robinson thought of the bonded labor who helped build the nation's Capitol. Brumidi's frieze centers on George Washington in the eye of the dome. Robinson writes, "Symbolizing the carapace of American liberty, sixty-odd robed figures are arranged in heroic attitudes around a majestic Washington, before whom a white banner is unfurled bearing the Latin phrase *E Pluribus Unum*, or *one out*

"SPIRITS RISING"

245

of many." Robinson seized on the irony of absence: "Although the practice of slavery lay heavily athwart the new country for most of the depicted age, the frieze presents nothing at all from this long, scarring period. No Douglass. No Tubman. No slavery. No blacks, period."[46] There is a small bust of Martin Luther King Jr. in the Rotunda, Robinson acknowledges, but Harriet Tubman has yet to be admitted into the most symbolically important public space in America.

There are ways other than monumental sculpture to memorialize historical figures on the American cultural landscape. In the wake of the assassination of Martin Luther King Jr., American cities named or re-named streets and boulevards in his honor. Naming roads and highways as a means to bind geographic space and American identity is an old practice. In 1913, the coast-to-coast link known as the Lincoln Highway (U.S. Route 30) was proposed. About the same time, the United Daughters of the Confederacy campaigned for the Jefferson Davis Memorial Highway, portions of which can still be traveled today.[47] There is no named cross-country route in honor of Tubman, though there are a number of streets named after her in communities here and there. Knoxville, Tennessee, has a Tubman Street, as do Augusta and Savannah, Georgia. U.S. Route 50, which runs east of Cambridge, Maryland, is now designated the Harriet Tubman Highway. In July 2002, the City Council of New York approved the renaming of Harlem's St. Nicholas Avenue from West 111th Street to West 141st Street as Harriet Tubman Avenue. Manhattan Borough President C. Virginia Fields commented on the meaning of the proposed re-naming as follows: "Harriet Tubman is one of the most important people in African American history, as well as the history of the United States. Her own flight from bondage and her efforts in leading other slaves to freedom using the 'underground railroad' demonstrated an unparalleled courage that has become legendary. Once the renaming becomes official, Harriet Tubman Avenue will be the first major thoroughfare in the City named for a woman. I say it's about time."[48]

Brooklyn honored Tubman on March 10, 2005, with the designation of Harriet Ross Tubman Avenue. New York City Comptroller William C. Thompson Jr. spoke at the unveiling, declaring: "Every man, woman or child of every race who looks up at the street signs bearing Harriet Tubman's name is instantly reminded of her great life and legacy."[49] Upset that the commemoration was only a co-naming of a stretch of Fulton Street running from Rockaway Avenue to Elm Place, some proponents of honoring black heroes dissented. Fred Laverpool of "Braggin' about Brooklyn," a campaign to promote tourism, charged that keeping Robert Fulton's name on a portion of the street was an insult to Harriet Tubman. Fulton's steamboats, Laverpool claimed, had been used to transport slaves. Having him linked with Tubman was "comparable to putting Oskar Schindler's name under that of Adolf Hitler."[50]

One might expect that Auburn, New York, would have a street or avenue bearing Tubman's name. Auburn does have a small Freedom Park, established in 1994, at 17 North Street to honor the city's famous resident, who is beter known to the general public now than her fellow Auburnian and longtime supporter William Henry Seward, twice governor of New York State and Lincoln's Secretary of State. In 2003, a proposal to designate Auburn's Arterial Highway the Tubman Arterial came from a group of women who claim to be descendants of Harriet's siblings in the wake of a failed proposal the previous November to rename Auburn's Genesee Elementary School after Tubman. The school-renaming controversy in Auburn had its roots as far back as 1985, when some students at the local high school walked out in protest of a proposal to rename their school after Tubman. It resurfaced in July 2002 when a member of the school board proposed the idea of renaming an elementary-school building.

Proponents of honoring Tubman by renaming the school drew heavily on the Tubman myth and argued that Black Moses had not been adequately memorialized in the community in which she had lived for most of her life. Opponents, including a majority of the school's faculty and staff, resisted, citing tradition and the cost of making the change. Press accounts of the controversy, especially those carried in the Syracuse papers, intimated that race was a factor in the dispute. Were white opponents of the renaming acting out of the fear of being identified with a school bearing the name of an African American? Black residents of Auburn expressed indignation at the notion that, if the school were renamed after Tubman, those who taught at and attended it would carry a stigma.[51] Emotions ran high on both sides of the question. An alternative proposal to name an auditorium after Tubman brought ridicule from outsiders. Trivial, they said. A Syracuse paper carried a cartoon showing a student quenching his thirst at a Harriet Tubman drinking fountain. In the end, the school board voted to name one of the school district's administration buildings after Tubman. I watched this parochial controversy with interest. It was, in microcosm, a playing out of the struggle over symbols that has engulfed much of America in the past several decades.[52]

Naming is as much a political act as an aesthetic one. Groups and institutions that take on Harriet Tubman as their moniker honor the woman and signal something about their nature and mission. For example, the Harriet Tubman Center of Minneapolis, an agency set up to assist victims of domestic violence, found inspiration in the charitable work done by the woman it honored in its appellation. A not-for-profit neighborhood social-service agency in Chicago called itself Harriet Tubman Place. The agency sponsored a food pantry, a work-placement service, voter-registration training, and counseling for young people confused about their sexual identity, and helped the victims of HIV/AIDS.[53] Housing for the homeless and for low-income families in New York City's West Harlem became known as the Harriet Tubman Houses.[54]

Boston has the distinction of having the oldest social agency bearing the Tubman name. The Harriet Tubman House was established for the poor in Boston's South End in 1904 and incorporated in 1906, while Tubman was yet alive and with her blessing. The house, an organized Christian home, gave its purpose as that of assisting "particularly the girl student and young women looking for work, many of them newcomers in Boston from the far South." A brochure stressed the hallmark virtues of the woman from Auburn, New York: "Bearing the torch of her name, the Harriet Tubman House pays homage to the grandeur of her living spirit in extolling courage, loyalty, high aspiration, and selfless devotion."[55] This is the only known example of a group or institution honoring Tubman in such a fashion before her death in 1913.

Some groups have invoked the Tubman name as a way to emphasize their antiestablishment politics or protest a particular act of discrimination and racial violence. Such was the case in Harlem in the early 1950s when black female activists, including the Reverend Mother Lena Stokes and Bessie Mitchell, were motivated to set up the Harriet Tubman Center on Lenox Avenue a few days after the "legal lynching of Willie McGee." The women wanted a "program for peace, jobs, better homes, an end to lynchings, frame-up and jimcrow—for true liberation of all those whose ancestors were kidnapped in Africa and brought to this country in chains." The women also declared that it was their goal to "raise Harriet Tubman to the place where she belongs to the consciousness of the American people." They demanded that a bust of her be put in "the Hall of Fame, among the great of the land" and that a Harlem housing project called the Stephen Foster House be named the Harriet Tubman Houses.[56]

Today, scores of American public and private organizations and institutions carry the Tubman name. They are located in the South as well as in the North. Macon, Georgia, has the Tubman African American Museum.[57] Several communities give out Harriet Tubman humanitarian achievement awards. In the United States, public and private schools, libraries and research centers, historical societies, church groups, fraternal societies, and a variety of other organizations have adopted the Tubman moniker and symbol. The practice has spread also to Canada. For example, the University of York in Toronto has the Harriet Tubman Resource Centre on the African Diaspora named in honor of the noted "feminist and political activist."[58] One of the most interesting appropriations of the Tubman name comes to us from the Canadian Union of Postal Workers. For a slogan, it adopted the line from the song "One night I dreamed I was in slav'ry/ 'Bout eighteen fifty/ the time sorrow was the only sign."[59]

On February 1, 1978, the U.S. Postal Service initiated its Black Heritage Series of commemorative stamps with a thirteen-cent stamp honoring Tubman (see Plate 9). The stamp design, done by Jerry Pinkney, an illustrator of children's books and a portrait painter, showed a middle-aged Tubman and the picture of a two-wheeled cart, recalling the incident in 1857 when Black Moses used a similar conveyance to carry her parents out of Maryland because her father wanted to bring along his best chicken coop and her mother insisted on taking along a feather bed. Robert G. Stewart, a great-grandson of John T. Stewart, a plantation owner to whom Harriet's owner hired her out, urged the U.S. Postal Service to hold the First Day of Issue ceremonies in Dorchester County, Maryland.[60] To his disappointment, and that of others favoring a first-day issue in Cambridge, Maryland, the Harriet Tubman stamp first appeared in Washington, D.C. Nevertheless, philatelists and Tubman admirers applauded the honor bestowed on Tubman in 1978 when her stamp was the inaugural stamp in the Black Heritage Series. Succeeding commemorative stamps have honored notables such as Martin Luther King Jr., Jackie Robinson, Sojourner Truth, Ida B. Wells, and W. E. B. Du Bois. A second commemorative honoring Tubman was issued in 1995, this time with a face value of thirty-two cents.

If I read their campaign accurately, many Tubman enthusiasts believe that their heroine will not be adequately honored until she has a holiday dedicated to her at both the state and national levels. Some activists have pushed for a national holiday on par with the one in January memorializing the life and legacy of Martin Luther King Jr. Responding to this public pressure, President George Bush Sr. proclaimed an informal "Harriet Tubman Day" in 1990, saying: "In celebrating Harriet Tubman's life, we remember her commitment to freedom and rededicate ourselves to the timeless principles she struggled to uphold. Her story is one of extraordinary courage and effectiveness in the movement to abolish slavery and to advance the noble ideals enshrined in our Nation's Declaration of Independence: 'We hold these truths to be self-evident, that all men are created equal, that they are endowed by their Creator with certain unalienable Rights, that among these are Life, Liberty and the pursuit of Happiness.'"[61] Bush asked Americans to honor Tubman "with appropriate ceremonies and activities" without specifying what these might be. Federal offices remained open, making it a token Tubman holiday, at best. Tubman-holiday activists pushed American politicians to do more. In March 2001, Elizabeth Rankin-Fulcher urged attendees at a forum of the National Action Network not to abandon the fight for a national Tubman holiday. "If we accomplish this mission," Rankin-Fulcher said, "she [Tubman] will be the first woman, Black or white, honored with a national holiday. We have always honored men; now it's our turn."[62]

Tubman-holiday promoters in New York State also engaged in a campaign to have a day on the calendar permanently dedicated to Black Moses. Most personal commemorative holidays use the birthdate of the honoree as the calendar date. Because Tubman's birthdate is not known, holiday advocates have chosen March 10, the day of her death, as the memorial occasion. Introduced in 1999, the Tubman Holiday initiative eventually got lost in the labyrinth of Albany politics. Opponents of the bill expressed concerns about a negative fiscal impact on the state budget and private businesses. Fiscal conservatives balked at the notion of having yet another paid holiday for state employees. An editorial writer for Syracuse's *Post-Standard* suggested a compromise: Make the Tubman Holiday a floating holiday. State employees could select it from the list of eleven holidays already designated for them. "And just in case a day honoring Tubman sounds somehow unnecessary," the editorialist added, "consider the fact that eight states honor Robert E. Lee, who fought for the Confederacy and slavery; two states celebrate the birth of Confederate President Jefferson Davis; and others honor Confederate Hero Day and Confederate Memorial Day."[63] Governor George Pataki did declare March 10 a statewide day of recognition for Harriet Tubman. This did not satisfy holiday advocates, who continued their petition and public-relations campaigns.

In 2001, two New York State legislators, Assemblyman Arthur O. Eve (D–Buffalo) and Assemblyman Michael F. Nozzolio (R–Auburn), re-introduced legislation to make March 10 a state holiday to honor Harriet Tubman. The bill passed the Assembly but ran into opposition in the Republican-controlled Senate. Politicians opposed to making March 10 an annual Tubman Holiday continued to drag their feet, concerned about an estimated 32 million dollar to 45 million dollar economic loss if state workers were given another day off and commerce were disrupted. In the aftermath of the State Senate's rejection of a fixed holiday, Assemblyman Nozzolio suggested a compromise. He advocated that the second Sunday of March be set aside to commemorate Tubman and noted that economic losses for a Sunday holiday, estimated by some at about 8 million dollars, could be offset by the economic benefits of tourism.[64]

The Tubman Holiday legislation languished in Albany, as did the proposal that Assemblyman Nozzolio introduced to have one of four state agency buildings honoring women named after Harriet Tubman.[65] Getting politicians to agree on how to honor Tubman has been far more difficult than in some other sectors of American institutional life. For example, in 1995 the Episcopal Church of the United States proposed placing Tubman on its Calendar of Saints, along with three of her contemporaries—Sojourner Truth, Elizabeth Cady Stanton, and Amelia Bloomer.[66] In 2003, Governor George Pataki's office announced that New York State would observe each forthcoming March 10 as a day of commemoration in honor of Harriet Tubman. Tubman enthusiasts vowed to press on with their campaign for a legal holiday.

While Tubman's revitalization in the American memory has not yet resulted in a state or national holiday for her, she fares well as a marketable symbol. Today Harriet Tubman is very collectible. There are multiple incarnations of her in doll form. Her representation in the Dor-a-bills Doll Historical Women Collection series shows her carrying a Bible. Other doll designers depict Tubman wearing clothing more likely worn by a white Southern belle. Today, the Tubman image shows up on

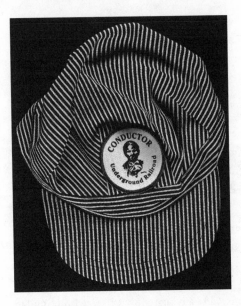

61. Conductor's cap. In the author's collection.

T-shirts, caps, coffee mugs, souvenir pins and postcards, puzzles, playing cards, posters, and assorted other souvenir items and collectibles. Some of these products raise eyebrows. The Harriet Tubman Brainy Babies key chain marketed by the Bishop Interactive Group of Cleveland, Ohio, bordered on a demeaning caricature.[67] In our consumer-orientated culture, Harriet Tubman's iconic representation is bought and sold as if she were a rock star or movie-screen idol. Having said all of this, I would not want to part with my Tubman conductor's cap (Figure 61).

Commercial establishments have joined in the effort to cash in on Tubman's current popularity. A funeral home uses her story to draw clients to its services. McDonald's offered a set of four African American Heritage Stamp pins, one of which depicted Harriet Tubman. The Seagrams Distillers Company sponsored a "Negro Historical Calendar" that included an illustration of Tubman. United Airlines put Tubman's image on a black history map with the theme "Celebrate Yesterday's Heroes. Save with United's Bicentennial Fare." Even such venerable institutions as the Smithsonian Institution tried to cash in on the resurgence of the public's interest in Tubman. An ad touted the Smithsonian's new credit card with pictures of Tubman and the words: "She used the Underground Railroad to plan great escapes. But all you need is this credit card."[68] While some Tubman enthusiasts had reservations about the commodification of her as symbol, others viewed the plethora of products bearing her image as proof of her increasing popularity.

When Earl Conrad was struggling to get his book about Tubman published in the early 1940s, he complained about how America had forgotten the woman whom he believed was the nation's greatest heroine. In the subsequent sixty years, Tubman's popularity as a symbol escalated in ways that Conrad could not have foreseen. Artists and sculptors, poets and singers, dramatists and dancers, and a variety of other creative minds tapped into the Tubman myth for inspiration. Communities put her name on public buildings, streets, bridges, and other markers on the landscape. A passionate group of Tubman admirers orchestrated campaigns to have a state and a national holiday set aside to commemorate her. By the end of the twentieth century, Tubman souvenirs and products had become highly marketable.

There is a striking irony in all of this. While Tubman's popularity increased in the post-Conrad decades, and most dramatically in the closing decades of the twentieth century, serious research lagged behind. The Tubman renaissance in popular culture drew on the Tubman myth crafted by Sarah Bradford and Tubman's other nineteenth-century mediators and by Earl Conrad's 1943 book. Memory had run ahead of history. In many respects, the Tubman revitalization of the second half of the twentieth century was merely a reinvigoration of the Tubman myth as crafted by her admirers and fueled by highly fictionalized versions of her life. Whereas Tubman's name was known to a small circle of friends and allies both before and after the Civil War, it was widely recognized by the end of the twentieth century. Name recognition, however, did not translate into an informed and critical understanding of the origins of the Tubman myth or of the life behind the symbol.

CHAPTER NINE

PRIDE OF PLACE

Americans search for ways to ground and thereby make tangible the historical figures whom they espouse as important symbols. The public honors former presidents at historic properties across the country, no matter how humble the places or fleetingly associated with those who occupied the White House. Heritage tourism thrives on being able to identify locations on the American landscape that invoke memories of individuals deemed worthy of veneration. Few designated historic sites, whether federal- or state-sponsored, currently honor African American women.[1]

Thus, endeavors to identify places that invoke the memory of Harriet Tubman are significant. Auburn, New York, and Dorchester County, Maryland, have been the strongest contenders for the title of Harriet Tubman's home ground. There are others, of course, but the following analysis of pride of place in the construction of Tubman as an American icon focuses for the most part on the region of her birth below the Mason–Dixon Line and on the part of upstate New York that Tubman called home for more than a half century.

Keepers of iconic memory traditionally become pilgrims, finding their way to sites, both sacred and secular, where they believe they can commune with heroic figures in some tangible way. Americans who want today to visit places that invoke reflection on the significance of Tubman's life fare better than at any time since Tubman's death. In November 2002, Congress mandated that the National Park Service conduct a special resource study to determine the feasibility of including places (buildings and sites) associated with Harriet Tubman into the national park system. This federally funded initiative fostered a renewal of interest in identifying and preserving structures and landscapes where Tubman's legacy could be invoked. As of this writing, the recommendations of the

National Park Service team have not been implemented, yet it is clear that the very process of examining how the federal government might honor Tubman has stimulated greater public interest in locating her in the American memory.[2]

In its preliminary survey of sites and structures worthy of investigation, preservation, and possibly restoration, the National Park Service team identified five in Auburn, New York: the Harriet Tubman Home for the Aged at 180 South Street, the Harriet Tubman Residence at 182 South Street, Tubman's burial site in Fort Hill Cemetery, the Thompson Memorial African Methodist Episcopal Zion church at 33 Parker Street, and the home of William Henry Seward at 33 South Street.

Auburn's notoriety because of Tubman's association with this upstate New York community has been a mixed blessing. On the one hand, Auburn residents take pride in having the woman whom many consider to have been the most important conductor on the Underground Railroad linked to their town. Indeed, as national interest in Tubman began to soar in the early 1990s and there was talk of erecting a memorial to Tubman, a representative of the neighboring Town of Fleming expressed a bit of jealousy. Donald A. Chase, supervisor of the Town of Fleming, wrote to the editor of the *Auburn Citizen*: "We read you find [*sic*] editorial regarding a monument for Harriet Tubman and we agree. However, Harriet Tubman lived and passed away in the Town of Fleming, not Auburn."[3] On the other hand, as we shall see, the Tubman–Auburn connection has sparked political controversy and community discord.

Today's Tubman Home historic site is situated on the Town of Fleming line, though property taxes are paid to the City of Auburn. In 1932, the New York State Department of Education placed a historical marker in front of what was then known as the Harriet Tubman Home (Figure 62). The marker reads: "Home of Harriet Tubman 'The Moses of Her Race' Underground Railroad Station in Slavery Days." As late as the 1990s, travelers in search of the grounded Tubman turned into the site and toured the two-story white clapboard house with the tin roof, unaware that the approximately eight-acre parcel on which the structure stands is not the sum total of what she once possessed. Nor is the wood-frame house her former residence. Unraveling the threads of the history of Tubman-related properties in Auburn is a complex task. What follows is not a definitive account of their legal patrimony but a summary of their history in light of this chapter's focus on the memorialization of place.

62. Harriet Tubman Home. Collection of the Cayuga Museum of History and Art, Auburn, New York.

With the help of William Henry Seward, Tubman first settled her elderly parents on the property just off South Street in the Town of Fleming in 1859, probably in the spring. The 6.253-acre parcel had been part of the Burton farm and was one of many pieces of real estate that Seward owned in and around Auburn. According to an abstract in the Seward Papers, Tubman took out a one thousand two hundred dollar mortgage for the property on May 25, 1859.[4] The payment schedule was characterized as being "on easy terms." In 1873, Tubman took owner-ship of this property by paying off a second mortgage for one thousand seven hundred fifty dollars to Frederick W. and Anna Seward, the son and daughter-in-law of William H. Seward. Her benefactor, the former New York State governor and later Secretary of State in the Lincoln ad-ministration, was dead by this time.

When Harriet's parents moved to the Auburn area from St. Catha-rines, having complained that the Canadian winters were too harsh, they most likely settled into a small wood-frame house. It no longer exists, having burned down in the 1880s. Nelson Davis, Harriet's second hus-

63. Brick house, Tubman residence, circa 1935. Photograph by Jane Searing. Original photograph courtesy Hazard Library, Poplar Ridge, New York.

band, knew the bricklaying trade and possibly constructed the red brick house (now at 182 South Street) that present-day visitors see (Figure 63). This structure seems to have replaced the wood-frame one that burned. A second wood-frame house and several small sheds or outbuildings also stood on the first piece of property, henceforth referred to as the small parcel.

In June 1896, Tubman borrowed one thousand dollars from an Auburn bank and, with an additional two hundred fifty dollars made up of personal loans and donations, purchased a 25.5-acre parcel to the north of the small one. Feeling, she would later recall, "like a blackberry in a pail of milk" as the only black person bidding, Tubman did so at public auction with the intent of using the property for a community farm cooperative and a place to expand and incorporate her home or hospital for the aged.[5] This second property, henceforth to be called the large parcel, contained two frame cottages, two barns, and one brick structure, which Tubman named John Brown Hall (Figure 64).[6] John Brown Hall opened in 1895 and was used to house elderly men, probably no more than six or seven at a time. John Brown Hall remained empty after the dissolution of

64. John Brown Hall, circa 1912. Courtesy Cayuga County Historian's Office, Auburn, New York.

the Harriet Tubman Home for the Aged, then burned in 1949 and subsequently was torn down.

During the seven years that Harriet Tubman owned the larger parcel, she was often hard pressed to pay the taxes and once had to sell off her cows to do so. In 1903, Tubman deeded the second parcel to the African Methodist Episcopal Zion denomination, which assumed debts on it totaling one thousand eight hundred dollars and gave Black Moses a pension. The Harriet Tubman Home for Aged and Indigent Colored Persons opened on June 22, 1908.[7] Tubman herself moved into it in her declining years. At the time of her death, the home served eight individuals. By 1915, only six remained, one of whom, Miss Winnie Johnson, was reportedly 113 years old.[8] In 1918, African Methodist Episcopal Zion leaders celebrated the burning of the mortgage on the Harriet Tubman Home. A newspaper account of the ceremonies claimed that, at long last, the "little home for aged colored people is free—free as the heroine for whom it was named, who escaped from the South during the Civil War days and came to Auburn to make her home."[9] Except for one similar facility in the South, the Harriet Tubman Home was, the paper asserted, unique.

As a refuge for aged African Americans, the Harriet Tubman Home was more important as a symbol than as a successful philanthropic enterprise. By 1926, a single person resided in the Harriet Tubman Home.[10]

The Harriet Tubman Home closed as the Great Depression settled in. Thereafter, the house was rented out for a number of years. Though the Tubman Home merited designation as a State Historic Site in 1932, it had stood empty since 1928. During the Depression years, vandals nearly destroyed it, taking wood framing for firewood and leaving only a skeleton of the original structure. During this period of neglect, neither the house nor the property was open to members of the public who wished to stand on ground that Tubman walked or tour a building she had lived in toward the end of her life. The historic Tubman property (the large parcel) went on sale because of unpaid taxes in 1943. It had to be redeemed by the Thompson Memorial church with the aid of a local philanthropist who provided the tax payment.[11] In 1944, the City of Auburn ordered that the Tubman Home, now a derelict structure exposed to the elements (Figure 65), be torn down. No action was taken.

When Tubman's estate was settled, ownership of the small parcel fell into the hands of a white family. Some of Tubman's friends and members of Auburn's African American community protested the manner in which the brick residence and approximately seven-acre parcel was lost. They claimed that they had not been given the opportunity to buy it, though they were prepared with the funds to do so. The lawyer whom Tubman had asked to settle her affairs countered that he was required by law to sell the property to the highest bidder to settle the debts carried in Tubman's estate.[12] As a result of the purchase of the small parcel by the Norris family, the African Methodist Episcopal Zion authorities were left with only the larger acreage containing the Harriet Tubman Home, John Brown Hall, and several other structures. The foundation of a second wood-frame house situated toward the front of the property and once used as a home by Tubman's brother John Stewart, awaits archaeological investigation. The Norris-owned property and brick house remained outside of the control of the African Methodist Episcopal Zion church until heirs of the Norris family put it up for sale in 1990.[13]

A campaign to restore the Harriet Tubman Home, led by African Methodist Episcopal Zion Bishop William J. Walls, took shape in the late 1940s. Eleanor Roosevelt consented to lend her name to the National Harriet Tubman Shrine Committee in an honorary capacity. Mary

65. Derelict Harriet Tubman Home, 1947. Photograph by Ruth Putter. Courtesy Ruth Putter.

McLeod Bethune was named second honorary chairman. Denominational officials took up the challenge of making the Auburn Tubman site "a shrine for our Zion and for our race."[14] According to its articles of incorporation, dated July 5, 1949, a legal entity called "The African Methodist Episcopal Zion Church Harriet Tubman Foundation" (sometimes referred to as the Harriet Tubman Corporation), was set up "to receive and administer funds for the restoration, development and perpetual upkeep of the Harriet Tubman homestead and property located in the City of Auburn, N.Y., which is now constituted property of the African Methodist Episcopal Zion Church by virtue of the bequest of the late Harriet Tubman, to the end that this property might become and remain a natural shrine to the memory of Harriet Tubman and an inspiration to all men, regardless of race, creed or color."[15] Bishop Walls successfully raised thirty thousand dollars to restore the frame house now known as the Harriet Tubman Home. It was rededicated on April 13, 1953. Though the African Methodist Episcopal Zion denomination used the property for memorial gatherings, the Tubman Home did not open to the public on a regular basis.

In the succeeding decades, the Northeastern Episcopal District of the African Methodist Episcopal Zion denomination attempted to keep the Tubman property well maintained, but it did so on a very modest budget. Even as public interest in Tubman was increasing and more and more pilgrims in search of a Tubman shrine arrived at the Auburn site, church officials struggled to manage the property effectively. For a while during the 1960s, the Reverend Samuel Brown lived in an upstairs apartment in the Tubman Home and acted as resident host. Then he was assigned to Buffalo, and the site closed to visitors. Brown came to Auburn once a week to check on the property. On one inspection trip, he discovered that the house had been broken into. Vandals damaged a showcase, tore down posters, and spattered glue about. A reporter for an Auburn newspaper wrote at the time, "The [African Methodist Episcopal] Zion church is hampered by lack of funds for maintaining the Tubman home, and in having administration of it at a distance from Auburn."[16]

Alarmed by the worsening state of affairs, a small group of Tubman admirers in Auburn known as the Harriet Tubman Boosters Club wrote denominational officials in June 1971. They warned of the possible loss of the South Street landmark. Failing to get a satisfactory response from the African Methodist Episcopal Zion episcopacy, the Boosters Club asked the Cayuga County Board of Supervisors to try to persuade denominational officials to take action to restore the Harriet Tubman Home.[17] An editorial writer for the Auburn press suggested that a local group take over the administration of the Tubman Home, an idea that the *Star of Zion*, the official denominational paper, forcefully rejected, saying, "We say just as earnestly and sincerely 'No,' A thousand times 'no.' The [African Methodist Episcopal] Zion has the know-how, the interest, the ability and means to restore in a first class manner, and operate this landmark."[18] African Methodist Episcopal Zion leaders were soon talking of restoring the Harriet Tubman Home and building a new domicile for "older, poor people" on the site in keeping with the vision of the home's namesake. They also proposed erecting a life-size illuminated statue of Tubman on the lawn.[19] Neither the domicile nor the statue came to be. As with the idea in the early 1950s of developing the property to include a rest station for needy farm migrants and more recent proposals to transform the Tubman property off South Street into a theme park focusing on the Underground Railroad and featuring an underground ride on a miniature train, the grasp exceeded the reach.[20]

In an editorial published in late 1971, George R. Metcalf, an Auburn native and longtime New York State senator, told the readers of an Auburn paper: "People who have resided in this area all or most of their lives tend to accept the life of Harriet Tubman as a local legend without realizing that her name and reputation knows no boundary. . . . Inside black America, as well as [in] all nations inside the so-called Third World, her fame continues to soar. She has become a top figure in the black world. For example, among the first acts of the Newark Board of Education, when it finally became black dominated this last summer, was to rename a city high school in her honor."[21] Metcalf advocated that the Tubman Home be turned into a national shrine and suggested that Representative Shirley Chisholm of Brooklyn, the sole black female member of the U.S. Congress, be persuaded to spearhead the project. Metcalf was one of Auburn's most passionate white advocates of enhancing the Tubman property and giving Black Moses her due.

He protested the installation of an electric power line at the rear of the Tubman property, arguing that the tall transmission towers violated the historic integrity of the site. "To pay tribute to her remarkable courage and hatred of human bondage," Metcalf wrote, "U.S. Negroes come to Auburn from long distances to visit, what is for them, a black shrine.

With this as background, it is particularly shocking to drive by this famed habitat and see enormous utility lines strung across the property, defiling the image of black heritage." Metcalf argued that if it was necessary to run utility wires across the William H. Seward homestead farther up on South Street, the utility company would be persuaded to bury them. "White America," he opined, "guards its white heroes at the same time it overlooks black men and women of heroic proportions. This is one reason of course, for the failure of blacks and whites to reach a closer relationship."[22]

After the departure of the Reverend Arthur E. May, the Reverend Guthrie Carter, who served a congregation in Saratoga Springs, became director in 1971. He would later admit that he knew little about Tubman at the time of his appointment. With obligations in Saratoga Springs, Carter traveled back and forth to Auburn as his schedule permitted. When interviewed in the early 1970s, he spoke about being a latecomer to the Harriet Tubman legend, though he was said to be "swiftly catching up." Carter, who was born the same year that Black Moses died was asked if he knew the woman whose fame was drawing busloads of children to Auburn. Carter responded, "Babies don't think well at that age."[23] Though the assignment of Guthrie Carter as manager of the Tubman site signaled renewed interest in developing it as a tourist destination, the African Methodist Episcopal Zion leadership still had a difficult task ahead.

For nearly two decades, Guthrie Carter acted as the primary ambassador to those in the public who desired to ground their memory of Tubman at the site in Auburn. Though he began his tenure as manager with little knowledge of Tubman's life and legend, he eventually became an enthusiastic custodian of her legacy. I met him during my first visit to the Tubman Home in 1975 and came away impressed by his dedication and service in spite of a limited budget and the lack of any staff. Because of his ministerial obligations in Saratoga Springs, a four- to five-hour drive from Auburn, Carter was unable to keep the Tubman Home open to visitors on a regular basis. It remained closed for most of the winter months. When Carter was present, he was tour guide, manager, and maintenance man.

In the early 1970s, cognizant of the importance of Tubman as a figure worthy of national honor, Bishop William J. Walls led another campaign to elevate the Tubman property on the denomination's list of priorities.

Walls chastised his fellow Zionites in 1972, observing "there never has been a regular board and no special place in the church economy for the Tubman Home." Instead, the Tubman Home, whose board of managers had not met for many years, had to rely on the charity and goodwill of a small number of Tubman admirers. Now in his nineties, Walls hoped to reverse this state of affairs, one that had relegated the Tubman home to a "parsimonious budget" and caused it to "slumber."[24] Opened in 1972 once again to visitors, the home appeared to have the support of church leaders. Visitors received a pamphlet which stated: "The hope of the [African Methodist Episcopal] Zion Church Connection is to continue the practice begun by Harriet Tubman by planning a National Non-Sectarian Group to expand the property into a home for the aged, a meeting place for youth conferences and a cultural enrichment center. This would fulfill her dream for making this property an institution for the service of all her people."[25]

Unfortunately, sufficient financial support for the Tubman Home and property never materialized. In 1977, the Harriet Tubman Home had a budget of only ten thousand dollars, a modest amount given the fact that the home had been declared a National Historic Landmark, the federal government's highest designation, three years earlier. At that time, only thirteen sites associated with the history of African Americans in the nation had a similar distinction.[26]

As public interest in Tubman escalated, Auburn's civic leadership attempted to help church officials. Cognizant that a revitalized Tubman property might bring in more tourism dollars and aware of the historical importance of the Tubman Home, a city official wrote to Bishop Walls asking if there were ways in which public funds could be used for the restoration. Solicitation of public funds to benefit the Tubman Home, a property under the control of a religious group, has been a complicated business. Opponents do not want tax dollars fostering a church enterprise. Denominational officials have been concerned that the acceptance of non-church-generated funds might imply diminution of church control. Nevertheless, the City of Auburn has from time to time contributed to the enhancement of the Tubman site. In 1976, the city made a contribution to the erection of brick pillars at the entrance to the Tubman Home.[27]

Tourists at the Harriet Tubman Home typically step into the parlor. From there, they look into a bedroom to the right, then go ahead into a kitchen and eating area. Given the wretched state of the home in the 1940s and the extensive rebuilding that had to be done, little that visitors see today is original. In 1949, when the contract was drawn up to rebuild the Harriet Tubman Home, press accounts described it as being "in ruins" and in a "tumbled down" state. African Methodist Episcopal Zion bishops came to inspect the property, saw an urgent challenge before them, and declared that it was a religious and racial duty to act lest the memory of "a great life . . . be buried in the sands."[28] So little of the historic structure then survived that the bishops spoke of building a "replica" on the existing ruins.[29] Jean Humez has written perceptively of the Harriet Tubman Home:

> The problems of maintaining a charitable institution through small voluntary donations by church members, year in and year out, overwhelmed the Harriet Tubman Home. Yet as a legacy of a national symbol of racial pride, the Home could not be allowed to fail. And so it went through a series of cycles of vacancy, decay, and vandalism, followed by indignant publicity and finger-pointing by city and church representatives, followed by fund-raising and efforts at restoration and renewal, throughout the twentieth century. Ultimately it evolved from a failed rest home into its present identity as historical shrine.[30]

The existing Tubman Home is a replica and not a restored structure. Visitors must imagine how it was furnished. "Because there are no pictures of the [interior of the] house before it was restored, we don't know how it was set up," the Reverend Paul G. Carter acknowledged in 1991.[31] On my tours of the home over the years, I have been told by the various docents, or guides, that the bedroom furniture, a Bible, and the treadle sewing machine belonged to Tubman. Subsequent investigations have raised questions about these claims. Only the Bible seems to have been one of Tubman's possessions. Gladys Bryant, the grandniece who was seven years old when "Aunt Harriet" died, donated the bed to the Tubman Home when it was being outfitted after restoration. Tubman did not own the bed during her lifetime.[32] When public interest in Tubman grew exponentially in the 1990s, home officials periodically made appeals hoping to obtain any items Tubman once owned. They prized most finding the medal and shawl that Queen Victoria supposedly requested be sent Tubman at the time of the Diamond Jubilee celebration of her reign in 1897.[33]

In 1979, a crowd estimated at five hundred witnessed the dedication of the Harriet Tubman Memorial Library, constructed on a site near the Harriet Tubman Home and funded entirely by the African Methodist Episcopal Zion connection.[34] In May 1984, during the annual Tubman Memorial Pilgrimage, leaders of the African Methodist Episcopal Zion church dedicated a multipurpose building built at a cost of approximately one hundred thousand dollars on the Tubman Home acreage. Equipped with a large meeting space and kitchen facilities, the Harriet Tubman Memorial Center offered better shelter for those attending the pilgrimages than did the tent the City of Auburn provided in earlier years. With the completion of the multipurpose structure, the Tubman Home property comprised the restored Tubman home (the white frame structure), a library building housing some Tubman artifacts and books on African American history, and the Harriet Tubman Memorial Center.[35] The purchase in 1990 of the small parcel on which Harriet had settled her parents in 1859 was significant. This acquisition restored the boundaries of the Tubman site as they existed at the time of her death in 1913.

In 1991, the Reverend Paul G. Carter, then thirty-nine, became director of the Tubman Home. He told a reporter from a Syracuse newspaper, "I'm here to get the Harriet Tubman Home back on the map, and operating as a full-time tourist attraction. Nothing's been going on down here, and I want to change that."[36] Carter and his wife, Christine, who actively joined in the effort to revitalize the Tubman Home for visitors, especially the many schoolchildren who came in large numbers each year, eventually moved into the brick house at 182 South Street, living there until efforts began to incorporate it more fully into a revived Tubman historic site through research and restoration.

In 1990, Congress authorized and funded a special resource study of the Underground Railroad. As the home's namesake was widely perceived as the most important Underground Railroad conductor of all, interest in her connections to Auburn escalated. The passage of the New York State Freedom Trail Act in 1997 also increased public awareness of Tubman's Auburn connection. Soon monies began to flow to the Tubman Home for various study and restoration projects. Speaking as bishop of the Northeastern Episcopal District of the African Methodist Episcopal

Zion church, George Washington Carver Walker Sr. told the press, "I think this country owes to Harriet's legacy all it can give."[37] Vince deForest, special assistant to the director of the National Park Service for the Underground Railroad initiative, underscored the centrality of Auburn's Tubman-related sites by saying, "Her story is the story of empowerment. The physical sites serve as benchmarks, help us tell those stories. Once we fully recognize Harriet's legacy, it can offer positive values for dealing with our (racial) situation in this country."[38]

As yet another indication of the revival of interest in Tubman-related properties, Professor Douglass V. Armstrong of Syracuse University offered his services and those of student archaeologists to the Tubman Home. Work began in the summer of 1998 at a field site set up to explore the ruins of the brick dormitory or infirmary occupied by some of the elderly Tubman cared for. Until Armstrong and his associates discovered and stabilized the structure's foundations, John Brown Hall, last occupied in the 1920s and destroyed in the 1940s, had been forgotten by the general public.[39] In the summer of 2003, the Syracuse University Archaeological Field School concentrated on the Harriet Tubman brick house with the intent of learning more about Tubman and those who lived there. Initial investigations suggested that it was built on the site of the original wood-frame house she and her parents moved into in 1859. It burned on February 10, 1880, early in the morning, perhaps due to a defective stovepipe.[40]

First Lady Hillary Rodham Clinton visited the Tubman Home in July 1998 as part of her Save America's Treasures tour. My wife and I were among the crowd estimated at one thousand strong that assembled on an extremely hot July day waiting for the First Lady's bus to arrive at the grounds on South Street.[41] I reflected on how different this occasion was from my first visit to the Harriet Tubman Home in 1975. Then, I was told that the wood-frame structure had been Tubman's personal residence. No mention was made of the brick house on the original, smaller parcel. The Carters, Paul and Christine, along with Bishop Walker welcomed Mrs. Clinton to the brick house, and afterward the entire party strolled to a podium set up before the Harriet Tubman Home. In her remarks to the large crowd of Tubman admirers, Clinton lauded Tubman as a true American hero, one whose legacy of humanitarian self-sacrifice ought to inspire present and future generations. Earlier, Clinton's office had announced a ten thousand dollar grant for the restoration of the Tubman

Home (given by the Washington, D.C., philanthropist Bitsy Folger). The wealthy were not the only benefactors during these years of increased interest in helping the Tubman Home. Children in a suburban Philadelphia elementary school donated one thousand dollars in pennies.[42]

No one was more effective at garnering financial support for the preservation and restoration of the Tubman-related historic structures in Auburn than Michael Long, city grants manager for capital improvement projects. Aided by his expertise in grant writing and passionate advocacy of the merits of the Tubman restoration effort, the Tubman Home obtained four hundred fifty thousand dollars from the federal government's Save America's Treasures fund for "brick and mortars" projects in 2000.[43] Earlier it had received a forty thousand dollar grant from the same source for planning and documentation. In 2001, New York Governor George Pataki's office announced a grant of two hundred eighty-four thousand dollars for emergency repairs and archaeological work on the brick house and the church on Parker Street. The governor released the following statement: "Harriet Tubman's dedication and commitment to helping so many slaves on the underground railroad has made her one of our Nation's historical figures, and it is fitting that we pay tribute to this great American champion of freedom. . . . Her remarkable courage in helping slaves find their way to freedom was an important part of the anti-slavery movement in the North, and we are honored that she made her home in New York."[44] New York State officials announced an award of one hundred thousand dollars in 2002 for restoration work on the Thompson Memorial church. By the end of 2003, more than one million dollars had been given or pledged by various sources toward the restoration and development of the Tubman-associated properties in Auburn.[45]

Fortunately, African Methodist Episcopal Zion officials charged with oversight of Auburn's Tubman sites responded favorably to the renaissance of public interest. In 2001, Bishop George W. Walker Sr. announced that the Northeastern Episcopal District would raise church funding to one hundred thousand dollars. This was a significant increase from the thirty thousand dollar annual budget the Harriet Tubman Home had subsisted on since at least the early 1970s. Ward DeWitt, appointed interim executive director of the Harriet Tubman Home in 2001, told the press: "Bishop Walker helped us understand that this [the Tubman property] can't just be held as a church shrine. It has to be shared for the national treasure that it is."[46] Without progressive thinking on the part of the African Methodist Episcopal Zion hierarchy, significant restoration and enhancement of the Tubman sites would have been impossible. Entrenched fears of losing control of the Tubman-related treasures to secular entities had to be overcome. The quality of the visitor's experience to the Tubman Home needed improvement. In 2002, representatives of Randall Travel Marketing of Mooresville, North Carolina, posed as tourists and came to the Tubman Home as part of a review of tourist attractions in the New York's Finger Lakes district. Their report described their experience as the worst they had had in twenty years of evaluating the tourism business.[47] In the wake of this unflattering review, De Witt urged staff at the site to improve what he called "customer service." He hoped to move beyond "a mom-and-pop kind of operation to a mega-premiere-historical-site operation."[48]

The National Park Service entered discussions in 2000 about the preservation and public use of Auburn's Tubman-related sites. Vijay Mital, director of planning and economic development for the City of Auburn, appeared before the Senate Subcommittee on National Parks, Historic Preservation, and Recreation to express support for Senate Bill 2345, a bill that would direct the Park Service to conduct a special resource study of sites associated with the Tubman legacy.[49] The following November, the National Park Service nominated the Tubman grounds, now including both parcels, and the African Methodist Episcopal Zion church on Parker Street to Secretary of the Interior Bruce Babbit for recognition as national historic sites. The brick home and the church became National Historic Landmarks in 2001.[50]

The Thompson Memorial African Methodist Episcopal Zion church on Parker Street (Figure 66) is also a popular destination on the Tubman pilgrimage trail. The existing structure was built in 1891, but the congregation's roots go back to about 1840. Legal incorporation took place in 1847. The members first met in various vacant buildings, including a black school on Washington Street, until they erected a building on Parker Street. The present house of worship was vacated in 1993 when the congregation moved into facilities on Wall Street that once belonged to a group of white Methodists. The congregation's name honors Bishop Joseph Jamison Thompson; he presided at the cornerstone laying on August 8, 1891. Thompson, born into slavery in Virginia, ran away and eventually came to Auburn where he studied theology privately with a professor at the Auburn Theological Seminary.[51]

66. Thompson Memorial African Methodist Episcopal Zion church, Auburn, New York, undergoing restoration, 2005. Photograph by the author.

67. Graveside ceremony, Empire State Federation of Women's Clubs, July 11, 1974. Gladys Bryant, who attended Tubman's funeral in 1913, is second from the left. From Bessie Cooper Noble, *Ain't Sleep, Ain't Gone: A Tribute to Harriett* [*sic*] *Tubman* (Fayetteville, N.Y.: Manlius Publishing, 1978).

    Tubman's final resting place in Fort Hill Cemetery also attracts visitors to Auburn (Figure 67).[52] In 1937, the Empire State Federation of Women's Clubs sponsored the erection of the present grave marker. An earlier one contained a mistake and had to be destroyed. A tall pine tree near Tubman's grave beckons contemporary pilgrims. Conflicting orally based accounts exist as to who planted it. One person told me that the pine was planted as a kind of exorcism and symbol of healing after someone, perhaps a member of the Ku Klux Klan, had desecrated the gravesite. Judith Bryant, however, explained that the tree was planted at the time her grandfather, William Henry Stewart, was buried in proximity to his sister Harriet.[53] Whatever the truth, the stately evergreen moves visitors to contemplate Tubman's significance. In the words of Nana Ama Pearl, an African American storyteller who sings praise songs about "Mama Moses": "When y'all go to her home place up there [Auburn], y'all can stop by the church. The peoples there is still involved with her property. Her grave is 'round there, too—got a great big ole pretty tree growing by it. So peaceful. I wanta go up there and just stand and ponder for a spell."[54] As a consequence of the public's interest in commemorating Tubman, leaders of the African Methodist Episcopal Zion denomination floated a proposal in the late 1990s to remove Tubman's remains from Fort Hill and bring them to the Harriet Tubman Home site for placement in a shrine-like structure. Descendants of Tubman's siblings, such as Judith Bryant, opposed the notion, as did officials representing the cemetery. Church leaders dropped the idea.

In 1991, Tubman admirers in Auburn successfully promoted the creation of a small park in her honor. Best described as a pocket park, the Harriet Tubman Freedom Park replaced a corner eyesore at the intersection of Dill and North streets. Hogan's Meats and Va Duzer Appliances, the former occupants, had been demolished in an urban-renewal project. Matthew Papkov and the other leaders of the memorial-park campaign envisioned a living monument to Tubman. They sold paving bricks to the public, raised over eighty thousand dollars in private funds, and got approximately one hundred forty thousand dollars' worth of in-kind services from city public-works employees free of charge.[55] A ground-breaking ceremony took place on July 5, 1993. Promoters planted fruit trees, installed benches, and built a kiosk shelter. But in the ensuing years, the park deteriorated; debris and weeds discouraged visitors. Pauline Copes Johnson, the most frequently quoted of those who claim to be a Tubman great-grandniece, told the press, "I always thought Aunt Harriet was worth something more than an eyesore. I think she should have had a larger park down there, something with some acreage where you could put her statue."[56] Copes Johnson said that she wanted Auburn to match what Boston had done in creating its monument honoring Tubman. Some observers viewed the dedication in 1994 of the Harriet Tubman Freedom Park as "a kind of communal exorcism"—a way of saying that white supremacy would not prevail and that the neo-Nazis who tried to march in Auburn a year earlier did not represent majority sentiment.

Aggressive racists have targeted Auburn from time to time with public displays of their symbols and rhetoric. In 1993, twenty members of the Philadelphia-based United States of America Nationalist Party came to Auburn with the intent of promoting their supremacist views. A large crowd surrounded the van carrying the out-of-towners as it attempted to reach Auburn's Harriet Tubman Freedom Park, a symbolically rich site on North Street.[57] Auburn authorities and a large assembly of counter-demonstrators prevented the interlopers from reaching the park, and the American Nationalists ended up giving their supremacist speeches from the steps of City Hall, all the while displaying the Confederate flag. After about an hour, the neo-Nazis, as they were called in press accounts, left under the protection of the police. As the white van drove away, one occupant, using a bullhorn, shouted, "Say 'yes' to white supremacy. George Washington was white. He owned slaves."[58] In May 1994, in the midst of preparations for the annual Harriet Tubman pilgrimage, some-one hung a Nazi flag on the front door of the Harriet Tubman Home, another indication that Tubman as symbol elicits strong emotions, some-times drawing the attention of individuals who harbor deep-seated racial animosities.[59]

According to local observers and residents with whom I have spoken, the City of Auburn shows something of a split personality. On the one hand, Auburn has its Tubman enthusiasts — chief of whom are individuals associated with the Tubman Home in one capacity or another, residents who claim to be descended from one of Tubman's siblings, advocates of elevating Auburn's tourism potential, and citizens who understand the historical significance of Tubman's life and work. On the other hand, some members of the community have expressed indifference, if not opposition, to local efforts to memorialize Tubman.

In 1979, an Auburn High School sociology teacher named Bill Kane encouraged students who formed a multicultural group to campaign to have their school renamed in honor of Tubman. They felt a need to re-spond in a positive way because flyers with racist messages had appeared in the hallways of the high school a year earlier. Kane told the press, "[It's] not a racial thing; it's not a woman thing. She was a great humani-tarian."[60] The campaign failed, but the debate it generated in the press and among the public was a harbinger of a controversy that erupted in 2002 over the renaming of an elementary school in honor of Tubman. School board officials, after five months of public debate, rejected a pro-posal to rename Genesee Elementary School after Tubman as well as a competing one to name an auditorium at the high school in her honor. As elsewhere in the nation where there have been attempts to place African American symbols on public institutions, the debate in Auburn fell out along racial lines, but not exclusively so. Tired of community discord, the Auburn school board pushed for a resolution of the matter in early 2003. They voted to rename a district office building at Thorton Avenue in honor of Tubman. Approximately two hundred attended the dedication ceremony in May 2004 and heard LeShonda Barnes, a high-school senior who introduced herself as a great-great-grandniece of Tubman, say, "Today . . . we dedicate this building as a center of vision in honor of that noble model, Harriet Tubman. I hope we can say we never lost a passenger as we ride on the train to a brighter future."[61]

With emotions still running high over the school-renaming issue, Auburn residents also began debating whether to put Tubman's name on a portion of Route 20 that runs through their community. The ensuing controversy drew the attention of outsiders, who were all too ready to offer advice and criticism. Editorials appeared in the principal newspaper of Syracuse, the *Post-Standard*, chastising Auburn city officials. In 2003, for example, the "Our Opinion" writer for the Syracuse paper noted that Representative Gary Bees of Wisconsin wanted a portion of a road in his state named in Tubman's honor—a road, ironically, that members of the Ku Klux Klan de-trashed under Wisconsin's Adopt-a-Highway program. "If a state assemblyman in Wisconsin can passionately advocate for Tubman's recognition, then the people from the place she called home should do no less," said the editorialist. "Otherwise, Auburn will be known as the city that did an injustice to the woman who fought so hard against injustice."[62]

Some Auburnites took umbrage at the holier-than-thou attitude expressed by outsiders during Auburn's renaming debates. Others explored ways to bridge the racial divisions that surfaced. For example, Gwen Jones, an African American woman whom the Auburn-Cayuga branch of the NAACP honored for her community service, became a facilitator of community dialogues on racism because of the discord over the renaming of Genesee Elementary School.[63] Naming a new school in honor of Tubman might have faced less opposition had the Auburn area not already had one school named after her.[64] This is the Harriet Tubman Residential Center, a facility for juvenile offenders (delinquent girls age fifteen to eighteen) east of Auburn. Most of the residents are African American girls referred to the center by juvenile court.[65]

Though some Tubman enthusiasts are not yet satisfied with how Auburn has commemorated their hero, the city's Tubman sites have been places of pilgrimage for a long time. In the early 1950s, the African Methodist Episcopal Zion denomination began sponsoring gatherings of its members at the Harriet Tubman Home, though these organized events stopped after a few years. Concerned that the denomination was neglecting the Tubman site, local Tubman admirers formed the Harriet Tubman Boosters Club in 1956. The Boosters disbanded in 1971, a sign that interest in Tubman was at a low ebb, and would not reconvene for another twenty years.[66] The Harriet Tubman Home Foundation Society revived the pilgrimage tradition in 1975. Sixty pilgrims showed up in 1976 at the second annual pilgrimage. Hattie M. Leake of Brooklyn was among them. She had been responsible for founding the first Harriet Tubman club in a local congregation. She spread the idea to other churches, and baked sweet potatoes and made jewelry to sell as she went around raising funds for the Harriet Tubman Home.[67]

The tradition of annual memorial pilgrimages continues to this day. Michael Lopez, a journalist for the Albany *Times Union*, caught the spirit well when he described the twenty-fifth anniversary pilgrimage conducted in 1999: "Once a year, a simple, pristinely white house, in the nearly all-white upstate city of Auburn, inspires a spiritual pilgrimage among hundreds of African-Americans who come to honor the slave who refused to be a slave: Harriet Tubman. . . . Here, at the end of South Street, Auburn's Victorian millionaire's row, travel-weary parishioners of African Methodist Episcopal Zion churches from throughout the nation descended busses to tour Tubman's home and the adjacent library."[68] At the pilgrimage Lopez witnessed, Lerone Bennett Jr., senior editor of *Ebony* magazine and well-known historian, spoke, urging his hearers to press the case for the federal government to "pay Harriet Tubman!" her due for her Civil War service. Women of the African Methodist Episcopal Zion church acted as guides dressed in Harriet Tubman garb, with appropriate head coverings and red kerchiefs. Various congregations in the connection competed for the honor of having raised the most money for the Tubman Home. Churches sponsored young contestants from among whom a "Miss Harriet Tubman" was chosen. The winner came from the congregation that had raised the most money. Bennett left the assembly of pilgrims with the message that the troubles besetting African Americans, such as poor housing and a disproportionate rate of cancer and AIDS, could be overcome. The solution, he said, was for people to "do the Harriet Tubman [thing]. . . . Each one, bring one out."[69]

The introduction of individuals described as "Tubman descendants" continues to be a highlight of the memorial pilgrimages. All have been women. They present themselves as links to the past. Generally called "grandnieces" or "great-grandnieces," they have their pictures taken and receive the good wishes of attendees. They are proud of their family connection to the great one, but the role of being a Tubman "descendant" has not always been easy. Tensions have existed among the various claimants, especially as the public eye has focused more intently on them and the press pleads for a comment on this or that development. Bernice Copes Johnson, perhaps because of her many years as a guide at the Tubman Home, has been the most frequently quoted "great-grandniece" in the public media. She and Joyce Jones of Syracuse, another so-called Tubman descendant receiving considerable media attention, trace their ties to Tubman through Ann Marie Stewart. Recent research suggests that Stewart was not one of Tubman's sisters. She may have been a niece, though this is unclear in the documentary record.[70]

Judith Bryant of Auburn traces her connection to Harriet through William Henry Stewart, one of Tubman's brothers. Of all of those living today who present themselves to the public as part of the Tubman "family," she has demonstrated the most interest in the new scholarship about her famous ancestor that has emerged in the last few years.[71] She may have inherited this enlightened spirit from her mother, Gladys Bryant. When interviewed by the columnist Richard Case in the *Syracuse Herald-Journal*, Gladys Bryant acknowledged that members of her extended family, not to mention the public, had little interest in a more accurate understanding of the Tubman story until the 1970s. She recalled how the emancipator's "house" had been ransacked for firewood when she was younger. Then came *Roots*, Alex Haley's book, in 1978 and the blockbuster television series that followed. The media besieged Tubman's "descendants" for stories about their famous ancestor. Gladys Bryant told Case, "I regret I didn't talk to older members of the family when they were alive. But most of the men in the family died when they were very young and for the rest it was a closed subject. We wanted to forget about slavery and having a price on your head. I think it took some outsiders to put it down."[72] Gladys was seven when she attended the funeral of Tubman in 1913.

Pilgrims to the Tubman historic sites in Auburn come for many reasons. Some find space where they can engage in ritual display of their political beliefs. In 1983, for example, members of the Women's Encamp-

ment for a Future of Peace and Justice located near the Seneca Army De-
port in Romulus, New York, visited the Tubman Home on South Street
and then marched to her gravesite in Fort Hill Cemetery. Accompanying
them was an African American woman known as Queen Mother Moore.
She reportedly admonished those present, saying, "We must work in
Harriet Tubman's name. It's not enough to eulogize her; we must work
in her spirit."[73] For the predominantly white feminists representing the
Women's Encampment, that spirit implied that they needed to work more
diligently to bridge the divide between white, middle-class women and
women of the so-called Third World. Kimberly Everett of the American
Friends Service Committee of Philadelphia told the Auburn press that
the pilgrimage to Auburn was intended to show "that our struggles are
combined."[74]

Black cultural nationalists have found Auburn's Tubman sites particularly inspirational. In 1998, the Association for the Study of Classical
African Civilizations came on a pilgrimage, first to the Tubman Home on
South Street and then to the Fort Hill Cemetery. They formed a circle
around Tubman's final resting place, performed a ritual oblation by pour-
ing water on the grave, and told each other to look to the one called
Black Moses for inspiration. Then a woman dressed as Harriet Tubman
appeared and spoke words of encouragement. Reverend Paul Carter
was present in the capacity of resident manager of the Harriet Tubman
Home. He told the pilgrims of the vision he had for the South Street
property—the building of a retreat facility, fitted out with lodging space,
a pool, a classroom, a gift shop, and an expanded library to accommodate
a research center.[75]

Most who make the pilgrim's journey to Auburn to honor Tubman
are schoolchildren, African Methodist Episcopal Zion church members,
Underground Railroad researchers, local and regional history devotees,
women's groups such as the Empire State Federation of Women's Clubs,
and the merely curious. They come, in the main, from the United States
and Canada, but the Harriet Tubman Home also has had its share of
visitors from abroad. For example, Vladimir Voina surprised many in the
Auburn community when he showed up in 1990. A Soviet journalist who
had written a brief biography of Tubman twenty-five years earlier, he
came to pay his respects to a long-time hero of his, someone that schoolchildren in the communist countries learned about in the 1950s.[76] In 2002,

68. Harriet Tubman sign on Green Briar Road, near the location of the old Brodess farm. Courtesy James A. McGowan.

an interfaith group calling itself "Peace Walkers" started in St. Catharines and trekked to Auburn in honor of Tubman. A Buddhist order known as Nipponzan Myohoji organized the Interfaith Walk for World Peace and Reconciliation.[77] Joining other Tubman admirers on pilgrimages to the Tubman Home in Auburn reportedly builds a sense of community and common purpose. Kay McElvey, a participant in a seven-day pilgrimage from Maryland to Canada and back to Auburn in 2002, recalled: "I came back with power. . . . It just made me feel like I can do all things."[78]

Dedicated Tubman pilgrims go beyond what Auburn offers in search of places where they can connect emotionally and spiritually with the woman whom they esteem so highly. Generally, this takes them to Maryland's Eastern Shore and specifically to Dorchester County. For many years, visitors came believing that "Minty" Ross (Harriet Tubman) was born near Bucktown approximately eight miles from the county seat of Cambridge. This is tidewater and rural country, low and flat. Except for a roadside marker on Green Briar Road (Figure 68), about a mile and half from its intersection with Bestpitch Road, erected by the Maryland Civil War Centennial Commission, Tubman pilgrims did not have much to guide them to historically important places in Dorchester County.

Bits and pieces of lore about Tubman's ties to the area circulated orally, especially among a small number of African American families, but they rarely surfaced to shape public attitudes. In 1984, Addie Clash Travers, claiming to be a distant relative of Tubman, told a journalist writing for the *Washington Post*, "I didn't have no black history in school. Growing up, I didn't really know too much about Harriet Tubman. You very rarely hear about her in Dorchester County."[79] Travers sought to compensate for this local amnesia by establishing a Harriet Tubman Day in the late 1960s. Initially, as Travers recalled, only a "pitiful" few, mostly individuals claiming to be Tubman relatives of one kind or another, attended.

One of the few whites in the region to take Tubman seriously has been John Creighton, an independent historical researcher. A poet and former teacher, he once served as groundskeeper of the Dorchester Historical Society. Though he has not published his findings at any great length, Creighton is an expert on the Maryland aspects of the Tubman story. In 1977, Robert G. Stewart, then senior curator of the National Portrait Gallery in Washington, D.C., aided Creighton's research through a fund he established at the Maryland Historical Society in memory of one of his aunts. Stewart believed that his great-great-grandfather was the John T. Stewart of Dorchester County to whom Tubman was bonded out for five or six years, though, as Kate Clifford Larson discovered, he was wrong.[80] More than a decade went by without the promised Creighton biography of Tubman, and the project eventually languished. Creighton acknowledged at one point that he had grown weary of the Tubman story, describing it as "a loss leader of sorts (an understatement) for the real picture on which I am trying to focus in Dorchester—an 'objective' reconstruction of its race & class relations." Weary of the grant-writing process and disappointed at not being able to get published, Creighton wrote to Stewart about "stopping altogether" and suggested that the remaining funds in the Esther T. Stewart Fund be used for other good purposes.[81] In 2001, Creighton promised to publish two newsletters, one to be called *Harriet Tubman Speaks!* and the other, *Harriet Tubman Lives!* in which he would report on his findings and give notice of Tubman and Underground Railroad–related events in his tricounty research area (Dorchester, Caroline, and Talbot counties). Neither newsletter appeared, but Creighton did participate in public hearings held by representatives of the National Park Service in charge of drafting a Tubman resource study. He also led a community history discussion group on Tubman and the Underground Railroad at meetings held at the Harriet Tubman Organization building, at 424 Race Street in Cambridge.

On my first visit to Dorchester County in 2000, the historical marker on Green Briar Road stood as a lonely sentinel at what many people at the time thought was the site of the Brodess farm on which Tubman was born in 1820 or 1821. My wife and I met Bonnie Ryan, then a graduate student in the Department of Archaeology and Anthropology at Syracuse University. She was conducting a summer dig in the soybean fields of a farmer whose land had been identified as the old Brodess property.[82] As we walked up to a white frame house set perhaps a thousand feet back from the road, I noticed a crudely lettered, hand-painted sign. It read: "Harriet Tubman DID NOT live here!!! Cripple Creek Hunting Camp." The "did not" was also underscored for emphasis (Figure 69). Apparently, the hunting club's members had tired of inquisitive Tubman trespassers. I read their warning as another indicator of the increased public interest in grounding the Tubman myth on the physical landscape. Ironically, of course, whoever put up the warning sign was correct: Tubman was not born on the Brodess farm.

Dorchester County began to offer Tubman pilgrims more to do after the creation of the Harriet Tubman Association of Dorchester County in 1983 by Travers and other local African American residents. Its members established the Harriet Tubman Museum in Cambridge at 424 Race Street. When I visited the museum in 2001, it appeared to be more a focal point for tourism than a collection of Tubman-related materials or exhibits. Visitors could purchase T-shirts, mugs, and other paraphernalia bearing Tubman's likeness or some symbol of the Underground Railroad. They could also register for guided tours of spots thought to be associated with Tubman's childhood years. This tour took them to the Brodess farm, of course, but also to the Bazzel Methodist Episcopal church (Figure 70) on Bestpitch Ferry Toad, one mile south of Green Briar Road.

Some mistakenly believe that Harriet Tubman worshiped in the Bazzel church before her escape. According to local memory, the present-day Bazzel church replaced an earlier small structure known as the "slave church" that had been attended by Tubman's family.[83] The site now contains two buildings. The larger one dates from about 1912. Formerly

69. "Harriet Tubman Did Not Live Here" sign at the old Brodess farm site. Photograph by the author.

70. Bazzel church. Courtesy James A. McGowan.

known as Scott's Chapel, it was donated by local whites to the congregation of black Methodists and moved to the present site sometime in the
early twentieth century. The smaller building may date to about 1876, the
approximate year when the land on which it is situated was given by local
whites for a black church.[84] During special commemorative services, held
on the third Sunday of June, participants celebrate the life and work of
Tubman on the present-day grounds of the Bazzel church.

The heritage-tour van usually takes visitors to a structure located
where Green Briar Road meets Bestpitch Road. Tubman admirers point
it out as the country store where Harriet was hit on the head while
coming to the aid of a runaway. We lack definitive proof of the building's
date of construction or its original location. The Bucktown Village Store
that Tubman pilgrims see today is a building owned by Jay and Susan
Meredith (Figure 71). Though the Merediths have outfitted the store as
they imagine it to have been when Tubman lived in Dorchester County,
complete with slave shackles and a two-pound counterweight, historians
remain highly dubious of the claim that the building was the one in which
Tubman suffered that head injury.[85]

The Blackwater National Wildlife Refuge, more than twenty-three
thousand acres of watery low country set aside in 1933 as sanctuary for

71. Crossroads store, Bucktown, Maryland. Photograph courtesy Kate Clifford Larson.

migratory birds, also attracts Tubman heritage seekers. Young Harriet trapped muskrats here. Given the paucity today of buildings or other physical remains in the Dorchester County area that can be reliably tied to Tubman's Maryland experience, heritage seekers are drawn to the landscape itself, to places like the Blackwater National Wildlife Refuge, which seems to have changed very little over the decades.

Though Maryland's Tubman admirers got a late start in the heritage-tourism business, they have not lacked enthusiasm. Helen Chapell, a writer for the *Washington Post*, sensed this passion when she visited Cambridge in 1996. Her description of her encounter with two Tubman tour guides is revealing at several levels and therefore worth quoting in its entirety:

> I'm sitting in a pocket park on Race Street in Cambridge, Md., talking to two 19-year old guys about Harriet Tubman. Nineteen-year old guys, I had previously thought, cared nothing at all about history, let alone the details of Harriet Tubman's remarkable life and career. Turns out that Leverne Simmons and Brian Hastings are volunteer guides for the Underground Railroad Gift Shop, which functions as the unofficial Harriet Tubman museum in town. It's their job to chaperon the Harriet Tubman tours for the seekers who

come here in search of history. The history books can tell you all the facts, but we three are talking about Harriet as if we all knew her. And in a way, maybe we do. This is the stuff of magical realism, the way the threads of the past and present are loosely woven into the daily fabric of old Dorchester County on Maryland's Eastern Shore. Harriet Tubman's spirit might be sitting on this bench with us; no one would be too startled.

"And," Brian's saying, "did you know that when they were going to sell her sister, at Spring Valley, over beside the courthouse, Harriet came down on a ship and rescued her?" No, I didn't know that, but I am learning, sitting here in the late afternoon sunlight. Long after the rich guys, the legislators and the generals have crumbled into obscure footnotes, Harriet Tubman, an African American woman born a slave, is remembered and celebrated here. Harriet Tubman was the ultimate escape artist.[86]

These young Tubman guides were simultaneously tapping into the collective memory of Tubman in the place they called home and re-shaping the story for present-day visitors to Dorchester County. The Tubman myth has evolved in similar fashion every place it has been told and retold.

Proponents of Tubman tourism in the region of her birthplace struggled at times to convince the public of the benefits of their campaign to raise awareness of her importance. In 1997, Cambridge city commissioners, by a vote of four to one, turned down a proposition to change Cedar Street to Harriet Tubman Boulevard. They cited the prohibitive costs of altering signs and letterheads. A writer for the *Washington Post* observed that this decision caused "barely a ripple in this Dorchester County seat, where race relations were once so tense." The journalist was referring to July 24, 1967, when Cambridge erupted after the black radical H. Rap Brown gave a streetcorner speech. Homes burned and businesses were left in ruin. The National Guard had to be ordered out to restore calm.[87] By way of contrast with events in 1997, the Maryland State Highway Administration named a fifteen-mile section of Route 50, beginning at the eastern edge of Cambridge, in honor of Tubman in 1998.

The effort to build up a Tubman tourism enterprise intensified in the late 1990s. Maryland tourism magazines now tout the Tubman connection: "An interest in history also brings many visitors to this region.

Dorchester is best known as the birthplace of Harriet Ross Tubman, who guided more than 300 slaves to freedom on the Underground Railroad."[88] Hoping to catch the eye of outsiders, another tourism brochure leads with the clever statement: "We had an Underground transportation system 100 years before Metro."[89] But, as Gail Dean acknowledges in one pamphlet, "Visitors are sometimes disappointed to find only a historic marker at the spot on Green Briar Road near the place where Harriet Tubman was born and raised."[90] In summary, Tubman admirers who want to walk the ground she walked as a child and young adult can do so in a general way in Dorchester County, Maryland. They will find few physical reminders on the landscape of places she lived or worked before her escape in 1849.

Whether they were willing to acknowledge it publicly or not, Tubman enthusiasts on Maryland's Eastern Shore were competing with the better-known Auburn-based Tubman historic properties for a share of the limelight and for whatever fiscal resources might accompany national recognition of the importance of identifying and preserving Tubman's legacy. In an effort to make the public more aware of Tubman's Maryland roots, Dorchester County Tubman enthusiasts supported the creation of Harriet Tubman Park, located just east of Cambridge along Route 50. Dedicated in 2000, the park is the site of African American cultural festivals, usually held each Labor Day. As with the members of Auburn's body politic, Maryland's Tubman promoters have struggled to articulate a shared vision of how best to tell their story. The Tubman question has sparked discussions of contemporary racial issues in Dorchester County, as it did up in Auburn. A brochure titled, "Harriet Tubman and the African American Story in Dorchester County," acknowledges: "Today, Dorchester County represents a microcosm of race relations in America where lingering notions of inequality and discrimination still remain among some members of the community."[91]

Like the Tubman enthusiasts in Auburn, proponents of the Tubman story in Maryland have had difficulty separating historically accurate information about Tubman out of the tangle of facts and fiction bequeathed to them by earlier generations. How Dorchester County Tubman promoters will adjust to the new information provided about Tubman's Maryland period by her contemporary biographers remains to be seen. As of this writing, that sign on Green Briar Road (pointing to the Edward Brodess farm as Tubman's likely birthplace) still stands.

In spite of Kate Clifford Larson's published research that questions the birthplace myth, there is still no historical marker near the former location of Anthony Thompson's plantation south of Madison in the Parsons Creek area. In May 2004, the *Washington Post* printed the synopsis of a road trip to Harriet Tubman's birthplace, directing travelers to Bucktown and the old historical marker. Readers were told that here visitors could see the birthplace of "the Moses of Her People" who guided "300 slaves north to freedom." The author also encouraged travelers to visit the Bazzel church — "the small white structure where Tubman attended services" — and visit the Bucktown Village Store, claiming that the store dates to the time of Jay Meredith's great-great-great-grandfather.[92] In late 2004, at a time when Kate Clifford Larson was already sharing her research regarding the improbability that Bucktown had been Tubman's birthplace, tourism promoters in Dorchester County presented a plan to attract visitors to the area that refused to accept the new findings. Curiously, they did so for practical rather than historical reasons. Though Larson was pointing to Harrisville near Taylors Island as a more likely Tubman birthplace, the Dorchester County plan stated: "Until research concludes that she was born along Harrisville Road, and its surface is improved, tourists should not be encouraged to travel this road."[93] The Bucktown sign remained.

Old and treasured myths take a long time to give way to new and better knowledge. Just how long it will be before the misleading Tubman birthplace sign on Green Briar Road is removed is open to speculation. As it stands, it is no more historically accurate than the brown sign at the junction on Maryland Route 328 in nearby Talbot County that reads "Birthplace of Frederick Douglass." Situated at the west end of the highway bridge that crosses the Tuckahoe River, the marker on old Matthewstown Road (now Route 328) is approximately six miles from the actual Douglass birthplace, which is closer to Tapper's Corner, situated at the intersection of Maryland Route 303 and Lewistown Road.[94]

Canadian Tubman enthusiasts want the public to know that "Black Moses" can be grounded in localities outside the United States. St. Catharines in eastern Ontario has been the primary contender in the competition to draw pilgrims to places other than Auburn, New York, and Dorchester County, Maryland. Tubman admirers are directed to Geneva Street and the historic Salem Chapel of the British Methodist Episcopal church, in front of which stands a sign (Figure 72) that reads:

HARRIET ROSS TUBMAN C. 1820–1913

A legendary conductor on the Underground Railroad, Harriet Tubman became known as the "Moses" of her people. Tubman was born
into slavery on a Maryland plantation and suffered brutal treatment
from numerous owners before escaping in 1849. Over the next decade she returned to the American South many times and led hundreds of freedom seekers north. When the Fugitive Slave Act of
1850 allowed slave owners to recapture runaways in the northern
free states Tubman extended her operations across the Canadian
border. For eight years she lived in St. Catharines and at one point
rented a house in this neighborhood. With the outbreak of the Civil
War, she returned to the U.S. to serve in the Union Army.[95]

While she was president of the Ontario Black History Society, Rosemary Sadlier wrote that, despite "racist stirrings that made St. Catharines a less than ideal place for Black people to start a new life," Tubman chose to settle in the community for practical reasons. It was close
to the American border, but not so close as to attract bounty hunters.
The Reverend Hiram Wilson, a white abolitionist who assisted Canada's
fugitive colonies, could provide aid. But most significant, St. Catharines
had a community of escapees from slavery in which Tubman could both
be useful and feel comfortable. She worshiped among fellow refugees
from the "peculiar institution" of United States, kept a boarding house at
11 North Street not far from Salem Chapel's location on Geneva Street,
and supported the interracial Refugee Slave's Friends Society, an agency
that assisted fugitives with housing, employment, and adjusting to life in
Canada.[96]

Adrienne Shadd has also written on the importance of Tubman to
Canadian history. A descendant of the famous African Canadian activist
Mary Ann Shadd, she contributed an essay on "Women and the Underground Railroad Movement" to a collection titled, *"We're Rooted Here
and They Can't Pull Us Up": Essays in African Canadian History*, first published in 1994. Shadd correctly observed that "the life of Harriet Tubman has come to symbolize in many ways the struggle of African people
for freedom and justice." She also noted that Tubman's name has come
to be "virtually synonymous" with the institution of the Underground
Railroad, though many more men than women have been celebrated as
conductors.[97] When the contributors to the volume on African Canadian

72. Tubman sign, St. Catharines, Ontario. Photograph by the author.

women's history in which Shadd's essay appeared grappled with what to call their publication, they selected one of Tubman's well-known aphorisms: "We're Rooted Here and They Can't Pull Us Up."[98]

Canadians have signaled their appropriation of the symbolic Tubman in other ways. The Welland Canals Centre in St. Catharines featured Tubman in an exhibit titled "Follow the North Star," recounting the history of the Underground Railroad, and put an image of her in the museum's brochure. The exhibit featured a copy of the 1858 Assessment Roll for the Town of St. Catharines. The document lists "Harriet Tubman" as the occupant of a dwelling whose owner was Joseph Robinson.[99] Tom Morton, a teacher at the John Oliver Secondary School in Vancouver, British Columbia, designed a learning module for tenth graders on the theme, "Issues in History: Harriet Tubman and Human Agency," for which he won the Governor General's Award for Teaching Canadian History in 1998. That Tubman should be the centerpiece of a unit in Canadian history illustrates how international a symbol she has become.[100]

Of the several contenders for primacy of place of Harriet Tubman remembered, Auburn, New York, is likely to remain at the top of list. The physical remains of Black Moses are there; it is the place she called home from 1859 until 1913. The Harriet Tubman Home and associated properties have attracted national attention during the past five years, helping to increase the flow of visitors, estimated at two thousand eight hundred people annually in 2000.[101] Federal and state monies have been allocated to the preservation of historic structures, funds that in their aggregate are impressive. It remains to be seen whether the African Methodist Episcopal Zion denomination can successfully manage the Auburn Tubman properties in cooperation with non-church agencies—local, state, and federal. There is still unfinished business—visionary proposals remain undeveloped. Tourism, the principal draw, overshadows the educational and research potential some Tubman admirers have wanted to see in Auburn.

Talk of a Harriet Tubman historic corridor facilitated by the National Park Service has generated considerable interest. One could imagine a driving and walking tour that would start in Maryland, have stops in Pennsylvania, reach Auburn, New York, and go on to St. Catharines, Canada. When I first heard of the proposal, I thought of a graduate student at Syracuse University in the 1970s who wanted to research and then walk Harriet Tubman's route(s) from slavery to freedom. His dissertation eventually turned on another subject, but he was so emotionally charged by the Tubman myth/memory that he reported having communicated with her spirit while meditating at her gravesite. Tubman devotees have gone to similar extraordinary measures to demonstrate their admiration for who she was and what she symbolizes. Several have made the trek from Dorchester County to the Tubman sites in New York State as demonstrations of their devotion, not unlike religious pilgrims who set out on a long journey, often at considerable personal sacrifice, to pay homage to a favored saint. Given the popularity and commercial viability today of what is often referred to as "heritage tourism," we can expect greater interest in locating Tubman on the American (and Canadian) landscape in the future. Secondary sites where some aspect of Tubman's life can be celebrated, such as the location of the Charles Nalle rescue in Troy, New York, also draw Tubman enthusiasts.

African Americans will continue to venerate Tubman "in place." They have been the most constant segment in the trickle that has now become a flood of visitors to Tubman sites. There was a time when the preservation of Harriet Tubman's memory on the American cultural landscape was viewed as primarily the responsibility of African Americans. But Tubman is now regarded as an icon for all Americans, a symbol located somewhere in the American concept of "we the people." As such, there will be a larger and more diverse number of Tubman admirers visiting sites associated with her life and legacy and an increasing demand for information about her in the future.

Finding Tubman on the American landscape requires time and money. One needs transportation, and, given the hundreds of miles separating the Tubman sites in Maryland and those in upstate New York and southeastern Ontario, only the most dedicated Tubman seekers make the entire trek, south to north, as she might have. Selectively visiting one or more of the Tubman historic settings is more the norm. No doubt, most individuals who wish to learn about Tubman do so not by going to Auburn, Dorchester County, or St. Catharines but by accessing information on the Internet. There they are likely to be overwhelmed by the volume of Tubman-related content, of varying quality, that is both free and downloadable. She has become a universal icon—no longer tied to any particular place. As such, her story can be told in geographic settings far removed from the grounded Tubman of the United States and Canada. She has become a citizen of the world.

CHAPTER TEN

HISTORIANS HAVE THEIR SAY

Auburn's *Advertiser-Journal*, where Earl Conrad worked when he was known as Earl Cohen, a local boy with aspirations of becoming a journalist, made much of his participation in the launching of the Liberty Ship ss *Harriet Tubman* at South Portland, Maine, in 1944, citing him as the principal speaker. The paper noted that until Conrad's biography of Tubman came out, little about her was known: "If he hadn't started the job about the time he did, much of her story would never have been written." Calling Conrad's book the first "comprehensive history" of the "great slave liberator," the *Advertiser-Journal* quoted one of Conrad's co-workers on the magazine *P.M.*: "The *book*, incidentally, was hawked all over the lot before it found a publisher. Twenty-nine of them passed it by, and the 30th brought it out."[1]

Sixty years would pass before new biographies about Tubman appeared, a fact that puzzles anyone familiar with the flourishing field of African American historiography, a growth area in academe and publishing since at least the early 1970s. How is it that the woman known as "Black Moses" should have existed for so long in the shadowy boundary land where myth and legend rule, a larger-than-life figure ignored by professionally trained historians? How are we to understand the meaning and significance of the appearance at the beginning of the twenty-first century of three new biographies about Tubman after so many years of silence? These questions will lead us to reflections on the place(s) Tubman occupies today in the American memory, an ever shifting landscape shaped as much by what Americans think they know about Tubman as by what the historians are now saying about her.

As this book has argued, the symbolic or "overdetermined" Tubman has had a life history, too, often one that obscured the story of the flesh-

and-blood person. This symbolic Tubman was there at the beginning when Thomas Wentworth Higginson and others introduced their "Black Moses" to the American public as a professional smuggler of the enslaved. Harriet Tubman helped craft the legend by telling her own story in so dramatic a fashion for so long. When various groups with causes of their own to advance needed a symbolic figure to represent the great struggle for freedom that eventually brought on the Civil War and then victory for the old abolitionist crusade, she was there to tell her story. When women, white and black, needed someone to inspire them, Harriet Tubman was there. Sarah Bradford's two books fueled the growth of the "Black Moses" myth by so intermixing biography and hagiography that even today readers have difficulty getting at the authentic history of the life of the woman who existed behind Bradford's constructions of her. Even Conrad, with his journalist's passion for getting at the facts, could not break loose of the power of Tubman the symbol. His admirable effort to rescue Tubman from the dustbin of American memory became, in the end, a work of reconstruction. Conrad's "Tubman" is the black revolutionary, the "new Negro" of the mid-twentieth century who is needed to resurrect a nation still in the clutches of racism and oppression.

Conrad's *Harriet Tubman*, in spite of his later claims, had only a modest impact on the American public. Sales were slow, and the book was difficult to find by the time of the late-twentieth-century explosion of interest in Tubman. Sarah Bradford's second book, *Moses*, in one of its reprint editions, was more likely to turn up in public libraries and school libraries than Conrad's more comprehensive and better-researched biography. Given the problematic nature of Bradford's highly bowdlerized *Moses*, this meant that most Americans were getting their understanding of Tubman through a heavily mediated source. Authors of fictionalized books about Tubman, such as Ann Parrish and Hildegarde Hoyt Swift, derived their understanding of her life history, in the main, from reading Bradford. The flood of books about Tubman written for the juvenile-literature market during the past quarter-century was, in turn, influenced by these fictionalized biographies. The sixty-year period during which no significant new research was being done on Tubman was a time when fiction paraded as fact and myth overpowered history. Harriet Tubman could be whatever an author wanted her to be, or needed her to be. Her symbolic uses seemed innumerable, sometimes appearing in surprising venues. For example, in a discussion of the question, "Is it ethical to lie to secure hospital admission?" the author of a 2001 article in the *Western Journal of Medicine* responded in the affirmative and included a picture of Tubman (the Robert Pius painting) with the caption: "Harriet Tubman's activities with the Underground Railroad were illegal but ethically sound."[2]

Given the overpowering nature of the symbolic Tubman by the end of the twentieth century, it would be no small challenge for any historian to write a new biography about someone who had come to occupy a place in the American memory of such heroic proportions. When Sarah Bradford's *Scenes* appeared in 1869, *Harper's Weekly* gave the "little volume" a brief notice saying, "It is a pitiful but profoundly interesting tale. It makes the nerves of an honorable man tingle, indeed, to think that it is not a romance of some dissolute and decrepit old country, but the true story of our American times and of a living woman."[3] Here was an admission of no small significance. Tubman's story was an American one, no matter how many people compared her to Joan of Arc, Florence Nightingale, or some other Old World heroine. Anyone writing about the life of Tubman—whether it was a Bradford, a Conrad, or a contemporary historian—would be writing about the struggle of Americans to bring their ideals in closer harmony with the lived experiences of every citizen, regardless of race, gender, or class. Tubman's story remains the quintessentially American story.

The publication at the end of 2003 and the beginning of 2004 of three new biographies about Tubman written by professional historians, coming as they did in the wake of renewed public interest in her, signaled an important moment in the evolution of the remembered Tubman. The three authors, all white women, broke through the curtain of silence academically trained historians had drawn down on Tubman. Jean Humez's *Harriet Tubman: The Life and the Life Stories* appeared in late 2003, followed by Kate Clifford Larson's *Bound for the Promised Land: Harriet Tubman, Portrait of an American Hero* and Catherine Clinton's *Harriet Tubman: The Road to Freedom*. Promotional notices, press commentary, and the early reviews of these new biographies almost invariably drew attention to the importance of their publication after so long a period of neglect. "It is astonishing that it has taken until today for Harriet Tubman, a central figure in the struggle against slavery, to find a modern biographer," said Eric Foner, DeWitt Clinton Professor of History at Columbia University, about Clinton's book.[4] A publisher's announcement for Larson's book hailed it as "the new, definitive biography of Harriet Tubman in more than a half century."[5] Of Humez's book, William L. Andrews, general editor of Wisconsin University Press's Studies in Autobiography, declared, "I see *Harriet Tubman: The Life and the Life Stories* as the most important book on Tubman in the last fifty years."[6] Gary Dorsey, a writer for the *Sun*, a Baltimore newspaper, took notice of this remarkable breaking of the silence on Tubman when he wrote on January 25, 2004: "So until this year—182 years after her birth, 139 years after the end of the Civil War, 91 years after her death—the world has known Tubman only through the grandly mythologized accounts of two amateur historians and the scores of children's books they inspired. Suddenly, three new books written by academic historians have appeared."[7]

Historical topics run hot and cold. Specialists in American diplomatic history fare far worse in publishing circles today than they did a generation or so ago. By way of contrast, feminist scholars, particularly those interested in the history of black women, find a ready market for their books in our time. It is not surprising, therefore, that the nearly simultaneous publication of three new biographies about Tubman should be welcomed, especially in the midst of great interest in the topic of the Underground Railroad. Book publishing is a commercial and competitive enterprise—in academic circles as well as non-academic ones. The timing of publication in the case of these new Tubman biographies may have been coincidental, but it highlighted the important question of why it has taken so long for professional historians to pay attention to Harriet Tubman in light of her immense symbolic stature in the American memory.

Each of the three new biographies has a unique genesis. Jean M. Humez, professor of women's studies at the University of Massachusetts, Boston, came to her Tubman project with a strong scholarly record of interest in women's spiritual autobiographies. She had already edited a collection of early Shaker writings on women and religion and a volume of the writings of the black Shaker Rebecca Cox Jackson. More to the point, she wrote a highly innovative and insightful essay dealing with strategies to recover Harriet Tubman's spiritual biography from a critical reading of Sarah Bradford's two books.[8] This essay would introduce many of the themes elaborated on in the analytical sections of Humez's Tubman book. Humez had also dealt with the *Narrative of Sojourner Truth*, another highly mediated text, in ways that portended her more complete discussion of how we can best understand the life of Tubman by close and careful reading of the mediated texts written about her.[9]

Humez tells us that her decision to focus on Tubman's life stories came out of a class she taught at Harvard Divinity School on spiritual autobiographies in 1990–91. Then in 1993, she received encouragement from William L. Andrews to place her Tubman book with the University of Wisconsin Press series he edited. Humez devoted almost a decade to an intensive search for primary documents that, in whole or in part, could form an extended text on Tubman's life story. Her sources included Bradford's two books, of course, but went far beyond them.

While researching and writing *Harriet Tubman: The Life and the Life Stories* (Figure 73), Humez received valuable assistance from James A. McGowan (Figure 74), the first contemporary Tubman admirer to take up the challenge of peeling away the layers of lore and legend that have so obscured the life history of a woman who could not write her own story. After ten years of research, McGowan began in 1993 to publish the *Harriet Tubman Journal*; the inaugural issue led with an essay titled, "Harriet Tubman: Facts and Fiction." In it McGowan, whose "life and letters" book about Thomas Garrett had appeared in 1977, recounted how it was that he began his passionate quest to rescue Tubman from "all of the inconsistencies, exaggerations, distortions and sensationalism" that had accrued to her iconic representation down through the generations. He was convinced "that *if the truth be told about Harriet Tubman, she will emerge a figure larger and truer than anything anyone has written about her.*"[10] McGowan's pioneering journal, never widely circulated, expired after a few years. Jim, as he is known among his wide circle of friends, intended to write a biography of his own about Tubman using the vast amount of Tubman-related material he had gathered. Unfortunately, health problems stemming from an injury he received when he was nineteen and living in Brooklyn flared up.

As a young man, McGowan was a promising baseball player. He also sang in a quartet known as the Starlight Toppers, making the rounds of Brooklyn's storefront churches singing spirituals and jubilee songs but eventually breaking out of the church setting and honing a style popularly known as rhythm and blues in a group called the Four Fellows. Gangs that engaged in "sham battles" and body punching plagued Brooklyn at the time. "To an outsider," McGowan writes in his memoirs, "a sham battle

73. Book cover from Jean M. Humez, *Harriet Tubman: The Life and the Life Stories* (Madison: University of Wisconsin Press, 2003).

74. James A. McGowan. Courtesy James A. McGowan.

could be a frightening thing to witness. With all the shouting, cursing, and violent punching, it had the appearance of an out-and-out war."[11] In June 1951, McGowan got in the way of one gang looking for another in Brooklyn's Bedford-Stuyvesant section and was stabbed with a sword.

Though complications from the stabbing would eventually confine him to a wheelchair, Jim has not shied away from challenges, large and small, throughout his life. Among other accomplishments, McGowan, who describes himself as a "Black American" with an Irish paternal grandfather, was the first paraplegic to attempt to swim the English Channel. He earned a bachelor's degree in liberal arts (1979) from Temple University and did graduate work in counseling psychology. Though he may think of himself as an "amateur historian," Jim had all of the credentials to write a more reliable Tubman biography, one that would build on Conrad's 1943 book, which he admires. He had to abandon the project when his health took another turn for the worse.

When new Tubman scholars, including Humez, contacted him about their research, Jim responded both enthusiastically and generously. In 2004, he launched the *Harriet Tubman Journal* on the Internet as a lodestar for scholarly interchanges among Harriet Tubman researchers and enthusiasts. Jim was also the inspiration and energy behind the production of a video titled "Whispers of Angels" that commemorates the life and work of Thomas Garrett, the Underground Railroad ally of Tubman to whose "station" in Wilmington, Delaware, Black Moses brought her passengers.[12] McGowan's enthusiasm for getting at the truth about Tubman has been infectious. Unlike some Tubman admirers with whom I have had contact, he does not feel that stripping away the legends that have built up about Harriet Tubman diminishes her historical importance. On the contrary, he steadfastly maintains that as Americans learn more about the "real Tubman," she will grow in stature in the American memory. It should not surprise us, therefore, that McGowan readily embraced the findings of the most detailed and best researched biography published to date: *Bound for the Promised Land: Harriet Tubman, Portrait of an American Hero*, by Kate Clifford Larson (Figure 75).

Larson's book developed from her doctoral dissertation at the University of New Hampshire.[13] She decided to work on a new biography about Tubman after reading about Black Moses to her young daughter and discovering that there was nothing available about this famous woman for

75. Kate Clifford Larson. Photograph by Christina M. Gillin, contributing photographer, *Syracuse Post-Standard*, Cayuga ed., February 24, 2004. Courtesy *Syracuse Post-Standard*.

adults. *Bound for the Promised Land* is the product of more than eight years of meticulous research, thousands of miles of travel, and many hours of interviewing sources, including individuals who claim to be descended from Tubman's siblings. In a review of Larson's book published in *Smithsonian*, Fergus M. Bordewich wrote, "It is risky business to tamper with a national icon and trickier still to convey the full dimension of the individual behind the legend. But Kate Clifford Larson has accomplished both in her brilliant biography of Harriet Tubman, whose name has become synonymous with selfless dedication to her people."[14]

The third new biography to appear after the long drought of scholarly work on Tubman was that by Catherine Clinton. Published in 2004, *Harriet Tubman: The Road to Freedom* came from the pen of a writer–historian with an impressive list of books to her credit, including several on Southern women, such as Fanny Kemble, the British stage star who married a Georgia plantation owner and became a critic of slavery.[15] Another of Clinton's books deals with the complex of stereotypes encapsulated in the "plantation myth" of the antebellum South, suggesting that Clinton would be well prepared to take on the challenge of demythologizing the larger-than-life and heavily romanticized Tubman.[16] In the preface to her Tubman biography, Clinton pointedly remarks:

> For the most part, the life of Harriet Tubman has been confined to the storybook world of "following the drinking gourd" and freedom quilts. These accounts are more folkloric than analytical, more riddled with inaccuracies than concerned with historical facts. Much like Sally Hemings before her, Harriet Tubman has been subjected to more fictional treatments than serious historical examinations, a reflection not of her place in the American past but of a failing on the part of the academy. This absence of scholarship must be recognized as a form of 'disremembering.' While Tubman was alive in the imagination of schoolchildren and within the popular and underground culture, she was a mystery to professional historians, who consistently mentioned her but failed even to set the record straight about her role and contributions.[17]

Just how successful Clinton, Humez, and Larson, all academically trained historians, have been in demythologizing the fictive Tubman is the question of the moment. The trio of new Tubman biographers first had to overcome the commonplace excuse of historians that few if any primary sources exist from which they could construct a more accurate reading of Tubman's life. Tubman's illiteracy, so it had been said, meant that her own voice was forever lost to us, except for faint soundings in heavily mediated texts. But, as Jim McGowan knew, and the new biographers would discover, primary sources do exist, scattered and elusive as they are. One of the cardinal virtues of Humez's "life and life stories" approach is that she reproduces a wealth of texts concerning Tubman in her book. Tubman enthusiasts, students, and scholars now have an easily accessible collection of "Stories and Sayings" in part 3 of *Harriet Tubman* and "Documents" in part 4. The earliest story about Tubman is a description written by Lucy Osgood in 1859 of the "unique entertainment" Tubman furnished at a gathering of white women in Boston. The last item in this section are selections from the 1940 correspondence between Earl Conrad and Carrie Chapman Catt. Humez begins the "Documents" section with the testimony Tubman gave Drew in 1856 and concludes with the account that Auburn's *Advertiser-Journal* gave of Booker T. Washington's address during the dedication of the memorial tablet in 1914. For

76. Judith Byrant. Photograph by John Berry, staff photographer, *Syracuse Post-Standard*, February 15, 2004. Courtesy *Syracuse Post-Standard*.

future Tubman scholars hungry to get at the sources, Humez's book is a feast.

Kate Clifford Larson deserves first honor for having pursued the evidentiary trail with the most zeal and persistence. Her book is rich in detail, so much so that in the early chapters the reader is sometimes overwhelmed by the introduction of facts relating to the complex kinship networks, black and white, in the world that Harriet inhabited while yet under the "whip and the lash." Countless hours spent poring over census and legal records, as well as listening closely to the refrains of family and regional lore still alive in the Eastern Shore of Maryland, enabled Larson to reconstruct Harriet Tubman's early years as no other author has done. Larson's reconstruction of Tubman's genealogical history (the Ross–Stewart family tree) is no small accomplishment in and of itself. Future Tubman biographers will amend and correct, perhaps, but they must forever build on Larson's meticulously researched biography. Judith Bryant (Figure 76), a descendant of William Henry Stewart Sr., Harriet Tubman's brother, aided and inspired Larson in her quest for accurate information, sometimes accompanying her on research trips. Bryant has spoken publicly of her own passion for removing the layers of myth that have accumulated about her famous ancestor over time and of her admiration and appreciation for Larson's *Bound for the Promised Land*. When Larson gave Bryant a copy of her new book, she inscribed it: "Harriet guided me to you."[18]

Humez's book devotes approximately 130 of its 471 pages to a narrative of Tubman's life. One journalist called it "a wisp of [a] biography."[19] Larson's *Bound for the Promised Land* is a more complete biographical treatment. The two books, one heavy on analysis and the presentation of texts and the other a detailed, chronologically organized biography of the more traditional kind, are complementary. Humez found Larson to be immensely helpful as her own book took shape. In working with Larson, a potential competitor, Humez tells us she found "a true collegial relationship."[20] When Larson constructed her long list of individuals to thank in the acknowledgments section of *Bound for the Promised Land*, the name of Jean Humez figured prominently, as did that of Jim McGowan.[21] As my bulging research files will attest, I, too, have benefited from Kate Clifford Larson's willingness to share her prodigious bank of knowledge about all aspects of the Tubman story. This collective and cooperative spirit would have pleased Tubman herself.

Catherine Clinton, because of a large publisher's subsidy, was able to hire research assistants to help her with the background work necessary to prepare *Harriet Tubman: The Road to Freedom*. Though she visited the Auburn area and Dorchester County and investigated some of the same primary sources that Larson and Humez mined so successfully, Clinton did so independently. Her book relies much more on secondary works than either of the other new Tubman biographies. Clinton may well be the best stylist of the three authors, but her research base is by far the weakest. As a consequence, Harriet Tubman is barely present in long sections—indeed, in entire chapters. These sections are informative and well written, but they are devoted primarily to contextual material. For example, chapter 4, "In a Free State," describes what Philadelphia was like for African Americans about the time that Tubman arrived there after her escape in 1849. Clinton says little about Tubman's actual experiences or activities in Philadelphia. Chapter 5, "The Liberty Lines," offers vignettes about contributions to the Underground Railroad by a covey of helpers—Tubman's story is deferred to the following chapter.

Given Clinton's reputation as a skilled writer, it is unfortunate that her book does not reflect the new discoveries made by Larson and Humez, correctives to the Tubman myth that Jim McGowan called for and began to initiate in the early 1990s. As discussed in an earlier chapter in this volume, the assertion that Tubman as "Black Moses" made nineteen trips rescuing at least three hundred individuals, an error that began with Sarah Bradford, cannot withstand scrutiny. Clinton writes that Tubman brought "hundreds out along liberty lines to freedom"—making "one trip a year, often two, deep into slave territory" beginning in 1852.[22] Larson and Humez persuasively demonstrate that a more accurate statement is that Tubman made twelve, perhaps thirteen, raids on Southern "property" and rescued approximately seventy individuals, most of them family members. That Clinton should reinforce the Bradford-derived numbers in her recently published Tubman biography is surprising. In her study of women, war, and the plantation legend, *Tara Revisited* (1995), Clinton wrote, "Tubman led several dozen runaways to freedom and became well-known as a 'conductor' on the Underground Railroad."[23] It is unclear why Clinton elected to go from "several dozen" to "hundreds" from one book to another. Clinton's Tubman biography needs to be read with Larson's better-researched volume set alongside as a corrective on many details, some of small consequence, but others central to what Clinton herself announces as her goal: redeeming the life of Harriet Tubman from the confines of "the storybook world of 'following the drinking gourd' and freedom quilts."[24] Of Clinton's book, Jean Thompson said in Baltimore's *Sun*, "Unfortunately, it sometimes falls back on assumptions about Tubman that Humez and Larson take pains to flesh out or debunk. It is a shame, in some ways, that Clinton did not wait for her colleagues' scholarship to come to the fore so she could cite it. Her volume would be improved by it."[25]

Early notices and reviews of the new Tubman biographies were generally favorable. The nearly simultaneous appearance of three books about Tubman written by professionally trained historians struck some observers as noteworthy in and of itself, given the six-decade drought.[26] Yet a definitive answer as to why Tubman was for so long ignored by historians and left for fiction writers and the authors of children's books remains illusive. Some explanations for the long silence point to racial myopia afflicting the academy; others focus on the purported faintness of the evidentiary trail. My personal view is that historians, like most Americans, thought that they knew all there was to be known about Harriet Tubman because she was seemingly everywhere as the romanticized symbol.

Clinton wrote that Tubman "cannot remain a 'Mammy' figure, a warm, nurturing historical caricature. Like Pocahontas before her, Tubman's life demands more than pop culture projections, and forces us to seek the underlying causes that make her legacy so powerful for us today."[27] In attempting to demythologize Tubman, the new biographies are less concerned with Tubman as symbol than with recovering the "flesh-and-blood" figure, to use a phrase borrowed from Clinton's book. The unstated assumption in this approach is that the historical Tubman—that is, the person behind the myth—can be found, in spite of her illiteracy and the heavily mediated texts historians contend with.

In the preface to her book, Clinton writes, "Though Harriet Tubman became an icon during the last years of the twentieth century, with this book I hope she might become human as well."[28] Biographers who intend to "humanize" their subjects by presenting them as fully grounded in the human condition, as opposed to retelling the old romanticized tales, generally discover that human beings are flawed creatures—"fallen angels," as it were. None of the three new Tubman biographies gives us examples of Tubman as imperfect in thought, word, or deed. She fails, of course—as she did in being unable to bring all of her family to freedom—but she fails in pursuit of an ultimately redemptive cause. She is afraid at times, as one would expect, given the life-and-death situations she found herself in. She was not always prescient or powerful enough to ward off harm to herself. In one instance, she fell victim to crooks who hoped to capitalize on her fame. But she is never depicted as having moral imperfections of her own. In these new biographies, Tubman is always the selfless one, helping others with righteous indignation in the face of injustice—society's evils born of the abuse of power. Her world is rife with inequity and iniquity in matters of race, class, and gender. Clinton, Humez, and Larson admire Tubman in this regard and, in trying to demythologize or humanize her, intend her to be a voice speaking to the ills of our time.

Humez in particular attempts to "construct a probable portrait of Tubman as a political and social thinker and activist"[29] by identifying the personal political and social agenda hidden or masked in the storytelling texts. Humez was particularly interested in what she called "the least mediated kinds of sources," those texts where Tubman's voice can be heard most directly. These "core stories," Humez believed, would reveal something of Tubman's own perspective on the critical matters such as racism, slavery, and women's rights. "The life story narrative of Harriet Tubman has been a complex, evolving cultural resource," Humez asserted, "much used in political debate and organizing from the 1860s to the present day."[30] Like that of Conrad, Humez's biography is an act of recovery and reconstruction. Tubman's voice must not be silenced or remain muted in heavily mediated texts. This "larger-than-life symbol of female heroism in resistance to the oppression of slavery and racism" lives on as a role model for today.[31] By giving us a clearer window on the life and life stories of the woman behind the legend, Humez has made a significant contribution to Tubman historiography.

Clinton's book on Tubman also casts her in the heroic mold. "Harriet Tubman," Clinton writes, "maintained an unblemished record of vigilance, creating a legacy of sacrifice and struggle that carried into the twentieth century."[32] Here again we have a portrait of a race heroine, albeit one of "broad humanitarian bent," who does not falter. Indeed, if I read Clinton correctly, her Tubman is nearly without fault. When Tubman fails, she does so in pursuit of a good cause. Her intentions are always honorable. There is no meanness of spirit in her, no grandstanding, no placement of self above others. In the one story where Tubman's motives might be questioned, Clinton leaves her readers swimming in a sea of speculation. Many books written by Tubman admirers omit the puzzling episode where Tubman goes back to Maryland and brings a child called Margaret to Auburn.

Clinton discusses this so-called kidnapping at some length, examining various possibilities, including the theory that Tubman might have had a daughter. In the end, Clinton dismisses this scenario, a reasonable conclusion given the total lack of any collateral evidence.[33] Strangely, Clinton does not entertain the possibility that a childless Harriet Tubman might have succumbed to an intense longing for a child companion, someone to raise and nurture. Her taking of the eight-year-old Margaret Stewart (Figure 77) — later known as Margaret Stewart Lucas, the mother of Alice Lucas Brickler, one of Earl Conrad's correspondents — might indeed have been a "kidnapping," not unlike the acts of desperation one reads about in today's press. Childless women enter hospitals in search of infants to fill a void in their lives. Clinton is correct, of course, to say that, given the available evidence, we cannot know what motivated Tubman. But to acknowledge that "no reasonable motive has been uncovered" does not preclude the possibility that Tubman acted irrationally, motivated by a need she herself did not fully understand.

If we are truly to make Tubman the icon more human, as is Clinton's

77. Margaret Stewart Lucas and Alice Lucas (later Brickler), her daughter, circa 1900. Conrad–Tubman Collection, Schomburg Center for Research in Black Culture, New York Public Library, New York City. Courtesy Photographs and Prints Division, Schomburg Center for Research in Black Culture, New York Public Library, Astor, Lenox, and Tilden Foundations.

announced goal, then we need to acknowledge what biographers of other American icons such as Thomas Jefferson and Abraham Lincoln have discovered. Saint and sinner war within the human condition. Sarah Bradford, especially in her second Tubman biography, dressed her subject in the garments of Christian righteousness. Bradford's Harriet Tubman is a Christian saint, albeit one whose religiosity is at the same time quaint and exotic. Tubman's modern biographers present her in the role of a secular saint—a social activist who should inspire the present generation to seek the greater good. In and of itself, this is a worthy endeavor. Biographers are not without their favorites and generally have empathy for the subjects for whom they have some personal affinity. Still, a question nags. How much have the new biographies broken free of the chorus of Tubman admirers that, down through the decades, have attended to the shrine of her iconic memory? Are these new biographies still in the tradition of writers who, for honorable reasons, used Tubman primarily for symbolic purposes? Are not the books by Clinton, Larson, and Humez also mediated texts? All biographers, whether in or out of the circles of professional historians, struggle to achieve full disclosure, aware that self and subject intertwine.

Larson's book about Tubman will strike readers as closest to the traditional genre of biography. The cradle-to-grave structuring of the narrative and an intense interest in recovering historical facts about Tubman's life are hallmarks of *Bound for the Promised Land*. Larson's research results astonish. Scores of new details become known in her book. Taken together, they deconstruct the older, romanticized Tubman based in large part on Bradford's volumes. It will be useful here to itemize the more important corrections Larson makes to the Tubman myth:

> Araminta "Minty" Ross was born in 1822, not 1820 or 1825, as earlier authors contended.

> Her birthplace was on Anthony Thompson's plantation in the Peter's Neck district, south of Tobacco Stick, not on the farm of Edward Brodess in Bucktown, Dorchester County.

> Araminta had eight, not eleven, siblings.

> Her parents, Ben and "Rit" Ross, were technically free people when she brought them out of the South, contrary to accounts that describe her as rescuing them from slavery.

Young Harriet received a blow to the head when struck by a weight thrown by an overseer trying to catch a runaway. Some older accounts have Tubman's "owner" throwing the weight at her.

Tubman liberated about seventy individuals, most of them related in some fashion to her, not three hundred, as is commonly believed.

She made twelve, possibly thirteen, trips, not the nineteen Bradford credited her with.

Claims of rewards of forty thousand dollars for her recapture cannot be substantiated.

Tubman settled in Auburn in 1859, not several years earlier, as most previous Tubman biographers would have us believe.

After much delay, the federal government did pay Tubman her due for services rendered as a nurse during the Civil War, as well as her pension as the widow of the soldier Nelson Davis.

The brick house in Auburn should be thought of as "Tubman's residence"—not the white frame structure called the "Harriet Tubman Home."

After Larson gave a lecture and book signing in February 2004 at Cayuga Community College in Auburn, the Syracuse *Post-Standard* reported: "Author Finds New Details on Tubman."[34] Larson's Tubman biography is indeed full of new details, such as the names of those rescued by Black Moses on specific missions. One reviewer lamented that *Bound for the Promised Land* overwhelms its readers with detail, especially in the early chapters, where Larson describes the world of slavery, symbolized by sweet gum and prickly burrs, of Maryland's Eastern Shore in the nineteenth century.[35] Readers of Larson's Tubman biography will encounter a wealth of details, some more important than others. Critics may find this plethora of detail distracting and feel no need to know all that Larson tells readers. Fellow Tubman researchers, however, will appreciate Larson's passion for mining the primary resources with such precision.

Given the paucity of historical scholarship centering on Harriet Tubman before the appearance of the Clinton, Humez, and Larson biographies, few reviewers of Larson's book had the credentials to sift wheat from chaff and recognize just how significantly *Bound for the Promised Land* breaks new ground. Larson's research findings challenge or amend the Harriet Tubman portrayed in the popular culture and imagination in so many important ways that it will be the benchmark biography for years to come. When yoked with the Tubman biography written by Humez, Larson's richly detailed narrative is even more informative.

By way of contrast, Clinton's *Harriet Tubman* is the least useful of the new biographies. There is in it, as Drew Gilpin Faust pointed out in her review of the book for the *New York Times*, a great deal of speculation. When Clinton writes about what she does not know or cannot know, she interjects phrases such as "one can imagine" or "there is every reason to believe."[36] As anyone who has devoted years to tracking down the documentary sources realizes, there is much about Harriet Tubman the historical person that we do not yet know and may never be able to know. Nevertheless, as the sampling of primary sources Humez includes in her book demonstrates, the sources, scattered and elusive though they are, are there. Humez and Larson went to the archives, drawing deeply from the documentary wellspring. Clinton went to the primary sources less often. In an essay on Tubman written for a collection published in 2004 to celebrate the opening of the National Underground Freedom Center in Cincinnati, Clinton stated: "Little is known about the details of Tubman's life, and some of the most basic information about her remains a matter of speculation."[37] This is true to a point, but less so now that Larson and others have diligently mined the surviving primary sources.

In her preface, Clinton writes, "During the research for this book, I found twenty-first-century scholarship and family lore from descendants as useful as the conflicting published accounts of the nineteenth century. I have tried not to privilege one set of sources over another, and to weigh competing accounts, rival agendas."[38] This is a useful approach, of course, but it is not without problems. Clinton's reference to drawing on "family lore from descendants" will puzzle anyone familiar with the risks of employing oral history in their historical detective work. These risks increase in the case of Harriet Tubman, whose own voice has been so heavily mediated, even in the documentary sources, and about whom so much legend and lore exist.

Clinton appears to have concentrated on one particular so-called descendant—Pauline Copes-Johnson of Auburn—as her access point to Tubman "family lore." As noted earlier, Copes-Johnson was for many

78. Pauline Copes-Johnson. Photograph by Michelle Gabel, staff photographer, *Syracuse Post-Standard*, August 16, 2005. Courtesy *Syracuse Post-Standard*.

years the "voice" of Harriet Tubman at the Harriet Tubman Home, giving tours and speaking on many occasions to the representatives of the press and others about being a great-grandniece of Tubman. She also served the Thompson Memorial African Methodist Episcopal church as choir director, accompanist, and clerk. Copes-Johnson grew up in Auburn, graduating from the high school there in 1945 and becoming Auburn's first black telephone operator. She has traveled to other parts of the country when groups elsewhere desire to have a living "descendant" of Harriet Tubman in their midst.[39] She represented Tubman at a ceremony on June 10, 2000, in Brooklyn, New York, in which Nana Harriet Ross Tubman-Davis was given a posthumous Enstoolment, a sacred Ghanaian honoring ritual.[40] In August 2005, Copes-Johnson went to Africa and received celebrity treatment by villagers in Aburi, a small village in southeastern Ghana (Figure 78). During a three-hour garden ceremony, she was honored as kin to "Ma" Tubman and witnessed the renaming of the Accra–Aburi road as Harriet Tubman Street and the dedication of a concrete statue of Tubman "standing with two slave children, their chains broken, her arms outstretched."[41]

Audiences who hear Copes-Johnson no doubt are surprised when she tells them that she did not know she was related to Harriet Tubman until she was twenty-five. Her parents never spoke of the family connection when Pauline was a child. She only learned about her famous ancestor when she was an adult—and then as accidental information rather than by direct knowledge after her mother had passed away. Copes-Johnson learned of her connection from her aunt Lida Gaskin Chaffin, the mother of Joyce Jones. This was sometime in the 1950s after the rededication of the Harriet Tubman Home in 1953.[42] Copes-Johnson then began her own research to confirm the family lore, a task still incomplete. Ann Marie Stewart, the great-grandmother claimed by Copes-Johnson, may have been a niece of Harriet Tubman's rather than a sister.[43] Whatever the case, Copes-Johnson acknowledged during a lengthy interview in 2003 that her knowledge of Harriet Tubman comes, in the main, from her research and the books she has read.

There is no unbroken chain of family lore, no intergenerational link to Tubman herself. When asked for any story about Tubman passed down in her family independent of what could be found in the Bradford books, Conrad's *Harriet Tubman*, or the numerous fictionalized works about Black Moses, Copes-Johnson mentioned the incident where Harriet holds a book upside down and pretends to read to throw off suspicion. While Copes-Johnson may first have heard this account of Tubman's ingenuity from a family member, various versions of this story are included in fictionalized versions of Tubman's life.[44] Copes-Johnson herself seems to have relied on works of fiction for knowledge about Tubman. For example, she contributed a short piece about Tubman to a collection of anecdotes about famous people of Cayuga County, published in 1999. In it, she used the novel by Marcy Heidish as a source: "According to author Marcie [*sic*] Heidish, Harriet was born about 1812 or 1813 as one of eleven children of Harriet and Benjamin Ross."[45] Copes-Johnson said in an interview that she tries to read as much as she can about Tubman and had "much to learn." Historians who make use of Tubman "family lore" need to listen closely. What they may be hearing are remnants of the Tubman legend or, as the case seems to be in the example discussed here, misinformation drawn from works of fiction.

Tubman family "descendants," to use a term the press frequently employs, have been much in demand during the renaissance of interest in the Underground Railroad. Journalists have sought them out for information about Harriet Tubman on the assumption that they will be able to tap into a deep reservoir of family lore and speak with authority about all aspects of Tubman's life. While some branches of the family tree have been faithful custodians of strands of memory related to Tubman, others demonstrated little interest in her until she became a "hot topic." In some instances, the so-called descendants, in their zeal to portray Tubman as the heroine for the ages, have given out errors of fact. I well recall being told by Pauline Copes-Johnson that a tunnel linked the Harriet Tubman Home (the white-frame structure on the big parcel) to William Seward's house. This tunnel, Copes-Johnson claimed, was used as part of the Underground Railroad, a contention that ignores the fact that the Harriet Tubman Home is a twentieth-century structure and the Seward house is several miles to the north.[46]

Though the extended network of Tubman "descendants" merits high marks for keeping the flame of memory burning, using its members as informants without cross-checking what they say against other sources—notably, the documentary record—invites problems. Clinton rightly argues that oral history or "family lore" is important, but it does not in and of itself offer proof of authenticity. Larson's more-than-eight-year quest for documents of one kind or another, as well as the approach taken by Humez, gives due credit to "family lore" but does so within the context of a richer collection of primary sources.

Fellow academics hailed *Bound for the Promised Land* as the most thoroughly researched and reliable Tubman biography to date. A few of these professional historians understood how large a challenge Larson had taken on as a doctoral candidate at the University of New Hampshire. "In the first scholarly biography of Harriet Tubman," Evelyn Brooks Higginbotham of Harvard University wrote, "Kate Clifford Larson rescues her from the 'underground' of knowledge, from unused and unseen primary documents, shedding new light on this American icon of freedom. Larson's painstaking research and vivid imagery separate truth from myth to reveal a life greater than legend."[47] Higginbotham's words of praise point to a critical matter. Is the Harriet Tubman that emerges out of the miasma of legend greater than the symbol or icon Americans have for so long embraced? Does the flesh-and-blood Harriet Tubman measure up to the heavily romanticized heroine whose symbolic power many and varied constituencies have invoked in their search for a usable past? One of the risks of poking around in the bin of communal memory is that we find that our iconic symbols are less than we had imagined.

Thomas Wentworth Higginson first sang the now familiar hymn of praise for Black Moses when he wrote in 1859 that she was "the greatest heroine of the age." Tubman admirers have echoed this refrain down through the years in one way or another. As the preeminent symbol of the Underground Railroad and, later, as a role model for activists championing a variety of good causes, Harriet Tubman the symbol overpowered the woman herself. David Mehegan of the *Boston Globe* has captured this tension between the Tubman of myth and memory and the Tubman the new biographies have attempted to recover for us. He began his review of the Clinton, Humez, and Larson books in this fashion: "The Harriet Tubman statue in Boston's South End, near the corner of Columbus Avenue and Pembroke Street, is about 8 feet tall, about 3 feet taller than the real Tubman. The scale is fitting, since the great conductor on the pre–Civil War Underground Railroad was truly a monumental figure. And yet, strange as it sounds, Tubman is only now, for the first time, getting the full attention of historians."[48] Monumental sculptures of our great public figures, be they presidents or generals, are generally larger than the individuals they portray. In Tubman's case, the larger-than-life monument in Boston is emblematic of what happened in the cultural memory of her.

Almost from the moment she entered into the collective consciousness of Americans in the nineteenth century, Harriet Tubman has been more important as a symbol than she has been as an ordinary human being, flaws and all. To apply the biographer's tool kit to the life of someone who is a cultural icon is no small challenge. There is always the risk that what emerges from close examination of the primary sources will disappoint.

All three authors of the new revisionist Tubman biographies explicitly disavow any intention to denigrate or diminish Tubman's reputation. On the contrary, they want their readers to know that they admire Tubman and wish to secure her a firmer place of honor in the American memory by getting closer to the real or historical person. Their argument seems to be that, as we come to know the real Tubman better, as opposed to hanging on to the Tubman of myth, her stature increases. "Tubman's remarkable life," Larson says in the introduction to her book, "is more powerful and extraordinary in its reality, is the stuff of legend and, ultimately of a true American hero."[49] "My goal," Clinton told Boston's *Globe*, "was to bring life to a character and take her off the children's shelves and put her where she belongs: in the pantheon of American patriots, a warrior as well as a humanitarian."[50] Of the three new Tubman biographers, Humez stands out as having had the best-articulated operational strategy to find the "real" Tubman cloaked for so long by heroic iconography. During ten years of research, she tried to discover how Harriet Tubman participated in the shaping of the public story that became the Tubman legend. In the end, Humez concluded that the "core" story is more powerful, more astonishing, and more meaningful than that of the mediated and mythologized Tubman.

The Tubman story that emerges collectively from the new biographies is, as we have seen, a story of diminished numbers. Tubman went on fewer trips than the old myth would have us believe. She rescued significantly fewer numbers than Sarah Bradford claimed. A reward for her recapture of forty thousand dollars, a very sizable sum in the 1850s, probably did not exist. Larson has demonstrated that other strands of the Tubman as symbol myth must also give way to better historical evidence. Some Tubman enthusiasts will see these corrections to the record as unwelcome and unsettling. That may be particularly so among African Americans who celebrate Harriet Tubman as a "race hero." Gary Soulsman, a staff reporter for the *News Journal*, writes that Larson told him, "I'm getting a little flak from the black community, who think I will destroy the myth of Harriet Tubman. It is not about the numbers. I hope that when people read the stories of people who ran away, they will understand how difficult it was. I hope that appreciation will replace any concern about numbers."[51] Adults, particularly those who grew up reading books depicting Harriet Tubman as the icon of the Underground Railroad, may have difficulty in coming to terms with the new, more historical Tubman the recently published biographies portray. This may be especially true in the African American community. where there has been a proprietary and protective interest in preserving the reputation of "our Harriet."

Though the new research by academic historians may challenge and upset individuals who engage in Tubman hero worship, it is unlikely that the symbolic Tubman will readily step aside to be replaced by the historic person. The iconic Tubman and the historical Tubman will live parallel lives in the American memory for as long as there is a felt need for the grandly mythologized Tubman. Access to more factual information about the woman who was already a legend in her own lifetime may not be an effective antidote to the inaccuracies and exaggerations that are embedded in American public memory.[52] In their search for a usable past,

Americans will continue to be selective, culling out that which serves their needs from the dross that does not. Historians do their work situated in their own times. Their lens on the past may also be clouded by the demands of the present. Humez acknowledged as much when she observed that Tubman's biographers, including her, have "used [Tubman] in different ways, depending on what their political objectives were and what the racial climate was like at the time."[53] This candid admission by one of Tubman's new biographers, all of whom are white women, suggests that their books also need to be read with the understanding that no writer, trained historian or not, can resurrect the "real" Tubman for us. Her voice has been stilled. But the human memory is a powerful venue. Harriet Tubman will live again for as long as there are storytellers honoring her and listeners eager to hear about her life and her life stories.

As all of the new biographies demonstrate so powerfully, Harriet Tubman's achievements were earned in the face of seemingly overwhelming personal and social obstacles. She became an enduring symbol of the causes she espoused and attained nearly mythical status in her own lifetime. Her persistent struggle and ultimate success against adversity have made her a continuing source of inspiration to this day. Harriet Tubman's significance as icon and inspiration falls somewhere within the realm of folklore or folk history and is not easily accommodated by the customary canons of historical scholarship. Nonetheless, now that historians have spoken, Americans can learn about the woman who inspired the myth and assess her "greatness" for themselves.

Tubman's reputation is today higher than it has ever been. Many and varied constituencies claim her. Her symbolic power has been tapped by groups advocating the rights of African Americans, women, the elderly, the disabled, children, the poor, victims of domestic violence, labor, and others with special interest in the welfare of those who feel excluded from the circles of power and influence. Her symbolic self also bridges societal divisions of race, class, gender, and nationality. Her name is known beyond the borders of the United States. She has become, in short, an all-comprehending symbol. The symbolic Tubman is a conflation of myth and history in our national memory. This collective memory is always undergoing growth and change, responding not only to new evidence but also to the felt needs of its custodians in varying social circumstances and times. The symbolic Tubman is alive and well today. Tubman's mortal remains may lie in Auburn's Fort Hill Cemetery, but she has not been forgotten, and her life will continue to inspire Americans, individually and collectively.

The iconic Tubman and the historical Tubman will thus coexist in our collective memory, in spite of the new research findings, for a long time. Gradually, however, correctives to now discredited notions about Tubman will begin to be reflected in publications written for both scholars and the general public. For example, the best and most comprehensive history of the Underground Railroad now available, published in 2005, fully embraces the more balanced and accurate accounts of Tubman's life given in the new biographies. In *Bound for Canaan: The Underground Railroad and the War for the Soul of America*, Fergus Bordewich simultaneously gives Tubman her due, honoring her unique place in the annals of the Underground Railroad, and sets the record straight. He writes that there was "no one quite like this incredibly single-minded, mystical, diminutive woman (she was barely five feet tall) who defied every antebellum notion about what women were supposed to be."[54] He also declares: "Tubman would lead at least seventy African Americans out of slavery in Maryland, and indirectly enable perhaps fifty others to escape to freedom on their own. (Her first biographer, Sarah Bradford, inflated these numbers for dramatic effect to nineteen trips and three hundred passengers.)"[55]

The power of Tubman as icon today derives essentially from the public's perception of her as an American hero. In spite of the difficulties of constructing an accurate history of her life, our individual and collective memories of her resonate so strongly because Harriet Tubman's life story causes us to reflect on both the good and the bad in the larger American story. Her struggles to be free and then her self-sacrificial efforts to help others underscore values that we as Americans treasure in custom and law, beginning with the founding of the Republic of the United States. Americans, at their best, aspire to be champions of freedom and great humanitarians. Our democracy's failures are mirrored, too, in Tubman's life. She knew the sting of racism, the pain of poverty, and the challenges of adversity. As long as some Americans believe that they suffer injustice, however defined, they will find Tubman a useful symbol of their struggle to achieve parity with those enjoying the full benefits of economic and political citizenship. Their Tubman may be more fiction than fact; our great mythic heroes and heroines are generally "over-determined," larger-than-life constructs of the imagination. To those who view the findings of the recent historical scholarship on Tubman disquieting, as if demytholo-

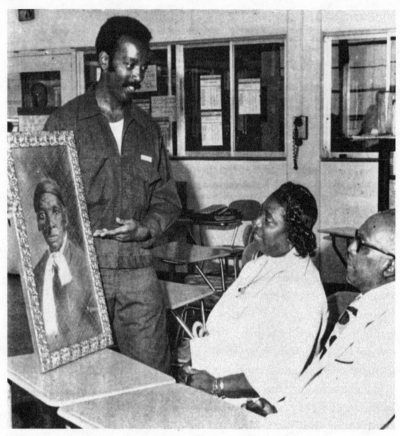

79. Dr. Bessie Cooper Noble and Reverend Guthrie Carter being shown Tubman portrait by the artist Alphonse Jenkins, a resident of the Auburn Correctional Facility, unveiled July 25, 1976, during a Bicentennial observance. From Bessie Cooper Noble, *Ain't Sleep, Ain't Gone: A Tribute to Harriet Tubman.* Fayetteville, N.Y.: Manlius Publishing, 1978).

gizing the symbol robs it of its power to comfort or inspire, I say: "Look again!" The Harriet Tubman who emerges from the pages of the new biographical research still deserves an honored place in the chronicle of the Story of America.

Tubman can still be creatively brought to life, as Beverly Lowry does in *Harriet Tubman: Imagining a Life*, published by Doubleday in 2007. A novelist with writing talents that some historians, including this one, envy, Lowry offers the caveat at the beginning of her book that it "does not pretend to be a work of intense scholarship." Readers familiar with the Larson biography of Tubman as well as the contributions to Tubman scholarship made Jean Humez, John Creighton, Jim McGowan, and others, cannot but conclude that Lowry's book would have been impossible a decade ago. Since historians have had their say in recent years, the knowledge base about the historical Tubman has expanded exponentially. Unfortunately, Lowry's reimagined life of Tubman perpetuates some of the myths about the woman who remains such an overpowering American icon. For example, Lowry writes that Tubman was able to make "as many as nineteen" trips. There are other errors of fact that mar an otherwise marvelous retelling of the Tubman story. Lowry insists on referring to Conrad's 1943 book as having the title *General Harriet Tubman*. Marketed as a biography, *Harriet Tubman: Imagining a Life* occasionally drifts into the shadowy and marginal land of imagination and "faction" where the historian fears to go but the novelist has more liberty to explore. In some ways, Lowry's book reminds one of the earlier Tubman biographies by writers such as Swift and Sterling, authors who moved freely between fact and fiction. But *Harriet Tubman: Imagining a Life* is vastly superior to the older works, more faithful to the historical evidence, and more respectful of the woman herself.[56]

Tubman triumphed because she was brave and full of faith, in her God and in her people. This ascent from slavery to freedom and from obscurity to public acclaim also taps into a quintessentially American myth: the notion that, with hard work and persistence, anyone can rise above the circumstances of their birth. This may be the most enduring legacy of Harriet Tubman. It is certainly the lesson that many Americans who admire Black Moses have come to know. Bessie Cooper Noble (Figure 79) grew up in Cincinnati, where she rode in the back of the bus and in segregated coaches on the railroad when she went to see relatives in Tennessee. When yet a child, she heard stories of the Underground Railroad—of how freedom seekers swam the Ohio River, bound for the "Promised Land." Years later, Noble settled in Syracuse, New York, where she taught hundreds of youngsters in the public school system. She also became interested in the life of Harriet Tubman and gained insight into the woman behind the myth from individuals such as Isabelle Williams, who had known Tubman personally. In 1978, Noble published her own tribute to Tubman in the hope of inspiring others to achieve beyond their circumstances. In closing the small volume, she wrote, "Harriet Tubman reminds us from her home on high to be about the business of loving each other. Again she prophetically reiterates, 'Ever' shut-eye ain't sleep; ever' good-bye ain't gone.'"[57]

APPENDIX

TUBMAN RESCUE MISSIONS:

THE NUMBERS QUESTIONS

Trip	Details of mission[a]	Count of res- cued	Cited in Larson (pages)	Cited in Humez[b]	Cited in Sanborn 1863
1. December 1850 to Balti- more	Niece Kessiah Bow- ley and two children (Sanborn's "Sister" is actually a niece)	3	89–90	yes	"Sister and two chil- dren"
2. "Few months later" to Baltimore	Brother Moses and two other men	3	90	yes	"Brother and two other men"
3. Fall 1851 to Dorchester County	Went to get husband; instead brings out a group of slaves	4–5?	90–91	yes	"A party of fugitives and brought them safely to Philadelphia"
4. Decem- ber 1851 to Dorchester County[c]	No details; may have just conveyed eleven to Canada who had already been brought out	11	92	Humez thinks this is the Christmas 1854 rescue.[d]	"Party of eleven," including "a brother and his wife"
5. Fall 1852 to Eastern Shore	Unidentified group of nine	9	96	yes	"From Cape May, in the fall of 1852, she went back once more to Maryland, and brought away nine more fugitives."
6. June 1854	Winnibar Johnson	1	106	yes	"Between 1852 and 1857 she made but two of these journeys."

Trip	Details of mission[a]	Count of rescued	Cited in Larson (pages)	Cited in Humez[b]	Cited in Sanborn 1863
7. Christmas Eve 1854 to Dorchester County[c]	Robert (*John Stewart*); Ben (*James Stewart*); Henry (*William Henry Stewart*); Jane, Ben's fiancée (*Catherine*); John Chase; Peter Jackson; George Ross; William Thompson	10–11	110–14	yes 10 or 11	
8. Sometime between 1855 and 1856	William Henry's wife, Harriet Ann, and son William Henry Ross Jr.; possibly a second son, John Henry Ross Jr.	2–3	124	yes	
9. December 1855	Brought out one man, Henry Hooper	1	125	yes	
10. May 1856	Four unidentified men	4	126	yes	
11. October 1856	Tilly, fiancée of refugee in Canada	1	131–32	yes	
12. Late November 1856	Josiah (Joe) Bailey; Brother Bill; Peter Pennington; Eliza Manokey	4[?]	133–36	yes	
13. May–early June 1857[e]	Parents' rescue from Caroline County; Ben (freed 1840) and Rit (also free)	2	143–44	"This brings us to ten or eleven trips, with 59–70 fugitives."	"In 1857 she made her most venturesome journey, for she brought with her to the North her old parents"

a. Names in italics are those taken after escaping slavery.

b. For a more complete discussion of the numbers questions by Humez, see her *Harriet Tubman*, appendix B, 349–52. A "yes" in the Humez column means that she counts the trip.

c. By conflating the December 1851 and 1854 trips, the total count of trips is reduced by one.

Trip	Details of mission[a]	Count of rescued	Cited in Larson (pages)	Cited in Humez[b]	Cited in Sanborn 1863
14. December 1860 from Dorchester area	(6 identified) Ennals family: Stephen; Maria, his wife; and children Harriet, Amanda, and a three month old. Also a man named John.	7	185–86	yes "Adding the last documented trip (December 1860) with its party of seven would make the grand total, by this conservative method, eleven (or twelve) trips, with 66–77 rescued."	"Her last visit was made after this in December 1860. . . . She brought away seven fugitives, one of them an infant."

d. Humez writes, "Sanborn also reported the rescue from the old neighborhood of a 'party of eleven' that included 'a brother and a wife,' and gave the date as December 1851. If we think of this as a separate trip not included in Garrett's four, we would need to increase the trip count by one, and the total number of fugitives by eleven. But I think Sanborn, writing in 1863 without Harriet Tubman there to ask, may have gotten the date wrong when remembering the Christmas rescue. Certainly the 1854 Christmas rescue involved a large party, and it included more than one brother, and probably a brother's wife as well" (Humez, *Harriet Tubman*, 351).

Humez also writes, "Harkless Bowley said that on the rescue of his mother and two older siblings, Harriet Tubman also took 'several others aboard the Underground Railroad to Canada' [Harkless Bowely Letter to Earl Conrad, August 8, 1939]. Assuming that Bowley's memory of the story he had been told was correct, the number rescued on these two earlier trips to Baltimore might be as many as perhaps a dozen. Adding this to the four trips discussed above would bring the total number of trips to six (or seven), and the total number of people rescued on southern trips by December 1855 would be 42–53" (ibid.).

According to Larson, "In total, she made approximately thirteen trips, spiriting away roughly seventy to eighty slaves, in addition to perhaps fifty or sixty more to whom she gave detailed instructions, nearly all from Dorchester and Caroline Counties in Maryland" (*Bound for the Promised Land*, 100).

Larson also says, "Over the next eleven years Tubman returned to the Eastern Shore of Maryland approximately thirteen times to liberate family and friends; in all, she personally brought away about seventy former slaves, including her brothers and other family and friends. She also gave instructions to approximately fifty more slaves who found their way to freedom independently. When Sarah Bradford published her first biography of Tubman in 1869, she flagrantly exaggerated those numbers to nineteen trips and three hundred rescued. Tubman herself claimed to have made only eight or nine trips and rescued approximately fifty people by the summer of 1859" (ibid., xvii).

e. If we do not think of this as a rescue of enslaved persons, then the total count of trips would be reduced to twelve after conflating trips 4 and 7.

NOTES

INTRODUCTION

1. Ravitch and Finn, *What Do Our 17-Year-Olds Know?* 53, 59, 60–61. Ravitch and Finn write, "Eleventh graders generally know what the former [Tubman] did. . . . But they do not understand the political context in which the Underground Railroad and Harriet Tubman operated": ibid., 76. They suggest that the high name recognition given to Tubman was influenced by the showing of the television drama *A Woman Called Moses* around the time of the history assessment in the spring of 1986.

2. This debate can be followed in Nash et al., *History on Trial*.

3. "*Biography of the Millennium* Names the Top 100 Most Influential People of the Past 1,000 Years," available online at www.biography.com/features/millennium/topten.html.

4. "Harriet Tubman 'Stamped' into Black History Month," *Jet*, vol. 53, February 23, 1978, 9.

5. Quarles, "Harriet Tubman's Unlikely Leadership," 57.

6. See Peterson, *"Doers of the Word,"* 24–55.

7. Blight, *Race and Reunion*, 332.

8. Quarles, "Foreword to the 1970 Edition," v.

9. Conrad, *Harriet Tubman* (1943).

10. Clinton, *Harriet Tubman*; Humez, *Harriet Tubman*; Larson, *Bound for the Promised Land*.

11. Good places to begin include Connerton, *How Societies Remember*; Thelen, *Memory and American History*.

12. Blight, *Beyond the Battlefield*; idem, *Frederick Douglass' Civil War*.

13. Kammen, *Mystic Chords of Memory*, esp. 1–14.

14. Peterson, *Lincoln in American Memory*.

15. Schwartz, *Abraham Lincoln and the Forge of National Memory*.

16. Blight, *Beyond the Battlefield*, 2.

17. Kammen, *Mystic Chords of Memory*, 9–10.

18. Schwartz, *Abraham Lincoln and the Forge of National Memory*, 9.

19. Ibid. Schwartz is drawing on the language used by Alfred Kroeber, the influential cultural anthropologist of the early twentieth century who believed that archaeology, including the study of monuments, serves as an important means for understanding the history of any society.

ONE. "MINTY"

1. Abdul-Jabbar and Steinberg, *Black Profiles in Courage*, 92.

2. Adams, *Grandfather Stories*, 269, 271. Bill Kauffman argues that Tubman "deserves better than today's mummification in dry textbooks" and celebrates her portrayal by Adams in his essay, "Harriet Tubman, Pre-Mummification." *American Enterprise* 17 (June 2006): 46.

3. Alice L. Brickler to Earl Conrad, July 19, 1939, CT.

4. Harkless Bowley to Earl Conrad, August 8, 1939, CT. Harkless Bowley's mother, Kessiah, was a niece of Araminta Ross (Harriet Tubman).

5. Vivian Carter Mason, "Cornbread Harriet Tubman," in National Council of Negro Women, *Historical Cookbook*, 28–29.

6. See Douglass, *Life and Times of Frederick Douglass, Written by Himself* (1881, 1892); idem, *My Bondage and My Freedom*; idem, *Narrative of the Life of Frederick Douglass, an American Slave, Written by Himself*.

7. Jacobs, *Incidents in the Life of a Slave Girl, Written by Herself*. See also Yellin, *Harriet Jacobs*.

8. For example, see Gaspar and Hine, *More than Chattel*.

9. Drew, *A North-Side View of Slavery*, 30.

10. Sanborn, "Harriet Tubman."

11. I am gleaning details about Tubman's early years from Larson, *Bound for the Promised Land*, esp. xvi, 16. It is the most thoroughly researched biography of Tubman written to date.

12. Ibid., 11. Because the Asante reputedly were a proud people with a tradition of having strong women leaders or ancestresses who acted as advisers, Tubman's admirers point to this African lineage as a means of underscoring her strength and courage.

13. Cited from Emma P. Telford, "Harriet: The Modern Moses of Heroism and Visions," typescript, ca. 1905, Cayuga County Museum, Auburn, N.Y., 4. Both Humez and Larson have chosen to render Tubman's language as found in the primary sources as standard English, or, to be more precise, transform what the authors of the sources put down as Tubman's manner of speaking by removing the plantation dialect spellings. There are problems with this approach, including differences in deciding what Tubman actually said. In this recollection of refusing milk, Humez interprets the word "shote" as found in Telford as meaning "shoat," a young pig. Larson understood the word to refer to a "shoot," a young plant: see Humez, *Harriet Tubman*, 206; Larson, *Bound for the Promised Land*, 37–38. Larson provides the language as found in the primary source—in this case, the circa 1905 memoir written by Telford, in the endnotes to her book (Larson, *Bound for the Promised Land*, 310). I have chosen to retain the spellings and dialect as found in the original sources, as these forms, however problematic, became part of the Tubman lore as it was passed down from generation to generation.

14. Sanborn, "Harriet Tubman."

15. Adler, *A Picture Book of Harriet Tubman*. For other examples of how books for younger readers treat the blow-to-the-head incident, see Ferris and Ritz, *Go Free or Die*, 25–27; and Benge and Benge, *Harriet Tubman*, 49–52.

16. Telford, "Harriet," 6. Few authors of books in the field of juvenile literature venture an explanation of these fits or spells other than attributing them to the injury Tubman suffered at the store. Recent biographers have done so. Larson suggests that the "blow to the head" may have caused Tubman to suffer from temporal lobe epilepsy. Clinton offers narcolepsy as an explanation of Tubman's sleeping spells.

17. See, for example, the illustration by Karen Ritz of Harriet chopping wood in Ferris and Ritz, *Go Free or Die*, 30.

18. Sanborn, "Harriet Tubman."

19. Bradford, *Scenes in the Life of Harriet Tubman*, 15.

20. Larson, *Bound for the Promised Land*, 63.

21. Sanborn, "Harriet Tubman."

22. "Three Hundred Dollars Reward," runaway advertisement, reproduced in Larson, *Bound for the Promised Land*, 79.

23. Bradford, *Scenes in the Life of Harriet Tubman*, 19.

24. Ibid.

25. Cheney, "Moses."

26. Bradford, *Scenes in the Life of Harriet Tubman*, 9–16.

27. Bradford, *Harriet, the Moses of Her People* (1886), 13–26.

28. Idem, *Harriet, the Moses of Her People* (1901), 135–36.

29. Conrad, *Harriet Tubman* (1943).

30. Pendleton, *A Narrative of the Negro*, 3.

31. Ibid., 140–42.

32. Brawley, *Women of Achievement*, 27.

33. Haynes, *Unsung Heroes*, 87–102. The Haynes material also appeared in Davis, *Lifting as They Climb*, 254–62.

34. Brown, *Homespun Heroines and Other Women of Distinction*, vii.

35. Ibid., 55.

36. Swift and Daugherty, *The Railroad to Freedom*, xi.

37. Ibid., xii.

38. Logan, "Review of *The Railroad to Freedom* by Hildegarde Swift."

39. Sterling, *Freedom Train*. Sterling did research for her Tubman book at the Schomburg Center for Research in Black Culture in New York City.

40. Ibid. *Freedom Train* was reissued by Scholastic Book Services in 1970, 1971, and 1974.

41. Sterling, *We Are Your Sisters*. For information on Sterling, see the book's foreword, by Mary Helen Washington, and Sterling's introduction. Sterling also wrote about Booker T. Washington, W. E. B. Du Bois, Mary Church Terrell, and James Weldon Johnson.

42. Quoted from an interview with Sterling done by Julia Mickenburg: Mickenburg, "Civil Rights, History, and the Left," 5.

43. Petry, *Harriet Tubman, Conductor on the Underground Railroad* (1983), note, inside back cover; "An Interview with Ann Petry" (*Artspectrum* [September 1988]: 3–4), cited in Mickenberg, "Civil Rights, History, and the Left," x.

44. Mickenberg, "Civil Rights, History, and the Left," 1. Mickenberg tells of the union activist and left-wing activist Alice Citron being fired from her teaching post in Harlem. In 1951, Citron criticized the school authorities for not teaching black children about Harriet Tubman and other freedom heroes.

45. McGovern, *Runaway Slave*; McGovern and Powers, *"Wanted Dead or Alive"*; Humphreville and Hodges, *Harriet Tubman*; Epstein et al., *Harriet Tubman* (1968, 1975); Winders and Plummer, *Harriet Tubman, Freedom Girl*.

46. Bradford, *Harriet Tubman*.

47. Johnston and Grifalconi, *A Special Bravery*.

48. Ibid.

49. Smith et al., *Gallant Women*.

50. Publisher's note in "The Saga of Harriet Tubman: 'The Moses of Her People,'" *Golden Legacy*, vol. 2 (New York: Fitzgerald Publishing, 1967) .

51. Tom Christopher, "Bertram A. Fitzgerald and the *Golden Legacy* Series of Black History Comics," available at www.tomchristopher.com (accessed June 27, 2007). Fitzgerald published sixteen issues in the Black History Comics series between 1966 and 1976, beginning with one on Toussaint L'Ouverture and the Birth of Haiti.

52. Grant, *Harriet Tubman*.

53. Johnson and Pileggi, *The Value of Helping*.

54. Quarles, *Black Abolitionists*.

55. Quarles, "Harriet Tubman," 57–63.

56. Examples include Sabin and Frenck, *Harriet Tubman*; Klingel et al., *Harriet Tubman*; Thompson-Peters, *Harriet Tubman*; Stone, *You Don't Own Me!*

57. Mims and Oleksy, "The Woman Called Moses," 14.

58. Meyer and Kerstetter, *Harriet Tubman*.

59. Polcovar and Bloch, *Harriet Tubman, What Was It Like?*

60. Carlson, *Harriet Tubman*.

61. Bentley, *Harriet Tubman*. Other examples are Adler and Byrd, *A Picture Book of Harriet Tubman*; Benjamin and Beier, *Young Harriet Tubman, Freedom Fighter* (1992); Burns, *Harriet Tubman*; Carter and Pinkney, *Harriet Tubman and Black History Month*; Clarke and Green, *Caring for Others*; Elish, *Harriet Tubman and the Underground Railroad*; Hoobler et al., *Next Stop, Freedom*; Jackson et al., *Listen for the Whippoorwill*; Kallen and Wallner, *The Civil War and Reconstruction*; McClard, *Harriet Tubman, Slavery and the Underground Railroad*; McMullan and Petruccio, *The Story of Harriet Tubman, Conductor of the Underground Railroad*; Ringgold, *Aunt Harriet's Underground Railroad in the Sky*; Taylor, *Harriet Tubman*.

62. Taylor, *Harriet Tubman*, 8.

63. Armstead, *Harriet Tubman*, preface.

64. McClard, *Harriet Tubman, Slavery and the Underground Railroad*, 7.

65. For more on the ideological wars over multicultural education, see Harlan, *The Degradation of American History*, esp. chap. 7.

66. Degler, "In Search of the Un-hyphenated American," 5.

67. Schlesinger, *The Disuniting of America*, 119.

68. Ibid., 136–37.

69. Nash and Crabtree, *National Standards for United States History*.

70. Cheney, "The End of History." For a critique of the Cheney critique, see Wiener, "Lynne V. Cheney's Baseless Attacks on the National Standards for History."

71. Elson, "Education: History, the Sequel," 64.

72. Hedstrom, *My American Heros*; Hedstrom and Martinez, *From Slavery to Freedom with Harriet Tubman*; Lilley, *Fighters against American Slavery*; Rowley, *Harriet Tubman: Lives and Times*; Taylor, *Black Abolitionists and Freedom Fighters*.

73. Schroeder and Pinkney, *Minty*.

74. Salvadore, "Review of *Minty: A Story of Young Harriet Tubman*," 589. See also Audrey Thompson, "Harriet Tubman in Pictures: Cultural Consciousness and the Art of Picture Books," *The Lion and the Unicorn* 25 (2001): 94–97.

75. Roehm and McCann, *Girls Who Rocked the World*.

76. Lutz, *Harriet Tubman*.

77. Rau, *Harriet Tubman*.

78. Nielsen, *Let Freedom Ring*.

79. Kulling and Flavin, *Escape North!*

80. Taverna and Hongell, "Meet Tubman," 42–45, 62.

81. See, e.g., "Kindergarten Lesson 2: Who Was Harriet Tubman?" available at http://www.eduref.org/Virtual/Lessons/crossroads/sec3/k2/unit6/u6kin12.htm (accessed January 18, 2007).

82. See, e.g., "Harriet Tubman," available at www.davis.ogsd.k12.ca.us/santa terresa/harriet%20.tubman.html (accessed March 4, 2005, no longer available).

83. Ringgold, *Aunt Harriet's Underground Railroad in the Sky*.

84. Wildflower Productions, *Brittany Meets Harriet Tubman*; Pitman, "Brittany Meets Harriet Tubman."

85. Harriet Tubman/The Underground Railroad Adventure Set by Child Light, LLC, P. O. Box 1563, Montpelier, Ver., 05602. Author's set.

86. Julia McCue, "Harriet Tubman," available at www/ash/udel/edu/ash/zine/poem/harriet_tubman.html (accessed January 27, 2001, no longer available).

TWO. "MOSES THE DELIVERER"

1. Sanborn, "Harriet Tubman," 1.

2. Holt, "A Heroine in Ebony," 461.

3. Born in the Northumberland village of Bamburgh, Grace Darling lived with her father, a lighthouse keeper of one of the Farne Islands. When the *Forfarshire* became stranded on another island on September 7, 1838, Grace Darling went out in an open rowing boat to attempt to rescue them. Victorian England embraced her as a heroine and erected a large memorial over her grave in Bamburgh.

4. Thomas Garrett's home in Wilmington, Delaware, was said to be the last station on the Underground Railroad before runaways crossed into the free state of Pennsylvania. Some sources credit Garrett (1789–1871) with aiding more than two thousand freedom seekers. African Americans thought so highly of him that, after the passage of the amendment giving black men the vote, a group of black celebrants, formerly enslaved, drew Garrett through Wilmington's streets in an open carriage bearing the inscription "Our Moses." See McGowan, *Station Master on the Underground Railroad* (2005).

5. Still, *The Underground Railroad*, 305. Garrett was also writing to Quaker allies in Scotland of Tubman's exploits years before Tubman became widely known to the American public. See his letters sent to Eliza Wigham, secretary of the Ladies' Emancipation Society of Edinburgh in 1855 and 1856, and to her sister Mary Edmundson in 1857, reprinted with commentary in McGowan, *Station Master on the Underground Railroad* (1977), 162–83.

6. Garrett to J. Miller Mckim, December 29, 1854, in Still, *The Underground Railroad*, 305–308.

7. Garrett letter, June 1868, in Bradford, *Scenes in the Life of Harriet Tubman*, 51.

8. Sanborn, "Harriet Tubman."

9. Brown, *The Rising Son*, 536–37.

10. Yerrington, "The Fourth at Framingham."

11. "New England Colored Citizens' Convention."

12. Thomas W. Higginson to mother, Louisa Storrow Higginson, letter, 1906, in Higginson, *Letters and Journals of Thomas Wentworth Higginson, 1846–1906*, 81. For an insightful discussion of Tubman's storytelling abilities, of how best to read

and identify the "core stories" in Tubman's repertoire, and of the problems of recovering an authentic voice in mediated texts, see Humez, *Harriet Tubman*, 133–94.

13. Yerrington, "The Fourth at Framingham."

14. Telford, "Harriet," in Humez, *Harriet Tubman*, 202.

15. Peterson, *"Doers of the Word,"* 17–22. Peterson's understanding of "liminality" draws on the theories of the noted anthropologist Victor Turner.

16. Brown, *The Rising Son*, 537.

17. Ibid.

18. Higginson, *Contemporaries*.

19. According to antebellum cultural theorists, the Yankees of the North, with their democratic and commercial characteristics, were descended from the Roundhead faction of the English Puritan Revolution, while the Southerners, especially the planter elite with their aristocratic and agrarian ways, were heirs to the royal party of the English Cavaliers. See Taylor, *Cavalier and Yankee*.

20. From a letter by Child to John Greenleaf Whittier, January 21, 1862, cited in Karcher, *The First Woman of the Republic*, 455.

21. Billington, *The Journal of Charlotte L. Forten*, 162.

22. Larson, *Bound for the Promised Land*, 169.

23. Garrett to Still, March 27, 1857, in McGowan, *Station Master on the Underground Railroad* (1977), 142–43. See also Still, *The Underground Railroad*, 662.

24. Hunter, *To Set the Captives Free*, chap. 6.

25. W. E. Abbot to Mr. Porter, November 29, 1856, Rochester Ladies' Anti-Slavery Society Papers, 1:9, William L. Clements Library, University of Michigan, Ann Arbor. The salutation is clearly meant for William Porter, though this letter is often mistakenly thought to be addressed to Maria Porter, his wife.

26. Sanborn, "Harriet Tubman."

27. Cheney, "Moses," 35.

28. Bradford, *Scenes in the Life of Harriet Tubman*, 72–87.

29. Ibid., 3.

30. Ibid., 21.

31. Ibid., 24.

32. Bradford, *Harriet, the Moses of Her People* (1886), 5–6.

33. Wyman, "Harriet Tubman," 111–12.

34. Siebert, *The Underground Railroad from Slavery to Freedom*, 186. Tubman apparently revealed some details of her Underground Railroad work. For example, she told Siebert that she did not use the mountain or Appalachian route, a claim made in Hinton, *John Brown and His Men*, 172–73.

35. Siebert, *The Underground Railroad from Slavery to Freedom*, 189; emphasis added.

36. Clarke, *Anti-Slavery Days*, 81–82; McDougall, *Fugitive Slaves*, 62.

37. Clarke, *Anti-Slavery Days*, 81–82.

38. Washington, *The Story of the Negro*, 222.

39. Work, *Negro Year Book, 1912*, 51.

40. Idem, *Negro Year Book, 1913*. Reference is made to the 1897 edition of Bradford's *Harriet, the Moses of Her People*.

41. Bradford, *Harriet, the Moses of Her People* (1897), 3.

42. Bradford, *Scenes in the Life of Harriet Tubman*, 53.

43. Conrad, *Harriet Tubman* (1943), 42.

44. Ibid., 42–43.

45. Ibid., 232.

46. Ibid., 112.

47. Ripley, *The Black Abolitionist Papers*, 5:222, fn. 7.

48. Napson-Williams, "Tubman, Harriet."

49. Sanborn to Higginson, May 30, 1859, Anti-Slavery Collection, Boston Public Library, reprinted in Humez, *Harriet Tubman*, 295.

50. Ibid.

51. Higginson to Louisa Storrow Higginson, June 17, 1859, in Higginson, *Letters and Journals of Thomas Wentworth Higginson, 1846–1906*, 81. In his 1899 volume entitled *Contemporaries*, Higginson wrote that Tubman "had gone back secretly eight times into the jaws of death to bring out persons she had never seen." Higginson's recollections were not entirely consistent. In 1905, he wrote that, after making her own escape from the land of slavery, Tubman made "eight or ten covert visits thither, each time bringing back by the underground railroad her little band of fugitives": Higginson, *Part of a Man's Life*, 18.

52. *Liberator*, December 16, 1860.

53. McGowan wrote: "Indeed, there were times when Sarah Bradford seemed to flatly deny the veracity of Harriet's stories! For example, it was *Sarah Bradford* who made the statement that 'according to the reckoning of her friends,' Harriet Tubman made *nineteen* trips into slave territory to rescue slaves, but Harriet Tubman never confirmed that statement": McGowan, "Harriet Tubman: According to Sarah Bradford," 9.

54. Larson, *Bound for the Promised Land*, 100.

55. Humez, *Harriet Tubman*, 352.

56. Garrett to Wigham, December 16, 1855. In McGowan, *Station Master on the Underground Railroad* (1977), 167–68.

57. Sanborn, "Harriet Tubman."

58. Humez, *Harriet Tubman*, 351.

59. See the appendix in this volume.

60. Du Bois, *Economic Co-Operation among Negro Americans*, 30.

61. Wendkos, *A Woman Called Moses*.

62. Bradford, *Scenes in the Life of Harriet Tubman*, 49–50.

63. Ibid., 53; emphasis added.

64. Ibid., 88.

65. Ibid., 32–33.

66. Sanborn, "Harriet Tubman."

67. Cheney, "Moses."

68. See the appendix in this volume.

69. Conrad, "I Bring You General Tubman."

70. Conrad, *Harriet Tubman* (1943), 232.

71. Ibid., 232–33.

72. Higginson to L. Higginson, June 17, 1859 in Higginsons, *Letters and Journals of Thomas Wentworth Higginson, 1846–1906*, 81.

73. Sallie Holley to Mr. Powell, letter, *National Anti-Slavery Standard*, November 30, 1867.

74. Bradford, *Scenes in the Life of Harriet Tubman*, 21–23.

75. Bradford, *Harriet, the Moses of Her People* (1886), 33–34.

76. Larson, *Bound for the Promised Land*, xviii.

77. Ibid., 191.

78. Bradford, *Scenes in the Life of Harriet Tubman*, 7.

79. Ibid.

80. Ibid., 1.

81. Cited in the appendix to Bradford, *Harriet, the Moses of Her People* (1901), 143.

82. Originally from an interview Earl Conrad did with Mrs. William Tatlock, August 15, 1939, CT.

83. Bradford, *Harriet, the Moses of Her People* (1886), 34–35.

84. The story of hiding in "potato holes" first appeared in Bradford's *Scenes* as part of her retelling of Tubman's rescue of Joe (Josiah) Bailey. See Bradford, *Scenes in the Life of Harriet Tubman*, 29. It was repeated in the obituary notice that appeared in the *Auburn Citizen* on March 11, 1913.

85. Bradford, *Scenes in the Life of Harriet Tubman*, 27.

86. Two versions of this story exist. The first is in Cheney, "Moses," 36, where Tubman tells others to persuade one member of a runaway party not to give up and go back: "I told the boys to get their guns ready, and shoot him. They'd have done it in a minute; but when he heard that, he jumped right up and went on as well as anybody." The second is from *Scenes*, where Tubman herself is said to have carried a revolver and said, "Dead niggers tell no tales. Go on or die": Bradford, *Scenes in the Life of Harriet Tubman*, 24–25.

87. Bradford, *Scenes in the Life of Harriet Tubman*, 25.

88. For the most comprehensive and well-researched recent history of the Underground Railroad, see Bordewich, *Bound for Canaan*.

89. As quoted in Pulfer, "Underground Railroad Museum Is Real Chance for Greatness." See Parker, *His Promised Land*.

90. Haskins, *Get on Board*, 34–38.

91. Blockson, *The Underground Railroad*, 188.

92. Fergus M. Bordewich to Milton Sernett, personal communication, February 21, 2004.

THREE. "GENERAL TUBMAN"

1. Cited in Jamie Stiehm, "I Will Not Disarm Harriet Tubman," *Baltimore Sun*, June 6, 2000.

2. Margie Hyslop, "The Sponsor of the Artwork Worries about the Weapon's Message," *Washington Times*, June 11, 2000.

3. Quoted in John Yocca, "Abolitionist's Rifle Engulfs N.J. Artist in Fray," *AgitProp News*, June 17, 2000.

4. Sara Rimensynder, "Disarming Harriet Tubman," *Reason*, December 1, 2000.

5. Julianne Malveaux, "Malveaux at Large: Disarming Tubman, Whitewashing Black History," *Sun Reporter*, vol. 57, June 29, 2000, 6.

6. The mural, at Ninth and Chestnut streets, was destroyed when the Goldburg building was torn down in 2002 to make space for a public parking garage: see http://www.katlindsey.com/potato_008.htm (accessed January 18, 2007).

7. Mike Alewitz, "What Are 'The Dreams of Harriet Tubman,'" *AgitProp News*, June 17, 2000.

8. See, e.g., Mabee, *Black Freedom*.

9. Bradford, *Scenes in the Life of Harriet Tubman*, introduction.

10. Adams, *Grandfather Stories*, 276.

11. Conrad, "I Bring You General Tubman," 5.

12. Wyman, "Harriet Tubman," 116.

13. Cited in Bradford, *Scenes in the Life of Harriet Tubman*, 5-6.

14. Conrad, *Harriet Tubman* (1943), 84.

15. John Brown Jr., letter, April 18, 1858, in Sanborn, *The Life and Letters of John Brown*, 452.

16. Clinton, *Harriet Tubman*, 129-30.

17. Conrad, *Harriet Tubman* (1943), 22.

18. Wyman, "Harriet Tubman," 116.

19. Ibid., 117.

20. As reported in Sanborn, "Harriet Tubman."

21. Renehan, *The Secret Six*, 154.

22. Conrad, *Harriet Tubman* (1943), 101.

23. Edwin Morton to Sanborn, letter, June 1, 1859, in Sanborn, *The Life and Letters of John Brown*, 468.

24. Douglass, *Life and Times of Frederick Douglass, Written by Himself* (1962), 320.

25. Sheila Tucker, "Tubman Held Messianic Beliefs about Brown," *Auburn Citizen*, February 21, 1977.

26. Sanborn to Higginson, Boston, May 30, 1859, Higginson Papers, Boston Public Library.

27. Cited in Renehan, *The Secret Six*, 188.

28. Lewis Hayden to John Brown, letter September 16, 1859, published in the *New York Herald*, October 25, 1859. The letter was discovered among Brown's personal effects after the raid at Harpers Ferry.

29. These secondary authorities generally cite a comment that Tubman was "probably in New Bedford sick" made by Franklin B. Sanborn in a letter to John Brown, August 27, 1859, in *Report of the Select Committee of the Senate Appointed to Inquire into the Late Invasion and Seizure of the Public Property at Harpers Ferry* (Washington, D.C.: Mason Committee, 1860), 67–68.

30. See Benjamin Quarles, *Allies for Freedom* (1974) and *Blacks on John Brown* (1972), reprinted as one volume (New York: Da Capo Press, 2001).

31. Franklin B. Sanborn to Sarah Bradford, letter, in Bradford, *Scenes in the Life of Harriet Tubman*, 54.

32. Cheney, "Moses," 37.

33. Martha Coffin Wright to William Lloyd Garrison II, January 10, 1869, Garrison Family Papers, Sophia Smith Collection, Smith College, Northampton, Mass.

34. Moncure D. Conway, "The Martyrdom of John Brown: The Proceedings of a Public Meeting Held in London on the 2nd of December, 1863, to Commemorate the Fourth Anniversary of John Brown's Death," pamphlet, Emancipation Society, London, 1864, vol. 9, John Brown Pamphlets, British Broadcasting System collection.

35. Christianson, "The Battle for Charles Nalle."

36. Cheney, "Moses," 37.

37. Bradford, *Scenes in the Life of Harriet Tubman*, 88–91.

38. The *Troy Whig* article estimated that the crowd at the time of Nalle's rescue from the commissioner's office "numbered nearly a thousand persons. Many of them were black, and a good share were of the female sex": *Troy Whig*, April 28, 1859, reprinted in *Liberator*, May 4, 1860.

39. "Statements Made by Martin I. Townsend, Esq., of Troy, Who Was Counsel for the Fugitive, Charles Nalle," in Bradford, *Scenes in the Life of Harriet Tubman*, 101–102.

40. Adams, *Grandfather Stories*, 276; Bradford, *Scenes in the Life of Harriet Tubman*, 91.

41. American Anti-Slavery Society, Executive Committee, *The Anti-Slavery History of the John Brown Year; Being the Twenty-Seventh Annual Report of the American Anti-Slavery Society* (1861), cited in Larson, *Bound for the Promised Land*, 183.

42. See, e.g., Sullivan, *Harriet Tubman*, 79–85.

43. Long after the Civil War ended, Tubman would tell Emma Telford that, to get into the South, she was to have gone as the "servant" of an officer. Arrangements were made for her to accompany a "gentleman from New York," but she took a dislike to him and decided to make her way alone to Baltimore, where she eventually found passage on a ship to Beaufort: Telford, "Harriet."

44. In Bradford, *Scenes in the Life of Harriet Tubman*, 68–69.

45. Billington, *The Journal of Charlotte L. Forten*, 161–62.

46. Bradford, *Scenes in the Life of Harriet Tubman*, 37.

47. Falk, "Black Abolitionist Doctors and Healers," 268. Falk drew on Bradford's *Scenes* for his information.

48. Prior to October 1863, Dix worked independently (and without salary) to recruit, assign, and support female nurses. They received a "certificate of approval" from Dix but reported to medical officers assigned to the military: see Stimson and Thompson, "Women Nurses with the Union Forces during the Civil War," 7.

49. Thoms, *Pathfinders*, 10.

50. Ibid., 7.

51. Hine, "Sisters on the Front Line."

52. "Manuscript History Concerning the Pension Claim of Harriet Tubman," HR 55A-DI Papers Accompanying the Claim of Harriet Tubman, Record Group 233, National Archives, Washington, D.C.

53. Cited in Bradford, *Scenes in the Life of Harriet Tubman*, 142.

54. P. K. Rose, "The Civil War: Black American Contributions to Union Intelligence," available online at www.odci.gov/csi/books/dispatches/dispatch .html (accessed January 18, 2007).

55. Hoefer, "They Called Her 'Moses.'"

56. Sanborn, "Harriet Tubman," gives the number liberated as 756, but the figure varies in other primary sources.

57. Tubman to Sanborn, dictated letter June 30, 1863, in Bradford, *Scenes in the Life of Harriet Tubman*, 87.

58. Adams, *Grandfather Stories*, 276–77.

59. Reported in Kwame Ansah, "Tubman Was the U.S. Army's First Woman General," *Philadelphia Tribune*, February 7, 1995.

60. Smith, *Aramenta*, 18.

61. Ibid.

62. Cited in Hoefer, "They Called Her 'Moses,'" 41.

63. Larson, "Bonny Yank and Ginny Reb," 33.

64. Ibid., 38.

65. The claim that Anna Ella Carroll devised a strategy that was ultimately responsible for General Ulysses S. Grant's victory at Vicksburg has sparked spir-

ited debate. T. Harry Williams opposed the idea in Williams, *Lincoln and His Generals*.

66. Larson, "Bonny Yank and Ginny Reb," 29. Larson cites Livermore, *My Story of the War*.

67. Larson, "Bonnie Yank and Ginny Reb," 46.

68. Conrad, *Harriet Tubman* (1943), 171.

69. Bradford, *Scenes in the Life of Harriet Tubman*, 39.

70. "Colonel Montgomery's Raid," *Wisconsin State Journal*, vol. 11, no. 237, June 20, 1863, p. 2, col. 4.

71. Conrad, *Harriet Tubman* (1943), 169.

72. Sanborn, "Harriet Tubman." Union reports say that the raid freed 725 slaves.

73. Conrad, "General Tubman on the Combahee," 13.

74. Swift, *The Railroad to Freedom*. "Hildegard[e] Hoyt, Author of Book, Praised in *Herald-Tribune* Review." Swift (1890–1977) was the author of the children's classic *The Little Red Lighthouse and the Great Gray Bridge* (1942).

75. Swift, *The Railroad to Freedom*, 311.

76. Hildegarde Hoyt Swift to Earl Conrad, September 8, 1939, CT. The story is also found in Taylor, *Harriet Tubman*, 13.

77. James E. Mason, *Then and Now, or The Soldier Spirit of Harriet Tubman*, address of October 14, 1930, at the Harriet Tubman Home, published by request. Copy in CT.

78. Hart, *Slavery and Abolition 1831–1841*, 209.

79. Washington, *The Story of the Negro*, 284–85.

80. Garrison, *Amazing Women of the Civil War*, 44.

81. "General Affidavit of Harriet Tubman Relating to Her Claim for a Pension," ca. 1898, available at www.archives.gov (accessed January 21, 2007).

82. Martha Coffin Wright to Marianna P. Mott, November 7, 1865, Garrison Family Papers, Sophia Smith Collection, Northampton, Mass.; Bradford, *Scenes in the Life of Harriet Tubman*, 46.

83. Frances Ellen Watkins Harper, speech, May 1866, reprinted in Foner and Branham, *Lift Every Voice*, 458–60.

84. Charles P. Wood, ms., 1868, House of Representative files, reprinted in Conrad, "Charles P. Wood Manuscripts of Harriet Tubman."

85. Conrad, *Harriet Tubman* (1943), 92.

86. Ibid.

87. "Harriet Tubman," Report No. 787, 43d Congress, 1st sess., House of Representatives, 1627.

88. General Affidavit, November 28, 1892, copy, Tubman file, Cayuga County Historian's Office, Auburn, N.Y. Members of Auburn's African American community, such as Thorton Newton, a friend of Tubman, and Margaret Stewart

Lucas, sometimes referred to as the "kidnapped niece," appeared before a notary public on June 15, 1893, to give a "Neighbors' Affidavit." The affidavit provides a few details about Nelson Davis, who is always overshadowed by Harriet Tubman in accounts of the Davis–Tubman marriage: "[Lucas and Newton] are also well and personally acquainted with her late husband Nelson Davis, the soldier above named about three years prior to his marriage to the above Harriet Tubman Davis and lived in the same house and family with him during those three years referred to, and at the time of said marriage and lived neighbors to them both up to the time of said Nelson Davis's death, and have lived neighbors to said Harriet Davis ever since. Affidavants further declare that said Nelson Davis came into the family as a boarder and as a single man, and so continued until his marriage to said Harriet Davis, and that said Nelson Davis had *not* been previously married. He was known and recognized in the family where he boarded and in the community where he lived, as an unmarried man until his marriage to the said Harriet Davis and they have heard it said that Harriet Davis had not been previously married." Neighbors' Affidavit, June 15, 1893, copy in Tubman file, Cayuga County Historian's Office.

89. For a factual and well-documented account of Tubman's various pension claims, see Larson, *Bound for the Promised Land*, 277–79.

90. "Petition of the residents of Auburn, New York, requesting that the claim of Harriet Tubman be called up, ca. 1898," available at www.archives.gov (accessed January 21, 2007).

91. Quoted from "A History of Pension Claim of Harriet Tubman written by Charles Wood," available at www.archives.gov (accessed January 21, 2007).

92. Mrs. William L. Garrison and Edna Dow Cheney (Boston), Mrs. D. M. Osborne and T. W. Osborne (Auburn), Joseph M. Clark and Mrs. C. B. Sedgwick (Syracuse), and Louisa Wilkinson Wilson (New York City) were among the co-signers.

93. The report quoted Seward's letter to General Hunter of July 25, 1865, and the Saxton and Montgomery endorsements and concluded: "These testimonials sufficiently show the character and value of the service rendered by Mrs. Davis during the war. She is now about 75 years of age, physically broken down and poor. This woman has a double claim on the Government. She went into the field and hospitals and cared for the sick and wounded. She saved lives. In her old age and poverty a pension of $25 per month is none too much." Committee on Invalid Pensions, House of Representatives, as cited in the Pension claim report written by Charles Wood.

94. "Harriet Tubman Davis," Report No. 1619, 55th Congress, 3d sess., U.S. Senate.

95. King, "In Search of Women of African Descent Who Served in the Civil War Union Navy," 306. See also Carnegie, *The Path We Tread*, 6.

96. "Senator Clinton Secures Funding to Repay Harriet Tubman Civil War

Pension," available online at http://clinton.senate.gov/~clinton/news/2003/
2003A30754.html (accessed November 4, 2003). The announcement, posted by
Senator Clinton's office, mistakenly quoted the House version not the final bill:
"By enacting H.R. 4982 on January 19, 1899, the 55th Congress authorized the
Secretary the Secretary of the Interior to pay Harriet Tubman a widow's pension
of $25 per month for the duration of her life, however Harriet Tubman received
only $20 per month until her death on March 10, 1913."

97. "Tubman's Back Pay Should Be Princely Sum," *Syracuse (N.Y.) Post-
Standard*, November 6, 2003.

98. As reported in *Amsterdam News*, November 12, 2003.

99. J. Zamgba Browne, "Harriet Tubman Slowly Getting Her Due," *Amsterdam News*, December 12, 2003; "Hillary Gets Funding for Harriet Tubman Pension," *New York Beacon*, November 6, 2003.

100. Major-General E. S. Adams of the Adjutant General's Office, War Department, responded on July 7, 1939 to Conrad's request for information on Tubman's wartime service with the statement, "A search of all records on file in this
Department thought likely to afford any information relative to the activities of
Harriet Tubman in the Civil War has resulted in the failure to find any record of
her as a nurse, civilian employee or in service in any other capacity whatsoever in
connection with the Union Army during the Civil War": Adams to Conrad, July
7, 1939, CT.

101. "Bill Introduced in Congress to Recognize Harriet Tubman's Civil War
Heroics"; Rahman, "Cultural Campaign for 'Medal of Honor' for Harriet Tubman."

102. See www.spymuseum.org/see/exhibit_perm.asp#spies (accessed January
19, 2007).

103. Earl Conrad to Samuel Hopkins Adams, March 11, 1940, CT.

FOUR. SARAH BRADFORD'S HARRIET TUBMAN

1. Cheney, "Moses," 38. Carleton Mabee suggests that Sojourner Truth's illiteracy "can best be understood as the interaction of her experience of slavery, the
development of her character, and her probable learning disability." Truth, Mabee
argues, used her illiteracy to her advantage, winning applause while on the lecture platform with lines such as, "I tell you I can't read a book, but I can read de
people": see Mabee and Mabee Newhouse, *Sojourner Truth*, 63–64. The women's
rights activist Lucy Stone said of Truth that she spoke "with direct and terrible
force, moving friend and foe alike" Stone, in *Woman's Journal*, August 5, 1876, as
cited in Mabee and Mabee Newhouse, *Sojourner Truth*, 65.

2. Several "dictated letters" purport to provide a more authentic Tubman. One
example is dated June 30, 1863. Sent from Beaufort, South Carolina, it is attached
to Sanborn, "Harriet Tubman." Written by someone, perhaps E. G. Duley, at

Tubman's request, the letter is voiced in the first person but has been purged of all indications of Tubman's pattern of speech. One primary source approximates a verbatim record of Tubman's own words. It is the testimony she gave on June 5, 1863, at the court-martial trial of Private John E. Webster, the superintendent of the Beaufort contraband camp. He faced accusations that he had sold government-supplied provisions for his own benefit. Tubman testified about the brown sugar Webster sold her: Guterman, "Doing 'Good Brave Work.'"

3. Bradford, *Scenes in the Life of Harriet Tubman*. I refer to this original printing in the text as Bradford, *Scenes*.

4. "Harriet Tubman," *Commonwealth*, January 9, 1869. Notice of the Bradford publication appears in the paper's "Minor Matters" section, which leads with the announcement that P. S. Gilmore, the "well-known and energetic band-leader," would be conducting at a three-day festival on the Boston Common "to celebrate [the] return of peace and integrity of the Union." The first edition of Bradford's book appeared while many Northerners were still in a triumphal mood and accounts of the exploits of fighters against slavery had the potential to sell well.

5. Bradford, *Harriet, the Moses of Her People* (1886). In the text, I cite this edition of the revised and enlarged biographical sketch as Bradford, *Moses*.

6. Idem, *Harriet, the Moses of Her People* (1897, 1901). The 1901 edition has additional material in an appendix.

7. Bradford, *Harriet Tubman*.

8. Hart, *The Presbyterian Presence in Geneva, New York, 1798–1998*, 92.

9. "Sarah Bradford, Authoress, Teacher, Historian, Gentlewoman," typescript, Sarah H. Bradford Collection, Box 58, Geneva Historical Society, Geneva, New York. Humez, "In Search of Harriet Tubman's Spiritual Autobiography" (*This Far by Faith*), 260, fn. 21.

10. Jennings, "Historian's Papers Never Found"; Nicholas, "Mrs. Sarah H. Bradford and Her History of Early Geneva." The Bradford house still stands in Geneva.

11. Julia A. Sill, "Obituary," copy in Sarah H. Bradford Collection, Box 58, Geneva Historical Society, Geneva, N.Y.

12. Sarah Bradford, "Poor Nina, the Fugitive," in idem, *Ups and Downs; or, Silver Lake Sketches*, 269–307. Nina is a pious and beautiful slave who is abused by an evil and debauched master. Bradford uses the story of Nina to underscore a core doctrine in Christian theology: Someday, God will raise up the poor and suffering to a place of honor while the rich and powerful will be humbled.

13. Bradford's pre-Tubman publications are exceedingly difficult to locate today because of their limited circulation. Several are in the Sarah Hopkins Bradford Collection, Box 58, Geneva Historical Society, Geneva, New York. Bradford wrote a history of Geneva that was published in Brigham's 1862 directory of Geneva, Seneca Falls, and Waterloo. She interviewed residents of Geneva who possessed memories of the community's pioneer period and employed primary sources with an eye to historical accuracy. This research experience would become useful in her later attempt to document the stories by and about Harriet Tubman. For commentary on Bradford's historical essay about Geneva, see Malcolm Sanders Johnston, "Sarah Hopkins Bradford, 1818–1912: Author, Historian, Teacher," *Geneva Daily Times*, October 2–3, 1944.

14. Hedrick, *Harriet Beecher Stowe*.

15. Stowe, "Sojourner Truth, the Libyan Sibyl." See also Lebedun, "Harriet Beecher Stowe's Interest in Sojourner Truth, Black Feminist"; Terry, "Sojourner Truth."

16. Bradford, *Scenes in the Life of Harriet Tubman*, 3.

17. Ibid., 22.

18. Adams, *A History of Auburn Theological Seminary, 1818–1918*, 115–16. Samuel Miles Hopkins completed his seminary training at Princeton Theological Seminary in 1836 and was ordained in 1840. Before coming to Auburn, he served Presbyterian pastorates in Corning, Fredonia, and Avon, New York. Though prominent in denominational, seminary, and community affairs, Hopkins lacks satisfactory historical treatment. John Quincy Adams, a seminary friend, commented: "No adequate biographical sketch has been printed doubtless because two weeks before his death, in some memoranda for his children, he wrote, 'I expressly and positively direct that there be not published any memorial of me'": ibid., 116

19. Emmons, *The Story of Geneva*, 463–65.

20. Bradford, *Scenes in the Life of Harriet Tubman*, i.

21. Two individuals, in addition to Smith and Phillips, are identified with places other than Auburn, New York: Timothy L. Barker of San Francisco and H. Ivison of New York City.

22. Bradford, *Scenes in the Life of Harriet Tubman*, 2.

23. Bradford (ibid., 9) also compared Tubman to Mary Ludwig Hays McCauly, better known as Molly Pitcher, the American Revolutionary heroine. McCauly (1754–1832) earned an honored place in American lore for her actions at the Battle of Monmouth on June 28, 1778. When her artilleryman husband fell wounded, she took the rammer staff from his hands and stepped forward in his place, acting as a matross (gunner) in the face of enemy fire. General George Washington made McCauly a noncommissioned officer, and thereafter she was called "Sergeant Molly."

24. Ibid., 22.

25. Ibid., 47.

26. For more on the historical origins of "come-outer" religion in Finney's Burned-Over District, see Sernett, *North Star Country*; Strong, *Perfectionist Politics*.

27. Curiously, the account of the wedding that appeared in the *Auburn Morning News* on March 19, 1869, a day after the wedding, gave the groom's name as William Nelson, not Nelson Davis.

28. Henry Fowler, letter, June 23, 1868, in Bradford, *Scenes in the Life of Harriet Tubman*, 71.

29. Ibid., 92.

30. Ibid., 88.

31. Ibid., 103.

32. Ibid., 104.

33. The "Bill of Sale" was not recorded until 1855: Larson, *Bound for the Promised Land*, 119–20.

34. Bradford, *Scenes in the Life of Harriet Tubman*, 108–109.

35. Ibid., 109–10.

36. Ibid., 111–12.

37. Ibid., 112.

38. Ibid., 113.

39. Ibid.

40. Ibid., 1.

41. Thomas Howard quote in Twain, *Personal Recollections of Joan of Arc*, back cover.

42. Bradford, *Scenes in the Life of Harriet Tubman*, 4.

43. Mitford, *Grace Had an English Heart*.

44. A museum memorializes Darling in the English town of Bamburgh. For a critical analysis of the sentimental use of Darling as a symbol, see Armstrong, *Grace Darling*.

45. Nightingale overshadowed the American-born Clara Barton, whose dates of birth (1821) and death (1912) approximate those of Harriet Tubman. Known as the "Angel of the Battlefield," Barton attended to the battlefield wounded during the Civil War as a volunteer and, in 1864, became the first superintendent of Union nurses. In 1881, Barton became the first president of the American Red Cross: Oates, *Woman of Valor*.

46. Cited in Bradford, *Scenes in the Life of Harriet Tubman*, 9.

47. Bradford, *Harriet, the Moses of Her People* (1886), 8.

48. Ibid., 7.

49. Ibid., 5.

50. Ibid., 10.

51. Ibid., 13–14.

52. Humez tells of trying to explore Tubman's spirituality using the Bradford biography with students so troubled by Bradford's language that "they could only read as racist—that they were unable to discern much value in the book." Humez took the pragmatic position that, given the paucity of primary sources on Tubman's life, "we need to make it yield as much as it can." With respect to the

1886 text, Humez says: "In fairness to Bradford, it seems likely that she censored Tubman's life story in the revision at least in part for fear of marring the image of a saintly African-American heroine that she was trying to construct for white readers in a post–Reconstruction era of virulent white racism." Humez argues that Bradford made Tubman "more saintly and less salty" in *Moses*: Humez, "In Search of Harriet Tubman's Spiritual Autobiography" (*This Far by Faith*), 240, 244.

53. Bradford, *Scenes in the Life of Harriet Tubman*, 19; idem, *Harriet, the Moses of Her People* (1886), 30.

54. Bradford, *Scenes in the Life of Harriet Tubman*, 26; idem, *Harriet, the Moses of Her People* (1886), 36–37.

55. Bradford, *Scenes in the Life of Harriet Tubman*, 26.

56. Bradford, *Harriet, the Moses of Her People* (1886), 37.

57. McGowan, "Harriet Tubman: According to Sarah Bradford," 4–5.

58. Ibid., 16.

59. Humez, "In Search of Harriet Tubman's Spiritual Autobiography" (*This Far by Faith*), 245.

60. Idem, *Harriet Tubman*, 150.

FIVE. SAINT, SEER, AND SUFFRAGIST

1. Penney and Livingston, *A Very Dangerous Woman*. Penney and Livingston generously shared their findings with me, including entries from Martha Coffin Wright's diaries that mention Tubman. On one occasion, on May 2, 1870, Tubman went to the Wright household to clean. There are numerous entries where Wright records going to the Tubman home and of giving Tubman monetary donations from herself and other women of Auburn. On November 29, 1873, Wright noted that Tubman had come to her house that day and "signed deed for lot at 19 acres," presumably referring to additional land Tubman purchased. David Wright, Martha's husband, was a lawyer.

2. Bradford, *Harriet, the Moses of Her People* (1886), 23.

3. Brown, *The Rising Son*, 538. For Brown's disparaging critique of the religious styles popular among the freed men and women of the post–Reconstruction South, see Brown, *My Southern Home*, 190–97.

4. Sanborn, "Harriet Tubman."

5. Ibid.

6. Bradford, *Scenes in the Life of Harriet Tubman*, 55–56.

7. Ibid., 56.

8. Bradford, *Harriet, the Moses of Her People* (1886), 75–76.

9. Bradford, *Scenes in the Life of Harriet Tubman*, 48–49.

10. Sanborn, "Harriet Tubman."

11. Holt, "A Heroine in Ebony," 459.

12. Bradford, *Harriet, the Moses of Her People* (1886), 80. The biblical allusion is to Exodus 13:21–22.

13. Humez, "In Search of Harriet Tubman's Spiritual Autobiography" (*This Far by Faith*), 243–44.

14. Ibid., 251–52.

15. Andrews, *Sisters of the Spirit*; Johnson, *God Struck Me Dead*; McMahon, *Gifts of Power*.

16. On Gabriel's revolt, see Bontemps, *Black Thunder*. On Turner's religious visions, see Greenberg, *The Confessions of Nat Turner and Related Documents*, xx.

17. Stevenson, *The Journals of Charlotte Forten Grimké*.

18. Bradford, *Scenes in the Life of Harriet Tubman*, 42–43.

19. Humez, "In Search of Harriet Tubman's Spiritual Autobiography" (*This Far by Faith*), 257.

20. According to an article that appeared in the *Auburn Citizen* shortly after Tubman's death, she had been operated on for the brain injury at the Massachusetts General Hospital. "There, despite the fact that the use of anesthesia had come into general use, Harriet insisted that the operation go on without ether, and it is recorded on good authority that the task was accomplished by the surgeons": "Harriet Tubman Is Dead," *Auburn Citizen*, March 11, 1913. The story first appeared in the new material Sarah Bradford added to the re-publication of the *Moses* book in 1901: see Bradford, *Harriet, the Moses of Her People* (1901), 152–53. Samuel Hopkins Adams heard the story directly from Tubman when he was a youth living in Auburn: Adams, *Grandfather Stories*, 277.

21. Conrad to Superintendent, Battle Creek Sanitarium, June 29, 1939, CT.

22. Ibid.

23. W. H. Riley to Conrad, July 12, 1939, CT.

24. Conrad to Riley, August 14, 1939, CT.

25. Riley to Conrad, August 21, 1939, CT.

26. Louis Casamajor to Conrad, September 1, 1939, CT.

27. Conrad to Mrs. Brickler, probably November 1939, CT.

28. Brickler to Conrad, January 27, 1940, CT.

29. Conrad to Brickler, March 11, 1940, CT.

30. Brickler to Conrad, April 16, 1940, CT.

31. Conrad, *Harriet Tubman* (1943), 19.

32. Ibid., 334–35.

33. The caul is the membrane that covers the head of a child at birth. Many cultures have ascribed mystical powers to one born with "the caul." On Turner, see Greenberg, *Nat Turner*.

34. Peter Hurkos (1911–88) acquired his psychic powers after falling from a ladder and suffering a brain injury in 1941. He specialized in psychometry. He would hold objects and see past-present-future associations: McGowan, "The Psychic Life of Harriet Tubman, Part I."

35. Sanborn, "A Negro Heroine."

36. In 1848, the Fox sisters of Hydesville, near Newark in Wayne County, sparked a spiritualist revival with their claims of having heard "rappings" from beyond the grave. E. W. Capron of Auburn promoted spiritualism and the Fox girls: Cross, *The Burned-Over District*, 345–52.

37. Bradford, *Harriet, the Moses of Her People* (1901), 138–39.

38. "Tribute Paid Harriet Tubman: Emma Paddock Telford Says City Is Honored in Perpetuating Story of a Great Life," *Auburn Advertiser-Journal*, June 11, 1914.

39. "The Mysterious Robbery," *Auburn Daily Advertiser*, Monday, October 6, 1873; "The Gold Swindle and the Greenback Robbery," *Auburn Daily Bulletin*, October 6, 1873. Larson, *Bound for the Promised Land*, 255–59.

40. See, e.g., Janney, *Harriet Tubman*, part of a series that includes biographies on Corrie ten Boom, Florence Nightingale, Susanna Wesley, Catherine Marshall, and other historical figures deemed exemplary "Women of Faith."

41. Johnson and Pileggi, *The Value of Helping*.

42. Noll, *Company of Prophets*.

43. Anthony Shafton, "African-Americans and Predicitive Dreams," available at www.asdreams.org/magazine/articles/african_prediction_dreams.htm (accessed January 19, 2007). See also Noll, *Company of Prophets*, 73.

44. Robert Moss, "Way of the Dreamer," available at www.mossdreams.com/tubman%20.excerpt.htm (accessed January 19, 2007).

45. *Rochester* (N.Y.) *Democrat and Chronicle*, November 19, 1896.

46. Ibid.

47. Conrad, "John Brown called Harriet Tubman: 'Most of a Man,'" 22.

48. Venet, *Neither Ballots nor Bullets*, 157.

49. Carrie Chapman Catt to Conrad, June 1, 1939, CT.

50. Catt would have examined Stanton et al., *History of Woman Suffrage*, which some historians claim downplays the importance of Lucy Stone and her organization in favor of the National Woman Suffrage Association, led by Anthony.

51. Catt to Conrad, June 8, 1939, CT.

52. Conrad to Catt, June 16, 1939, CT. Villard wrote to Conrad on June 6, 1939, "Harriet Tubman once came to our house when I was a boy and I remember seeing her. My mother and my uncles knew her, of course, and often talked of her. I have a book about her, but very little else. I think she did play a part in the suffrage campaign, and I think my mother spoke with her on one occasion, probably in Syracuse": Oswald Garrison Villard to Conrad, June 6, 1939, CT.

53. Conrad to Catt, August 5, 1939, CT.

54. Catt to Conrad, August 11, 1939, CT.

55. Conrad to Catt, August 14, 1939, CT.

56. Ibid., November 14, 1939, CT.

57. Catt to Conrad, January 25, 1940, CT.

58. Conrad to Catt, February 3, 1940, CT.

59. Catt to Conrad, February 17, 1940, CT.

60. Lucy E. Anthony to Conrad, August 29, 1939, CT.

61. Alice Stone Blackwell to Conrad, July 24, 1939, CT.

62. Conrad to Alice Stone Blackwell, July 23, 1939, CT.

63. Conrad to Eleanor Roosevelt, August 5, 1939, CT.

64. Conrad to Catt, April 2, 1940, CT.

65. Conrad, *Harriet Tubman* (1943), 200.

66. Anne Fitzhugh Miller and her husband, Dudley Miller, lived in Geneva on their Lochland estate. She was president of Geneva's Political Equality Club for many years: Huff, "Anne Miller and the Geneva Political Equality Club, 1897–1912."

67. Clarke, "An Hour with Harriet Tubman," 118.

68. West and Blumberg, *Women and Social Protest*, 16.

69. Jordan, *Broken Silences*, 31.

70. Terborg-Penn, *African Women in the Struggle for the Vote, 1850–1920*, x.

71. Catt to Conrad, June 27, 1939, CT.

72. The 1850 edition can be found as Washington, *Narrative of Sojourner Truth*.

73. Mabee and Mabee Newhouse, *Sojourner Truth*, 81.

74. Ward, *Not for Ourselves Alone*, 51.

75. White, *Ar'n't I a Woman?* 13–14.

76. Ibid., 5.

77. I have borrowed this apt wording from a letter Boyd B. Stutler wrote Earl Conrad, November 13, 1939, CT.

78. Stetson and David, *Glorying in Tribulation*, 104.

79. Ibid., 194.

80. Painter, "Sojourner Truth in Life and Memory," 365.

81. Idem, *Sojourner Truth*, 3.

82. Peterson, *"Doers of the Word,"* 24.

83. Painter, *Sojourner Truth*, 3.

84. Ibid., 4.

85. *Commonwealth*, August 17, 1864; Holt, "A Heroine in Ebony," 462; Painter, *Sojourner Truth*, 203–207.

86. *Liberator*, December 23, 1864.

87. Sterling, *We Are Your Sisters*, 398–99.

88. Giddings, *When and Where I Enter*, 94.

89. Mabee and Mabee Newhouse, *Sojourner Truth*, 184.

90. Peterson, *"Doers of the Word."* 52.

91. *Auburn Citizen*, March 11, 1913.

SIX. THE APOTHEOSIS OF "AUNT HARRIET"

1. Majors, *Noted Negro Women.*

2. Holt, "A Heroine in Ebony."

3. Ibid., 459, 461.

4. Mabee and Mabee Newhouse, *Sojourner Truth*, 244. Truth's funeral took place in Battle Creek's Congregational and Presbyterian church. Two white clergymen were the principal speakers.

5. Hart, *Slavery and Abolition*, 209.

6. "Moses of Her Race Ending Her Life in Home She Founded," *World* (New York), June 25, 1911.

7. Frank C. Drake, "The Moses of Her People," *New York Herald*, September 22, 1907.

8. This information is from the introductory biographical note written by William Edgar Easton, who appended Clarke's sketch of Tubman, "A Hour with Harriet Tubman," to his *Christophe*: Easton, *Christophe*, 106–108.

9. Clarke's version of what Tubman sang omitted the last line, "Come along! Come along! Don't be a fool. Uncle Sam's rich enough to send us all to school!"

10. Clarke, "An Hour with Harriet Tubman," 121.

11. Ibid.

12. Taylor, *Harriet Tubman*, 15.

13. Ibid., 16. Taylor's reference to Tubman's brother, "several years her senior," most likely points to John Stewart.

14. Ibid.

15. Ibid., preface and introduction.

16. Siebert, *The Underground Railroad from Slavery to Freedom*, 118.

17. Ibid., 189.

18. Wyman, "Harriet Tubman," 117–18.

19. "To End Days in Home She Founded," newspaper clipping, September 4, 1911, Harriet Tubman Files, Cayuga County Historian's Office.

20. Copy from Harriet Tubman Files, Cayuga County Historian's Office.

21. "Harriet Tubman Dying," *New York Times*, March 11, 1913.

22. Tubman was drawing from John 14:2–3. According to the *Auburn Daily Advertiser*, Tubman's very last word following the biblical citation was a simple, "Goodbye": "Death of Aunt Harriet," *Auburn Daily Advertiser*, March 11, 1913.

23. "Harriet Tubman Is Dead," *Auburn Citizen*, March 11, 1913. The *Auburn Daily Advertiser*, March 11, 1913, reported that Tubman expired at 8:40 P.M., a puzzling but not surprising discrepancy of ten minutes from the account given in the *Auburn Citizen*.

24. Conrad, *Harriet Tubman* (1943), 224.

25. "Harriet Tubman Davis, 98, Dead after Brief Illness," *Syracuse Post-Standard*, March 11, 1913.

26. "Harriet Tubman Davis," New *York Times*, March 14, 1913.

27. In 1911, shortly before Aunt Harriet moved to the home, a reporter queried her about her age. She was quoted as responding, "Indeed I don't know, Sir, I am somewhere's about 90 to 95." The reporter had been impressed with how "unusually clear" Tubman's mind was at the time of his interview with her. *Auburn Citizen*, March 11, 1913.

28. Ibid.

29. "Aunt Harriet Was Very Old," *Auburn Daily Advertiser*, March 12, 1913.

30. "At Church of Zion: Body of Harriet Tubman Davis Will Lie in State," *Auburn Citizen*, March 12, 1913.

31. "To Aunt Harriet: Hundreds Pay Tribute at Funeral Services," *Auburn Citizen*, March 13, 1913.

32. "'Aunt Harriet's' Funeral," *Auburn Daily Advertise*r, March 13, 1913; *Auburn Citizen*, March 13, 1913. The Smith quote is taken from a report dated March 13, 1913, and filed from the *Syracuse Post-Standard*'s branch office in Auburn: "Mrs. Harriet Tubman Davis Is Laid at Rest in Auburn," *Syracuse Post-Standard*, March 14, 1913.

33. *Syracuse Post-Standard*, March 14, 1913.

34. "Harriet Tubman Davis," *New York Tribune*, March 13, 1913.

35. There is an oral tradition in Syracuse that Tubman was baptized at Bethany Baptist church, an African American congregation, late in her life, but I have been unable to uncover supporting evidence.

36. *Auburn Daily Advertiser*, March 13, 1913.

37. "A Race of Harriets Would Secure the Future of the Negro, Says Bishop Blackwell," *Auburn Citizen*, March 14, 1913. The *Auburn Daily Advertiser* quoted Talbert as having recalled Tubman's remark as, "I've been firing up for the journey for some time": *Auburn Daily Advertiser*, March 13, 1913.

38. *Auburn Citizen*, March 14, 1913.

39. Ibid., March 13, 1913.

40. The lot was purchased on August 1, 1913, in Harriet Tubman's name, though it is unclear who paid for it. According to the records of Brew's funeral home, Tubman's funeral expenses came to one hundred dollars. Brew's register listed Tubman's age at the time of death as ninety-eight, though it was more likely closer to ninety-one, if we accept 1822 as her birth year: Harriet Tubman Files, Cayuga County Historian's Office.

41. Rosell, *Images of Auburn's Fort Hill Cemetery*, 8.

42. "Monument over Harriet Tubman Grave Unveiled," *Auburn Citizen-Advertiser*, July 8, 1937.

43. "Describes Tablet to Be Unveiled in Memory of Harriet Tubman," *Auburn Advertiser-Journal*, May 25, 1914.

44. Ibid.

45. "Pays Tribute to Harriet Tubman," *Auburn Advertiser-Journal*, June 6, 1914.

46. Ibid.

47. Harlan, *Booker T. Washington*.

48. "All This since '81: Word of Wonderful Growth of Tuskegee Institute," *Auburn Citizen*, June 8, 1914.

49. Ibid., 1914. The *Auburn Advertiser-Journal* of June 9, 1914, may have created confusion, and thereby reduced the potential windfall for Tuskegee Institute and the home, by stating that the programs would be given free to those who attended the unveiling ceremony: "Committee Plans Tubman Program," *Auburn Advertiser-Journal*, June 9, 1914.

50. The second page bears the title, "Program of the Unveiling of Bronze Tablet in Memory of Harriet Tubman at Burtis Auditorium Friday Evening, June the Twelfth Nineteen Hundred and Fourteen at Eight O'Clock. Under Auspices of Auburn Business Men's Association and Cayuga County Historical Society, Auburn, New York." I examined an original copy found in the Harriet Tubman Files, Cayuga County Historian's Office.

51. "Editorial," *Auburn Citizen*, June 10, 1914.

52. "Let's All Display Flags on the Morrow!" *Auburn Citizen*, June 11, 1914.

53. Brevet Lieutenant-Colonel Myles Walter Keogh, an Irish-born adventurer who once joined the army of Pope Pius IX in Italy, married into a wealthy Auburn family, the Martins of the Willowbrook estate. Keogh died, as the Civil War re-enacters who participate in Auburn's annual Myles Keogh Weekend will attest, not during the Civil War but at the Battle of the Little Big Horn. Auburn's fascination, past and present, with the Keogh story is an interesting analogue to its interest in perpetuating the memory of Tubman: Langellier, *Myles Keogh*.

54. "Fitting Memorial of Harriet Tubman Davis Is Appropriately Unveiled: Booker T. Washington Was the Orator," *Auburn Citizen*, June 13, 1914.

55. Ibid.

56. Letter, March 12, 1913, included in the article "A Race of Harriets Would Secure the Future of the Negro, Says Bishop Blackwell," *Auburn Citizen*, March 14, 1913. John W. Jones, a freedom seeker from Loudon County, Virginia, served as the chief agent of the Underground Railroad in Elmira, New York, and is credited with helping more than eight hundred freedom seekers. During the Civil War, Jones took charge of the burial of the Confederate soldiers who died at Elmira's prison camp.

57. *Auburn Citizen*, June 13, 1914.

58. Ibid.

59. Ibid.

60. Ibid.

61. "Editorial," *Auburn Citizen*, June 13, 1914.

62. "Tribute Paid Harriet Tubman," *Auburn Citizen*, June 11, 1914.

SEVEN. EARL CONRAD

1. Cyril Briggs, "Dear Editor," Crusader News Agency, December 19, 1939, 1, copy in CT.

2. Idem, "Seeks Data on Life of Harriet Tubman," Crusader New Agency, June 26, 1939, 7, copy in CT.

3. Idem, "Dear Editor."

4. Conrad, *Harriet Tubman* (1943).

5. Ibid., vii.

6. Conrad to Arlene Donovan, February 5, 1963, EC.

7. Conrad to Don, March 31, 1966, EC.

8. Conrad to Paul Eriksson, April 26, 1969, EC.

9. Conrad, *Harriet Tubman* (1969, 1974); published simultaneously in the Dominion of Canada by Fitzhenry and Whiteside, Ontario.

10. Idem, "Author's Note," in *Harriet Tubman* (1969).

11. Conrad and Conrad, *General Harriet Tubman*.

12. Anna Alyse Conrad, "Foreword," ibid., xii.

13. Ibid., xi–xii.

14. Publicity, Doubleday, 1954, EC.

15. Conrad to Elmer A. Carter, June 27, 1939, CT.

16. Conrad to Hildegarde Hoyt Swift, July 4, 1939, CT.

17. Swift and Daugherty, *The Railroad to Freedom*.

18. Conrad to Angelo, October 22, 1941, EC.

19. Anna Alyse Conrad, "Foreword," in Conrad and Conrad, *General Harriet Tubman*, xi.

20. Ibid.

21. Conrad, *Horse Trader*.

22. Copy for Contemporary Authors, Gale Research Company, EC.

23. Promotional copy, Doubleday, 1954, EC.

24. Ibid.

25. Diary, entries for January 8, 15, 17, 19, 26, and 29, EC.

26. Promotion, Doubleday, EC.

27. Conrad to "My dear Friend [Harkless] Bowley," March 11, 1940, CT.

28. Ibid.

29. Richard Wright moved to New York City from Chicago after breaking from the Communist Party there in 1937 and became Harlem editor of the *Daily Worker*. He supported himself, as did Conrad, by writing for various leftist journals and working on the New Deal Federal Writers' Project. For a useful overview of African American authors of the 1930s, see Young, *Black Writers of the Thirties*.

30. Conrad to "My dear Friend [Harkless] Bowley."

31. See, e.g., Haynes, *Unsung Heroes*, 87-104. See also Howard W. Coles, "Harriet Tubman: 'The Joan of Arc of America and the Moses of Her People,'" in idem, *The Cradle of Freedom*, 91-99.

32. Katharine Rose Foster, "A Moses in War-Time Maryland: Harriet Tubman Led Many Slaves through the Lines to Freedom," Maryland newspaper clipping, April 21, 1924, copy in CT.

33. Swift, *The Railroad to Freedom*, xi.

34. Ibid., xii.

35. Logan, "Review of *The Railroad to Freedom* by Hildegade Swift."

36. Parrish, *Slavery*, 6-7.

37. In an undated letter, written probably in late 1939, Conrad tells Swift that he had seen the review of her book in the *Journal of Negro History*, CT.

38. Conrad to Hildegarde Hoyt Swift, July 4, 1939, CT; Swift, *The Railroad to Freedom*, 333-41.

39. Swift to Earl Conrad, September 8, 1939, CT.

40. Cleghorn, *The True Ballad of Glorious Harriet Tubman*.

41. Copy in CT, along with the Conrad note.

42. Sickels, *In Calico and Crinoline*, 223-37. I have not discovered evidence that Conrad knew of the Sickels book.

43. Lawson, "Harriet Tubman—Born a Slave—Became Known as the 'Moses of Her People'"; Conrad note, CT.

44. "Between Ourselves," *New Masses*, vol. 31, May 16, 1939.

45. Conrad to editor, Viking Press, October 2, 1939, EC.

46. Ibid., Houghton, Mifflin Company, September 3, 1939, EC.

47. Ehrlich, *God's Angry Man*.

48. Conrad to Leonard Ehrlich, June 4, 1939, CT.

49. Ehrlich to Conrad, June 14, 1939, CT.

50. McHenry, "Newspaperman Is Inspired by Heroine of His Book on Harriet Tubman."

51. Conrad, "White Author of Tubman Biography Explains the Reason for His Book," newspaper clipping, ca. 1943, EC.

52. Conrad to Father Divine, June 7, 1939, CT.

53. Conrad to Brickler, August 3, 1939, CT.

54. Brickler to Conrad, August 14,1939, CT.

55. Ibid., "Dear Mr. Conrad" note, n.d., CT.

56. Ibid., September 6, 1939, CT. As might be surmised, Alice Brickler taught French. She graduated from the Auburn Academic High School (Garden Street) in 1919. Her husband, a native of Denver, graduated from engineering college.

57. Brickler to Conrad, January 13, 1940, CT.

58. Bowley to Conrad, January 4, 1939, CT.

59. Ibid., August 8, 1939, CT.

60. Conrad to Bowley, March 11, 1949, CT.

61. Bowley to Conrad, May 1, 1940, CT.

62. Mrs. E. S. Northrup to Conrad, April 1, 1940, CT.

63. Conrad to Northrup, n.d., probably April 1940, CT.

64. George S. Schuyler to Conrad, September 1, 1939, CT.

65. Conrad, "Prospectus," typescript, n.d., CT. See also Conrad's typescript of a biographical article titled, "General Tubman: The Most of a Man," CT.

66. Conrad to Helen Sellers Garrett, June 17, 1939, EC.

67. Conrad to Angus Cameron, February 3, 1940. E.C. Forrest Wilson's biography of Harriet Beecher Stowe, which was published in 1941 on the heels of an intensive publicity campaign under the title *Crusader in Crinoline*, won a Pulitzer Prize in 1942.

68. Flyer, June 26, 1932, copy in CT.

69. Conrad to Malliet, February 7, 1940, EC.

70. Malliet to Conrad, February 15, 1940, EC.

71. Conrad to Cameron, February 26, 1940, EC.

72. Ibid., February 3, 1940, EC.

73. Ibid., February 26, 1940. Conrad was referring to the monumental official history edited by Elizabeth Cady Stanton, Susan B. Anthony, and Matilda Joslyn Gage: Stanton et al., *History of Woman Suffrage*.

74. Conrad to Willis N. Bugbee Company, November 15, 1940, EC.

75. Michael Curtiz, dir., *Santa Fe Trail* (film, 1940). The original screenplay was by Robert Bukner.

76. Ira Rich Kent to Conrad, February 27, 1940, EC.

77. Quincy Howe to Conrad, May 5, 1940, CT. Howe's response was particularly upsetting. Conrad now believed that the "regular" publishing houses wanted to "rip out the guts" of his Tubman book and vented some of his anger in a letter to Richard Moss:

> A few words as to H. Tubman. The note I got from Howe was pretty jarring. I guess he expressed what they all think. The only chance of finding a publisher in an established house would be to locate an editor with understanding on the Negro question, and influential enough to get the thing across to his bosses, and I don't know of any such. Even the progressives—and Quincey Howe rates as a liberal, are as confused as the out and out s.o.b.'s. Howe was candid at least when he referred to the theme as "almost a freak subject," where the others were evasive. It is certainly a look-in on the mental processes of our "educators," which is what the editors regard themselves as. But I'm confirmed in the subject itself, because of the Howe note. I see that I have Negro-angled it so far. Then, as I suggested, there is always the liklihood [*sic*] (in this case very probable) that a publisher could abandon the project immediately after putting it out if it didn't happen to catch on quickly

enough to suit his fancy, or for other reasons. Moreover I feel that they are all wrong. The only significant books in America have in one way or another dealt with the Negro. From *Uncle Tom's Cabin*, to *Gone with the Wind*, and again to *Native Son*. Steinbeck's *Wrath* is the one of the few exceptions and even this, by implication deals with the oppressed—all. (Conrad to Richard Moss, carbon copy of a letter, n.d. [probably written in May 1940], EC.)

78. Carter G. Woodson to Conrad, January 8, 1940, CT.

79. Conrad to Woodson, February 15, 1940. Sterling Brown was also one of the editors of the massive literary anthology *The Negro Caravan*, which was published in 1941. From 1936 through 1939 Brown served as editor on Negro affairs for the Federal Writers' Project. He did not complete a biography of Tubman.

80. Angus Cameron to Conrad, October 4, 1940, CT.

81. Harold Strauss to Conrad, November 28, 1940, CT.

82. Earl Conrad, "Some Facts about Harriet Tubman," Crusader News Agency, January 1, 1940, 2. Cyril Briggs informed readers that, as of January 1940, twenty-two papers had subscribed to the serial publication of Conrad's "I Bring You General Tubman," which, as matter of fact, was far from complete.

83. D. S. Gilmore, "How to Defend Democracy" *Friday* May 1940: 2; Earl Conrad, "John Brown Called Harriet Tubman: 'Most of a Man,'" *Friday*, May 1940.

84. Conrad to Elmer A. Carter, April 29, 1940, CT.

85. Edward Lawson to Conrad, June 6, 1940, CT.

86. Earl Conrad, "A Great Leader–Harriet Tubman," *Negro World Digest*, August 1940, 46–50; idem, "General Tubman on the Combahee," *Negro World Digest*, December 1940, 13–16.

87. Idem, "General Tubman at Troy," *Crisis*, vol. 48, March 1941 78, 91.

88. Arthur B. Spingarn, "Books by Negro Authors in 1940," *Crisis*, vol. 48, March 1941, 76–77.

89. Conrad, "'General Tubman, Composer of Spirituals," *Etude Music Magazine*, vol. 60, May 1942, 305, 344, 352; idem, "Fighting Slave," *Negro Digest*, vol. 1, June 1943, 66–67, condensed from *PIC*. Even after *Harriet Tubman* came out, Conrad used the medium of the popular black magazines to tell of Tubman. See, e.g., idem, "Tubman Tales," *Negro Digest* (October 1943): 28–29.

90. Conrad to Arthur B. Spingarn, March 24, 1941, EC.

91. Helen Lincoln to Conrad, March 14, 1941, EC.

92. Conrad to Mary T. Littlejohn, May 22, 1941, EC.

93. Conrad to Spingarn, March 24, 1941, CT.

94. Spingarn to Conrad, April 1, 1941, EC.

95. See the typescript "Conrad/Tubman Collection, Inventory of Archives, Number 15, Date Completed: August, 1971," CT, which is also available on reel 1 of the Scholarly Resources microfilm edition.

96. See the finding aid compiled by Douglas O. Michael, "Earl Conrad: An Inventory of the Papers at Cayuga Community College," Auburn, N.Y., April 1983.

97. W. W. Norton to Conrad, January 26, 1942, EC. Norton had another concern: "I feel the book suffers by an obvious effort to make it a definitive and documentary life."

98. Richard J. Walsh to Conrad, May 4, 1942, EC.

99. Conrad, *I Heard a Black Man Sing Last Night*, 1.

100. Conrad to Roy Wilkins, April 1, 1941, CT. Younger readers of the *Fraternal Outlook*, the official publication of the International Workers' Order, had already been introduced to Harriet Tubman in an essay about her written for the Junior World section by Otto Hall and published in January 1941. Otto Hall, "'Let My People Go,'" *Fraternal Outlook*, January 1941, 18–19.

101. Foner, *Paul Robeson Speaks*, 203, 234, 283–84, 299, 303, 312, 316, 321, 368–69, 387, 425, 465.

102. Conrad, *Harriet Tubman* (1942).

103. Woodson to Conrad, July 8, 1942, EC.

104. Woodson wrote to Conrad, "I am of the opinion that the title of your book should drop the word 'General.' It will look too much like stretching things to call Harriet Tubman 'General.' Such a title will have the effect of losing your audience before you find it. The fact that she was referred to as 'General' is well taken care of in the book itself. Kindly give this serious attention": ibid., August 20, 1942, EC.

105. Arthur E. Burke, book review of *Harriet Tubman*, *Crisis*, 1943, clipping in EC.

106. Sidney L. Jackson, "Harriet Tubman," clipping, *New York Tribune*, 1943, EC.

107. Eugene Gordon, "In the Cause of Freedom," clipping, *Worker*, 1943, EC.

108. Ben Burns, "Books," *Chicago Defender*, September 15, 1943.

109. Langston Hughes, clipping, *Chicago Defender*, 1943, EC.

110. Adam Clayton Powell, clipping, *People's Voice*, 1943, EC.

111. Walter Winchell, clipping, *Daily Mirror*, 1943, EC.

112. "*Harriet Tubman* a Fine Seller," *Negro History Bulletin* 7 (February 1944): 110.

113. Conrad, "Author's Note," in *Harriet Tubman* (1969).

114. He also wrote several novels with race as text or subtext, including *Crane Eden* (1962); *Typoo: A Novel* (1969); and *Club: Novel* (1974). In addition, Conrad wrote a biography of Billy Rose (*Billy Rose, Manhattan Primitive* [1968]) and was the ghostwriter of Errol Flynn's autobiography *My Wicked, Wicked Ways* (1979).

115. Conrad, *Harriet Tubman* (1943), copy in the Norman F. Bourke Memorial Library, Cayuga Community College, Auburn, N.Y.

EIGHT. "SPIRITS RISING"

1. Quoted from a Bennett College bulletin in "The Aaron Douglas Fresco of Harriet Tubman," *Crisis*, vol. 39, January 1932, 449. Douglas taught art at Fisk University from 1937 until his retirement in 1966. On his life and career, see Kirschke, *Aaron Douglas*.

2. Quoted in *Amsterdam News*, June 17, 1944; *Portland Evening Express*, June 3, 1944.

3. *Auburn Citizen-Advertiser*, August 16, 1973. The ss *Robert L. Vann*, named in honor of the publisher and editor of the *Pittsburgh Courier*, was the first.

4. *Amsterdam News*, June 17, 1944.

5. Claude A. Barnett to Conrad, April 2, 1940, CT.

6. Lawrence remembered that he first learned of Tubman "from my mother and from the many schoolteachers and librarians within New York's Harlem community": Lawrence, *Harriet and the Promised Land*, author's foreword. When Lawrence's narrative paintings of Tubman first appeared in 1968 in a picture book for children, several critics thought them unsuitable, given the stark and angular look and disturbing theme.

7. Cited from Ellen Harkins Wheat, *Jacob Lawrence: The Frederick Douglass and Harriet Tubman Series of 1938–40* (Seattle: Hampton University Museum and Univ. of Washington Press, 1991), 30. See also Wheat, *Jacob Lawrence*. Purchased in 1940 by the Harmon Foundation, the Tubman paintings were given to Hampton University in 1967: Hills, "Jacob Lawrence as Pictorial Griot."

8. Buckmaster, *Let My People Go* (1941, 1959, 1992). Henrietta Buckmaster was the pseudonym of Henrietta Henkle, a journalist, book reviewer, and writer with strong pro-civil rights convictions. Her story of the Underground Railroad and the growth of the abolition movement brought African American activists to center stage, an emphasis absent from earlier books on the same theme. Though Buckmaster devoted fewer than four pages to Tubman, her book effused a moral vision that was neo-abolitionist in perspective and provided a useful antidote to previous accounts of the Underground Railroad that depicted African Americans as largely passive in a white-led crusade against slavery. In the preface to the 1959 edition of *Let My People Go*, Buckmaster says: "Having been born in Ohio, I had heard of the Underground Railroad most of my life—that daring, clandestine venture which smuggled slaves out of the South into Canada–but I had given it little thought." In the process of doing research for an article on the "railroad" for a magazine, Buckmaster/Henkle pored over old court records, newspapers, diaries, letters, and books. As a result, she recalled many years later, she was set afire. She thought she had discovered something of "the *mystique* of the United States" and came away "with the conviction that if we knew more about the courage, faith, idealism, and practical good sense which went into the fight against the monolithic slave power, we would be better equipped to deal with present problems."

9. Parrish, *A Clouded Star*.

10. McGowan, "Harriet Tubman: According to Anne Parrish," 4.

11. Ibid., 9.

12. Eusebius, "A Modern Moses: Harriet Tubman," 16. Eusebius based her thesis on Sarah Bradford's biographical portrait of Tubman.

13. McGovern, *Runaway Slave*.

14. Moon, *Reel Black Talk*, 246–47.

15. CBS-TV, *The Great Adventure: Go Down Moses*, November 1, 1963. Ruby Dee played Tubman.

16. John Getz to Mr. Stewart (Robert G. Stewart), letter, February 19, 1979, courtesy of Robert G. Stewart.

17. Mary Taylor, "Actress Studies Tubman," *Auburn Citizen*, October 24, 1977; see also *Auburn Citizen*, December 3, 1978. Hollie I. West, "The Woman behind 'A Woman Called Moses,'" *Washington Post*, December 12, 1978, B11. West quotes Heidish as expressing some anxiety about the reactions of African American intellectuals in taking up Tubman as the subject of her first novel: "I worried about critics, especially following the barrage of criticism by blacks that met William Styron's book, *The Confessions of Nat Turner*, after its publication a decade ago."

18. The *Newsweek* quote figured prominently in the promotion of *A Woman Called Moses*.

19. McGowan, "'A Woman Called Moses," 26.

20. Idem, "Harriet Tubman: According to Marcy Heidish," 33.

21. Ibid., 32.

22. Wendkos, *A Woman Called Moses*.

23. *Flight to Freedom: The Underground Railroad* (WXXI Television, Rochester, N.Y., 1995; dist. Films for the Humanities and Sciences, Princeton, N.J.). Other examples of films or video recordings about the Underground Railroad that highlight Harriet Tubman's role as a conductor include *Steal Away: The Harriet Tubman Story* (National Geographic Television, Washington, D.C., 1997), and *Struggle for Freedom* (video, 1993, dist. Simitar Entertainment, Plymouth, Minn.).

24. For example, Troll Associates, *Harriet Tubman* (filmstrip, 43 frames, 1969).

25. Barbara Rothman, "In Praise of African American Women: Female Images in the Plays of Alice Childress" (unpublished Ph.D. diss, New York University, New York), 33.

26. Will Crutchfield, "Harriet Tubman as Opera Heroine," *New York Times*, February 24, 1985.

27. Cited from composer's note, available at https//theamusgrave.com/html/harriet_woman_called_moses.html (accessed January 19, 2007).

28. Nelson Pressley, review of *Harriet's Return*, *Washington Post*, April 17, 2001.

29. Quoted at "General Moses," available at www.earthsvoices.org/moses .html (accessed February 19, 2006).

30. Carolyn Gage, *Harriet Tubman Visits a Therapist*, Twenty-Third Annual Off-Off Broadway Original Short Play Festival, Samuel French, New York, ca. 1994, 1999.

31. Chrisman, "Go Down Moses," 784–85.

32. Cited in Brown-Guillory, *Wines in the Wilderness*, 100. See May Miller, "Harriet Tubman," in Richardson and Miller, *Negro History in Thirteen Plays*, 265– 88.

33. Kander mistakenly uses Garrett's mother's name, Sarah, for his wife. Garrett's first wife was Mary and his second wife was named Rachel. See McGowan, *Station Master on the Underground Railroad* (1977), 158.

34. Neil Novelli, "Tubman's Life Well-Illustrated in 'Passenger': Schoolchildren Enthralled by the Opera about Tubman and the Underground Railroad," *Syracuse Post-Standard*, February 14, 2002, D6.

35. See the website at www.oldtownschool.org/resources/songnotes/song notes_S.html (accessed January 23, 2007).

36. Partial lyrics from Woody Guthrie, "The Ballad of Harriet Tubman," on *Long Ways to Travel: The Unreleased Folkways Masters, 1944–49* (Smithsonian Folkways CD, 40046).

37. Adapted from Walter Robinson, "Harriet Tubman," recorded by Holly Near (Shawnee Press, Delaware Water Gap, Penn., 1977). Compare with Margaret Walker, "Harriet Tubman," *Phylon 5* (Fourth Quarter, 1944): 326–30.

38. Wynton Marsalis, "Harriet Tubman," on *Thick in the South: Soul Gestures in Southern Blue, Volume 1* (audio CD, Columbia, 1991).

39. Pam Louwagie, "Mural Instills Pride, Work Ethic," *Times-Picayune* (New Orleans), August 13, 1998.

40. Sernett, *North Star Country*, 270, image 273.

41. There were two other statues honoring women in Boston on state-owned property (on the Massachusetts State House Lawn). One called to mind Mary Dyer, hanged in 1660 for her Quaker beliefs. The other honored Anne Hutchinson, whom the Massachusetts Bay Puritan authorities banned as a heretic.

42. Cindy Rodriquez, "A Long-Overdue Tribute: Harriet Tubman Statue Will Be First of a Black Woman on City Property," *Boston Globe*, March 20, 1999. See also, Joe Yonan, "Tubman Leads the Way Again: Sculpture to be First of Woman on City Land," *Boston Globe*, April 24, 1997.

43. Available online at http://faculty.brenau.edu/lewis/tubman.html (accessed January 19, 2007).

44. Mike Householder, "Underground Railroad: Memorials to Those Who Helped Slaves," *Stamford Advocate*, November 18, 2001.

45. "Learning by Doing," *Loyola Magazine*, available at www.luc.edu/publica

tions/loyolamag/fa112001/learning.htm (accessed July 21, 2006). The article points out that Luciano's proposal evolved to include art and sculpture honoring minority women of other cultures, including Asian, Native American, Jewish, and Hispanic.

46. Robinson, *The Debt.*

47. Richard F. Weingroff, "Jefferson Davis Memorial Highway," Federal Highway Administration website, available at www.fhwa.dot.gov/infrastructure/jdavis .htm (accessed June 29, 2007).

48. J. Zamgba Browne, "Harriet Tubman's Legacy Gets a Square Deal," *Amsterdam News*, March 21, 2001. In July 2005, Fields presided over a groundbreaking ceremony for the construction of the Harriet Tubman Triangle at the intersection of St. Nicholas Avenue, Frederick Douglass Boulevard, and West 122nd Street. Plans included the erection of a thirteen-foot-tall bronze sculpture of Tubman.

49. Press release, "Thompson on Designation of Harriet Ross Tubman Avenue in Brooklyn," PR05–032, March 10, 2005.

50. Nayaba Arinde, "Harriet Tubman Avenue," *Black World Today*, March 9, 2005, available online at http://tbwt.org.

51. "Black Auburn Residents Say Racial Overtones Came across Loud and Clear," *Syracuse Post-Standard*, March 16, 2003.

52. David L. Shaw. "Board to Discuss Renaming of School," *Syracuse Post-Standard*, September 24, 2002; Robert Taylor, "Fresh Start on Tubman," *Auburn Citizen*, November 13, 2002.

53. Deborah Bayliss, "Harriet Tubman Place PathFinders Answers Community's Needs," *Chicago Weekend*, vol. 26, December 1, 1966, 4.

54. J. Zamgba Browne, "Harriet Tubman Houses Open in Historic Harlem Building," *Amsterdam News*, January 2, 1993.

55. Cited from *Harriet Tubman House* (Boston), 25–27 Holyoke, brochure, CT. The brochure states: "In the roster of women immortals, no signature more sublimely commemorates Heroism than that of Harriet E. [*sic*] Tubman." See also United South End Settlement Records, 1892–1973, Social Welfare History Archives, University of Minnesota, Minneapolis. The Harriet Tubman House merged in 1950 with other settlement houses in the Boston area to become United South End Settlements.

56. Betty Feldman, "Harriet Tubman Center," ca. 1951, EC.

57. See the museum's website at www.tubmanmuseum.com (accessed January 19, 2007).

58. See Harriet Tubman Resource Centre on the African Diaspora, University of York, Toronto, website at www.yorku.ca/nhp (accessed January 19, 2007).

59. See www.geocities.com/CapitolHill/7840/song1.htm (accessed January 19, 2007).

60. Robert G. Stewart to Donald MacDowell, Stamp Development Branch, U.S. Postal Service, letter, August 5, 1977; copy courtesy Robert G. Stewart.

61. *Congressional Record*, vol. 136, no. 12, February 20, 1990. Vivian Abdur-Rahim, president of the Harriet Tubman Historical Society in Wilmington, Delaware, led the effort to obtain congressional approval of a national Tubman Day: Joint Resolution to Designate March 10, 1990, as "Harriet Tubman Day," S. J. Res. 257, 104 Stat. 99, Public Law 101–252.

62. Herb Boyd, "Petition Circulating to Honor Tubman with a Holiday," *Amsterdam News*, March 14, 2001.

63. "Editorial," *Syracuse Post-Standard*, February 17, 2000.

64. Erik Kriss, "New Plan Offered for Tubman Holiday," *Syracuse Post-Standard*, March 5, 2002.

65. The other three buildings were to be named after, respectively, Eleanor Roosevelt, Susan B. Anthony, and Mother Frances Cabrini. The measure passed the New York State Assembly in 2001.

66. "Episcopal Church Honors Harriet Tubman's Life," *Washington Post*, February 18, 1995. The Episcopal General Convention acted favorably on the nomination in 1997.

67. In the author's collection, as are many of the other items.

68. Leach Garchik, "Sit, Stay, Play Dead," *San Francisco Chronicle*, September 19, 1997.

NINE. PRIDE OF PLACE

1. The National Park Service does support the Mary McLeod Bethune Council House National Historic Site, 1318 Vermont Avenue N.W., in Washington, D.C., in honor of the founder of the National Council of Negro Women, and the Maggie L. Walker National Historic Site at 600 North Second Street, Richmond, Va., to commemorate the life of a successful African American entrepreneur.

2. National Park Service, Northeast Region, "Notice of Intent to Prepare an Environmental Impact Statement and Hold Public Meetings for Harriet Tubman Special Resource Study," *Federal Register*, vol. 68, February 7, 2003, 6508–509.

3. David A. Chase, letter to the editor, *Auburn Citizen*, March 20, 1991.

4. Abstracts of Seward's Personal Estate, William H. Seward Papers, folder 6557, reel 192.

5. Tubman's account of outbidding the "white folks" appears in Bradford, *Harriet, the Moses of Her People* (1901), 149–50.

6. "Gives History of Tubman Home" *Auburn Advertiser-Journal*, June 11, 1914; "Harriet Tubman Home and Christening of John Brown Hall," *Auburn Daily Advertiser*, June 20, 1903. For a generally accurate and recent portrayal of the Harriet Tubman Home written for a general audience, see Marc Ferris, "Aunt Harriet's Home," *American Legacy*, vol. 10, Summer 2004, 63–66.

7. "Dedication of Harriet Tubman Home," *Auburn Daily Advertiser*, June 24, 1908.

8. "Tubman Home Report," *Auburn Advertiser-Journal* January 8, 1915.

9. "Mortgage on the Tubman Home Is but Memory Now," *Auburn Citizen*, October 5, 1918.

10. *Auburn Advertiser-Journal*, July 22, 1926.

11. "Harriet Tubman Home 'Rescued': Church to Keep It," *Auburn Citizen-Advertiser*, June 17, 1943.

12. "Wanted to Buy Tubman Property," *Auburn Advertiser-Journal*, June 9, 1914.

13. "House Linked to Tubman Offered for Sale," *Auburn Citizen*, February 25, 1990.

14. "Restoration of Harriet Tubman Home Definite," *Auburn Citizen*, June 27, 1949.

15. "New Harriet Tubman Home to Be Dedicated as Shrine to 'Moses of Her Race,'" *Auburn Citizen-Advertiser*, July 5, 1949.

16. "Auburn's Shrine to Faithful Slave Now Silent Dark," *Auburn Citizen-Advertiser*, December 24, 1971.

17. "Tubman Boosters Urge Action by Supervisors," *Auburn Citizen-Advertiser*, November 9, 1971.

18. Cited in "AME Zion Rejects Takeover of Harriet Tubman Home," *Auburn Citizen-Advertiser*, February 24, 1972.

19. Dick Bandy, "Home for the Aged Planned at Auburn's Tubman House," *Syracuse Herald-American*, December 3, 1972.

20. The proposal for the rest station for migrant farmworkers can be found in *Program of the Dedication of the Harriet Tubman Home* (April 13, 1953). Conceptual plans for a new conference center, with a one-thousand-seat auditorium, retreat facilities for about two hundred people, and twenty-four overnight cottages were being floated in 2000: Dave Tobin, "Tubman Is Receiving Her Due," *Syracuse Post-Standard*, February 17, 2000.

21. George R. Metcalf, "Tubman," *Auburn Citizen-Advertiser*, November 17, 1971. Metcalf, an Auburn native, served fifteen years in the New York State Senate, where he sponsored legislation in support of civil rights, fair housing, and better public health. He taught courses on "black history" at the community college in Auburn during the 1970s. In the 1980s, Metcalf served as board chairman of the Columbian Rope Company in Auburn, a firm started by the Metcalf family in 1903. A longtime public servant, active philanthropist, and opponent of injustice wherever he encountered it, Metcalf gave much needed support for the renovation of the Tubman and Seward homes over the years. He died in 1992.

22. "America's Heritage—Black and White," *Auburn Citizen-Advertiser*, April 1, 1970.

23. Richard Case, "The Legend of Auburn's Aunt Harriet Continues to Grow," *Syracuse Herald-Journal*, May 26, 1986.

24. Irene C. Tallman, "Future of Tubman Home Discussed by Clergy," *Auburn Citizen-Advertiser*, April 10, 1972.

25. Fordham, "The Harriet Tubman Home and Museum."

26. "Auburn Home Cited," *Syracuse Post-Standard*, July 11, 1974; Cantor, *Historic Landmarks of Black America*.

27. "Tubman Pillars Okayed," *Auburn Citizen*, August 3, 1976.

28. "Restoration of Harriet Tubman Home Definite," *Auburn Citizen-Advertiser*, June 27, 1949.

29. "New Harriet Tubman Home to Be Dedicated as Shrine to 'Moses of Her Race,'" *Auburn Citizen-Advertiser*, July 5, 1949.

30. Humez, *Harriet Tubman*, 128.

31. Molly Fennell Manchenton, "Tubman's Home for Aged Aided Poor," *Syracuse Herald-Journal*, February 1, 1999.

32. As told to me by Judith Bryant, daughter of Gladys Bryant.

33. Some people believe that the medal placed in Tubman's coffin at the time of her burial was the one sent to her by Queen Victoria. Others say that the medal in question was stolen by unnamed individuals at some point in time. The *Auburn Daily Advertiser* gave an account of what mourners saw when they passed by the casket as Tubman lay in state on March 13, 1914: "The body was clothed in a black dress on which was pinned a medal which was presented to 'Aunt Harriet' by Queen Victoria in recognition of her great work in freeing the slaves and her remarkable work on the battlefield."

It is likely, however, that Queen Victoria did not have a medal made especially to honor Tubman but, as was her custom, sent one of the ubiquitous tokens made for her Silver Jubilee celebration in 1896. James F. Clarke wrote in 1911 that Susan F. Miller, the granddaughter of Gerrit Smith, inquired about the medal and was told by Tubman that she had given it to the daughter of a brother. Miller visited the home of this unnamed Tubman niece and saw the medal bearing the likeness of Queen Victoria." Clarke, "A Hour with Harriet Tubman." In 2004, the eBay online shopping network listed one of the Jubilee Silver Medals with a starting bid of nine dollars. As to the shawl, Earl Conrad (then using the name Earl Cohen) wrote to Henry Johnson in 1939: "Mrs. Carter tells me that Queen Victoria sent Harriet a shawl along with a letter and a medal. I am particularly familiar with this episode through the Clarke memoir, but I have not heard that she was given a shawl, and I also understand that the shawl disappeared": Cohen to Johnson, June 29, 1939, CT. Rosemary Sadlier is shown wearing the white silk scarf or shawl in a photograph in *Harriet Tubman and the Underground Railroad*, 65. She found the shawl in the possession of Marline Wilkins of Philadelphia. Wilkins is also shown displaying glassware supposedly used by Tubman and the boxed bottle that was used to christen the *SS Harriet Tubman* (Sadlier, *Harriet Tubman and the Underground Railroad*, 67). Wilkins represented herself as another of Tubman's great-grandnieces.

34. Sheila Tucker, "Tubman Library Dedicated," *Auburn Citizen*, May 21, 1979.

35. "Bishops of AME Zion Church Dedicate Harriet Tubman Memorial Center," *Syracuse Impartial Citizen*, May 16–31, 1984.

36. Shawn Carey, "New Director Aims to Put Tubman's Home on the Map," *Syracuse Herald-American*, February 3, 1991.

37. As quoted in Dave Tobin, "Tubman's Life, Legacy Languishing," *Syracuse Post-Standard*, September 2, 2000.

38. deForest as quoted ibid.

39. Judy Holmes, "Students Unearth the Past at Auburn's Tubman Home," *Syracuse Record*, July 26, 1999, supp., A1, A4–A5. For a report on the findings of the archaeological investigations of John Brown Hall, see Ryan and Armstrong, *Archaeology of John Brown Hall at the Harriet Tubman Home*.

40. Beth Beer Cuddy, "Evidence of Tubman Home Fire Unearthed," *Syracuse Post-Standard*, April 12, 2004. On the date of the fire, see "Another Conflagration," *Evening Auburnian* 6, no. 4 (February 10, 1880). I thank Beth Crawford for discovering this.

41. Scott Rapp, "Inspiring First Lady Gets Warm Reception," *Syracuse Herald-Journal*, July 16, 1998.

42. Kathy Kiely and Richard Benedetto, "Clintons Visit a Treasure in Need," *USA Today*, September 2, 1999. The article reports that, since Clinton's first visit to the Tubman Home site in 1998 as part of her Save America's Treasures tour, the total number of visitors, usually five thousand or six thousand a year, had gone up two thousand annually.

43. The original grant request was for nine hundred thousand dollars and included monies for the restoration of the church on Parker Street. The National Park Service reduced the award to four hundred fifty thousand dollars and restricted its use to the Harriet Tubman Home because using tax dollars for the church would be unconstitutional: Pam Greene, "Tubman Home Receives $450K 'Save America Treasures' Grant: Will Expand Tubman Home," *Syracuse Post-Standard*, July 8, 2000.

44. "Governor Announces $284,000 to Restore Harriet Tubman Home," press release, March 9, 2001, copy in author's possession.

45. Some of the grants were competitive matching grants. The total came to approximately 1.2 million dollars, according to Michael Long, personal communication, July 2, 2004.

46. Suzanne Montalalou, "Emerging from the Underground," *Syracuse New Times*, May 23–30, 2001. See also Eric Sorensen, "Tubman Home Welcomes New

Director," *Auburn Citizen*, February 28, 2001. DeWitt resigned at the end of 2003.

47. Dorothy Long, "Tourism Review Pans Tubman Home Staff," *Auburn Citizen*, February 17, 2002.

48. Quoted in an interview with DeWitt by Beth Beer, "Talking Tubman Home," *Syracuse Post-Standard*, March 2, 2002.

49. "Official Pitches Tubman Home Project to Congress," *Syracuse Post-Standard*, August 10, 2000. Mital, a close student of the philosophy of Mahatma Gandhi and the connections between the American Civil Rights Movement and struggles for human dignity in India, felt a special affinity to the effort to preserve the memory and legacy of Harriet Tubman. The enabling legislation sent to the Secretary of the Interior is Public Law 106–516 of the 106th Congress, cited as the "Harriet Tubman Special Resource Study Act."

50. Pam Greene, "Landmark Decision for Tubman Home Recommendation Must Clear One More Hurdle," *Syracuse Post-Standard*, Cayuga ed., November 18, 2000; "New York Properties Declared National Historic Landmarks," *New York Preservationist*, vol. 5, Fall–Winter 2001, 6.

51. Brochure, Thompson Memorial African Methodist Episcopal Zion church, Service of Dedication, 69 Wall Street, Auburn, N.Y., in my possession.

52. Fort Hill has an interesting history. William H. Seward and many of his family are buried there. Authorities buried the body of Leon F. Czolgosz, who was electrocuted in 1901 at the state prison in Auburn for the assassination of President William McKinley at the Pan-American Exposition in Buffalo, in Potter's Field near Fort Hill. When the cemetery was expanded in the 1930s to take over the ground designated Potter's Field, the remains found there—including, presumably, those of Czolgosz—were removed to Soule Cemetery, outside the Auburn city limits: Jennifer Plotnick, "Electric Chair: Treasured or Torched," *Auburn Citizen*, February 27, 2002.

53. William H. Stewart, formerly Henry Ross, was one of Harriet's brothers. He died in Auburn in 1912, a year before his famous sister.

54. Excerpt from Nana Ama Pearl, "Mama Moses' Spirit," available at http://members.tripod.com/~Amasewa/MamaMoses (accessed June 25, 2007).

55. David Tobin, "Buy a Brick, Pay Tribute to the Moses of Her People," *Auburn Citizen*, January 22, 1992.

56. Quoted in idem, "Tiny Tribute to Tubman Left to Weeds, Uncut Trees," *Syracuse Post-Standard*, September 2, 2000. See also David L. Shaw, "Brick Sales Pave Way: Auburn Plans Park Honoring Harriet Tubman," *Syracuse Post-Standard*, September 3, 1992.

57. Tobin, "Tiny Tribute to Tubman Left to Weeds, Uncut Trees."

58. "Opponents Stop March of Neo-Nazis in Auburn," *Albany (N.Y.) Times Union*, September 26, 1993.

59. "Law Guarantees Rights of Picketers," *Albany Times Union*, May 27, 1994.

60. Carmen Livingstone, "Students: Rename School for Tubman," *Syracuse Post-Standard*, March 10, 1995.

61. David L. Shaw, "Decision Due on Honor for Tubman," *Syracuse Post-Standard*, January 5, 2003; Sean Kirst, "If History's Any Guide, Tubman a Good Icon," *Syracuse Post-Standard*, January 8, 2003. The Barnes quote is from David L. Shaw, "Auburn Dedicates a Building to Tubman," *Syracuse Post-Standard*, May 28, 2004. Opponents of the renaming of Genesee Elementary School made the point that there was little if any support for the proposal among the staff and school community: see David L. Shaw, "Move to Rename School Fails by One Vote," *Syracuse Post-Standard*, January 8, 2003.

62. "Taking the Highway," *Syracuse Post-Standard*, December 8, 2003. Mayor Melina Carnicelli proposed renaming the highway to the Auburn City Council. It did not come to a vote because of a technicality, and her term expired. Nevertheless, the editorialist faulted the Auburn politicians and, with a note of sarcasm, reported: "One council member cited safety concerns about the potential confusion with the existing Tubman Lane, which is, ironically, a dead-end street." Tubman Lane first appeared in the Auburn city directory in 1986. See also Beth Beer, "Group Suggests Tubman Arterial," *Syracuse Post-Standard*, December 22, 2002.

63. Beth Beer Cuddy, "Honoring Her Strength: Auburn Woman Overcame Racism, Stayed Compassionate," *Syracuse Post-Standard*, January 29, 2004.

64. Richard Case, "Cry of Racism Stings in Flap over Renaming Auburn High," *Syracuse Herald-Journal*, March 22, 1995.

65. A teacher familiar with the Harriet Tubman Residential Center told me that she thought many Auburn parents and schoolchildren feared being identified with the "step-down" facility if Auburn's high school were renamed in honor of Tubman.

66. The group came back together in 1991 after the historian and Underground Railroad expert Charles Blockson spoke at the Tubman Home and urged a revival: "Group Revives to Honor Tubman," *Syracuse Herald-Journal*, March 27, 1991.

67. Linda Grotke, "Harriet Tubman Day Draws Sixty Pilgrims," *Auburn Citizen*, May 25, 1976.

68. Micheal Lopez, "Ancestral Affinity Pilgrimages to Auburn Honor the Spirit of Harriet Tubman," *Albany Times Union*, July 4, 1999.

69. Cited ibid.

70. Ann Marie Stewart, born about 1845 in Dorchester County, Maryland, married Thomas Elliott and lived in Auburn. Her parents are not known, though Kate Clifford Larson suggests that one of them may have been a sibling of Harriet Tubman. See Larson's depiction of the Ross–Stewart family tree in *Bound for the Promised Land*. Joyce Jones and Pauline Copes-Johnson have conducted their own research concerning their link to Tubman. Neither woman has been able to confirm that Ann Marie Stewart, their great-grandmother, was one of Tubman's sisters. Nevertheless, the public has been led to believe that Jones and Copes-Johnson are "great-grandnieces" of the famous Harriet Tubman. Jones's efforts to discover the "missing link" by going to Dorchester County and meeting with Tubman descendants are recounted in "Syracuse–Auburn Link to Harriet Tubman: City Hall's Joyce Jones Traces Roots," *Syracuse Impartial Citizen*, July 1, 1984, 5. Despite her inability to resolve how she is actually related to Tubman, Jones produced a videotape with the title, *A Conversation with a Living Relative of Harriet Tubman*, using the Proud Heritage Productions label, and began working on a book (yet unpublished) about her "Aunt Harriet" in the early 1970s: Lynn McNicol, "'Aunt Harriet' Tubman," *Auburn Citizen*, October 26, 1992. Bernice Copes-Johnson served the Harriet Tubman Home in Auburn as a docent for many years, giving tours and telling stories about Tubman. Frequently quoted in the press as representing Tubman's "descendants," she has been invested with the honorific title of "Harriet Tubman II" by a group in Brooklyn.

71. Richard Case, "Keeper of Tubman Legacy Has History to Spare," *Syracuse Post-Standard*, February 15, 2004.

72. Idem, interview with Gladys Bryant, in "The Legend of Auburn's Aunt Harriet Continues to Grow," *Syracuse Herald-Journal*, May 26, 1986.

73. Eve Holberg, "Tubman's Life Inspires Women," *Auburn Citizen*, August 21, 1983.

74. Idem, "Tribute Targets Women," *Auburn Citizen*, August 19, 1983.

75. Toni Johnson, "Group Hails Harriet Tubman's Legacy," *Syracuse Herald-American*, July 19, 1998.

76. Charley Hannagan, "Soviet Writer Visits Home of His Hero: Harriet Tubman Biographer Thrilled by Trip to Auburn," *Syracuse Herald-Journal*, June 18, 1990.

77. Colin Richards, "Interfaith 'Peace Walkers' Remember Harriet Tubman," *Michigan Citizen*, vol. 19, April 5, 1997, A1.

78. Talibah L. Chikwendu, "Pilgrimage Builds Belief That We Can Change the World," *Baltimore Afro-American*, June 16, 2000.

79. Kaye Thompson, "Eastern Shore Honors Its Harriet Tubman: Bucktown Seeks to Mark Birthplace of 'Underground Railroad' Leader," *Washington Post Maryland Weekly*, July 19, 1984.

80. Larson, *Bound for the Promised Land*, 55–56, 116. Robert G. Stewart is a descendant of John T. Stewart, son of Levin Stewart and a known Union sympathizer. The John T. Stewart to whom Harriet was bonded was the son of Levin's brother Joseph, a farmer living at Tobacco Stick (now Madison). Three of Tubman's brothers (Robert Ross, Ben Ross, and Henry Ross) took the Stewart name after they escaped. Robert became John Stewart; Ben became James Stewart; and Henry took the name William H. Stewart. Why they did so remains a mystery,

though it was not uncommon for successful runaways to take on aliases; Kate Clifford Larson to Milton C. Sernett, personal correspondence, July 20, 2004.

81. Creighton to Stewart, undated correspondence, and other documents relating to the Esther T. Stewart Fund, courtesy of Robert G. Stewart.

82. Ryan was then the Jessie Ball du Pont Scholar at Washington College in Chestertown, Maryland, on leave from her librarian's post at Syracuse University. John Seidel, professor of archaeology at Washington College, joined in the project at the Bucktown farm once owned by the Brodess family. Though little of significance was unearthed and Ryan would later acknowledge the possibility that Kate Clifford Larson is correct in her claim that Tubman most likely was born elsewhere, the excavations drew considerable public interest and enhanced efforts to better understand Tubman's connections to Maryland's Eastern Shore.

83. Thompson, "Eastern Shore Honors Its Harriet Tubman."

84. The myth that Tubman attended religious services at the Bazzel church stems from the mistaken assumption that the wife of the original minister, Nathan Bazzel, a woman named Soph Ross, was Harriet Tubman's sister: Larson to Sernett, personal communication, April 15, 2004. I am also indebted to John Creighton for helping me understand the complicated intertwining of myth and history (particularly oral history) in the Bazzel church story. Unfortunately, the myth lives on. *Multicultural Maryland*, a tourism brochure produced by Maryland's Department of Business and Economic Development, describes the "Bazel Church[*sic*]" in this fashion: "A small wooden church where Harriet Tubman worshiped in the mid-1800s." The pamphlet is in my possession.

85. The *Dorchester Star* reported in 2002 that the Merediths did not intend to the sell the property to the National Park Service should a Harriet Tubman National Park be established: Gail Dean, "National Park Service Discusses Tubman Park Plans," *Dorchester Star*, July 26, 2002. I thank John Creighton, Kate Clifford Larson, and Bonnie Ryan for helping sort out myth and history as they relate to the Bucktown Country Store. In 2002, Jay Meredith told a journalist representing the *Philadelphia Inquirer* that the structure Tubman tourism promoters claim as the Bucktown Country Store today probably is not the original one that his great-great-grandfather owned. Angie, "Secret Paths to Freedom," *Philadelphia Inquirer*, available at http://www.cambridgemd.org/articles/harriettubman.html (posted February 24, 2002; accessed January 19, 2007).

86. Helen Chappell, "Present Too Tense? Tubman's Eastern Shore Still Holds Secrets of the Way Out," *Washington Post*, January 10, 1996.

87. Eugene L. Meyer, "Eastern Shore Town Prefers to Put Its Racially Torn Past behind It," *Washington Post*, August 10, 1997.

88. Gail Dean, "Leave the Fast Lane and Discover Dorchester," *Discover Dorchester: The Heart of Chesapeake Country*, pamphlet, 3, in my possession.

89. Ibid., statement inside front cover.

90. Gail Dean, "Explore the Heart of Chesapeake County," ibid., 3.

91. Brochure in author's possession.

92. Suzanne White, "Roadtrip: Harriet Tubman Birthplace," *Washington Post*, May 2, 2004.

93. Cited in Gail Dean, "Presentation of Tubman Legacy Focus of Hearing Locating Important Places in Her Life Proving Problematic," Easton, Md., *Star Democrat*, December 2, 2004.

94. Preston, *Young Frederick Douglass*, 34–45.

95. The Ontario Heritage Foundation, Ministry of Culture and Communications, sponsored the sign.

96. Rosemary Sadlier says that her interest in Tubman's life in Canada arose in part because her mother's ancestors came via the Underground Railroad to Ontario: Sadlier, *Harriet Tubman and the Underground Railroad*, 46–49. Sadlier claims that she was "instrumental in making the celebration of Black History Month a national event in Canada": see www.bookrapport.com/profiles/rosemary-sadlier.htm (accessed June 25, 2007).

97. Adrienne Shadd, "'The Lord Seemed to Say "Go"': Women and the Underground Railroad Movement," in Bristow, *"We're Rooted Here and They Can't Pull Us Up,"* 54–55.

98. This phrase is reported in "New England Colored Citizens' Convention."

99. Welland Canals Centre brochure, in my possession.

100. "John Oliver Secondary School, Vancouver, BC," www.coedcomm.com/gg/98morton.html (accessed January 19, 2007).

101. Jon Hand, "Tubman Sites to Receive Grant," *Syracuse Herald-Journal*, January 8, 2000.

TEN. HISTORIANS HAVE THEIR SAY

1. "'Harriet Tubman,' New Liberty Ship Launched in Maine," *Auburn Advertiser-Journal*,

2. Graber, "Is It Ethical to Lie to Secure Hospital Admission?" 220.

3. Literary notices, *Harper's Weekly*, April 3, 1869.

4. Dust jacket comment in Clinton, *Harriet Tubman*.

5. Book announcement, Random House, in my possession.

6. Press kit, available at www.wisc.edu/wisconsinpress/Presskits/Humez.html (accessed January 27, 2007).

7. Gary Dorsey, "A Legend Unshackled," *Baltimore Sun*, January 25, 2004.

8. Humez, *Gifts of Power*; idem, *Mother's First-Born Daughters*; idem, "In Search of Harriet Tubman's Spiritual Autobiography" (NWSA *Journal*).

9. Idem, "Reading the Narrative of Sojourner Truth as a Collaborative Text."

10. McGowan, "Harriet Tubman: Facts and Fiction," 1.

11. McGowan, *Hear Today, Here to Stay*, 20.

12. The *Harriet Tubman Journal* is available at http://www.harriettubman

journal.com (accessed January 19, 2007). Information about *Whispers of Angels: A Story of the Underground Railroad*, which was narrated by McGowan and written, produced, and directed by Sharon K. Baker (Teleduction, 2001), is available at http://www.whispersofangels.com (accessed January 19, 2007).

13. Kate Clifford Larson maintains an extremely useful website that features information about her book and Tubman's life at http://www.harriettubman biography.com (accessed January 19, 2007).

14. Fergus M. Bordewich, "Review of *Bound for the Promised Land*," *Smithsonian*, vol. 35, April 2004, 123.

15. Clinton, *Fanny Kemble's Civil Wars*; idem, *The Plantation Mistress*; idem, *Half Sisters of History*.

16. Idem, *Tara Revisited*.

17. Idem, *Harriet Tubman*, xi.

18. Case, "Keeper of Tubman Legacy Has History to Spare."

19. Jean Thompson, "Harriet Tubman's Three Biographies," *Baltimore Sun*, February 1, 2004.

20. Humez, *Harriet Tubman*, xii.

21. Larson, *Bound for the Promised Land*, viii.

22. Clinton, *Harriet Tubman*, 85.

23. Idem, *Tara Revisited*, 69.

24. Idem, *Harriet Tubman*, xi.

25. Thompson gives examples of where Clinton repeated old claims that Larson and Humez dispute, such as the oft repeated notion that there was a forty thousand dollar reward for the capture of Black Moses. She also points out that Larson's research turned up important facts that Clinton could only describe as unconfirmed, such as the date of Tubman's first escape attempt: Thompson, "Harriet Tubman's Three Biographies."

26. Lev Grossman, writing for *Time* magazine, described Clinton's *Harriet Tubman: The Road to Freedom* as "the first major biography of Tubman in more 100 years"—an indication that he was not aware of Conrad's book: Lev Grossman, "'Reader, My Story Ends with Freedom,'" *Time*, February 9, 2004.

27. Clinton, *Harriet Tubman*, xii–xiii.

28. Ibid., xiii.

29. Humez, *Harriet Tubman*, 156.

30. Ibid., 194.

31. Ibid.

32. Clinton, *Harriet Tubman*, xii.

33. Ibid., 117–23.

34. Beth Beer Cuddy, "Author Finds New Details on Tubman," *Syracuse Post-Standard*, February 23, 2004.

35. Drew Gilpin Faust, "The General," book review, *New York Times*, February 15, 2004.

36. Ibid.

37. Catherine Clinton, "'Slavery Is War': Harriet Tubman and the Underground Railroad," in Blight, *Passages to Freedom*, 197.

38. Clinton, *Harriet Tubman*, xii. Clinton writes, "It is nearly impossible to attach details or particulars, especially dates, to many of Tubman's various escapes": ibid., 95. Larson has demonstrated that it is possible to reconstruct a far more detailed and coherent narrative of Tubman's rescue missions than Clinton provides in her book. Clinton claims that Tubman made "abductions" from Virginia: ibid., 85. There is no evidence for this in the primary sources. Clinton also frequently misidentifies individuals whom Tubman rescued, confuses and conflates one rescue story with another, and overlooks important rescues, such as the last trip, when Tubman, failing to find her sister Rachel alive, brought out the Ennals family. Readers who compare the Clinton book with the more detailed and better-researched Larson biography will discover that many of the errors perpetuated in Clinton's book are due to her confusion over the identities of Tubman's relatives and failure to dig deep enough in the primary sources.

39. See, e.g., "Descendants of the World's Most Famous Female Abolitionist to Visit Georgetown College Campus," for a story about a visit to a Baptist college in Georgetown, Kentucky in 2003, available at http://spider.georgetown college.edu/ugrr/harriet/harriet.htm (accessed January 6, 2004).

40. Linda Cousins-Newton, a Brooklyn poet and storyteller, organized the ceremony and helped bring Nana Yiadom from Ghana to officiate.

41. As reported by Molly Hennessy-Fiske, "A World Away . . . Tubman Relatives 'Part of the Family,'" *Syracuse Post-Standard*, August 16, 2005.

42. Milton C. Sernett and Elizabeth Crawford, interview with Pauline Copes-Johnson, July 31, 2002, Auburn, N.Y. When asked why she thought her parents kept the Tubman connection from her, Copes-Johnson asserted that a fear of retaliation from Rebels and racists caused them to keep the secret. See also Amie Bisignano, "Tubman's 'Relative' Effect," *Auburn Citizen*, February 27, 2000. Bisignano quotes Copes-Johnson as saying, "My parents never told me. It was a well-kept secret. In fact, they took it with them to their graves."

43. "Ross–Stewart Family Tree," in Larson, *Bound for the Promised Land*. Pauline Copes-Johnson said in the 2002 interview that she did not know who Ann Marie's mother was.

44. Earl Conrad heard this story from Mrs. William (Helen Woodruff) Tatlock in 1939 and included it in his book: see Conrad, *Harriet Tubman* (1943), 65–66.

45. Copes-Johnson, "Harriet Tubman Davis."

46. Copes-Johnson said that the children frequently asked her if she had been a slave: Sernett and Crawford, interview with Copes-Johnson.

47. Evelyn Brooks Higginbotham, quote from publisher's flyer, Random House, in my possession.

48. David Mehegan, "Up from the Underground," *Boston Globe*, February 5, 2004.

49. Larson, *Bound for the Promised Land*, xxi.

50. Quoted in Mehegan, "Up from the Underground."

51. Quoted in Gary Soulsman, "Projects Pay Fresh Tribute to Freedom Fighter's Legacy," Wilmington, Del., *News Journal*, August 11, 2003.

52. See Michael B. Chesson, "Schoolbooks Teach Falsehoods and Feel-Good Myths about the Underground Railroad and Harriet Tubman," in *Textbook Letter*, vol. 12, no. 13 available at http://www.textbookleague.org/121tubby.htm (accessed January 27, 2007). Even after the Larson and Humez books showed that Tubman did not rescue the proverbial "three hundred," exaggerated claims continue. An editorial writer for the *Brooklyn Paper* said: "An escaped slave, she returned repeatedly to pre-Emancipation Maryland to rescue, by her estimate, 7,000 slaves." Editorial, "Name 'Park' for a Hero," *Brooklyn Paper* 30, no. 4 (January 27, 2007), 6.

53. Gary Dorsey, "A Legend Unshackled," *Baltimore Sun*, January 25, 2004.

54. Bordewich, *Bound for Canaan*, 346–47.

55. Ibid., 351.

56. Beverly Lowry's *Harriet Tubman: Imaging a Life*, 1, 7, 204, 377.

57. Noble, *Ain't Sleep, Ain't Gone*. Noble consistently spells Tubman's first name "Harriett." In conversations with her in May 2005, Bessie Cooper Noble told me of her belief that Gladys Bryant, the mother of Judith Bryant, had the most authentic claim to be one of Tubman's kin.

BIBLIOGRAPHY

This is a selected bibliography of sources consulted and used. For a fuller bibliography, see the chapter notes. All Tubman students and scholars should refer to the detailed bibliography of archival, manuscript, and printed sources compiled by Jean Humez and included in *Harriet Tubman: The Life and the Life Stories* (Madison: University of Wisconsin Press, 2003), 409–41. Humez has published many of the most important primary sources in part 3, "Stories and Sayings," and part 4, "Documents." Though Kate Clifford Larson's book *Bound for the Promised Land: Harriet Tubman, Portrait of an American Hero* (New York: Ballatine Books, 2004) does not have a formal bibliography, Tubman researchers will be richly rewarded by carefully reading her extensive documentation in the notes. Although my research investigations began several years prior to the publication of the Larson and Humez books, I am indebted to both authors for directing my attention to some of the more elusive primary sources used in this volume.

The amount of Tubman-related material on the Internet can be overwhelming, as a search using Google demonstrates. Much of what is posted on the Internet is useful only for understanding the extent of the mythology that has grown up around Tubman. Historically accurate information is now beginning to filter on to the Internet as a result of the publication of the Larson and Humez books. James A. McGowan, publisher of the *Harriet Tubman Journal* in the 1990s, has designed the best and most reliable website for Tubman enthusiasts and scholars. It can be found at http://www.harriettubmanjournal.com. The National Park Service's Harriet Tubman Special Resource Study site, at http://www.harriet tubmanstudy.org, is also useful.

ARCHIVES AND MANUSCRIPT COLLECTIONS

The first and most important is the Earl Conrad–Harriet Tubman Collection, 1939–41, 1946, at the Schomburg Center for Research in Black Culture, New York Public Library, New York City. This collection consists of seven boxes (three linear feet). It is also available on two reels of microfilm. This valuable archive contains the research correspondence, notes, newspaper clippings, interviews, manuscripts, and other materials Conrad gathered. I used the microfilm version (Scholarly Resources, Wilmington, Del., 1995), which is cited as CT.

Conrad also donated many materials related to his efforts to publish his Tubman book to Cayuga Community College in Auburn, New York. This collection is at the Norman F. Bourke Memorial Library and contains duplicates of some of the items he gave to the Schomburg Center. See *Earl Conrad: An Inventory of Papers at Cayuga Community College* (April 1983), compiled by Douglas O. Michael. I cite the Caygua Community College Collection as EC.

Tubman researchers should also consult the Ellen Jean Mahoney Collection at the Seymour Public Library in Auburn, New York. Located in the Mary Van Sickle Wait History Room, the scrapbooks consist of copies (not originals) of newspaper stories, articles, photographs, and other documents compiled by Mahoney over many years. The Harriet Tubman Files at the Cayuga County Historian's Office in Auburn, New York, contain valuable items. Many of them are in the better organized Mahoney Collection.

A variety of other manuscript and archival collections contain isolated items pertaining to Harriet Tubman and those who helped make her a national icon. Among the more useful are

Garrison Family Papers, Sophia Smith Collection, Smith College.

Gerrit Smith Papers, George Arents Research Library, Syracuse University.

Pension Files, National Archives, Washington, D.C.

William H. Seward Papers, Rare Books Department, Rush Rees Library, University of Rochester.

Franklin B. Sanborn Papers, Special Collections, American Antiquarian Society, Worcester, Mass.

Osborne Family Papers, George Arents Research Library, Syracuse University.

ARTICLES AND ESSAYS

Newspapers served as important vehicles for shaping the public's views of Harriet Tubman. The Auburn press carried many stories about Tubman, particularly after she had become a national icon; in recent decades, the Syracuse press and Baltimore press have featured articles about Tubman and her legacy. Articles about Tubman have also appeared in the black press, but not with the frequency one might expect, given her status as a "race" hero. These sources are cited in the notes. National outlets such as the *New York Times* only occasionally carried stories useful for this study of Tubman and the American memory. Since these are few in number, I cite them in this section.

"Acquittal of a Murderer." *Baltimore American*, December 23, 1867.

Boyd, Herb. "Petition Circulating to Honor Tubman with a Holiday." (New York) *Amsterdam News*, March 14, 2001.

Browne, J. Zamba. "Harriet Tubman Slowly Getting Her Due." (New York) *Amsterdam News*, December 12, 2003.

———. "Harriet Tubman Houses Open in Historic Harlem Building." (New York) *Amsterdam News*, January 2. 1993.

Carter, George C. "Harriet, the Moses of Her People." *Woman's Journal* (Boston), August 1, 1908.

Cheney, Edna Dow. "Moses." *Freedmen's Record*, vol. 1, March 1865, 34–38.

Cheney, Lynne V. "The End of History." *Wall Street Journal*, October 20, 1994.

Chrisman, Robert. "Go Down Moses: An Introduction." *Michigan Quarterly Review* 37 (fall 1998):782.

Christianson, Scott. "The Battle for Charles Nalle." *American Legacy* 2 (winter 1997): 31–35.

Clarke, James B. "An Hour with Harriet Tubman." Pp. 115–22 in William Edgar Easton, *Christophe: A Tragedy in Prose of Imperial Haiti*. Los Angeles: Press Grafton, 1911.

Conrad, Earl. "Charles P. Wood Manuscripts of Harriet Tubman." *Negro History Bulletin* 13 (January 1949): 90, 92–95.

———. "The Fighting Slave." *Pic Magazine*, April 13, 1943, clipping in CT.

———. "General Tubman at Troy." *Crisis* 48 (March 1941): 78, 91.

———. "'General Tubman,' Composer of Spirituals." *Etude* 5 (May 1942): (60) 305, 344, 352.

———. "General Tubman on the Combahee." *Negro World Digest* (December, 1940): 13–16.

———. "A Great Leader-Harriet Tubman." *Negro World Digest* (August, 1940): 46–50.

———. "I Bring You General Tubman." *Black Scholar* 1, no. 3 (1970): 2–7.

———. "Most of a Man." *Negro World Digest* 1 (November, 1940): 88.

Copes-Johnson, Pauline. "Harriet Tubman Davis." P. 25 in *Back to Before: Anecdotes from the Twentieth Century in Cayuga County, New York*. Auburn, N.Y.: Donning Company, 1999, 25–27.

Crutchfield, Will. "Harriet Tubman as Opera Heroine." *New York Times*, February 24, 1985.

Degler, Carl. "In Search of the Un-hyphenated American." *New Perspectives Quarterly* 8 (1991): 5.

Dennis, Charles. "The Work of Harriet Tubman." *Americana Magazine* 6 (November 6, 1911): 1067–71.

Du Bois, W. E. B. "David Livingston and Harriet Tubman." *Crisis*, March, 1913.

Earle (Mathews), Victoria. "Harriet Tubman." *Woman's Era* (Boston) (June 1896): 8.

Elson, John. "Education: History, the Sequel: A Controversial New Set of Recommendations Generates a Debate on What's Important about America's
Past." *Time*, November 7, 1994, 64.

"Episcopal Church Honors Harriet Tubman's Life." *Washington Post*, February
18, 1995.

Eusebius, Mary. "A Modern Moses: Harriet Tubman." *Journal of Negro Education*
19 (Winter 1950): 16–27.

Falk, Leslie A. "Black Abolitionist Doctors and Healers." *Bulletin of the History of
Medicine* 54 (1980): 258–72.

"Fatal Shooting Affray." *Baltimore Sun*, October 4, 1867.

Ferris, Marc, "Aunt Harriet's Home," *American Legacy* 10, 2 (summer 2004): 63–
68.

Fordham, Monroe. "The Harriet Tubman Home and Museum." *Afro-Americans
in New York Life and History* 1 (January 1977): 106.

Garrison II, William Lloyd. "The Story of Harriet Tubman." *Boston Evening
Transcript*, April 13, 1897.

Graber, Mark A. "Is It Ethical to Lie to Secure Hospital Admission?" *Western
Journal of Medicine* 175 (October 2001): 22–21.

Grossman, Lev. "Reader, My Story Ends with Freedom." *Time*, February 9,
2004.

Guterman, Benjamin. "Doing 'Good Brave Work': Harriet Tubman's Testimony
at Beaufort, South Carolina." *Prologue: Quarterly of the National Archives and
Records Administration* 32 (Fall 2000): 155–65.

"Harriet Tubman." *Commonwealth*, July 10, 1863.

"Harriet Tubman." *Commonwealth*, August 4, 1864.

"Harriet Tubman." *Commonwealth*, August 12, 1864.

"Harriet Tubman." *Commonwealth*, January 9, 1869.

"Harriet Tubman: A Colored Woman with a Remarkable History Revisits Boston." *Boston Sunday Herald*, October 31, 1886, 10.

"Harriet Tubman Davis." *New York Times*, March 14, 1913.

"Harriet Tubman Davis." *New York Tribune*, March 13, 1913.

"Harriet Tubman Davis." *Springfield (Mass.) Republican*, March 14, 1913.

"Harriet Tubman Davis Dies Monday at Auburn, N. Y." *New York Age*, March 13,
1913.

"Harriet Tubman Dying." *New York Times*, March 11, 1913.

"Harriet Tubman Ill and Penniless." *New York Age*, June 8, 1911.

"Harriet Tubman Penniless." *New York Times*, June 2, 1911.

"Hillary Gets Funding for Harriet Tubman Pension." *New York Beacon*, November 6, 2003.

Hills, Patricia. "Jacob Lawrence as Pictorial Griot: The Harriet Tubman Series."
American Art 7 (Winter 1993): 40–59.

Hine, Darlene Clark. "Sisters on the Front Line." *Heart and Soul* (Spring 1994): 58–61.

Hoefer, Jean M. "They Called Her 'Moses': Harriet Tubman, a Heroine of the Underground, Goes to War." *Civil War Times Illustrated*, vol. 26, February 1988, 37–41.

Holt, Rosa Belle. "A Heroine in Ebony." *Chautauquan*, vol. 23, July 1896, 459–62.

"Home of Harriet Tubman Dedicated as a National Shrine." *Ithaca (N.Y.) Journal*, May 6, 1953.

Hopkins, Pauline E. "Famous Women of the Negro Race. III. Harriet Tubman (Moses)." *Colored American Magazine* (January–February, 1902): 210–16.

Huff, Robert A. "Anne Miller and the Geneva Political Equality Club, 1897–1912." *New York History* 65 (October 1984): 325–48.

Humez, Jean M. "In Search of Harriet Tubman's Spiritual Autobiography." *National Women's Studies Association* (NWSA) *Journal* 3 (1993): 162–82.

———. "In Search of Harriet Tubman's Spiritual Autobiography." Pp. 239–61 in *This Far by Faith: Readings in African-American Women's Religious Biography*, ed. Judith Weisenfeld and Richard Newman. New York: Routledge, 1996.

———. "Reading the Narrative of Sojourner Truth as a Collaborative Text." *Frontiers* (Spring 1996): 29–52.

Kauffman, Bill. "Harriet Tubman, Pre-Mummification." *American Enterprise* 17 (June 2006): 46.

Kiely, Kathy, and Richard Benedetto. "Clintons Visit a Treasure in Need." *USA Today*, September 2, 1999.

King, Lisa Y. "In Search of Women of African Descent Who Served in the Civil War Union Navy." *Journal of Negro History* 83 (Fall 1998): 302–9.

Larson, C. Kay. "Bonny Yank and Ginny Reb." *Minerva: Quarterly Report on Women in the Military* (1990): 33–48.

Lawson, Elizabeth. "Harriet Tubman—Born a Slave—Became Known as the 'Moses of Her People.'" *Daily Worker*, February 19, 1938.

Lebedun, Jean. "Harriet Beecher Stowe's Interest in Sojourner Truth, Black Feminist." *American Literature* 46 (1974): 359–63.

"Liberty Ship Harriet Tubman Launched with Many Celebrities Participating." *New York Amsterdam News*, June 17, 1944.

Logan, Rayford W. "Review of *The Railroad to Freedom* by Hildegarde Swift." *Journal of Negro History* 18 (April 1933): 213–14.

McGowan, James A. "Harriet Tubman: According to Anne Parrish." *Harriet Tubman Journal* 3 (August 1995): 1–10.

———. "Harriet Tubman: According to Marcy Heidish." *Harriet Tubman Journal* 2 (April 1994): 1, 23–25, 32–33.

———. "Harriet Tubman: According to Sarah Bradford." *Harriet Tubman Journal* 2 (January 1994): 1–10.

————. "Harriet Tubman: Facts and Fiction." *Harriet Tubman Journal* 1 (October 1993): 1, 3–4, 12–13, 15–16, 19.

————. "The Psychic Life of Harriet Tubman, Part I." *Visions* (March 1995): 1–3.

————. "A Woman Called Moses: The Television Drama." *Harriet Tubman Journal* 2 (April 1994): 26, 34.

McHenry, Beth. "Newspaperman Is Inspired by Heroine of His Book on Harriet Tubman." *Daily Worker*, September 13, 1943.

"Memorial to Harriet Tubman." *New York Age*, June 18, 1914.

Mickenburg, Julia. "Civil Rights, History, and the Left: Inventing the Juvenile Black Biography." *MELUS* 27 (Summer 2002): 65–93.

Miller, Anne Fitzhugh. "Harriet Tubman." *American Magazine*, vol. 74, August 1913, 420, 422.

Mims, Peg, and Walter Oleksy. "The Woman Called Moses." *Cobblestone* 2 (February 1981): 9–14.

"Moses of Her People, The: Proposed Memorial to Harriet Tubman, A Negress." *New York Sun*, May 2, 1909.

"Moses of Her Race Ending Her Life in Home She Founded." *New York World*, June 25, 1911.

"Moses of the Negroes, The." *Literary Digest* 46 (April 19, 1913): 913–15.

Napson-Williams, Theresa D. "Tubman, Harriet." Pp. 786–77 in *The Oxford Companion to United States History*, ed. Paul S. Boyer. New York: Oxford University Press, 2001.

"New England Colored Citizens' Convention." *Liberator*, August 26, 1859.

"Oldest Ex-Slave Given Reception." *Boston Journal*, May 26, 1905 (reprint. as "Harriet Tubman at the Hub," *Auburn Daily Advertiser*, May 30, 1905).

Painter, Nell Irvin. "Sojourner Truth in Life and Memory: Writing the Biography of an American Exotic." *Gender and History* 2 (Spring 1990): 3–16.

Pitman, R. "Brittany Meets Harriet Tubman." *Video Librarian*, May 11, 1997, available online at http://www.elibrary.com, accessed February 2, 2001.

Pulfer, Laura. "Underground Railroad Museum Is Real Chance for Greatness." *Cincinnati Enquirer*, March 30, 1997.

Quarles, Benjamin. "Foreword to the 1970 Edition." Pp. v–viii, in William Still, *The Underground Rail Road* (1872), reprint. ed. Chicago: Johnson Publishing, 1970.

————. "Harriet Tubman." Pp. 57–63 in *Heritage of '76*, ed. Jan P. Dolan. South Bend, Ind.: University of Notre Dame Press, 1976.

————. "Harriet Tubman's Unlikely Leadership." Pp. 43–57 in *Black Leaders of the Nineteenth Century*, ed. Leon Litwack and August Meier. Urbana: University of Illinois Press, 1988.

Rahman, Ali. "Cultural Campaign for 'Medal of Honor' for Harriet Tubman." *New York Beacon*, May 31, 2000.

"Report of the Committee of Teachers." *Freedmen's Record* 1 (April 1865): 54–55.

Salvadore, Maria B. "Review of *Minty: A Story of Young Harriet Tubman.*" *Horn Book Magazine* 72 (September 19, 1996): 589.

Sanborn, Franklin B. "Concerning Harriet Tubman and Fugitive Slaves." *Springfield* (Mass.) *Republican*, March 19, 1913.

———. "Harriet Tubman." *Commonwealth*, July 17, 1863.

———. "A Negro Heroine—Scenes in the Life of Harriet Tubman." *Springfield Republican*, January 25, 1869.

Stimson, Julia C., and Ethel C. S. Thompson. "Women Nurses with the Union Forces during the Civil War." *Military Surgeon* 62 (January 1928): 1–17, 208–30.

Stowe, Harriet Beecher. "Sojourner Truth, the Libyan Sibyl." *Atlantic Monthly*, vol. 11, April 1863, 473–81.

Taverna, Patty, and Terry Hongell. "Meet Tubman: The Story of a Website." *Learning and Leading with Technology* 27 (March 2000): 42–45, 62.

Terry, Esther. "Sojourner Truth: The Person behind the Libyan Sibyl." *Massachusetts Review* 26 (Summer–Fall 1985): 425–55.

Thompson, Audrey. "Harriet Tubman in Pictures: Cultural Consciousness and the Art of Picture Books." *The Lion and the Unicorn* 25 (2001): 81–114.

Thompson, Priscilla. "Harriet Tubman, Thomas Garrett, and the Underground Railroad." *Delaware History* (Spring–Summer 1986): 22.

"Tubman, Conductor on Greatest Railroad." *New York Age*, June 15, 1911.

"Unveil 'Tubman' Memorial." *Cleveland Advocate*, July 17, 1915, 2, I.

Walker, Margaret. "Harriet Tubman." *Phylon* 4 (Fourth Quarter, 1944): 326–30.

White, Suzanne. "Roadtrip: Harriet Tubman Birthplace." *Washington Post*, May 2, 2004.

Wiener, Jon. "Lynne V. Cheney's Baseless Attacks on the National Standards for History." *New Republic*, vol. 212, January 2, 1995, 9.

Wyman, Lillie B. Chace. "Harriet Tubman." *New England Magazine*, n.s. 14, March 1896, 110–18.

Yerrington, James M. W. "The Fourth at Framingham." *Liberator*, July 8, 1859.

BOOKS

Abdul-Jabbar, Kareem, and Alan Steinberg. *Black Profiles in Courage: A Legacy of African American Achievement*. New York: William Morrow, 1996.

Abraham, Philip. *Harriet Tubman*. New York: Children's Press, 2002.

Adams, John Quincy. *A History of Auburn Theological Seminary, 1818–1918*. Auburn, N.Y.: Auburn Seminary Press, 1918.

Adams, Russell L., and Eugene Winslow. *Great Negroes, Past and Present*, 3d ed. Chicago: Afro-Am, 1969.

Adams, Samuel Hopkins. *Grandfather Stories*. New York: Random House, 1947.

Adler, David A. *A Picture Book of Harriet Tubman*. New York: Scholastic, 1994.

Adler, David A., and Samuel Byrd. *A Picture Book of Harriet Tubman*. New York: Holiday House, 1992.

African-Americans Who Made a Difference: 15 Plays for the Classroom. New York: Scholastic Professional Books, 1996.

Altman, Susan, Susan Lechner, and Byron Wooden. *Followers of the North Star: Rhymes about African American Heroes, Heroines, and Historical Times*. Many Voices, One Song. Chicago: Children's Press, 1993.

Andrews, William, ed. *Sisters of the Spirit: Three Black Women's Autobiographies of the Nineteenth Century*. Bloomington: Indiana University Press, 1986.

Anner, John. *Beyond Identity Politics: Emerging Social Justice Movements in Communities of Color*. Boston: South End Press, 1996.

Aptheker, Herbert. *The Negro in the Civil War*. New York: International Publishers, 1938.

Armstead, Reed S. *Harriet Tubman: Stand and Deliver*. Indianapolis: AESOP Enterprises, 1991.

Armstrong, Richard. *Grace Darling: Maid and Myth*. London: J. M. Dent, 1965.

Ashby, Ruth, and Deborah Gore Ohrn. *Herstory: Women Who Changed the World*. New York: Viking, 1995.

Bains, Rae, and Jenna Whidden. *Harriet Tubman: The Road to Freedom*. Mahwah, N.J.: Troll Associates, 1982.

Baldwin, Louis. *Women of Strength: Biographies of 106 Who Have Excelled in Traditionally Male Fields, A.D. 61 to the Present*. Jefferson, N.C.: McFarland, 1996.

Beckner, Chrisanne. *One Hundred African-Americans Who Shaped American History*. San Francisco: Bluewood Books, 1995.

Benge, Janet, and Geoff Benge. *Harriet Tubman: Freedom Bound*. Lynnwood, Wash.: Emerald Books, 2002.

Benjamin, Anne, and Ellen Beier. *Young Harriet Tubman, Freedom Fighter*. Troll First-Start Biography. Mahwah, N.J.: Troll Associates, 1992.

Bentley, Judith. *Harriet Tubman*. New York: Franklin Watts, 1990.

Billington, Ray Allen, ed. *The Journal of Charlotte L. Forten: A Free Negro in the Slave Era*. New York: Dryden Press, 1953.

Blake, Nelson Manfred, and Carol V. R. George. *"Remember the Ladies": New Perspectives on Women in American History, Essays in Honor of Nelson Manfred Blake*. Syracuse, N.Y.: Syracuse University Press, 1975.

Bledsoe, Lucy Jane, Corinn Codye Scott, and James Balkovek. *Harriet Tubman*. Biographies from American History. Belmont, Calif.: Fearon/Janus, 1989.

Blight, David W. *Beyond the Battlefield: Race, Memory, and the American Civil War*. Amherst: University of Massachusetts Press, 2002.

———. *Frederick Douglass' Civil War: Keeping Faith in Jubilee*. Baton Rouge: Louisiana State University Press, 1989.

————. *Race and Reunion: The Civil War in American Memory.* Cambridge, Mass.: Harvard University Press, 2001.

Blight, David W., ed. *Passages to Freedom: The Underground Railroad in History and Memory.* Washington, D.C.: Smithsonian Books, 1994.

Blockson, Charles L. *The Underground Railroad: Dramatic Firsthand Accounts of Daring Escapes to Freedom.* New York: Berkley Books, 1987.

Bontemps, Arna. *Black Thunder.* New York: Macmillan, 1936.

Bordewich, Fergus M. *Bound for Canaan: The Underground Railroad and the War for the Soul of America.* New York: HarperCollins, 2005.

Boyd, Herb. *Autobiography of a People: Three Centuries of African American History Told by Those Who Lived It.* New York and London: Doubleday, 2000.

Bradford, Sarah Hopkins. *Harriet, the Moses of Her People.* New York: G. R. Lockwood and Son, 1886.

————. *Harriet, the Moses of Her People,* 2d ed. New York: Geo. R. Lockwood and Son, 1897.

————. *Harriet, the Moses of Her People,* rev. ed. New York: J. J. Little, 1901.

————. *Harriet Tubman: The Moses of Her People.* New York: Corinth Books, 1961.

————. *Scenes in the Life of Harriet Tubman.* Auburn, N.Y.: W. J. Moses, 1869.

————. *Ups and Downs; or Silverlake Sketches.* Auburn, N.Y.: Alden, Beardsley, 1855.

Bragg, George F. *Heroes of the Eastern Shore.* Baltimore: G. F. Bragg, 1939.

————. *Men of Maryland.* Baltimore: Church Advocate Press, 1914.

Brawley, Benjamin Griffith. *Women of Achievement.* Chicago: Woman's American Baptist Home Mission Society, 1919.

Braxton, Joanne M. *Black Women Writing Autobiography: A Tradition within a Tradition.* Philadelphia: Temple University Press, 1989.

Breault, Judith Colucci. *The World of Emily Howland, Odyssey of a Humanitarian.* Millbraw, Calif.: Les Femmes, 1974.

Bressler, Joyce, et al. *Harriet Tubman 1820 to 1913: Leader of Escaping Slaves, Civil War Scout and Spy.* Brooklyn, N.Y.: TABS, 1986.

Brin, Ruth F. *Contributions of Women: Social Reform.* Minneapolis: Dillon, 1977.

Bristow, Peggy, ed. *"We're Rooted Here and They Can't Pull Us Up": Essays in African Canadian Women's History.* Toronto: University of Toronto Press, 1994.

Brouk, Joanna, and Bob Lewis. *Harriet Tubman.* San Francisco: Jabberwocky, 1981.

Brown, Hallie Quinn. *Homespun Heroines and Other Women of Distinction.* Xenia, Ohio: Aldine, 1926.

Brown, William Wells. *My Southern Home, or, The South and Its People.* Boston: A. G. Brown, 1880.

————. *The Rising Son, or The Antecedents and Advancement of the Colored Race.* Boston: A. G. Brown, 1874.

Brown-Guillory, Elizabeth, ed. *Wines in the Wilderness: Plays by African-American Women from the Harlem Renaissance to the Present*. New York: Praeger, 1990.

Buckmaster, Henrietta. *Let My People Go: The Story of the Underground Railroad and the Growth of the Abolition Movement*. New York: Harper and Brothers, 1941.

———. *Let My People Go: The Story of the Underground Railroad and the Growth of the Abolition Movement*, 2d ed. Boston: Beacon Press, 1959.

———. *Let My People Go: The Story of the Underground Railroad and the Growth of the Abolition Movement*, reprint. ed. Columbia: University of South Carolina Press, 1992.

———. *Women Who Shaped History*. New York: Collier Books, 1966.

Burns, Bree. *Harriet Tubman*. Junior World Biographies. New York: Chelsea Juniors, 1992.

Cantor, George. *Historic Landmarks of Black America*. Detroit: Gale Research, 1991.

Carlson, Judy. *Harriet Tubman: Call to Freedom*. New York: Fawcett Columbine, 1989.

Carnegie, Mary E. *The Path We Tread: Blacks in Nursing, 1854–1990*. New York: National League for Nursing Press, 1991.

Carter, Polly, and J. Brian Pinkney. *Harriet Tubman and Black History Month*. Englewood Cliffs, N.J.: Silver Burdett Press, 1990.

Chadwick, John White. *A Life for Liberty: Anti-slavery and Other Letters of Sallie Holley*. New York: G. P. Putnam's, 1899.

Chappell, Helen. *The Chesapeake Book of the Dead: Tombstones, Epitaphs, Histories, Reflections, and Oddments of the Region*. Baltimore: Johns Hopkins University Press, 1999.

Cheney, Edna Dow. *Reminiscences*. Boston: Lee and Shepard, 1902.

Childress, Alice, and Charles Lilly. *When the Rattlesnake Sounds, a Play*. New York: Coward, McCann and Geoghegan, 1975.

Clark, Sara. *Harriet Tubman: Total Learning Resource and Activity Book*. Animated Hero Classics. Irving, Tex.: Nest Entertainment, 1996.

Clarke, Brenda, and Gwen Green. *Caring for Others: Tales of Courage*. Austin: Steck-Vaughn Library Division, 1990.

Clarke, James Freeman. *Anti-Slavery Days: A Sketch of the Struggle which Ended in the Abolition of Slavery in the United States*. New York: John W. Lovell, 1883.

Cleghorn, Sarah N. *The True Ballad of Glorious Harriet Tubman* (1933), reprint. ed. Radical Pamphlets in American Collections: Anarchism Collection. Alexandria, Va.: Chadwyck-Healey, 1987.

Clinton, Catharine. *Fanny Kemble's Civil Wars*. New York: Oxford University Press, 2000.

———. *Harriet Tubman: The Road to Freedom*. New York, Little, Brown, 2004.

————. *The Plantation Mistress: Woman's World in the Old South*. New York: Pantheon, 1983.

————. *Tara Revisited: Women, War and the Plantation Legend*. New York: Abbeville Press, 1995.

Clinton, Catharine, ed. *Half Sisters of History: Southern Women and the American Past*. Durham: Duke University Press, 1994.

Coles, Howard W. *The Cradle of Freedom: A History of the Negro in Rochester, Western New York and Canada*. Rochester, N.Y.: Oxford Press, 1942.

Colman, Penny. *Spies! Women in the Civil War*. Cincinnati: Betterway Books, 1992.

Commager, Henry Steele. *Crusaders for Freedom*. Garden City, N.Y.: Doubleday, 1962.

Connerton, Paul. *How Societies Remember*. Cambridge: Cambridge University Press, 1990.

Conrad, Earl. *Harriet Tubman*. Washington, D.C.: Associated Publishers, 1943.

————. *Harriet Tubman*, reprint. ed. New York: Paul S. Eriksson, 1969.

————. *Harriet Tubman*, reprint. ed. New York: Paul S. Eriksson, 1974.

————. *Harriet Tubman: Negro Soldier and Abolitionist*. New York: International Publishers, 1942.

————. *Horse Trader: The Story of a Real David Harum*. New York: Thomas Y. Crowell, 1953.

————. *I Heard a Black Man Sing Last Night*. New York: National Education Department, International Workers' Order, 1941.

Conrad, Earl, and Anna Alyse Conrad. *General Harriet Tubman*. Reprint of 1943 edition with new title. Washington, D.C.: Associated Publishers, 1990.

Cross, Whitney R. *The Burned-Over District: The Social and Intellectual History of Enthusiastic Religion in Western New York, 1800–1850*. Ithaca, N.Y.: Cornell University Press, 1950.

Daniel, Sadie Iola, Charles H. Wesley, and Thelma D. Perry. *Women Builders*. Washington: Associated Publishers, 1970.

Davis, Charles T., and Henry Louis Gates Jr., eds. *The Slave's Narrative*. New York: Oxford University Press, 1985.

Davis, Elizabeth Lindsay. *Lifting as They Climb*. Washington, D.C.: National Association of Colored Women, 1933.

Dean, Phillip Hayes, et al. *Black Heroes: Seven Plays*. New York, N.Y.: Applause Theater Books, 1989.

Douglass, Frederick. *Life and Times of Frederick Douglass, Written by Himself*. Hartford, Conn.: Park Publishing, 1881.

————. *Life and Times of Frederick Douglass, Written by Himself*, rev. ed. Boston: DeWolfe, Fisk, 1892.

————. *Life and Times of Frederick Douglass, Written by Himself* (1892), reprint. ed. London: Collier-Macmillan, 1962.

————. *My Bondage and My Freedom*. New York: Miller, Orton and Mulligan, 1855.

————. *Narrative of the Life of Frederick Douglass, an American Slave, Written by Himself*. Boston: Anti-Slavery Office, 1845.

Drew, Benjamin. *A North-Side View of Slavery: The Refugee, or The Narrative of Fugitive Slaves in Canada, Related by Themselves, with an Account of the History and Condition of the Colored Population of Upper Canada*. Cleveland: Johan P. Jewett, 1856.

Du Bois, W. E. B. *Economic Co-Operation among Negro Americans*. Atlanta: Atlanta University Press, 1907.

Easton, William Edgar. *Christophe: A Tragedy in Prose of Imperial Haiti*. Los Angeles: Press Grafton Publishing, 1911.

Edelman, Marian Wright. *Lanterns: A Memoir of Mentors*. Boston: Beacon Press, 1999.

Educational Resources Information Center. *Myself and Women Heroes in My World: Sojourner Truth, Harriet Tubman, Queen Liliuokalani, Amelia Earhart, Maria Tallchief, Sonia Manzano*. Windsor, Calif.: National Women's History Project, U.S. Department of Education, Office of Educational Research and Improvement, Educational Resources Information Center, 1994.

Ehrlich, Leonard. *God's Angry Man*. New York: Press of the Reader's Club, 1932.

Elish, Dan. *Harriet Tubman and the Underground Railroad*. Brookfield, Conn.: Millbrook Press, 1993.

Emmons, E. Thayles. *The Story of Geneva*. Geneva, N.Y.: Geneva Daily Times, 1931.

Epstein, Sam, Beryl Williams Epstein, and Paul Frame. *Harriet Tubman: Guide to Freedom*. Champaign, Ill.: Garrard, 1968.

————. *Harriet Tubman: Guide to Freedom*, reprint. ed. New York: Dell, 1975.

Fabre, Geneviève, and Robert O'Meally, eds. *History and Memory in African-American Culture*. New York: Oxford University Press, 1994.

Felder, Deborah G. *The One Hundred Most Influential Women of All Time: A Ranking Past and Present*. Secaucus, N.J.: Carol Publishing, 1996.

Ferguson, Mary Anne. *Images of Women in Literature*, 5th ed. Boston: Houghton Mifflin, 1991.

Ferris, Jeri, and Karen Ritz. *Go Free or Die: A Story of Harriet Tubman*. Minneapolis: Carolrhoda Books, 1988.

Fields, Mamie Garvin, and Karen Fields. *Lemon Swamp and Other Places: A Carolina Memoir*. New York: Free Press, 1983.

Foner, Philip S., ed. *Paul Robeson Speaks: Writings, Speeches, Interviews, 1971–1974*. New York: Brunner, Mazel, 1978.

Foner, Philip S., and Robert James Branham, eds. *Lift Every Voice: African American Oratory, 1787–1900*. Tuscaloosa: University of Alabama Press, 1998.

Forrest, Diane. *The Adventurers Ordinary People with Special Callings.* Nashville: Wood Lake Books, 1984.

Gara, Larry. *The Liberty Line: The Legend of the Underground Railroad.* Lexington: University of Kentucky Press, 1961.

Garrison, Webb. *Amazing Women of the Civil War.* Nashville, Tenn.: Rutledge Hill Press, 1999.

Gaspar, David Barry, and Darlene Clark Hine. *More than Chattel: Black Women and Slavery in the Americas.* Bloomington: Indiana University Press, 1996.

Gayle, Sharon, and Felicia Marshall. *Harriet Tubman and the Freedom Train.* Ready-to-Read Level 3. New York: Aladdin, 2003.

Gersh, Harry. *Women Who Made America Great.* Philadelphia: Lippincott, 1962.

Giddings, Paula. *When and Where I Enter: The Impact of Black Women on Race and Sex in America.* New York: William Morrow, 1984.

Gittings, Joan Grenville, and T. Robbins. *Let My People Go: A Story of Escaped Slaves.* Round the World Histories. Amersham, U.K.: Hulton, 1971.

Gosda, Randy T. *Harriet Tubman.* Edina, Minn.: ABDO Publishing, 2002.

Grace Products Company. *The Quest for Freedom: In Search of Heroes.* Richardson, Tex.: Grace Products, 1992.

Grant, Callie Smith. *Harriet Tubman: "Moses" of Her People.* Uhrichsville, Ohio: Barbour Publishing, 1999.

Grant, Matthew G., John Keely, and Dick Brude. *Harriet Tubman: Black Liberator.* Mankato, Minn.: Creative Education, 1974.

Greenberg, Kenneth S. *Nat Turner: A Slave Rebellion in History and Memory.* New York: Oxford University Press, 2003.

Greenberg, Kenneth S., ed. *The Confessions of Nat Turner and Related Documents.* Boston: Bedford Books, 1996.

Greenfield, Eloise. *Honey, I Love, and Other Love Poems.* New York: Crowell, 1978.

Greenwood, Barbara. *The Last Safe House: A Story of the Underground Railroad.* Toronto: Kids Can Press, 1998.

Harlan, David. *The Degradation of American History.* Chicago: University of Chicago Press, 1997.

Harlan, Louis R. *Booker T. Washington: The Wizard of Tuskegee, 1901–15.* New York: Oxford University Press, 1983.

Harlow, Ralph. *Gerrit Smith: Philanthropist and Reformer.* New York: Henry Holt, 1939.

Halvorsen, Lisa. *Harriet Tubman.* San Diego, Calif.: Blackbirch Press, 2002.

Harriet Tubman, Freedom Fighter. Social Studies Series. Tigard, Ore.: C.C. Publications, 1986.

Hart, Albert Bushnell. *Slavery and Abolition, 1831–1841.* New York: Harper and Brothers, 1906.

Hart, J. Richard. *The Presbyterian Presence in Geneva, New York, 1798–1998*. Geneva, N.Y.: Presbyterian Church in Geneva, 1997.

Haskins, Jim. *Get on Board: The Story of the Underground Railroad*. New York: Scholastic, 1993.

Haynes, Elizabeth (Ross). *Unsung Heroes*. New York: DuBois and Dill, 1921.

Hedrick, Joan D. *Harriet Beecher Stowe: A Life*. New York: Oxford University Press, 1994.

Hedstrom, Deborah. *My American Heroes*. Sisters, Ore.: Gold'n'Honey, 1999.

Hedstrom, Deborah, and Sergio Martinez. *From Slavery to Freedom with Harriet Tubman*. Sisters, Ore.: Multnomah Publishers, 1997.

Heidish, Marcy. *A Woman Called Moses: A Novel Based on the Life of Harriet Tubman*. New York: Houghton Mifflin, 1976.

Hernblad, Gladys Kinard. *Harriet Tubman Rising: A Historical Novel*. N.p.: Xlibris Corporation, 2000.

Higginson, Mary Thacher, ed. *Cheerful Yesterdays*. Boston: Houghton Mifflin, 1898.

———. *Letters and Journals of Thomas Wentworth Higginson, 1846–1906*. Boston: Houghton Mifflin, 1921.

Higginson, Thomas Wentworth. *Contemporaries*. Boston: Houghton Mifflin, 1899.

———. *Part of a Man's Life*. Boston: Houghton Mifflin, 1905.

Hill, Errol, et al. *Black Heroes: Seven Plays*. New York: Applause Theatre Book Publishers, 1989.

Hinton, R. J. *John Brown and His Men*. New York: Funk and Wagnall's, 1894.

Hoobler, Dorothy, et al. *Next Stop, Freedom: The Story of a Slave Girl*. Englewood Cliffs, N.J.: Silver Burdett Press, 1991.

Hughes, Langston. *Famous American Negroes*. Famous Biographies for Young People. New York: Dodd, Mead, 1954.

Humez, Jean M. *Harriet Tubman: The Life and the Life Stories*. Madison: University of Wisconsin Press, 2003.

Humez, Jean M., ed. *Gifts of Power: The Life and Writings of Rebecca Cox Jackson, Black Preacher, Shaker Eldress*. Amherst: University of Massachusetts Press, 1984.

———. *Mother's First-Born Daughters: Early Shaker Writings on Women and Religion*. Bloomington: Indiana University Press, 1993.

Humphreville, Frances T., and David Hodges. *Harriet Tubman: Flame of Freedom*. Boston: Houghton Mifflin, 1967.

Hunter, Carol M. *To Set the Captives Free: Reverend Jermain Wesley Loguen and the Struggle for Freedom in Central New York, 1835–1872*. New York: Garland Publishing, 1993.

Jackson, Dave, Neta Jackson, and Julian Jackson. *Listen for the Whippoorwill*. Minneapolis: Bethany House, 1993.

Jacobs, Harriet A. *Incidents in the Life of a Slave Girl, Written by Herself*, ed. Jean Fagan Yellin. Cambridge, Mass.: Harvard University Press, 1987.

Janney, Rebecca Price. *Harriet Tubman*. Women of Faith Series. Minneapolis: Bethany House, 1999.

Johnson, Ann Donegan, and Steve Pileggi. *The Value of Helping: The Story of Harriet Tubman*. La Jolla, Calif.: Value Communications, 1979.

Johnson, Clifton H., ed. *God Struck Me Dead: Voices of Ex-Slaves*, 2d ed. Cleveland: Pilgrim Press, 1993.

Johnson, LaVerne C., and Craig Rex Perry. *Kumi and Chanti Tell the Story of Harriet Tubman*. Chicago: Empak Enterprises, 1992.

Johnston, Johanna, and Ann Grifalconi. *A Special Bravery*. New York: Dodd, Mead, 1967.

Jordan, Shirley, ed. *Broken Silences: Interviews with Black and White Women Writers*. New Brunswick, N.J.: Rutgers University Press, 1993.

Kaland, William J., Westinghouse Broadcasting Company, and John Hope Franklin. *The Great Ones*. New York: Washington Square Press, 1970.

Kallen, Stuart A., and Rosemary Wallner. *The Civil War and Reconstruction: A History of Black People in America, 1830–1880*. Minneapolis: Rockbottom Books, 1990.

Kammen, Michael. *Mystic Chords of Memory: The Transformation of Tradition in American Culture*. New York: Vintage Books, 1993.

Karcher, Carolyn L. *The First Woman of the Republic: A Cultural Biography of Lydia Maria Child*. Durham: Duke University Press, 1994.

Kay, Elizabeth. *Harriet Tubman*. San Diego, Calif.: Young People's Press, 1997.

Kelton, Nancy, and Peg Zych. *Rebel Slave*. Milwaukee: Raintree Editions, 1977.

Kent, Deborah, and Kathryn A. Quinlan. *Extraordinary People with Disabilities*. New York: Children's Press, 1996.

Kinard, Lee, and Daryl Shon Anderson. *Harriet Tubman's Famous Christmas Eve Raid*. Nashville: James C. Winston Publishers, 1995.

King, Coretta Scott. *Salute to Historic Black Achievers*. New York: Chelsea House, 1992.

King, Wilma. *Stolen Childhood: Slave Youth in Nineteenth-Century America*. Bloomington: Indiana University Press, 1995.

Kirschke, Amy Helene. *Aaron Douglas: Art, Race, and the Harlem Renaissance*. Biloxi: University of Mississippi Press, 1995.

Klingel, Cynthia Fitterer, John Keely, and Dick Brude. *Harriet Tubman: Black Liberator (1820–1913)*. Mankato, Minn.: Creative Education, 1987.

Kraus, Joanna Halpert, Janet Rubin, and Nellie. McCaslin. *Women of Courage: Five Plays*. Woodstock, Ill.: Dramatic, 2000.

Kudlinski, Kathleen. *Harriet Tubman: Freedom's Trailblazer*. New York: Simon and Schuster, 2002.

Kulling, Monica, and Teresa Flavin. *Escape North! The Story of Harriet Tubman*. New York: Random House, 1999.

Langellier, John P. *Myles Keogh: The Life and Legend of an "Irish Dragoon" in the Seventh Cavalry*. El Segundo, Calif.: Upton and Sons, 1991.

Larson, Kate Clifford. *Bound for the Promised Land: Harriet Tubman, Portrait of an American Heroine*. New York: Ballantine Books, 2004.

Lawrence, Jacob. *Harriet and the Promised Land* (1968), reprint. ed. New York: Aladdin Paperbacks, 1997.

Lawrence, Jacob, and Albright-Knox Art Gallery. *Jacob Lawrence: The Harriet Tubman Series, January 18–March 2, 1986, Albright-Knox Art Gallery, Buffalo, New York*. Buffalo: Buffalo Fine Arts Academy, 1986.

Lilley, Stephen R. *Fighters against American Slavery*. San Diego, Calif.: Lucent Books, 1999.

Livermore, Mary A. *My Story of the War: A Woman's Narrative of Four Years' Personal Experience in the Sanitary Service of the Rebellion*. Hartford, Conn.: A. D. Worthington, 1888.

Lowry, Beverly. *Harriet Tubman: Imagining a Life*. New York: Doubleday, 2007.

Lutz, Norma Jean. *Harriet Tubman*. Philadelphia: Chelsea House, 2000.

Mabee, Carleton. *Black Freedom: The Nonviolent Abolitionists from 1830 through the Civil War*. London: Macmillan, 1970.

Mabee, Carleton, and Susan Mabee Newhouse. *Sojourner Truth: Slave, Prophet, Legend*. New York: New York University Press, 1993.

Majors, M. A. *Noted Negro Women: Their Triumphs and Activities*. Chicago: Donohue and Henneberry, 1893.

Mara, Wil. *Harriet Tubman*. New York: Children's Press, 2002.

Mazzarella Communications Company and Sunburst Communications. *Heroes of Today and Yesterday: Harriet Tubman*. Pleasant, NY: Sunburst Communications, 1999.

McClard, Megan. *Harriet Tubman, Slavery and the Underground Railroad*. Englewood Cliffs, N.J.: Silver Burdett Press, 1991.

McDonough, Yona Zeldis. *Who Was Harriet Tubman?* New York: Grosset and Dunlap, 2002.

McDougall, Marion G. *Fugitive Slaves*. Boston: Ginn, 1891.

McGovern, Ann. *Runaway Slave: The Story of Harriet Tubman*. New York: Four Winds Press, 1965.

McGovern, Ann, and Richard M. Powers. *"Wanted Dead or Alive": The True Story of Harriet Tubman*. New York: Scholastic, 1965.

McGowan, James A. *Hear Today, Here to Stay: A Personal History of Rhythm and Blues*. Ampler, Penn.: Akashic Press, 1983.

———. *Station Master on the Underground Railroad: The Life and Letters of Thomas Garrett*. Moylan, Penn.: Whimsie Press, 1977.

————. *Station Master on the Underground Railroad: The Life and Letters of Thomas Garrett*, rev. ed. Jefferson, N.C.: McFarland, 2005.

McLoone, Margo. *Harriet Tubman: A Photo-Illustrated Biography*. Mankato, Minn: Bridgestone Press, 1997.

McMahon, Jean, ed. *Gifts of Power: The Writings of Rebecca Jackson, Black Visionary, Shaker Eldress*. Amherst: University of Massachusetts Press, 1981.

McMullan, Kate, and Steven Petruccio. *The Story of Harriet Tubman, Conductor of the Underground Railroad*. New York: Dell, 1991.

Meltzer, Ida S. *Harriet Tubman, the Moses of Her People*. Brooklyn, N.Y.: Book-Lab, 1971.

Merritt, Susan E. *Her Story: Women from Canada's Past*. St. Catharines, Ont.: Vanwell Publishing, 1993.

Metcalf, Doris Hunter. *Portraits in Black*. Carthage, Ill.: Good Apple, 1990.

Metcalf, George R. *Black Profiles*. New York: McGraw-Hill, 1968.

Meyer, Linda D., and J. Kerstetter. *Harriet Tubman: They Called Me Moses*. Windsor, Calif.: Parenting Press, 1988.

Miller, John. *Legends: Women Who Have Changed the World through the Eyes of Great Women Writers*. Novato, Calif.: New World Library, 1998.

Mitford, Jessica. *Grace Had an English Heart: The Story of Grace Darling Heroine and Victim*. London: Viking, 1988.

Moon, Spencer. *Reel Black Talk: A Sourcebook of Fifty American Filmmakers*. Westport, Conn.: Greenwood Press, 1997.

Mosher, Kiki. *Learning about Bravery from the Life of Harriet Tubman*. New York: PowerKids Press, 1996.

Myers, Mildred D. *Miss Emily: Emily Howland, Teacher of Freed Slaves, Suffragist and Friend of Susan B. Anthony and Harriet Tubman, with Excerpts from Her Diaries and Letters*. Charlotte Harbor, Fla.: Tabby House, 1998.

Nash, Gary B., and Charlotte A. Crabtree. *National Standards for United States History: Exploring the American Experience*. Los Angeles: National Center for History in the Schools, 1994.

Nash, Gary B., Charlotte Crabtree, and Ross E. Dunn. *History on Trial: Culture Wars and the Teaching of the Past*. New York: Vintage Books. 2000.

National Council of Negro Women. *The Historical Cookbook of the American Negro*. Washington, D.C.: Corporate Press, 1958.

National Women's History Week Project. *Harriet Tubman and the Underground Railroad*. Santa Rosa, Calif.: Project, 1982.

Nielsen, Nancy J. *Let Freedom Ring: Harriet Tubman*. Mankato, Minn.: Capstone Press, 2002.

Nies, Judith. *Seven Women: Portraits from the American Radical Tradition*. New York: Viking Press, 1977.

Noble, Bessie Cooper. *Ain't Sleep, Ain't Gone: A Tribute to Harriett [sic] Tubman*. Fayetteville, N.Y.: Manlius Publishing, 1978.

Noll, J. E. *Company of Prophets: African American Psychics, Healers and Visionaries.* St. Paul, Minn.: Llewellyn Publications, 1991.

Oates, Stephen B. *Woman of Valor: Clara Barton and the Civil War.* New York: Free Press, 1994.

Painter, Nell Irvin. *Sojourner Truth: A Life, a Symbol.* New York: W. W. Norton, 1996.

Paris, Peter J. *Slavery: History and Historians.* New York: Harper and Row, 1989.

Parker, John. *His Promised Land,* ed. Stuart Seely Sprague. New York: W. W. Norton, 1996.

Parrish, Anne. *A Clouded Star.* New York: Harper and Row, 1948.

Pendleton, Leila Amos. *A Narrative of the Negro.* Washington, D.C.: Press of R. L. Pendleton, 1912.

Penney, Sherry H., and James D. Livingston. *A Very Dangerous Woman: Martha Wright and Women's Rights.* Amherst: University of Massachusetts Press, 2004.

Perkins, Kathy A., et al. *Black Female Playwrights: An Anthology of Plays before 1950.* Blacks in the Diaspora. Bloomington: Indiana University Press, 1989.

Peterson, Carla L. *"Doers of the Word": African-American Women Speakers and Writers in the North (1830–1880).* New York: Oxford University Press, 1995.

Peterson, Merrill D. *Lincoln in American Memory.* New York: Oxford University Press, 1994.

Petry, Ann (Lane). *Harriet Tubman, Conductor on the Underground Railroad.* New York: Crowell, 1955.

———. *Harriet Tubman, Conductor on the Underground Railroad,* reprint. ed. New York: HarperCollins, 1983.

Polcovar, Jane. *Harriet Tubman.* Stamford, Conn.: Longmeadow Press, 1988.

Polcovar, Jane, and Alex Bloch. *Harriet Tubman, What Was It Like?* Chicago: Children's Press Choice, 1988.

Potter, Joan, and Constance Claytor. *African Americans Who Were First Illustrated with Photographs.* New York: Cobblehill Books, 1997.

Preston, Dickson J. *Young Frederick Douglass: The Maryland Years.* Baltimore: Johns Hopkins University Press, 1980.

Quarles, Benjamin. *Black Abolitionists.* New York: Oxford University Press, 1969.

Rau, Dana Meachen. *Harriet Tubman.* Compass Point Early Biographies. Minneapolis.: Compass Point Books, 2000.

Ravitch, Diane, and Chester E. Finn Jr. *What Do Our 17-Year-Olds Know? A Report on the First National Assessment of History and Literature.* New York: Harper and Row, 1987.

Ready, Dolores, and Rick Cooley. *Harriet Finds a Way: A Story about Harriet Tubman.* Stories about Christian Heroes. Minneapolis, Minn.: Winston Press, 1978.

Renehan Jr., Edward J. *The Secret Six: The True Tale of the Men Who Conspired with John Brown*. Columbia: University of South Carolina Press, 1997.

Richardson, Willis, and May Miller. *Negro History in Thirteen Plays*. Washington, D.C.: Associated Publishers, 1935.

Riggs, Marcia. *Can I Get a Witness? Prophetic Religious Voices of African American Women: An Anthology*. Maryknoll, N.Y.: Orbis Books, 1997.

Ringgold, Faith. *Aunt Harriet's Underground Railroad in the Sky*. New York: Crown Publishers, 1992.

Ripley, C. Peter, ed. *The Black Abolitionist Papers*, 5 vols. Chapel Hill: University of North Carolina Press, 1992.

Robinson, Randall. *The Debt: What America Owes to Blacks*. New York: E. P. Dutton, 2000.

Roehm, Michelle, and Jerry McCann. *Girls Who Rocked the World: Heroines from Harriet Tubman to Mia Hamm*. Hillsboro, Ore.: Beyond Words, 2000.

Rolka, Gail Meyer. *One Hundred Women Who Shaped World History*. San Francisco: Bluewood Books, 1994.

Rollins, Charlemae Hill. *They Showed the Way: Forty American Negro Leaders*. New York: Crowell, 1964.

Rosell, Lydia J. *Images of Auburn's Fort Hill Cemetery*. Charleston, S.C.: Arcadia Publishing, 2001.

Rowley, John. *Harriet Tubman: Lives and Times*. Des Plaines, Ill.: Heinneman Interactive Library, 1998.

Ryan, Bonnie Crarey, and Douglas V. Armstrong. *Archaeology of John Brown Hall at the Harriet Tubman Home: Site Report*. Syracuse University Archaeology Research Report, vol. 13, Syracuse University, Syracuse, N.Y., 2000.

Sabin, Francene, and Hal Frenck. *Harriet Tubman*. Mahwah, N.J.: Troll Associates, 1985.

Sadlier, Rosemary. *Harriet Tubman and the Underground Railroad: Her Life in the United States and Canada*. Toronto: Umbrella Press, 1996.

———. *Leading the Way, Black Women in Canada*. Toronto: Umbrella Press, 1994.

Salley, Columbus. *The Black One Hundred: A Ranking of the Most Influential African-Americans, Past and Present*. Secaucus, N.J.: Carol Publishing Group, 1992.

Sanborn, Franklin B. *Recollections of Seventy Years*, 2 vols. Boston: R. G. Badger, 1909.

Sanborn, Franklin B., ed. *The Life and Letters of John Brown*. New York: Negro Universities, 1885.

Schlesinger Jr., Arthur M. *The Disuniting of America: Reflections on a Multicultural Society*. New York: W. W. Norton, 1992.

Schraff, Anne E. *Harriet Tubman: Moses of the Underground Railroad*. African-American Biographies. Berkeley Heights, N.J.: Enslow, 2001.

Schroeder, Alan, and Jerry Pinkney. *Minty: A Story of Young Harriet Tubman*. New York: Dial Books for Young Readers, 1996.

Schwab, George. *Harriet Tubman, Who Led Slaves to Freedom*. African Home Library. London: Sheldon Press, 1900.

Schwartz, Barry. *Abraham Lincoln and the Forge of National Memory*. Chicago: University of Chicago Press, 2000.

Schwartz, Marie Jenkins. *Born in Bondage: Growing Up Enslaved in the Antebellum South*. Cambridge, Mass.: Harvard University Press, 2000.

Sernett, Milton. *North Star Country: Upstate New York and the African American Freedom Struggle*. Syracuse, N.Y.: Syracuse University Press, 2002.

Sickels, Eleanor. *In Calico and Crinoline*. New York: Viking Press, 1935.

Siebert, Wilbur H. *The Underground Railroad from Slavery to Freedom*. New York: Macmillan, 1899.

Singerton, Ronald. *Harriet Tubman and the Underground Railroad*. Northvale, N.J.: Santiliana, 1981.

Smith, Donald N. *Harriet Tubman (a Play)*. New York: New Dimensions, 1970.

Smith, Helene. *Aramenta: America's Most Unsung Civil War General*. Greensburg, Penn.: MacDonald and Sward, 1998.

Smith, Kathie Billingslea, and James E. Seward. *Harriet Tubman*. New York: Simon and Schuster, 1988.

Smith, Margaret Chase, H. Paul Jeffers, and Paul Giovanopoulos. *Gallant Women*. New York: McGraw-Hill, 1968.

Stanton, Elizabeth Cady. *Eighty Years and More: Reminiscences 1815–1897* (1898), reprint. ed. New York: Shocken Books, 1971.

Stanton, Elizabeth Cady, Susan B. Anthony, and Matilda Joslyn Gage, eds. *History of Woman Suffrage*, 6 vols. New York: National American Woman Suffrage Association, 1881–1922.

Sterling, Dorothy. *Freedom Train: The Story of Harriet Tubman*. Garden City, N.Y.: Doubleday, 1954.

Sterling, Dorothy, ed. *We Are Your Sisters: Black Women in the Nineteenth Century*. New York: W. W. Norton, 1984.

Sterling, Philip, Rayford Whittingham Logan, and Charles White. *Four Took Freedom: The Lives of Harriet Tubman, Frederick Douglass, Robert Smalls, and Blanche K. Bruce*. Garden City, N.Y.: Doubleday, 1967.

Stetson, Erlene, and Linda David. *Glorying in Tribulation: The Lifework of Sojourner Truth*. East Lansing: Michigan State University Press, 1994.

Stevenson, Brenda, ed. *The Journals of Charlotte Forten Grimké*. New York: Oxford University Press, 1988.

Still, William. *The Underground Railroad* (1872), reprint. ed. Chicago: Johnson Publishing, 1970.

Stone, Melissa. *You Don't Own Me!* Irvine, Calif.: Steck-Vaughn National Education Corporation, 1989.

Strong, Douglas M. *Perfectionist Politics: Abolitionism and the Religious Tensions of American Democracy*. Syracuse, N.Y.: Syracuse University Press, 1999.

Stuart, Marie. *Harriet Tubman. Black Leaders in the Freedom Struggle.* Bristol, U.K.: Central Bristol Adult Education Centre, 1991.

Sullivan, George. *Harriet Tubman.* New York: Scholastic, 2001.

Swift, Hildegarde Hoyt. *The Railroad to Freedom* reprint. ed. New York: Harcourt, Brace and World, 1960.

Swift, Hildegarde Hoyt, and James Henry Daugherty. *The Railroad to Freedom; a Story of the Civil War.* New York: Harcourt, Brace and World, 1932.

Taylor, John M. *William Henry Seward, Lincoln's Right Hand.* New York: HarperCollins, 1991.

Taylor, Kimberly Hayes. *Black Abolitionists and Freedom Fighters.* Minneapolis: Oliver Press, 1996.

Taylor, Marian. *Harriet Tubman.* New York: Chelsea House, 1991.

Taylor, Robert W. *Harriet Tubman: The Heroine in Ebony.* Boston: George E. Ellis, 1901.

Taylor, William R. *Cavalier and Yankee: The Old South and American National Character.* New York: George Braziller, 1961.

Terborg-Penn, Rosalyn. *African Women in the Struggle for the Vote, 1850–1920.* Bloomington: Indiana University Press, 1998.

Thelen, David, ed. *Memory and American History.* Bloomington: Indiana University Press, 1990.

Thompson-Peters, Flossie E. *Harriet Tubman: Freedom Fighter.* Los Angeles: Atlas Press, 1988.

Thoms, Adah B. *Pathfinders: A History of the Progress of Colored Graduate Nurses.* New York: Kay Printing House, 1929.

Troy, Don. *Harriet Ross Tubman.* Chanhassen, Minn.: Child's World, 1999.

Twain, Mark. *Personal Recollections of Joan of Arc,* reprint. ed. San Francisco: Ignatius Press, 1989.

Van Deusen, Glyndon G. *William Henry Seward.* New York: Oxford University Press, 1967.

Venet, Wendy Hammand. *Neither Ballots nor Bullets: Women Abolitionists and the Civil War.* Charlottesville: University of Virginia Press, 1991.

Voina, Vladimir Alekseevich. *Konduktor "Tainoi Zheleznoi Dorogi": Garriet Tabmen, 1820- 1913; Stranitsy Geroicheskoi Zhisni.* Moscow: Mysl, 1965.

Ward, Francis, and James Edward Davis. *Harriet Tubman, Leader of the Underground Railroad.* New York: Scott, Foresman, 1970.

Ward, Geoffrey C. *Not for Ourselves Alone: The Story of Elizabeth Cady Stanton and Susan B. Anthony.* New York: Alfred A. Knopf, 1999.

Washington, Booker T. *The Story of the Negro: The Rise of the Race from Slavery.* New York: Doubleday, 1909.

Washington, Margaret, ed. *Narrative of Sojourner Truth.* New York: Vintage Books, 1993.

Washington, Mary Helen. *Invented Lives: Narratives of Black Women, 1860–1960*. Garden City, N.Y.: Doubleday, 1987.

Watson, Daniel W., et al. *Harriet Tubman: The Road to Freedom*. Reading Instruction through Literature: Teachers' Reference Guide, Fifth Grade. Clovis, Calif.: Clovis Unified School District, 1986.

Weidt, Maryann N. *Harriet Tubman*. Minneapolis: Lerner Publications, 2003.

Weisenfeld, Judith, and Richard Newman, eds. *This Far by Faith: Readings in African-American Women's Religious Autobiography*. New York: Routledge, 1996.

West, Guida, and Rhoda Lois Blumberg, eds. *Women and Social Protest*. New York: Oxford University Press, 1990.

Wheat, Ellen. *Jacob Lawrence: American Painter*. Seattle: University of Washington Press, 1986.

White, Deborah Gray. *Ar'n't I a Woman? Female Slaves in the Plantation South*. New York: W. W. Norton, 1985.

Williams, T. Harry. *Lincoln and His Generals*. New York: Alfred A. Knopf, 1952.

Wilson, Forrest. *Crusader in Crinoline*. New York: J. B. Lippincott, 1941.

Winders, Gertrude Hecker, and William K. Plummer. *Harriet Tubman, Freedom Girl*. Indianapolis: Bobbs-Merrill, 1969.

Wolff, Christian, and Susan Griffin. *I Like to Think of Harriet Tubman*. New York: C. F. Peters, 1985.

Woodward, Helen Beal. *The Bold Women*. New York: Farrar, Straus and Young, 1953.

Work, Monroe. *Negro Year Book, 1912*. Tuskegee, Ala.: Negro Yearbook Publishing, Tuskegee Institute, 1912.

———. *Negro Year Book, 1913*. Tuskegee, Ala.: Negro Yearbook Publishing, Tuskegee Institute, 1913.

Yellin, Jean Fagan. *Harriet Jacobs: A Life*. Boulder, Colo.: Basic Civitas Books, 2004.

Young, James O. *Black Writers of the Thirties*. Baton Rouge: Louisiana State University Press, 1973.

MULTIMEDIA

Bagwell, Orlando, et al. *The American Experience*. WETA-TV, 1990.

Benjamin, Anne, and Ellen Beier. *Young Harriet Tubman, Freedom Fighter*. Macintosh/Windows software, v. 1.0. Troll Communications, Mahwah, N.J., 1996.

Brannon, Jean Marilyn, and Dorothy Washington. *The Negro Woman*. Folkways Records, 1966.

Bright Morning Star (musical group). *Arisin.'* Rainbow Snake Records, Greenfield, Mass., 1981.

Brittany Meets Harriet Tubman. Wildflower Productions, Athens, Ala., 1996.

Edwards, Leo, and Anthony Martone. *Lullaby from Harriet Tubman: For High Voice with Piano Accompaniment*. Willis Music, Cincinnati, 1983.

Elder, Lonne, et al. *A Woman Called Moses*. Xenon Home Video, Santa Monica, Calif., 1992.

Fabian, Rhonda, et al. *Harriet Tubman*. Black Americans of Achievement Video Collection. Schlessinger Video Productions, Bala Cynwyd, Penn., 1992.

Foster, Gloria., et al. *The Great Ones: Excerpts from a Series of Radio Programs Broadcast by Group W*. Westinghouse Broadcasting Company, 1971.

Franks, Saundra Dunson, et al. *"Hats": A Tribute to Harriet Tubman*. Theatrical History, 1981.

Guthrie, Woody, and Cisco Houston. *Long Ways to Travel*. Smithsonian/Folkways Records, Washington, D.C., 1994.

Harriet Tubman (musical group). *I Am a Man*. Knitting Factory Records, New York, 1998.

Harriet Tubman. Juba Series. International Instructional Television Cooperative and Washington Educational Telecommunications Association, Washington, D.C., 1977.

Harriet Tubman and the Underground Railroad. CRM McGraw-Hill Films, New York, 1972.

Harriet Tubman Tells Her Story. America's Multicultural Heroes. Society for Visual Education, Chicago, 1993.

Harrison, Michael. *Harriet Tubman: Leader of Slaves*. Idiom Controlled Readers, Biographies from American History. Activity Records, Freeport, N.Y., 1978.

Hurtz, William, et al. *The Gift of the Black Folk*. Pyramid Film and Video, Santa Monica, Calif., 1978.

Logan, Michael, et al. *Black Americans of Achievement*. Schlessinger, Bala Cynwyd, Penn., 1992.

Mannucci, Mark, dir. *Reading Rainbow: Follow the Drinking Gourd*. Lancit Media Productions and Great Plains National Instructional Television Library, Lincoln, Neb., 1993.

Near, Holly, and Ronnie Gilbert. *Lifeline*. Redwood Records, Oakland, Calif., 1983.

Nelson, Novella, et al. *Harriet Tubman and the Underground Railroad: You Are There*. CBS News and BFA Educational Media, New Brunswick, N.J., 1971.

Petry, Ann, and Peter Francis James. *Harriet Tubman, Conductor on the Underground Railroad*. Biography on cassette. Recorded Books, Prince Frederick, Md., 1999.

Rich, Richard, et al. *Harriet Tubman*. Animated Hero Classics. Warner-Nest Animation, Irving, Tex., 1996.

Richards, Lloyd. *Harriet Tubman and the Underground Railroad*. Phoenix/BFA Educational Media, New Brunswick, N.J., 1971.

Robbins, John, et al. *The Legend of Harriet Tubman*. Juba Series. PBS Video, Alexandria, Va., 1978.

Smith, Harry, et al. *Biography of the Millennium: One Hundred People, One Thousand Years*. Arts and Entertainment Home Video and New Video Group, 1999.

Taylor, Marian, et al. *Harriet Tubman: Antislavery Activist*. Black Americans of Achievement Series. Schlessinger Video Productions, Bala Cynwyd, Penn., 1992.

Troll Associates. *Harriet Tubman*. Filmstrip, 43 frames, 1969.

Wendkos, Paul, dir. *A Woman Called Moses*. Xenon Home Video, Santa Monica, Calif., 1992.

Wiley, Foster, et al. *Steal Away: The Harriet Tubman Story*. National Geographic Society Television Educational Films, Washington, D.C., 1997.

INDEX

Note: HT refers to Harriet Tubman.

Auburn, New York (*continued*)
39, 75, 94, 98, 100, 112, 145, 149, 152,
156, 161, 165, 167, 171, 200, 211, 227,
234, 236, 248, 256, 259–60, 262, 272,
309, 316; struggle to honor HT and,
247, 251, 274–75; support for HT in,
5, 12, 93, 95, 97–98, 111, 113, 115–17,
132, 147, 179, 183, 186–87, 262–63,
265, 269–70, 273–74; visits by
notables to, 235–56, 278, 303, 309
Auburn Theological Seminary, 111–12,
270
*Aunt Harriet's Underground Railroad in
the Sky* (Ringgold, 1992), 37, *plate 4*

Bailey, Josiah (Joe), 53, 322
Barnes, LeShonda, 275
Barnes, Paul, 159
Barnes, V. K., 86, 116
Barnett, Claude A., 228
Barton, Clara, 30, 342 n.45
Bazzel Methodist Episcopal Church,
281–82, 283 (*fig.* 70), 287, 366 n.84
Beaufort, South Carolina, 53, 86, 88,
116, 170
Bennett, Lerone, Jr., 276
Bentley, Judith, 32
Bethune, Mary McLeod, 29, 226
biographers of HT. *See* Bradford,
Sarah H.; Cheney, Edna B. Dow;
Clinton, Catherine; Conrad, Earl;
Humez, Jean M.; Larson, Kate
Clifford; Lowry, Beverly; Mc-
Gowan, James A.; Petry, Ann; Sad-
lier, Rosemary; Sanborn, Franklin
B.; Sterling, Dorothy; Swift, Hilde-
garde Hoyt
*Biography of the Millennium: 100
People—1, 000 Years* (Smith, 1999), 1
Black Abolitionist Papers (Ripley, ed.),
62
Black Moses: artistic interpretations

of, 15, 228; as name for HT, 4–5,
48, 50, 67, 83, 94, 105, 110, 117–19,
124–25, 127, 130, 132, 166–67, 170,
172, 178–80, 183–84, 234, 244, 247,
249–50, 259, 263–64, 278, 290, 299,
309, 312, 314, 318, 319; pointing to
biblical Moses, 4, 13, 15, 17, 41, 44,
49–50, 52–54, 66, 68, 72, 75, 87, 95,
101, 105, 108, 114, 130–31, 149, 168,
172, 241, 287–88, 293–94, 304
Blackwater National Wildlife Refuge,
283–84
Blackwell, Alice Stone, 154–55
Blackwell, G. L., 180
Blatch, Harriet Stanton, 155
Blight, David, 3, 7
Blockson, Charles L., 71
Bloomer, Amelia, 251
bloomer dress, 112, 161, 251
Bordewich, Fergus, 71, 300, 317
Boston, Massachusetts: abolitionists
in support of HT and, 49, 57, 113,
301; HT's visits to, 48–50, 53, 77, 79,
81–82, 93, 113, 153–55, 161, 172; John
Brown in, 80; monument to HT in,
244–45, 314
*Bound for Canaan: The Underground
Railroad and the War for the Soul of
America* (Bordewich, 2005), 317
*Bound for the Promised Land: Harriet
Tubman, Portrait of an American
Hero* (Larson, 2004), 20, 295, 299–
300
Bowley, Harkless, 12, 211
Bowley, Kessiah, 321, 326 n.4
Brackett, Edward A., 81
Bradford, John Melancthon, 108
Bradford, Sarah H., 4, 12, 109 (*fig.*
30); apology of, for hasty prepara-
tion of *Scenes*, 115; appearance of,
108; biographical sketch of, 107–9;
family of, 108–9; Geneva back-

ground of, 111-12; influence of, on
other authors, 4, 92, 102, 132, 204-5;
on John Tubman, 17; Nalle rescue
and, 82-85; on number of people
HT rescued, 60, 304; on question of
number of HT's trips, 58-59, 63-66,
304; on question of size of reward,
66-67; on religious character of HT,
131, 135-39; religious views of, 132;
as source of myths about HT, 44,
53, 58-59, 61, 64, 66-67, 82, 253,
294, 317, 323; writings and publications of, 21, 108-9, 340 n.12. See
also *Harriet, the Moses of Her People*
(Bradford, 1886); *Scenes in the Life
of Harriet Tubman* (Bradford, 1869)
Brickler, Alice Lucas, 12, 142-43, 189,
210-13, 306-7, 351 n.56
Briggs, Cyril, 195, 353 n.82
Briley-Strand, Gwendolyn, 240
Brister, Charles W., 187, 190
Brittany Meets Harriet Tubman (Wild-
flower Productions, 1996), 37
Brodess, Edward, 15, 143, 239, 286,
308
Brodess, Eliza Ann, 19, 119
Brooks, E. U. A., 149, 175-77, 180-81,
186-87, 193
Brown, Hallie Q., 25
Brown, Jeannetta Welch, 227
Brown, John, 21, 72, 76, 77 (*fig. 23*),
78-82, 181, 189, 216-17, 220, 258
Brown, John, Jr. 80
Brown, Sterling, 216-18, 353 n.79
Brown, William Wells, 47, 50, 129,
134, 343 n.3
Bryant, Gladys Stewart, 182, 266, 277
Bryant, Judith, 273, 277, 302 (*fig. 75*),
303, 370 n.57
Buckmaster, Henrietta, 230, 355 n.8
Bucktown, Maryland, 15, 39, 279 (*fig.
68*), 283-84, 287, 308

Bucktown Village Store, 283, 284 (*fig.
71*), 287, 366 n.85
Burns, Ken, 159
Burroughs, Margaret Taylor Goss,
243
Bush, President George H. W., 250
Byrd, Samuel, 16, 18

Cameron, Angus, 214-15, 217
Canada West, 12, 41, 56, 79, 211. *See
also* St. Catharines, Ontario
Canadian Union of Postal Workers,
249
Carlson, Judy, 31
Carnicelli, Melina, 364 n.62
Carroll, Anna Ella, 90
Carter, Christine, 267-68
Carter, Elmer A., 200, 218
Carter, Florence, 13
Carter, Guthrie, 236-37, 264, 318 (*fig.
79*)
Carter, Paul G., 266-68, 278
Carver, George Washington, 11, 23,
233, 268
Casamajor, Louis, 141
Catt, Carrie Chapman, 152 (*fig. 39*),
153, 155, 301
Cazenovia Anti-Fugitive Slave Law
Convention, 43 (*fig. 11*)
Central Presbyterian Church
(Auburn, N.Y.), 117, 179, 187
Chaffin, Lida Gaskin, 312
Chapell, Helen, 284
Charles, Nelson, 96. *See also* Davis,
Nelson
Charles E. Stewart Relief Corps, 181
Chase, Donald A., 256
Chatham, Canada West, 79, 211
Cheney, Edna B. Dow, 21, 82, 96
Cheney, Lee, 146 (*fig. 36*)
Cheney, Lynne, 35, 329 n.70
Child, Lydia M., 52

children and slavery, 14

Childress, Alice, 157, 238

Citron, Alice, 328 n.44

Civil War: HT's pension and pay claims from, 95–97, 99–100, 104, 276, 309, 337–38 n.88; 338 n.93; 338–89 n.96; HT's service in the, 2, 4, 22, 39, 53, 72, 75, 85–87, 89, 92–94, 100, 102, 134, 150–52, 160–61, 170, 172, 175, 181, 189–90, 309, 314, 339 n.100

Clark, James Freeman, 59

Clarke, James B., 156, 169

Cleghorn, Sarah N., 206–7

Clinton, Catherine, 78, 295, 300–303, 306, 314, 369 n.38. See also *Harriet Tubman* (Clinton, 2004)

Clinton, Senator Hillary Rodham, 99, 245, 268, 338–39, n.96

Clouded Star (Parrish, 1948), 230–32

Cobblestone, 31

Cohen, Earl, 201, 293. *See also* Conrad, Earl

Collins, Paul, 68, *plate 6*

Colman, Lucy, 161

Combahee River raid, 88, 89 (*fig. 26*), 90–92, 218, 337 n.72

Commager, Henry Steele, 31, 33

commodification and commercialization of HT name, 38, 251, 252 (*fig. 61*), 253

Commonweath (Boston newspaper), 15, 21, 46, 56–58, 91–92, 107, 118

Conrad, Anna Alyse, 198–99

Conrad, Earl: Alice H. Brickler and, 12, 210–11; biographical sketch of, 200–203; Carrie Chapman Catt and, 152–59; death of, 198, 224; Eva S. Northrup and, 212–13; Harkless Bowely and, 13, 142–44, 211–12; Hildegarde Swift's book and, 92, 204–6; on HT and Combahee raid,

91–92; on HT and John Brown, 78–79; on HT as black heroine, 61, 66, 101, 195–96; on HT as "General Tubman," 74–78; on HT as suffragist, 152; on HT's death, 176; on HT's pre-escape life, 22; on HT's religious self, 142–44; on HT's visionary experiences, 139–43; left-wing politics of, 203, 207; as "modern abolitionist," 198–200, 209–10; Paul Erlich and, 208–9; poem on Paul Robeson and, 220–21; publishing record of, 224, 354 n.114; question of number of HT's trips and, 61–62; question on number of people HT rescued and, 65–66; ss *Harriet Tubman* and, 227; Wood manuscript and, 101–2. See also *Harriet Tubman* (Conrad, 1943)

Conway, Moncure D., 81

Cooley, Rick, 17

Cooper, James Fenimore, 47

Copes-Johnson, Pauline, 273, 310, 311 (*fig. 78*), 312–13, 364–65 n.70, 369 n.42, 369–70 n.43

Coppin, Fanny Jackson, 162, 164

Creighton, John, 280–81, 318

Crisis (NAACP), 218, 220, 223

Crusader News Agency, 195–96

Cunningham, Fern, 244–45; HT Boston monument and, 244 (*fig. 60*)

Daily Worker, 207, 209

Darby, J. C., 74, 75, 103

Darling, Grace, 44, 68, 114, 121–22, 123 (*fig. 34*), 330 n.3, 342 n.44

Davis, Charles Nelson. *See* Davis, Nelson

Davis, Danny, 245

Davis, Gertie, 146 (*fig. 36*)

Davis, Jefferson, 37, 121, 246, 251

Davis, Nelson (husband of HT), 96–

97, 116, 146 (*fig. 36*), 147, 257, 309,
337–38 n.88

Dean, Gail, 286

DeDecker, Jane, 245

Degler, Carl, 34

dialect usage, 326–27, n.13

dictated letters, 107, 339–40 n.2

Dix, Dorothea, 29, 86, 336 n.48

D. M. Osborne and Company, 147,
187

Dolan, Jay P., 31

Donovan, Sam, 74

Dorchester County, Maryland: denial
of memorial to HT, 285; HT's birthplace in, 15, 287, 308; HT's early
years in, 15, 20, 56, 280, 283, 287;
HT's rescue trips from, 56, 62, 80;
remembering HT in, 246, 249, 279,
281, 283, 285–87

Douglas, Aaron, 225, 256 (*fig. 54*), 355
n.1; *plate 7*

Douglass, Frederick, 61; as American
icon, 2, 7, 23, 67, 169, 192, 358 n.48,
plate 5; birthplace of, 166–67, 287;
death of, 215; Earl Conrad's admiration of, 215; HT and, 67, 137, 166;
John Brown and, 79; literacy of, 105,
129, 169, 179, 183, 215; monument of,
244; religious status of, 179

Drake, Frank C., 168–69

dramatists and HT, 239–41

dreams and foreknowledge of HT, 22,
39, 79, 115, 120–21, 134–44, 149

Drew, Benjamin, 15, 41

Du Bois, W. E. B., 32, 64, 185, 221,
234, 249

Durant, Henry K., 86

Dwight, Ed, 245

Dyer, Mary, 357 n.41

Ehrlich, Leonard, 208

Emancipation Proclamation, 148, 167

Empire State Federation of Women's
Clubs, 177, 181–82, 272 (*fig. 67*), 278

Ennals family, 323, 369 n.38

Episcopal church, 251

Eponyms for HT, 2

Epstein, Beryl, 28

Epstein, Sam, 28

Eriksson, Paul, 197

Escape North! (Kulling, 1999), 36 (*fig.
10*), 37

Eusebius, Mary, 232

Evans, Ilene, 239

Eve, Arthur O., 251

Fairbanks, Calvin, 71

Fairfield, John, 71

Falk, Leslie A., 86

Federal Writers' Project, 26, 203

Fifteenth Amendment, 153

Fifty-fourth Massachusetts Regiment
Volunteer Infantry, 92, 93, 175

films, videos, and TV programs about
HT, 37–38, 64, 234–38, 325 n.1, 356
n.23

Finn, Chester, 1

Finney, Charles G., 108, 112

First South Carolina Volunteers, 50

Fitzgerald, Bertram A., Jr., 30, 328
n.51, *plate 3*

Flavin, Teresa, 36–37, 71

Flight to Freedom (WXXI TV, Rochester,
1995), 235

Fort Hill Cemetery (Auburn, N.Y.),
181, 182 (*fig. 44*), 187, 194 (*fig. 48*),
256, 272, 278, 316, 363 n.52

Fort Wagner assault, 92–94, 177, 206

Forten, Charlotte, 53, 86, 139, 162

Foster, Katharine Rose, 204

Fourteenth Amendment, 131

Fowler, Henry, 83, 116–18

Framingham, Massachusetts, 48

Frederick Douglass monument, 244

Humez, Jean M. (*continued*)
144, 266, 295–98, 301–16, 318, 321–
23, 326 n.13, 342–43 n.52, 370 n.52.
See also *Harriet Tubman: The Life
and the Life Stories* (Humez, 2003)
Humphreville, Frances T., 28
Hunter, David, 85–86, 88
Hurkos, Peter, 344 n.34
Hutchinson, Anne, 357 n.41

iconic status of HT, 15, 49, 63, 149,
163–64, 248–49
iconic stories about HT: apple trees,
planting of, 168–69; battle for
Charles Nalle, 84; book, reading
of, upside down, 68, 70 (*fig. 18*),
312; chopping wood, 17, 18 (*fig. 2*);
chickens, diversionary use of, 69, 70
(*fig. 19*); escape, 21; flax-processing
work, 17; head injury, 16–17, 18
(*fig. 1*); gun, use of, 69, 71 (*fig. 20*),
241, 333 n.86; herbs and roots, use
of, 86; laudanum, use of, to quiet
infants, 57; manure pile, hiding in,
214; muskrat-trap work, 16, 284;
never lost a passenger remark, 68;
onions and garlic, 48; pigs, eating
with, 19 (*fig. 3*), 22; potato holes,
hiding in, 69, 333 n.84; quilt, given
by, 21; railway car incident, 94,
sleeping fits, 140–41, 239, 327 n.16;
sugar, stealing of, 17, 22; weaving
work, 116; whippings, 21
illiteracy of HT, 49, 104–6, 301, 305
International Publishers, 221
International Workers Order, 215, 354
n.100
Internet and HT, 37, 87, 291, 299

Jacobs, Harriet A., 14
Jaeckel, John, 179, 187

Jeffers, H. Paul, 30
Joan of Arc, 25, 68, 114, 121, 122 (*fig.
33*), 123, 145, 185, 196, 214, 238, 295
John Brown Hall, 258, 259 (*fig. 64*),
268
Johnson, Ann Donegan, 30
Johnson, James Weldon, 167, 218
Johnson, Oliver, 125, 166, 181
Johnson, William, 229, *plate 8*
Johnston, Johanna, 29
Jones, Gwen, 275
Jones, John W., 189, 349 n.56
Jones, Joyce, 277, 312, 364–65 n.70
Journal of Negro History, 26, 34
juvenile literature and HT, 11–12, 23,
25, 29, 30, 40, 233

Kammen, Michael, 7, 39
Kander, Susan, 241, 357 n.33
Keogh, Myles, 187, 349 n.53
King, Coretta Scott, 32–33
King, Martin Luther, Jr., 11, 29, 232,
246, 249–50
Ku Klux Klan, 272, 275
Kulling, Monica, 36–37, 71

Larson, C. Kay, 90
Larson, Kate Clifford, 15, 19, 20, 54,
63–64, 67, 90–91, 280, 287, 295,
299, 300 (*fig. 75*), 301–15, 321–23,
326–27 n.13, 327 n.16, 364 n.70, 368
n.13, 369 n.38. See also *Bound for
the Promised Land: Harriet Tubman, Portrait of an American Hero*
(Larson, 2004)
Lawrence, Jacob, 15, 228, 229 (*fig. 56*),
355 n.6, *plate 1, plate 2*
Leake, Hattie M., 276
Let My People Go (Buckmaster, 1941),
230, 355 n.8
Lewis, Edmonia, 165

Moses (Old Testament prophet), 42, 117–18, 137

Mott, Lucretia Coffin, 133 (*fig. 35*)

Musgrave, Thea, 238

musicians and HT, 241–43

Myohoji, Nipponzan, 279

Nalle, Charles, 82–84, 85 (*fig. 24*), 118, 218, 290, 335 n.38

naming HT in public spaces, 38, 246–48

National American Woman Suffrage Association (NAWSA), 153

National Association for the Advancement of Colored People (NAACP), 30

National Association of Colored Women (NACW), 25, 162, 163 (*fig. 41*)

National Council for History Standards, 1, 34–35

National Council of Negro Women (NCNW), 13, 226–27

National Freedom Trail Act of 1990, 238, 243

National Park Service, 255–56, 268, 270, 290, 359 n.1, 362 n.43

National Standards for United States History (1994), 34–35

Near, Holly, 241–42

Negro History Bulletin, 223

Negro History in Thirteen Plays (Miller and Richardson, 1935), 240–41

Negro World Digest, 218

New Bedford, Massachusetts, 80, 202, 335 n.29

New England Freedmen's Aid Society, 57

New York State Woman Suffrage Association, 150

Newman, Allen G., 183

Nightingale, Florence, 68, 114, 121, 123–24

Noble, Bessie Cooper, 182, 272, 318 (*fig. 79*), 319, 370 n.57

Norris family, 260

Northrup, Eva Stewart, 68, 114, 121, 123–24, 205, 212–13, 295

North-side View of Slavery (Drew, 1856), 15

Nozzolio, Michael F., 251

nursing profession, 87

O'Brien, Charles, 147

oral history (orature), 50, 53–54, 130, 310, 313

Osborne, Eliza Wright, 133 (*fig. 35*), 154

Osgood, Lucy, 301

Oxford Companion to American History (2001), 62

Painter, Nell Irvin, 160

Papkov, Matthew, 273

Parker, John D., 69

Parrish, Anne, 26, 230

Parsons Creek, 15, 287

Pataki, Governor George, 180, 251

Payne, Daniel A., 25

Payne, Sereno E., 97–98

Pearl, Nana Ama, 272

Pendleton, Leila Amos, 23–24

Peterson, Carla, 3, 49, 160, 163

Peterson, Eliza E., 175

Peterson, Merrill D., 7

Petry, Ann, 26–27, 232

Phillips, Wendell, 113, 115, 137, 181, 215

Pinkney, Jerry, 35–36, 249

Pitcher, Molly (Mary Ludwig Hays McCauly), 341 n.23

Pius, Robert, 243, 295

Plowden, J., 91
poets and HT, 38–39, 240–43
Porter, Alex, 243
Port Royal Experiment, 85, 88, 162

Quakers, 21, 44, 52, 132, 188, 205, 241
Quarles, Benjamin, 3–4, 30–31

Railroad to Freedom (Swift, 1932),
    25–26, 76 (*fig. 22*), 92–93, 112, 201–3,
    204 (*fig. 51*), 205–10
Rankin-Fulcher, Elizabeth, 250
Ravitch, Diane, 1
Ready, Dolores, 17, 19
Reconstruction, 2, 4, 96, 127, 131, 138
Reddick, L. D., 219
Renehan, Edward J., Jr., 79
reward for HT's capture, 66–68, 309,
    315
Riley, W. H., 140–41
Rimensnyder, Sara, 73
Ringgold, Faith, 37
Rit, 119, 211. *See also* Green, Harriet
    "Rit"
Robinson, Randall, 245–46
Robinson, Walter, 242
Rochester Ladies' Anti-Slavery So-
    ciety, 55
Rochester Women's Rights Conven-
    tion, 68
Roosevelt, Eleanor, 30, 155, 206–7, 226,
    260, 359 n.65
Ross, Araminta (Minty), 15, 22, 35, 50,
    97, 308. *See also* Tubman, Harriet
Ross, Benjamin (brother of HT). *See*
    Stewart, James
Ross, Benjamin (father of HT), 15, 110,
    119–20, 135, 308, 312
Ross, Harriet Green "Rit" (mother of
    HT), 119, 211, 308
Ross, Harriet. *See* Tubman, Harriet

Ross, Henry (brother of HT). *See*
    Stewart, William Henry
Ross, Robert (brother of HT). *See*
    Stewart, John T.
Runaway Slave (McGovern, 1965), 28,
    29 (*fig. 7*), 233
Ryan, Bonnie, 281, 366 n.82

Sadlier, Rosemary, 288, 361–62 n.33,
    367 n.96
Salem Chapel, British Methodist
    Episcopal Church, St. Catharines,
    287–88, 289 (*fig. 72*)
Sanborn, Franklin, B., 46 (*fig. 14*);
    battle for Charles Nalle and, 82;
    Combahee raid and, 91; *Common-
    wealth* article on HT and, 15–19;
    dependence of other authors on, 21,
    24, 50, 58, 118; description of HT's
    religiosity and, 137, 139; enumera-
    tion of HT's rescue missions and, 56,
    62–65, 80–81, 321–23; interpretation
    of HT's importance and, 21, 42,
    46–47, 52, 57, 125, 145, 208; report
    of HT's reaction to death of John
    Brown and, 81; views of, on HT as
    conductor, 134–36
Saxton, Rufus B., 87–88, 115, 338 n.93
Scenes in the Life of Harriet Tubman
    (Bradford, 1869), 21, 24, 116 (*fig.
    32*); comparison of, to *Moses* (1886),
    127–29; description of, 107; eclec-
    tic structure of, 115–20, 125; hasty
    preparation of, 58, 112; influence of,
    on other HT books, 21, 102, 230, 253,
    294; printer of, 117; publication of,
    340 n.4; purpose for, 112–13, 125;
    Sarah Bradford's efforts to corrobo-
    rate, 125; sources for, 114–15; sub-
    scriptions for, 113–15
Schlesinger, Arthur M., Jr., 34

Stone, Lucy, 153–54

Stowe, Harriet Beecher, 30, 33, 110, 138, 145, 214–15, 232

Strauss, Harold, 217

Stutler, Boyd B., 160

Suspension Bridge, 53, 54 (*fig. 16*), 55–56

Swift, Hildegarde Hoyt, 25, 76, 92, 201, 204–10, 230, 294, 319, 337 n.74

Swift, Isabella, 112

tablet in honor of HT, 5, 24, 178, 183–84, 186–87, 189–90, 191 (*fig. 47*), 193–94, 301

Talbert, Mary Burnett, 164, 179–81, 190, 192

Tatlock, Helen, 353 n.82, 370 n.44

Taylor, Marian W., 32

Taylor, Robert W., 171–72

Taylor, Susie King, 99 (*fig. 27*)

television programs, films, and videos about HT, 37–38, 64, 234–38, 325 n.1, 356 n.23

Telford, Emma Paddock, 49, 147, 187, 193–94

Terrell, Mary Church, 162

Thalinger, Frederic Jean, 230, 231 (*fig. 57*)

Thirteenth Amendment, 55, 131

Thompson, Anthony, 15, 19, 287

Thompson, Joseph Jamison, 270

Thompson, Thelma, 182

Thompson Memorial African Methodist Episcopal Zion Church (Auburn, N.Y.), 178, 256, 260, 269–70, 271 (*fig. 66*), 311

tourism, HT: in Auburn, N.Y., 248, 256, 262, 264–67, 270, 272, 276–79, 290; in Bucktown, Md., 279–81, 283, 287; in Cambridge, Md., 281, 284–87, 290; in Dorchester County, Md., 279–81, 283, 285–87, 290; in St.

Catharines, Ontario, 287, 290; in Troy, N.Y., 290

Towns, Edolphus, 101

Travers, Addie Clash, 280–81

Trickster (HT as) 69, 130

Troy, New York, 82–85, 88, 118, 290

True Ballad of Harriet Tubman (Cleghorn, 1933), 206–7.

Truth, Sojourner, 3, 22–24, 31, 37, 48–49, 110, 153, 157, 158 (*fig. 40*), 159–64, 167, 179, 234, 240, 249, 251, 296, 339 n.1

Tubman, Harriet, 51 (*fig. 15*), 103 (*fig. 28*), 106 (*fig. 29*), 146 (*fig. 36*), 173 (*fig. 42*), 174 (*fig. 43*); Abraham Lincoln and 52, 161–62; Auburn, N.Y., friends and supporters of, 111–12, 132–32; back-pay and pension claims of, 94–95, 134–35; baptism of, 345 n.35; birth of, 15–16; brain surgery on, 344 n.20; burial of, 182 (*fig. 44*), 183, 256; Canadian stay of, 41–42; charitable activities of, 120–21, 145–48; Charles Nalle rescue and, 82–85; Combahee raid and, 88–90; comparison of, to Florence Nightingale, 68, 114, 121, 123–24, 295; comparison of, to Grace Darling, 44, 68, 114, 121–23; comparison of, to Joan of Arc, 2, 25, 68, 121–23, 145, 185, 196, 214, 238, 195; cradle name of, 35; death of, 166, 171–76, 347 n.22; escape of, 19–21; Fort Wagner and, 93; freedmen's relief efforts and, 118–20; funeral of, 14–16, 176–83; guns and, 73–75, 102; head injury of, 16–17, 18 (*fig. 1*), 118, 140, 144–45; Home for the Aged and, 148–49; illiteracy of, 105–7, 169, 301, 305; interview of, by Frank C. Drake, 167–69; interview of, by James B. Clarke,

Tubman, Harriet (*continued*)
169–72; interview of, by William G. Siebert, 172–73, 331 n.34; last words of, 347 n.22, 348 n.37; marriage of, to John Tubman, 17–18; marriage of, to Nelson Davis, 96, 101, 116–17; memorial services for, 183–94; memorial tablet for, 189–92; National Association of Colored Women and, 162; nursing activities of, 85–87; pension claims of, 96–101, 337–38 n.88, 338 n.93; property purchase by, 257–58; poverty of, 166, 171–72; psychic powers of, 134–35, 145, 147, 148–49; public neglect of, 2, 125, 165, 176, 214, 260, 295; question of number of rescued by, 64–66; question of number of trips of, 56–64; relationship of, to Margaret Stewart, 12, 306–7; relationship of, with Sarah Bradford 112–13, 124, 129–30, 132, 139; religious character of, 132–45; reward for capture of, 66–67, 368 n.25; reward notice for, 20 (*fig. 4*), Robert Gould Shaw and, 93; settlement of parents of, in Auburn, N.Y., 110–11; sleeping spells of, 15, 120, 140–41; Sojourner Truth and, 160–62; spying and scouting activities of, 76 (*fig. 22*), 87–93; storytelling abilities of, 12–14, 48–49, 53–54, 114, 124–25, 305, 330–31 n.12; tactics of, as Underground Railroad conductor, 68–69; train injury and, 94–95; Underground Railroad reputation of, 44–46, 55–65, 67–71; as victim of gold scam, 147–48; views of, on *Uncle Tom's Cabin*, 110, 138; women's suffrage and, 1, 5, 67, 95, 150–58, 159, 161–62; work experiences of, 16–17, 21. *See also* ancestry and family of

HT; appearance of HT; Araminta; Black Moses; Civil War; Combahee River raid; dreams and foreknowledge of HT; General Tubman symbol; Harriet Tubman Home for the Aged; Harriet Tubman residence; iconic status of HT; iconic stories about HT; Underground Railroad; veteran's status and HT
Tubman, John, 17, 39, 96–97, 236
Turner, Nat, 72, 139, 144
Tuskegee Institute, 171–72, 185–86, 188, 192
Twain, Mark, 121–22
Tyson, Cicely, 64, 234–35, 238

Uncle Tom's Cabin (Stowe, 1852), 30, 33, 109–10, 138, 142, 203, 219, 232
Underground Railroad, 57 (*fig. 17*); description of, 13, 39, 41, 44, 53, 55, 114; HT as conductor of, 1, 4, 13, 17, 24, 27–28, 35, 37, 39, 44, 48, 53, 55, 57, 62–63, 67–69, 134, 150, 156, 158, 190, 241–43, 256, 267, 288, 304, 314, 317; HT as icon of, 4, 12, 31, 41, 44, 60, 62, 68, 158, 168, 184, 237–38, 246, 267, 288, 314–15, 317; operatives on, 44, 47, 55, 69, 71, 125, 188, 205, 299; passengers on, 12–13, 53, 57, 60, 62
Underground Railroad (Still, 1872), 44
Underground Railroad from Slavery to Freedom (Siebert, 1899), 59–60, 172–73, 331 n.34
United States of America Nationalist Party, 273
Unsung Heroes (Haynes, 1921), 24
Urban Arts Training Program, 243

veteran's status and HT, 1, 96, 98, 100–102

MILTON C. SERNETT is retired professor of African American studies and history and retired adjunct professor of religion at Syracuse University. He is the author of *North Star Country: Upstate New York and the Crusade for African American Freedom* (2002); *Bound for the Promised Land: African American Religion and the Great Migration* (Duke, 1997); *Abolition's Axe: Beriah Green, Oneida Institute, and the Black Freedom Struggle* (1986); *Geographic Considerations in Afro-American Religious History: Past Performance, Present Problems, and Future Hopes* (1981); and *Black Religion and American Evangelicalism: White Protestants, Plantation Missions, and the Flowering of Negro Christianity* (1975). He is also the editor of *African American Religious History: A Documentary Witness* (Duke, 1985; 2d ed., 1999).

Library of Congress Cataloging-in-Publication Data
Sernett, Milton C., 1942–

Harriet Tubman : myth, memory, and history / Milton C. Sernett.
p. cm.
Includes bibliographical references and index.
ISBN 978-0-8223-4052-2 (cloth : alk. paper)
ISBN 978-0-8223-4073-7 (pbk. : alk. paper)
1. Tubman, Harriet, 1820?–1913—Influence. 2. Tubman, Harriet, 1820?–1913—Public opinion. 3. African American women heroes. 4. Legends—United States. 5. Memory—Social aspects—United States. 6. Tubman, Harriet, 1820?–1913. 7. Underground railroad. 8. African American women—Biography. 9. Fugitive slaves—United States—Biography. 10. Slaves—United States—Biography. I. Title.
E444.T82S45 2007
973.7′115092—dc22
[B]   2007015126